Sandra L. Bloom, MD
Michael Reichert, PhD

Bearing Witness
Violence and Collective Responsibility

Pre-publication
REVIEWS,
COMMENTARIES,
EVALUATIONS . . .

"**T**his is a magnificent book that analyzes the damaging consequences of violence. . . . I have never read such a well-documented contribution to a complex problem. Although based on American conditions, it is relevant and convincing to the European reader also. . . . From now on there is no excuse for being just a bystander—here is a tool for action for professionals and laymen in medicine, social work, law, mass media, and legislation."

Ingrid Leth
Department Head,
Institute of Clinical Psychology,
University of Copenhagen,
Denmark

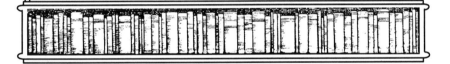

More pre-publication
REVIEWS, COMMENTARIES, EVALUATIONS . . .

"**B**loom and Reichert have made a totally convincing argument documented by reams of terrible, chilling factual evidence that violence is the number one public health problem in the world today. This book demands careful study by all elected representatives, the clergy, the mental health and medical professions, representatives of the media, and all those unwittingly involved in the repressive perpetuation of this catastrophic global problem. Their work is hopeful in that it suggests solutions involving all levels of individual societies as well as the world community. We delay getting on with the compassionate solutions suggested by Bloom and Reichert at our peril."

Harold I. Eist, MD
Past President,
American Psychiatric Association

"**B**loom and Reichert write clearly and with a minimum of jargon, thus making their book accessible. To survey the escalating violence of our world is so depressing that the instinct is to shut our eyes. Yet for the triumph of evil all that is necessary is that good men should do nothing and it is greatly to the authors' credit that they examine and explain today's violence, with a wealth of evidence. Much praise is due to Bloom and Reichert."

Sir Richard Bowlby
Boundary House,
London

"**T**his is a book of immense importance, in which with wisdom, the secrets of the consulting room and the scientific knowledge base are integrated and applied as a way of understanding our responsibilities to one another and to ourselves."

Stuart Turner, MD
The Traumatic Stress Clinic,
London

"**F**illed with an important blend of scientifically based information, practice, and advocacy, this is a very useful manual. Its trauma-based principles for intervention can be applied internationally in different cultures and in different regions of the world."

Sahika Yuksel, MD
Medical Director,
Istanbul Psychosocial Trauma
Program and ESTSS Board Member,
Istanbul University Medical School
of Psychiatry

Bearing Witness
Violence and Collective Responsibility

THE HAWORTH MALTREATMENT AND TRAUMA PRESS
Robert A. Geffner, PhD
Senior Editor

New, Recent, and Forthcoming Titles:

Sexual, Physical, and Emotional Abuse in Out-of-Home Care: Prevention Skills for At-Risk Children by Toni Cavanagh Johnson and Associates

Cedar House: A Model Child Abuse Treatment Program by Bobbi Kendig with Clara Lowry

Bridging Worlds: Understanding and Facilitating Adolescent Recovery from the Trauma of Abuse by Joycee Kennedy and Carol McCarthy

The Learning About Myself (LAMS) Program for At-Risk Parents: Learning from the Past—Changing the Future by Verna Rickard

The Learning About Myself (LAMS) Program for At-Risk Parents: Handbook for Group Participants by Verna Rickard

Treating Children with Sexually Abusive Behavior Problems: Guidelines for Child and Parent Intervention by Jan Ellen Burton, Lucinda A. Rasmussen, Julie Bradshaw, Barbara J. Christopherson, and Steven C. Huke

Bearing Witness: Violence and Collective Responsibility by Sandra L. Bloom and Michael Reichert

Sibling Abuse Trauma: Assessment and Intervention Strategies for Children, Families, and Adults by John V. Caffaro and Allison Conn-Caffaro

From Surviving to Thriving: A Therapist's Guide to Stage II Recovery for Survivors of Childhood Abuse by Mary Bratton

"I Never Told Anyone This Before": Managing the Initial Disclosure of Abuse Re-Collections by Janice A. Gasker

Breaking the Silence: Group Therapy for Childhood Sexual Abuse, A Practitioner's Manual by Judith A. Margolin

Bearing Witness
Violence and Collective Responsibility

Sandra L. Bloom, MD
Michael Reichert, PhD

For Philadelphia Physicians
for Social Responsibility

HMTP

The Haworth Maltreatment and Trauma Press
An Imprint of The Haworth Press, Inc.
New York • London

Published by

The Haworth Maltreatment and Trauma Press, an imprint of the The Haworth Press, Inc., 10 Alice Street, Binghamton, NY 13904-1580

Cover design by Jennifer M. Gaska.

Quoted material in the Introduction taken from *Family Album* by Mikal Gilmore. Reprinted by permission of International Creative Management, Inc. Copyright © 1991 by Mikal Gilmore.

Excerpted text by Thomasma in Chapter 8 is an excerpt reprint from the *Journal of Allied Health*. Reprint permission granted May 1998.

Library of Congress Cataloging-in-Publication Data

Bloom, Sandra L., 1948-
    Bearing witness : violence and collective responsibility / Sandra L. Bloom, Michael Reichert.
       p. cm.
    Includes bibliographical references and index.
    ISBN 0-7890-0478-X (alk. paper)
    1. Violence—Psychological aspects. 2. Violence—Social aspects. 3. Violence—Prevention.
I. Reichert, Michael. II. Title.
RC569.5.V55B53   1998
616.85'82—dc21
                                                              98-29059
                                                                  CIP

The childhood shows the man
As morning shows the day

John Milton, *Paradise Regained*

ABOUT THE AUTHORS

Sandra L. Bloom, MD, is Founder and Executive Director of "The Sanctuary," a specialized inpatient hospital program for the treatment of adults traumatized as children, which is located at Friends Hospital in Philadelphia, Pennsylvania, the oldest private psychiatric hospital in the United States. She is also founder and President of the Alliance for Creative Development, a multidisciplinary private practice and psychiatric management company with offices in three counties in Pennsylvania and fourteen years of inpatient management experience. A Board-Certified psychiatrist and fellow of the College of Physicians of Pennsylvania, Dr. Bloom served as the 1997-1998 President of the International Society for Traumatic Stress Studies. She is currently the President of the Philadelphia chapter of Physicians for Social Responsibility and is Clinical Assistant Professor in the Department of Psychiatry at Temple University. Dr. Bloom chairs the statewide Task Force on Family Violence for Mike Fisher, Attorney General of Pennsylvania. She has lectured nationally and internationally on various topics related to post-traumatic stress, has published in various books and journals, and is the author of *Creating Sanctuary: Toward the Evolution of Sane Communities.*

Michael C. Reichert, PhD, is founder and partner of Bala Psychological Resources, a multidisciplinary outpatient group, and Director of the "On Behalf of Boys" Project of The Haverford School, a center for research and discussion on boys' lives. A child and family psychologist, he has worked in clinical and community settings for the past twenty years. Dr. Reichert is a board member of the Philadelphia chapter of Physicians for Social Responsibility, co-chaired its Psychosocial Taskforce, and currently serves as Clinical Supervisor for its Peaceful Posse project, an antiviolence project serving early adolescent boys. He has lectured widely on many topics related to children and families, most recently specializing on the subject of caring for boys.

CONTENTS

Preface

Alienation as our present destiny is achieved only by outrageous violence perpetrated by human beings on human beings. No man can begin to think, feel, or act now except from the starting point of his or her own alienation.

R. D. Laing,
The Politics of Experience

In every crisis there is an opportunity. From the perspective of mental health practitioners, the social crisis engendered by escalating levels of violence provides an opportunity for a new level of public awareness. We are forced to make the startling realization that conventional wisdom does not help us to understand why people treat each other so badly. This realization provides the impetus to broaden our search for answers.

The Philadelphia chapter of Physicians for Social Responsibility has embarked on a campaign to make a substantial contribution to the effort to stem all forms of violence. Working with existing neighborhood and government groups, creating coalitions, developing grant projects in new areas, PSR has thrown its expertise, resources, and energy into the fight.

The Task Force on Psychosocial Causes of Violence was created to provide a theoretical framework to these efforts, to ensure that all of the various projects embodied our most sophisticated understanding of human behavior. Through the development of this manual, the Task Force has distilled a great mass of information into a readable form that will be used to introduce all PSR projects to this point of view.

The Task Force consists of a diverse group of clinicians who share the experience of working with perpetrators and victims of violence. From juvenile justice settings, psychiatric hospitals, clinical training programs, outpatient services of many kinds, women's programs, men's groups, and independent practices we have developed a point of view about the causes of violence. Our specialties cover a broad range; underlying the different populations and problems, however, is the central theme of trauma and its effects on human behavior.

Among our group are therapists and consultants who have provided assistance to people in the most affluent areas of the Delaware Valley as well as in the poorest sections of Philadelphia. The group includes clinical professionals who have been seasoned through extensive contact with a great diversity of cultures, races, and classes. Individually, most of us have worked with community groups, agencies, and schools to lend a psychological perspective to efforts to address social problems. Clinicians are not usually on the scene at times of violence. Our involvement comes after the fact, in offices with individuals, families, or groups. Our tool is an in-depth understanding of the therapeutic process of what happens when people are heard, understood, and can feel emotionally safe. From our work with clients we have learned how to access, explore, and restore people's sense of identity, confidence, and self-esteem.

In addition to our clinical experiences, the members of the Task Force have a common concern about society. Many of us have a history of social activism; all of us feel alarmed by the impact of violence in our patients' lives. Because we have dedicated ourselves to careers as healers, we take seriously all factors that affect the well-being of our clients. We have come to recognize that no one escapes completely the impact of violence in the culture. As a child, a spouse, an innocent pedestrian, or community resident, violence seeps into most all relationships, creating an invidious presence that influences behavior, development, and progress. Where individuals, families, and whole communities organize to cope with problems of safety and violence, there is a stress level that pervades all relationships.

The work we do in our offices and clinics, therefore, is not separate from these stresses and social forces. As healers, we are affected in our ability to accomplish our work; we are also affected as witnesses. All who minister to victims of violence are likely to experience secondary trauma, or "vicarious traumatization" (Figley, 1995; McCann and Pearlman, 1990; Stamm, 1995). We believe that a necessary response to this exposure to trauma is social activism. We must bring our concern, care, and commitment to our society's battle with violence, as much for our own sakes as for our patients'. To be passive in the face of hurt is to hurt oneself. The alternative is to be a helpless bystander, watching the parade of violent perpetration, unable or unwilling to do anything to prevent it.

Health care professionals are simultaneously practitioners and educators; healers, teachers, and role models. An extensive body of research-based knowledge is now available to everyone that explains how violence affects people at all levels of function: the biological, the psychological, the social, and the moral. Physicians for Social Responsibility is committed to providing as much public education as possible on the short-term and long-term, individual and social results of trauma for children and their families. In service of this goal, the following material is presented as a framework for understanding the various psychosocial components of violence using post-traumatic stress theory as the theoretical basis. In the following pages we will start by focusing attention on the various aspects of the problem of violence in the vital arenas of our social and political life. We will then look at normal human development in the context of attachment theory, and then what occurs as a result of disrupted attachment bonds. Nest, we will delve into the various aspects of trauma—what trauma does to the body, the mind, the emotions, and relationships before beginning to formulate proposals for initiating processes that will lead to problem solving.

Throughout this book we hope we have conveyed one essential message: that it is a fundamental and absolute moral responsibility that we each find a way to *bear witness* to the pain and suffering that is all around us, and that starting from the position of this testimony we must join together to liberate the human body, mind, and soul from the rack of traumatic reenactment that is stretching our social body to the limit of endurance.

Sandra Bloom, MD, Task Force Co-Chair
Michael Reichert, PhD, Task Force Co-Chair

Task Force Members:
Margaret Baker, PhD
Ellen Berman, MD
Joel Chinitz, MD
Sandra H. Dempsey, MSS, MLSP
Carol Dolinskas, MD
Robert Garfield, MD
Elizabeth Kuh, MD
Diane Perlman, PhD
Marlene Watson, PhD

Introduction

STATEMENT OF PROBLEM: VIOLENCE AND COMMUNITY

From every corner of the United States comes a growing concern with the problem of violence. In urban areas, in our homes, in relationships between men and women, parents and children, the elderly and their caregivers, the problem has reached a level of awareness that some call epidemic. Crime is one of the top issues in political debates. According to the FBI, one violent crime occurs every eighteen seconds (Federal Bureau of Investigation, 1996). Five out of six people will be victims of violent crimes at least once in their lifetimes (National Victim Center, 1993). In 1995, U.S. residents age twelve or older experienced approximately 38.4 million crimes (U.S. Department of Justice, 1995). The cost of crime to victims is an estimated $450 billion a year when the cost of pain, suffering, and the reduced quality of life is taken into consideration (Miller, Cohen, and Weirsema, 1996). More pervasive even than the actual effects of crime is the fear it generates. Sixty percent of all Americans limit the places they go by themselves, where they go shopping, and where they work due to fear of crime. This fear particularly limits the behavior of women (National Victim Center, 1993). Despite the fact that incarceration for crime has been increasing without notably positive results, our approach continues to be skewed toward punishment; we have a record number of jails and prison inmates—to the detriment of understanding and prevention. Nationally, only 19 percent of the population has a "great deal" or "quite a lot" of confidence in the criminal justice system (Gallup Organization, 1996). Sixty-two percent of Americans say that they would pay higher taxes to improve the criminal justice system (National Victim Center, 1993). However, a tax consensus is unlikely to be reached about such things as banning corporal punishment, early neonatal home visitation, or job training programs.

These days, just reading the morning newspaper or switching on the evening news can be an overwhelming experience. Violence, lies, and betrayals are such a daily occurrence that it feels as if we are riding a train without an engineer, careening out of control down a steep hill, destined for a painful end. Everybody tries to produce some explanation for the violence that at least provides an illusory sense of control. For some the problem is a lack of something—discipline, religion, mothers at home, involved fathers, poverty, fair play, rights of all sorts. Others believe the causes of our social disintegration are to be found in excesses of something—welfare, permissiveness, attention, material goods, rights of all sorts. But whatever the finger points to as THE cause, almost everyone will admit to feeling powerless and helpless to bring about any substantial or meaningful change. It seems that we have reached the limits of our present knowledge. The old ways of thinking and acting do not seem to be working—our problems just get bigger, more life threatening, more extreme.

New problems require a new way of understanding, new problem-solving methods, new solutions. But to formulate new solutions we need a comprehensive model of the way the world works that explains things better than the old model and that aids us in our quest for answers. Too often, learned people cloak their own ignorance or confusion behind inexplicable concepts that lie far afield from most people's everyday experience. Fortunately, the material we are going to present is really relatively simple to understand and should stand up to the test of "common sense" as long as common sense is informed by compassion.

Understanding the causes of violence is not actually all that difficult, and is, to a large extent, knowledge we have had since childhood. As one of the world's great simplifiers, Robert Fulgham, has pointed out, "Everything we ever really have needed to know we learned in kindergarten." This includes rules such as share everything, play fair, don't hit people, and say you're sorry when you hurt somebody (Fulgham, 1989). A rapidly accumulating body of scientific knowledge now supports the reality of a self-perpetuating cycle of violence that originates in the hurts—great and small—that we inflict on each other from childhood, through adolescence, and into adult life.

We are beginning to understand, in fact, that virtually all of our human systems are organized around trauma and the prolonged, transgenerational, and often permanent, effects of traumatic experience. This is not surprising. Our evolutionary history has been a difficult one. We are an extremely intelligent, extraordinarily sensitive species with very long and far-reaching memories. But, in evolutionary terms, we have also been quite vulnerable to all kinds of environmental threats that have cost us dearly in terms of damaging and disrupting our attachment bonds to each other and to the ecology surrounding us. People do not necessarily heal spontaneously from trauma. Healing requires certain situations that are only too rare in our present circumstances: safety, the ability to form compassionate attachments with other people, the ability to communicate feelings, and the opportunity to turn the nonverbal experience of trauma into verbal expression that can be integrated internally and can be shared with others.

Instead, there are many forces in our society that help us avoid dealing with old hurts. These attitudes can be best expressed through such folk aphorisms as "What you don't know won't hurt you," "Out of sight, out of mind," "Children forget," "The past is the past, just let it be," "Children should be seen but not heard," "Big boys don't cry," "Spare the rod, spoil the child," and other kinds of social indoctrination characteristic of what Alice Miller has termed "poisonous pedagogy" (Miller, 1983). As each generation teaches the next to act out their emotional conflicts rather than work them through via language and relationship, the society—or at least the most damaged portion of it—becomes increasingly skewed toward violence and anarchy, its members cut off from any ability to relate to other human beings. We become socially dead—"robopaths" (Yablonsky, 1992).

The violence in our culture now can only be perceived as a "cry for help," the old-fashioned but still relevant explanation for many psychiatric symptoms. Before the individual patient actually reaches out for help, he or she often has to reach some bottom or depth, manifesting symptoms that have become life threatening. Our entire culture is doing the same thing—manifesting such extremes of pathology that we no longer can deny that something is pervasively wrong. We manifest this cry for help in our rate of firearm deaths, crimes of violence, and in the recent epidemic of child-on-child assaults. But we also demonstrate a need for help in our preoccupation with sex divorced from love and intertwined with violence, our escalating abandonment of the underprivileged, our continued sexism and racism, and our profound unwillingness to protect our future through protecting our children.

The root cause, the lowest common denominator for violence, is that perpetrated against children. And this includes all forms of violence—allowing children to go hungry in the midst of plenty, permitting homelessness, lack of medical care, lack of other sustaining adults to support overwhelmed families, and oppressive policies that make good parenting virtually impossible. Nothing will change for the better until we take seriously our supposed and stated concern for the well-being of our children. The U.S. Advisory Board on Child Abuse and Neglect stated in their 1992 Board Report:

> Adult violence against children leads to childhood terror, childhood terror leads to teenage anger, and teenage anger too often leads to adult rage, both destructive toward others and self-destructive. Terror,

anger, rage—these are not the ingredients of safe streets, strong families, and caring communities. (U.S. Advisory Board, 1992)

In this book we intend to address this cycle of violence by discussing some of the biological, psychological, social, and even moral issues that determine whether a person will become a victim, perpetrator, or bystander to violent events and what happens to an individual when he or she is in one or all three of these roles.

In the following pages we will examine a number of these intersecting factors which we believe play an interdependent role in creating a culture that promotes, supports, and even encourages violence. First, we will survey forces that we think of as "traumatogenic"—backdrops against which the chances of exposure to violent perpetration and violence as a problem solver are increased. These factors include some long-standing child-rearing practices, such as corporal punishment, which send a message to the developing child that violence is acceptable. Our cultural standard of disavowing our normal emotional experience sets the stage for repeated and regular empathic failure. Sexism produces an unhealthy imbalance of power between the genders, which is maintained by violence or the threat of violence and is strongly reinforced by male conditioning to violence. Economic inequality breeds extremes of poverty and racism that serve to justify the scapegoating of people of color, situations that are breeding grounds for violence. In addition, the rapid changes in modern society and the breakdown of the traditional family structure all contribute to a level of social stress that promotes violence. The combined effect of all of these factors is to create a sense of existential confusion, a profound questioning of purpose and meaning that so characterizes the social environment of the late twentieth century.

In the next section we explore the most important places within which violence occurs in order to further illustrate the magnitude of the problem and the lack of safety that permeates the entire culture. This includes violence in the family, in the workplace, and in the schools—all the places in society to which people turn for security. We will also look at the structural violence that is a part of our religious heritage as well, since that has so influenced all of our other cultural institutions in ways that may no longer be visible as religious, but that continue to influence our thinking.

Next, we will examine the ways in which the culture actively provides support for various forms of violence by promoting and encouraging violence. This support is often denied by those who economically benefit from it or who are concerned with the preservation of individual rights. This section points out the critical need for some value decisions on the part of society, and raises many important questions. How do we balance the right to bear arms and the right of free speech against the need to create safe environments? When, by their behavior, a people indicate their lack of social responsibility, do rights need to be curbed, at least temporarily? How can we create safety without losing hard-earned freedoms? The main topics of discussion in this section are firearms, substance abuse, pornography, and media violence.

We next focus our attention on our social responses to violence, the ways in which our responses decrease or increase the likelihood of further violence. In this section we discuss whether punishment really works as an effective method of stopping further violence. Then we will look at the "bystander effect"—is anyone really an innocent bystander? What is the role of other people in diminishing or increasing the likelihood of violence? We will also view more subtle factors that permeate the entire social climate, factors considered here under the concept of "robopathology." But, not everyone who is traumatized suffers the long-term effects of trauma, so in this section some of the protective factors that are involved in resilient types of responses to violence are explored.

After looking at many of the social forces that influence violence in our culture, we will turn to an exploration of the fundamental nature of human beings. This section examines the ways in which trauma affects our minds, bodies, and souls, thus altering the way we think, remember, feel, relate to others, and make sense of the world. Our bodies respond in certain predictable, biologically evolved ways when we are very frightened or upset. Our physical, emotional, and social responses have a great deal to do with how we respond to subsequent events in our lives and basically explain why we have become so trapped in a cycle of repetitive violence that is psychologically and socially destabilizing. This knowledge base, called "trauma theory" is relatively new, originating largely with the study of veterans of the Vietnam War, and in the two decades drawing upon research with other survivor groups. The impact of traumatic experience on issues of spirituality and meaning is discussed and we touch upon the age-old question about the nature of evil. We will make the case that our society has become organized around unresolved traumatic events and discuss how recognition of this formerly hidden constellation of thoughts, feelings, and behaviors contaminates our social milieu. Finally, since thought ideally precedes action, we explain how our thinking has to change if we are to create a better world.

Once this knowledge base has been established, certain inevitable conclusions can be drawn about our present situation and implications for future change. The final section of this book will suggest the beginnings of an outline for reorganizing society with the aim of establishing a community that is responsive to the basic human need for safety and peace. We have taken a public health approach to the problem of trauma in our society because we believe it will take a total approach to contain and ultimately eliminate the disease we call "violence." This section is certainly not intended to be the final word on social change. But we think it can serve as a preliminary blueprint, a starter for any community seeking to face the problem head on. We have touched on all of the major social institutions and provided some ideas that we believe are necessary for system change as well as some examples of ideas and programs that are working.

Let's start by reading a portion of a story of one famous criminal's troubled life, because in some ways it raises questions we have yet to honestly answer about our own lives and the society we live in.

A Criminal Tale

> You have to learn to be hard. You have to learn to take things and feel nothing about them: no pain, no anger, nothing. And you have to realize, if anybody wants to beat you up, even if they want to hold you down and kick you, you have to let them. You can't fight back. You shouldn't fight back. Just lie down in front of them and let them beat you, let them kick you. Lie there and let them do it. It is the only way you will survive. If you don't give in to them, they will kill you. (Gilmore, 1991, p. 17)

The man who spoke these teenage words of advice to his little brother was Gary Gilmore, a man who was executed in 1977 for the cold-blooded murder of two innocent men. The man who recounts these words is Gary's youngest brother, Mikal, an accomplished writer.

In July 1976, Gary Gilmore was thirty-five years old. He had already spent most of his adolescent and adult life in jail for various criminal and violent offenses. In jail he had been repeatedly brutalized, had witnessed violence perpetrated upon others, and had inflicted violence himself. On news reports he appeared cold-blooded, arrogant, and mean. It was easy to call this man an aberration, an anomaly, a monster, deserving whatever he got.

Easy, that is, until you hear the whole story. How do we correlate this image of a sociopathic killer with the other images his younger brother described: a man who as a child had nightmares of being beheaded; a gifted artist who drew paintings of children, ballet dancers, and boxers; a man who slashed his wrists in his cell when the prison authorities denied him the right to attend his abusive father's funeral; a man who insisted on his right to die with the words, "I've lost my freedom. I lost it a long time ago. I don't want you to think I'm some 'sensitive' artist because I drew pictures or wrote poems. I killed—in cold blood" (Gilmore, 1991, p. 37); a man capable of holding a sobbing cellmate in his arms to comfort him; a condemned man who wrote a reply to an eight-year-old boy's malicious letter, "You're too young to have malice in your heart. I had it in mine at a young age and look what it did for me" (Gilmore, 1991, pp. 40-41).

Look further and the story becomes more eerie. We learn about a mother apparently obsessed by at least one childhood traumatic experience of her own—being forced by her brutal and abusive father to witness the execution by hanging of a condemned murderer at a public execution, an occasion of warning for all the children of the community. We learn of a father, raised among spiritualists, vaudevillians, and circus performers, who grew up to be both handsome, charming, and an alcoholic, who beat his wife when she refused to abort the fetus that was to become Gary, and hated his son from that moment on. We learn of a family in which violence, cruelty, and brutality was as much a part of the home as the family television set, but in which a young son could still witness a scene in which "My father was crying, and my mother was petting his hand" (Gilmore, 1991, p. 24).

We also learn that the murderer killed two innocent men that night in July, to keep himself from killing two other innocent people: the woman that he loved, and his youngest brother, who was the only real recipient of their father's love.

There are a few things about this story that are clear. Gary Gilmore was clearly responsible for his crimes and he suffered the highest penalty. The men who were murdered and the families that survived them were helplessly victimized by Gilmore's criminal behavior. There are none left in the Gilmore family except Mikal who raises his author's voice and clearly asks "Why?" Why did this happen? Bearing the mark of Cain from his familial associations, Mikal wants his readers to recognize that blaming the victims—even the perpetrating victim—gives only a partial answer to a very complex question. Mikal says:

> Murder has worked its way into our consciousness and our culture in the same way that murder exists in our literature and film: we consume each killing until there is another, more immediate or gripping one to take its place. . . . Each murder will be solved, but murder itself will never be solved. You cannot solve murder without solving the human heart or the history that has rendered that heart so dark and desolate. (Gilmore, 1991, p. 50)

In the pages that follow we are going to explore the human heart—and the human brain—and the history that has been so devastating to our families and our people. Gary Gilmore knew he was a killer—he wanted to die for it and he did. What we hope for is that there can come a time when those whose hearts are darkened with pain and trauma can be understood and helped and that the culture that spawns their hurt can play a useful role in supporting their recovery.

PART I:
A TRAUMA-ORGANIZED SOCIETY?

In Part I of this book we are going to make the case that we live in a society that is "organized" around unresolved traumatic experience. By making this claim, we intend to show that the effects of multigenerational trauma lie like an iceberg in our social awareness. All we see is the tip of the iceberg that is above the surface—crime, community deterioration, family disintegration, ecological degradation. What lies below the surface of our social consciousness is the basis of the problem—the ways in which unhealed trauma and loss have infiltrated and helped determine every one of our social institutions. As statistics show, the majority of the population will be exposed to an event considered traumatic and this exposure places them at risk for many other physical, emotional, and social problems. This rate of exposure is dramatically increased for those members of the community who are raised in "traumatogenic environments." A traumatogenic environment is one in which human beings are at increased risk for experiencing traumatic events. There are many traumatogenic forces in our society, including child-rearing practices that encourage the use of violence directed at children or that impair the ability of parents to adequately provide for their children, poverty, sexism, racism, male conditioning to use violence as a means of control, and many other kinds of social stresses, all of which are embedded within a religious and philosophical belief system that permits, and even encourages, the use of violence. Today, violence is all around us and we will examine how we provide both passive and active support for that violence. We will also explore how we currently are responding to violence and how effective those responses are. Finally, we briefly survey the important research on resilience to see if we can gather some hints about how to make even dangerous environments safer.

Chapter 1

Looking at the Numbers

More than twenty years ago, Murray Straus and Suzanne Steinmetz called the family the "cradle of violence" (Steinmetz and Straus, 1973). Recent surveys of U.S. households support that observation. Hitting children is virtually universal; a quarter of infants one to six months are hit and this rises to half of all infants by six months to a year (Straus, 1994). Sibling violence occurs in 800 per 1,000 children (Finkelhor and Dziuba-Leatherman, 1993). Moving from "normative" violence to the more extreme end of the continuum, the government-sponsored Third National Incidence Study of Child Abuse has presented alarming data. The number of abused and neglected children grew from 1.4 million in 1986 to over 2.8 million in 1993. During that same period, the number of seriously injured children *quadrupled* and these increases cannot be attributed to increased sensitivity on the part of reporters (U.S. Department of Health and Human Services, 1996). The number of sexually abused children rose by 83 percent in that period. Every incident of child sexual abuse costs the victim and society $99,000 (Miller, Cohen, and Wiersema, 1996).

Of the children who met the strictest criteria, the Harm Standard, child protective services only investigated 28 percent of the reports—a significant decrease from the 44 percent investigated in 1986 when the Second National Incidence Study of Child Abuse was performed (U.S. Department of Health and Human Services, 1996). A 1995 Gallup Poll of parents estimated that as many as 49 children per 1,000 in the population suffered physical abuse and 19 per 1,000 suffered sexual abuse (Gallup Organization, Inc., 1995). Nearly 1,000 children were known by child protective services to have died as a result of abuse or neglect (U.S. Department of Health and Human Services, 1997).

More than six out of ten of all rape cases (61 percent) occur before victims reach age eighteen; 29 percent of all forcible rape occurs before the age of eleven. (National Victim Center, 1993). Overall, in terms of the effects of all forms of violence on boys, a Massachusetts study estimated that one in forty-two teenage boys receive hospital treatment for some form of assault (Guyer et al., 1989). Of the adolescents ages twelve to seventeen in the United States, an estimated 8 percent have been victims of serious sexual assault; 17 percent have been victims of serious physical assault; and 40 percent have witnessed serious violence (Kilpatrick and Saunders, 1997).

And then there is violence to the woman of the house. In 1994, 62 percent or 2,981,479 of the victimizations of females were by persons whom they knew, while 63 percent or 3,949,285 of the victimizations of males were by strangers (Craven, 1997). Gelles and Straus (1988) have estimated, based on probability sampling, that from two to three million women are assaulted by male partners each year in the United States and that from 21 to 34 percent of all women will be assaulted by an intimate male during adulthood. More than 50 percent of all women will experience some form of violence from their spouses during marriage; more than one-third are battered repeatedly every year; 15 to 25 percent of pregnant women are battered (National Victim Center, 1993). According to a nationwide survey released by the Family Violence Prevention Fund, more than one in three Americans have witnessed an incident of domestic violence (1993). In homes where spousal abuse occurs, children are abused at a rate 1,500 percent higher than the national average (National Victim Center, 1993).

Every year, domestic violence results in almost 100,000 days of hospitalizations, almost 30,000 emergency room visits, and almost 40,000 visits to physicians (National Victim Center, 1993). In a New York study of fifty battered women, 75 percent said that their batterer had harassed them while they were at work, 54 percent reported missing an average of three days per month because of the beatings, and 44 percent of the women had lost at least one job for reasons directly related to the abuse (Friedman and Cooper, 1987). Domestic violence already costs companies nationwide $3 to $5 billion annually in absenteeism, reduced productivity, and increased health care costs (Anfuso, 1994).

According to a 1996 National Institute of Justice study, domestic crime against adults accounts for almost 15 percent of the total crime costs— over $67 billion a year (National Institute of Justice, 1996).

Estimates for sexual assault also support the proposition that most violence directed against women is perpetrated by intimates: 14 percent of ever-married women in one study reported being raped by husband or ex-husband (twice the rate for stranger assault). One out of every eight adult women, or at least 12.1 million American women, will be victims of forcible rape sometime in their lifetimes (Kilpatrick, Edmunds, and Seymour, 1992). In 1990, 683,000 American women were forcibly raped and of these, only 16 percent were reported to the police (Kilpatrick, Edmunds, and Seymour, 1992). In 1991, 28 percent of all female murder victims were slain by their husbands or boyfriends and in fact, family violence kills as many women every five years as the total number of Americans who died in the Vietnam War (National Victim Center, 1993).

Given the dangers of marriage, divorce might seem to be a solution. Not so. A recent survey of divorced Philadelphia-area women found that 70 percent were abused by their spouses. Nineteen percent cited the violence as their primary reason for leaving the marriage. Fifty-four percent had suffered several incidents of violence and sustained injury from their ex-husbands. Even after separation, nearly one-half of the women experienced violence from their estranged husbands. Not surprisingly, 30 percent feared further violence during child support negotiations, and, of this subset, 66 percent did not receive regular child support payments (Kurz, 1996).

While men are the chief perpetrators of violent acts, they are also the chief victims. Men are twice as likely as women to be victims of violent crime (Farrell, 1993). In addition to hurting each other, men hurt themselves at a rate much higher than women. Teenage boys commit suicide at a rate four times greater than females; that difference grows through young adulthood, until at age 85, the rate is 1,350 percent greater (Farrell, 1993). There is evidence that these differences reflect pressures that may be even greater in poorer neighborhoods. Self-inflicted injury affecting males aged ten to forty-four grew by 76 percent over the four years of a study of a Philadelphia African-American neighborhood (Schwarz et al., 1994). Matching the deterioration of their communities, suicide rates for black males in Philadelphia grew steadily during the decades since the 1950s.

Community life in urban neighborhoods reflects a significant deterioration over the past several decades. A four-year study of Philadelphia neighborhoods completed in 1990 found that gun-related violence increased 179 percent over the time of the study period. The same study reported that during the four years of the study 94 percent of men in the age group twenty to twenty-nine had to go to an emergency room at least once with an injury, caused 41 percent of the time by violent encounters (Schwarz et al., 1994). The 1960s upsurge of violence primarily involved males, but the introduction of wholesale drug trafficking has made violent death more common for people who are not involved with gangs or drugs: young women, middle-aged women, children (Nightingale, 1993). Factors other than poverty account for these increases because when comparisons are made among groups of similar socioeconomic status there is considerable variation in the homicide rates.

Violence as a cause of community deterioration or violence as a reflection of community disintegration are the oversimplified attributions made in the face of these data. Like the effort of the culture to assimilate the perspective of trauma theory with respect to children, so too we can see a parallel struggle to recognize the interplay between broad social forces such as poverty, racism, culture, and violence. The statistical picture painted by male children who face a lifetime of deprivation, humiliation, harsh treatment by society's caregivers, exacerbated by mean streets and unforgiving institutions, bears powerful witness to the relevance of a psychology of perpetration. What we can make out in these data since 1960 is a spiral, in which a variety of factors reinforce each other to produce the sense of a system out of control.

In fact, though, such a spiral argues powerfully for a new set of premises guiding our policy interventions. People have not changed in any fundamental way; it must be that our understanding of what is affecting behavior and how to improve conditions to prevent such distortions are off target. As we mentioned, to date the overriding response of society to this spiral has been to punish the perpetrator and hope to deter others. According to the Justice Department, from 1980 to 1992 the state and federal prison population in America soared nearly 150 percent, from 139 to 344 jailed for every 100,000 of total population—the Western world's highest ratio (Starer, 1995). By 1992, 1.3 million persons were in state and federal prisons and the number keeps rising. More people are behind bars in America than in any other country in the world (Forer, 1994). Juveniles held in public or private facilities increased 30 percent since 1975. In 1992 there were more than 100,000 children in correctional institutions (Forer, 1994). Of women in prison, 75 percent are mothers, and 88 percent of their children are under the age of eighteen. It is estimated that at the end of 1992, 167,000 children had mothers in prison (Forer, 1994).

While insights from clinical work with perpetrators argue for a strong system of accountability and limits to acting-out behaviors, it is also clear from this work that punishment and deterrence alone will do little to resolve the compulsive quality of perpetration. Our efforts to gain a foothold on the problem of the spiral of violence and community deterioration must begin with a more sophisticated appreciation for what makes some people hurt other people. Understanding that, we can take the next steps as a society to eliminating the conditions that produce these problems.

To do this, we may have to look at the possibility that our entire culture has become "trauma-organized" (Bentovim, 1992), meaning trauma and its immediate and long-term effects have become a central organizing principle for our entire social structure. A number of studies in recent years have shown that up to three-quarters of the general population in the United States have been exposed to some event in their lifetime that can be defined as traumatic (Green, 1994; Norris, 1992; Resnick et al., 1993, Sutker, Allain, and Winstead, 1993). This exposure to overwhelming stress has long-term as well as immediate consequences for the survivors and for their families, friends, colleagues, employers, and fellow citizens. In one study of young adults in the Midwest, life threat, seeing others killed or badly injured, and physical assault all produced a lifetime rate of post-traumatic stress disorder (PTSD) of around 25 percent (Breslau et al., 1991). In another recent study 39 percent of women who had experienced aggravated assault developed post-traumatic stress disorder, as did 35 percent of those who were raped (Kilpatrick and Resnick, 1993). In a study by Kubany and colleagues, 33 to 83 percent of battered women met criteria for PTSD (1996). The severity of symptoms tends to be directly proportional to the amount and intensity of exposure to trauma (March, 1993). The effects of trauma are not short-lived. In one follow-up of a disaster, one-quarter of the survivors studied showed continuing and significant psychopathology (Green et al., 1990). As Dr. Bonnie Green notes, "There is clear evidence that PTSD is a long-lasting disorder in many individuals. Up to half of those who develop the disorder may continue to have it decades later without treatment" (Green, 1994).

Worse yet, post-traumatic stress disorder rarely occurs alone; it most commonly coexists with major depression and substance abuse, and with other psychiatric, physical, and social problems as well (Green, 1994). There have been reports connecting PTSD with fibromyalgia (Amir et al., 1997), chronic pain (Benedikt and Kolb, 1986; Geisser et al., 1996; Walling et al., 1994), irritable bowel syndrome (Irwin et al., 1996; Walker et al., 1996), asthma (Davidson et al., 1991); peptic ulcer (Davidson et al., 1991); other gastrointestinal illness (Drossman, 1995), chronic pelvic pain (Badura et al., 1997; Drossman, 1995; Walker et al., 1996; Walling et al., 1994), panic disorder and social phobia (Orsillo et al., 1996), borderline personality disorder (Ellason et al., 1996; Herman, Perry and Van der Kolk, 1989; Perry et al., 1990), somatoform disorders (Rogers et al., 1996; Saxe et al., 1994), obsessive-compulsive disorder (Bleich et al., 1994; Pitman, 1993), panic disorder (Orsillo et al., 1996; Vasile et al., 1997) and anxiety disorders (Fierman, 1993).

In addition to the proximal exposure to trauma and its effect in this generation, a burgeoning amount of literature indicates the very real dangers of intergenerational transmission of the effects of trauma. This has been studied most thoroughly in children of Holocaust survivors (Danielli, 1985) and is succinctly summed up in one sentence, "The children of survivors show symptoms which would be expected if they actually lived through the Holocaust" (Barocas and Barocas as quoted in Herzog, 1982). Transgenerational transmission has also been well-documented among populations who have been abused and neglected in childhood (Egeland and Susman-Stillman, 1996; Main and Hess, 1990; Oliver, 1993; Zeanah and Zeanah, 1989).

If our society is, in fact, organized around trauma, what are the forces in the society that permit or promote the occurrences of overwhelming stress, forces that may be controllable if we can properly identify them? If we only look at the crimes themselves, we decontextualize a complex situation and in doing so are less likely to be able to change the most important factors in determining violent behavior. This is the approach best characterized by the criminal justice system. Solutions to the problems of crime that completely rely on punitive measures such as more police or incarceration, though sometimes necessary, are not sufficient. They are like closing the barn door after the horse is gone. Violent perpetration is the final outcome of a multitude of intersecting factors that determine the life course of a person beginning in childhood, factors that we believe are "traumatogenic," providing the breeding ground for the twisting of a mind, a body, and a soul.

Chapter 2

Traumatogenic Forces in Society

Although we may experience traumatic episodes as isolated events, unpredictable and shockingly distinct from those considered "normal," statistical aggregates of these separate acts point to clear patterns. Significantly higher rates of sexual abuse for females suggest that gender is relevant in understanding this form of violence. The high proportion of teenage boys in urban neighborhoods whose violence-caused injuries force an emergency room visit tells us something about life in urban neighborhoods. The higher proportion of child abuse cases found in impoverished families implicates the stressor of economic deprivation in the etiology of child battering.

What we can say about psychological trauma, in fact, is that there is an intimate connection between traumatizing behaviors and the social conditions that support them. As the culture wrestles with definitions of date and acquaintance rape, for example, awareness of these acts of violence grows and the society's tolerance for them diminishes; women may expect a day when they have less to worry about from an intimate. Parental behavior that used to be accepted or at least tolerated is now considered abuse. The growing awareness of the incidence of child abuse should lead to a growing intolerance of such behavior and a greater willingness to actively protect children. Through an organized education campaign, law enforcement agencies have become more sensitized to the issue of domestic violence and more willing to actively offer protection for the battered woman rather than turning away from the "family squabble."

But social conditions can also foster the occurrence of trauma. The social ideology that has defined children as their parent's property plays a key role in the freedom adults still have to batter and abuse children. Our refusal to understand the importance of providing emotional support for each other establishes a climate of cruel disregard for other's feelings. Gender images of women as inferior, less capable, submissive, emotional, and stupid and men as superior, more competent, dominant, rational, and intelligent have supported deeply sexist assumptions and practices that are extremely detrimental and even dangerous to healthy human functioning.

Racist images of African Americans and other minority groups have supported cultural perceptions of these population groups that have generated a host of threats to their existence.

In the jargon of trauma theory, traumatogenic forces are those social practices and trends that cause, encourage, or contribute to the generation of traumatic acts. As we will see in our review of attachment theory, for example, certain conditions generate optimal infant development. In particular, nurturance from adult caregivers is critical for mental, emotional, and social development. But in a culture where parenting is not an activity supported by the society, parents must do it as a hobby or a forced necessity and find time for nurturing only after basic bread and butter needs have been satisfied, if at all. When the culture fails to support the work of parents, a traumatogenic force is created that fosters the neglect of children's attachment needs.

The organization of society may support or mitigate the individual's experience of crippling psychological trauma. There are indications that in some ways, society makes deliberate efforts to reduce the incidence of trauma. It was the recognition that segregated schools were inherently inferior that led to a massive cultural effort to ensure more respectful handling of minority children's education. The "rule of thumb" originally referred to a judicial ruling that limited men to beating their wives with sticks no stouter than their thumb, and until the growth of the women's movement, assaulting your wife was not considered a crime commensurate to assault on a stranger. DeMause (1982) has carefully documented the many cruelties that were imposed on children in the past, practices such as beatings that are now labeled as abuse, but that were then considered a part of normal childrearing.

When we accept the perspective that social conditions can either directly traumatize people or make it more likely that they will be traumatized, the organization of our society becomes a critical focus. In the folk saying, "What goes around comes around," we understand in a new way the relatedness of social justice, psychological trauma, and cultural habitability. In a very compelling way, being "against" violence means that we must be "for" the humane treatment of all other human beings. We neglect conditions that foster mistreatment only at the expense of the general climate we live in. This section outlines some important traumatogenic forces that are related to violence. Just as the basics of human development theory yield an advocacy perspective, so we expect that making the connections between these social forces and their effects will create social advocates of us all.

CHILDREARING CONDITIONS AND PRACTICES

A child may not be subjected to physical punishment or other injurious or humiliating treatment.

Parenthood and Guardianship Code,
Sweden, 1979

In 1979, Sweden became the first country to ban the spanking of children. Since then, Finland, Denmark, Norway, and Austria have all joined Sweden in their efforts to stop the physical punishment of children. This move represents continuing progress in efforts to understand the needs of children that have been developing for generations. To understand the significance of this change, we must take a quick look at the history of childhood.

DeMause (1982) has chronicled the improvement in treatment of children from ancient times through modern societies. His theory of psychohistory proposes that each generation, with the benefit of hindsight, was able to improve treatment of their children over the treatment received from their parents. He divides the history of childhood into stages, ranging from an Infanticidal Stage, roughly until 400 A.D., when killing unwanted children was acceptable practice, through an Abandonment Stage, when it was no longer acceptable to kill children although it was acceptable to abandon them, to an Ambivalent Mode, when parents' task was seen as molding children into shape, to an Intrusive Mode, a Socialization Mode, and finally to the Helping Mode. This most recent child-rearing mode began after the Second World War and according to DeMause is the first time in history that the needs of the children are placed ahead of the child satisfying the needs of the parents. The progress of history, according to these ideas, is the story of increasing involvement and attachment between parents and children and the continuing problems of history are related to continuing failures or deficits in this critical attachment. Psychological processes governing parents' ability to identify and empathize with children, and thereby to be sensitive to their needs, are thought to be central to the culture's overall conception of children's place in society. The nature of childhood, including fundamental issues of life, death, work, and nurturance, is determined by the ability of the caretaking generation to process its traumatic childhood experiences.

The thrust of DeMause's psychogenic theory is to contest the sway of purely economic interpretations of history. But other historians of childhood have established the influence of economic conditions on the society's treatment of its children. Sommerville (1982) has described the impact of tightening family finances on child-rearing practices and attitudes of parents toward children in general. Whereas in 1950, 12 percent of preschool-aged children had working mothers, thirty years later 65 percent of mothers were working. This simple fact is fraught with consequence for America's families. Overall, he reported that we have seen twenty years of decline in the amount of time parents spend with children. Even the decision to have a child has been altered: fertility rates plunged from 278 per 1,000 women in 1800 to 65 per 1,000 in 1980. His point was that we cannot understand attitudes toward children independent of the economic conditions affecting parents' decisions.

Others have shown the relatedness of economic and social conditions to parenting attitudes. Nightingale (1993) found in his ethnographic study of an inner-city Philadelphia neighborhood that the harshness of parental childhood, especially in terms of experiences with racism, poverty, and violence, contributed to a characteristic parenting style that included frequent use of corporal punishment. As we will discuss later in this monograph, this intergenerational transmission of trauma is best understood in terms of the psychology of traumatic experience.

Child-rearing practices and attitudes, then, tell us something about the mental health and social well-being of the adults in a particular culture. Just as the fabled mine canary in West Virginia coal mines told miners when the air was unhealthy, the dependent status of children means they are subject to the circumstances of parents' lives, including their psychological status, and that cultural attitudes develop to rationalize and promote child-rearing practices consistent with these conditions.

From this perspective of culture and history we can consider it significant that currently American children cannot expect an end to corporal punishment such as that experienced in Scandinavian countries. In fact, the laws in each state presently give parents the right to hit a child with an object, provided no serious injury results (Straus, 1994). Ninety-nine percent of parents studied in Sears, Macoby, and Levin's 1957 landmark study, *Patterns of Child Rearing,* hit their children. Hitting children is one of the few child-rearing practices that most parents agree upon. Results of a Los Angeles study indicated that one-quarter of one- to six-month-old infants were spanked, and by the second half of the infant's first year, nearly half were being spanked (Straus, 1994). More than 90 percent of American parents use corporal punishment on toddlers and more than half continue this into the early teen years. According to a recent Gallup poll, nothing much has changed in the last fifty years. Sixty-five percent of Americans approve of spanking children, down only slightly from the 74 percent who approved of spanking in 1946. This approval also appears to apply to actual practice: almost exactly the same number of today's adults, 81 percent, say that they were spanked as a child as did Americans who were asked the same question in 1947 (Gallup Organization, Inc., 1997). The corporal punishment of children has an established place in cultural history. The physical punishment of children is rooted in beliefs about the need to "break children's wills" and a basic belief that self-will is evil and sinful. Although "spare the rod, spoil the child" is not actually in the Bible, the Old Testament certainly does make reference to this concept, according to Philip Greven in *Spare the Child: The Religious Roots of Punishment and the Psychological Impact of Physical Abuse* (1990). As he points out: "More than two thousand years of physical violence and painful assaults against the bodies and wills of children have been justified by these proverbs, scattered through the Old Testament collection of sayings attributed to Solomon" (Greven, 1990, p. 49). But then, the Old Testament is noted for its vivid descriptions of violence and "righteous" warfare.

The New Testament is far less clear on the matter. In fact, Greven points out that:

> When a Christian parent tells a child who is about to be punished that "Jesus teaches that you must receive the rod," he cannot justify this with any text from the Gospels. Jesus never advocated any such punishment. Nowhere in the New Testament does Jesus approve of the infliction of pain upon children by the rod or by any other such implement, nor is he ever reported to have recommended any kind of physical discipline of children to any parent. (Greven, 1990 p. 51)

Despite this finding, Protestant fundamentalism is closely linked to favorable attitudes toward corporal punishment of children in the home and the school. According to a recent study, greater personal religiosity and adherence to a punitive image of God account for very little of the relationship. Instead, the emphasis on biblical literalness among fundamentalists appears to be a major source of their advocacy of corporal punishment (Grasmick, Bursik Jr., and Kimpel, 1991).

In terms of DeMause's evolutionary perspective, the supposed "socializing function" of corporal punishment continues to dominate much thinking about children and helps to rationalize the use of corporal punishment. A recent advocate of the physical punishment of children wrote:

> If the punishment is of the right kind it not only takes effect physically, but through physical terror and pain, it awakens and sharpens the consciousness that there is a moral power over us, a righteous judge and a law which cannot be broken. (Christianson, L. as cited in Greven, 1990, p. 71)

A number of myths perpetuate corporal punishment in child-rearing practices in the United States. As indicated by Straus (1994), these are:

1. Spanking works better.
2. Spanking is needed as a last resort.
3. Spanking is harmless.
4. One or two times won't cause any damage.
5. Parents can't stop without training.
6. If you don't spank, your children will be spoiled or run wild.
7. Parents spank rarely or only for serious problems.
8. By the time a child is a teenager, parents have stopped.
9. If parents don't spank, they will verbally abuse their child.
10. It is unrealistic to expect parents never to spank.

One of the principles used to justify the use of corporal punishment is fear.

> Fear acts as a catalyst for love. He who fears God most will love him best. If God, the perfect Father, so disciplines His children as to inspire fear, then we should follow the same pattern in dealing with our children. (Greven, 1990, p. 64)

Through the study of trauma, we now know that fear does amazing things to a person, that fear increases our attachment, even to abusing objects, that it inhibits our ability to think clearly and thus makes us more blindly obedient, that it alters the way we remember and learn things, that it dramatically changes the way we relate to ourselves and other people. Fear does not inspire or serve as a catalyst for love. It does, however, provide the means of control, the method of manipulating others in service of the abuse of power.

An abundance of evidence now exists linking corporal punishment to social and psychological problems. Straus (1994) recently reviewed numerous studies conducted over the last fifty years showing the connection between the uses of physical punishment, depression, and suicide. The finding was quite clear: the more corporal punishment, the greater the chances of being depressed as an adult and the more likely to have thoughts about killing oneself.

There are gender differences when it comes to punishment. In a recent study, boys received higher amounts of harsh discipline on all outcome measures. For boys, growing up in an impoverished home was predictive of the greater likelihood of receiving harsh punishment. And "strict" discipline even seems to affect one's intelligence. Using IQ at age three as the outcome measure, girls were found to be vulnerable to persistent harsh discipline and lack of maternal warmth. Maternal harsh discipline in a context of low maternal warmth was associated with IQ scores for girls that are twelve points lower than the IQ scores of girls who received low punishment and high warmth (Smith and Brooks-Gunn, 1997).

In another study, researchers at the Family Research Lab wanted to test the hypothesis that the use of corporal punishment by parents to correct antisocial behavior in their children instead increased the antisocial behavior. They studied families for two years and found that parental physical punishment designed to stop antisocial behavior had the opposite effect (Straus, Sugarman, and Giles-Sims, 1997). Results of an eighteen-year longitudinal study of the effects of physical punishment were recently released. The study drew three major conclusions: (1) those exposed to harsh or abusive treatment during childhood are an at-risk population for juvenile offending, substance abuse, and mental health problems; (2) much of this elevated risk arises from the social context within which harsh or abusive treatment occurs; and (3) nonetheless, exposure to abuse appears to increase risks of involvement in violent behavior and alcohol abuse (Fergusson and Lynskey, 1997).

Violent adults were violent children and violent children learn about violence at home. Many studies have shown that physically and sexually abused children have high rates of violence and crime later in life (Eisenman, 1993; Laub and Lauritsen, 1995; Sheridan, 1995; Straus, 1994; Widom and Ames, 1994). Of course, the reasons parents give for administering the physical abuse is usually punishment and discipline. As Straus says:

> A relatively large amount of research has been done on the link between corporal punishment and aggression and delinquency. Almost all of those studies show that children who are hit by their parents tend to have higher rates of hitting and other aggression. (Straus 1994, p. 100)

Straus has also reviewed the connection between corporal punishment, violence, and crime. Studies have shown a connection between corporal punishment and increased aggression and violence in children. Children whose parents hit them are twice as likely to attack a brother or sister. Adults who were hit as adolescents are more likely to hit their spouses. Teenagers who were hit by their parents are more likely to steal and physically assault someone. The more corporal punishment parents use, the greater the chances of delinquent behavior among their children. States where teachers are allowed to hit children have a higher rate of student violence. Corporal punishment and physical abuse overlap: the more a parent was hit as an adolescent, the greater was the chance the parent would physically abuse his or her own child (Straus, 1994).

In many families, physical abuse is disguised as discipline, carrying on an intergenerational pattern of using violence in an attempt to manage children. And parents, being only human, sometimes lose control and what was meant as a slap turns into a punch, a kick, a serious injury, and sometimes even death. There can be a fine line between physical punishment and physical abuse. A growing body of evidence clearly demonstrated the connection between physical abuse and many other problems including: increased likelihood of the use of alcohol, marijuana, and almost all other drugs for both males and females (Harrison, Fulkerson, and Beebe, 1997); more lifetime and current episodes of depression, post-traumatic stress, and substance abuse (Duncan et al., 1996); a significant impact on the likelihood of arrest for delinquency, adult criminality, and violence (Maxfield and Widom, 1996); increased rates of psychopathology, sexual difficulties, decreased self-esteem, and interpersonal problems (Mullen et al., 1996); increased risk for promiscuity, prostitution, and teenage pregnancy (Widom and Kuhns, 1996); increased risk for later aggressive behavior as well as the development of deviant patterns of processing social information which may mediate the development of aggressive behavior (Dodge, Bates, and Pettit, 1990).

In addition to what we know now about the effects of abuse, John Bowlby noted over thirty years ago that there are three basic experiences that can produce a sociopathic character: (1) lack of any opportunity for forming an attachment to a mother figure during the first three years; (2) deprivation of contact with a loving maternal figure for a limited period—at least three months and probably more than six—during the first three or four years; and (3) changes from one mother figure to another during the same period. Bowlby's words ring out down through the decades, "Yet so far, no country has tackled this problem seriously . . . the twin problems of neglectful parents and deprived children are viewed fatalistically and left to perpetuate themselves" (Jones, 1968, p. 122).

In summary, corporal punishment has also been highly correlated with attacks on siblings, attacks on spouses, increased street crime, juvenile delinquency, and a generally accepted, socially learned acceptance and encouragement of violence (Straus, 1994). Children learn that violence is a way to express feelings, solve problems, get what you want, feel strong, feel safe, and feel good. Some children learn these lessons better than others. Some children never try anything else, because the violence always works. These kids are labeled "bad" everywhere—in school, by their families, by their peers, and neighbors. We know that many of these children are acting out the covert pathology of their family systems, at least at first. But after awhile, being "bad" becomes an identity—a way of defining yourself and reality. Unfortunately, in our culture being "bad" carries a great deal of status. It is certainly preferable to being "weak," a "sissy," or "childish." Can you imagine how much glamour would be lost if the violent bully on television was widely viewed as an overgrown two-year old throwing tantrums instead of as a tough guy?

Given these facts, which have been accumulating from studies over the past fifty years, we can conclude that it would be best if parents could learn to use other forms of managing children. Without encouragement to do so by their cultural milieu, however, it is unlikely that the sea change suggested by DeMause in the shift to a Helping Mode from the Socializing Mode can be accomplished despite such clear indications of widespread negative effects. What can be said with confidence at this point is that child-rearing practices, including normative violence from parents to children, is one of the key factors underlying society's problem with violence.

Obviously, not everyone who has been hit as a child ends up as a criminal. Many other factors in a loving family attenuate the affects of violence. Still, as we will discuss in detail later, we know that any experience of physiological hyperarousal experienced in association with helpless terror can have profound and far-reaching negative consequences for the child. Whenever a child is hit we must be willing to make an informed decision about whether it is really "worth it," whether the supposed gain is ever worth the very real risks. Since adult behavior is conditioned by childhood experience, it is time that we asked ourselves the more general question of whether hitting children results in producing adults who are prepared to run a democracy. Do we want adults who are fearful, who think poorly under stress, who are blindly obedient to authority, and who see violence as the appropriate response in dealing with others? If not, then we had better consider ending the routine abuse of power between adults and children.

DISAVOWAL OF EMOTIONS AND EMOTIONAL NUMBING

It looks more and more as if our emotions are the source of many of the problems that have plagued human beings throughout our long and tortured history. Actually, it is not the emotions themselves, but rather our failure to learn how to adequately manage them that cause the problems. This should come as no surprise to a generation raised with *Star Trek*. The pointy-eared Mr. Spock descended from a race of humanoids who had such trouble with emotions that they had learned to virtually eliminate them from their social intercourse. Unlike Vulcans, we humans cannot eliminate our emotions—at least not without paying an inordinately high price. Emotional experience is part of our mammalian heritage, hard-wired into every aspect of our physical and psychological being, and apparently necessary for our health, well-being, and sense of being alive.

According to Silvan Tomkins, the psychologist who spent a lifetime studying our emotional nature, we are each born with nine basic "affects." Affect is the term used to describe the biological origins of emotional experience. Affects are innate, hard-wired, the biological givens, genetically determined, and therefore beyond our conscious control. As we add experience, biographical information, time, and associations, affects develop into feelings, emotions, and moods. But all humans have affects in common. The nine basic affects, according to Tomkins' scheme are: interest/excitement, enjoyment/joy, startle/surprise, fear/terror, distress/anguish, anger/rage, shame/humiliation, disgust/dismell (Nathanson, 1992). Each affect determines a specific pattern of facial expression and a specific pattern of internal physiological arousal (Ekman, Levenson, and Friesen, 1983).

Our complex affect system has been biologically evolving over millions of years. Why? What survival value do emotions have? Harber and Pennebaker (1992) have looked at the cognitive functions of emotions. We use our emotions as sensitive mental radar, which give us vital information about what we should pay attention to in the environment, including other people. We begin forming cognitively and emotionally based mental files from the time we are born and each bit of new information has to be categorized into one of our files. Any disruption in these file categories or conflict with established expectations or beliefs will evoke emotions. Anything—an experience, a perception, an emotion—that does not fit into one of our files will keep bothering us until we find some way to categorize it or until we make a new file for it. In this way, we are constantly drawn toward any discrepancies in our surroundings. This can be very important, even life-saving information. Noticing that something is not right, or just does not fit, can be the first inkling we get that there is some sort of danger. Gavin de Becker has called this the "gift of fear" (1997).

We are extremely susceptible to "emotional contagion." This concept refers to the "tendency to automatically mimic and synchronize facial expressions, vocalizations, postures, and movements with those of another person and consequently to converge emotionally" (Hatfield et al., 1994, p. 5). In conversation we all tend automatically and continuously to mimic each other and synchronize our faces, voices, postures, and movements with the people around us. This synchronization happens so quickly that it has been noted that "for people to match their behaviors within 50 milli-seconds requires some mechanism unknown to man" (Condon, W. as cited in Hatfield, Cacioppo, and Rapson, 1994, p. 28). Hatfield and colleagues have reviewed the research data on emotional contagion. They found that we respond to other people's affect states in measurable ways— by changes in heart rate, blood pressure, and skin conductance as well as muscle activity, motor behavior, and an entire pattern of autonomic system activity that is different for each emotion.

Through these very rapid, nonverbal, and generally unconscious forms of communication, we are "catching" each other's emotions from moment to moment. Not only are we feeling what other people are feeling, but also their affect is affecting *our* basic biological functions. Ethologists believe that this imitation of emotional expression constitutes a phylo-genetically ancient and basic form of intraspecies communication that has an extremely high survival value for a social species (Hatfield, Cacioppo, and Rapson, 1994). As you might suppose, there is also clear evidence that parents "catch" their children's emotions and that children "catch" their parents emotions as well, and that for both, physiological patterns are synchronized according to the affect elicited.

A growing body of evidence indicates that in order to stay healthy, we need to express our emotions. A tendency to avoid disclosure of emotional states has been associated in a number of studies with cancer, coronary ailments, and other illnesses. Likewise, a tendency to disclose has shown an improved prognosis in bereavement and among patients suffering from breast cancer (Harber and Pennebaker, 1992). Across many studies, failure to disclose traumatic experiences surrounding death, sexuality, divorce, and so forth, has consistently been associated with self-reported and actual physician visits for illness, as well as major and minor health complaints in both retrospective (Pennebaker and Susman, 1988) and prospective studies (Pennebaker, 1989).

According to James Pennebaker and his associates, inhibiting emotional expression is related to impairments in the capacity to think clearly and impairs the processing of events by inhibiting translation into language that promotes assimilation. The unexpressed emotions are likely to arise anew as ruminations, preoccupations, dreams, and other forms of intrusions that interfere with thought. These effects have emerged with a variety of samples including people who have experienced the sudden death of a spouse, corporate employees, a large national sample of magazine readers, and college students. These effects hold when statistically controlled for social class, sex, nature of trauma, education, and social support. Likewise, confronting traumatic memories helps negate the effects of inhibition both physiologically and cognitively. When they studied college students who were instructed to simply write about their traumatic experiences for fifteen to twenty minutes, three to four days in a row, the health benefits to these students were significant and lasted two to four months after the writing experience (Harber and Pennebaker, 1992).

The implications of this research are enormous. First of all, we must begin to understand that there is something called "emotional intelligence"—the ability to monitor one's own and others' feelings and emotions, to discriminate among them and to use this information to guide one's thinking and actions (Mayer and Salovey, 1997). Our capacity for empathy and sympathy with the emotional experience of others is innate and evolved because it had significant survival value for the species. In a study comparing mothers who were judged to be at high-risk for physically abusing their children with low-risk mothers, the high-risk mothers showed a lack of empathy and the presence of negative emotions preceding abusive behavior. These mothers seem be more affected by emotional contagion from their infants' negative states than they were by empathy for the baby. They could not respond with compassion to a crying baby, but instead experienced an increase in sadness, distress, hostility, unhappiness, and less quietness themselves when faced with a crying baby (Milner, Halsey, and Fultz, 1995). In other studies, mothers who used less power strategies for disciplining their children and more empathy developed children who had better socialization skills, were more prosocial, and had better internalized their mothers' values and rules (Kochanska, 1997; Krevans and Gibbs, 1996).

If we consistently teach children to suppress their emotions, then we must accept the fact that we are probably doing harm to their physical bodies as well as their ability to relate to others, as more evidence accumulates that emotional inhibition has harmful health effects. If we do not respond empathetically to children's emotional needs, then they will cut off their emotional responsiveness to others and grow into adults incapable of empathy. This is particularly true for men, who are culturally brainwashed from a very early age that the expression of any emotion except anger is not entirely acceptable. Certainly, there is evidence that women are more comfortable expressing emotions, become less aroused by their own emotions, and are more nonverbally expressive then men (Hatfield, Cacioppo, and Rapson, 1994).

The development of empathy is also intimately tied to the development of a healthy prosocial conscience. Stilwell and associates have been looking at the connection between attachment, empathy, and moral development. In normal development, there appears to be a progression of stages as the child's attachment to a loving parent impacts the child's moral growth. First, the child's sense of security and empathic responsiveness become paired with a sense of moral obligation; caretaker rules are then incorporated; an understanding of how empathy modifies strict rule-following develops; idols and ideals are chosen that reflect earlier learning in attachment relationships; finally, a visualization of the self as moral standard-bearer or teacher unfolds (Stilwell et al., 1997). In a study of the effects of maltreatment on moral development, children who endured maltreatment prior to thirty-six months had developmental delays and more interference with conscience functioning than those who were either spared such experiences or who endured maltreatment later in life (Galvin et al., 1997).

This research also points to very important areas of social concern in which we often fail to provide for each other the responses that we are biologically programmed to provide. Presumably, the role of emotional contagion is to guarantee a group response to stimuli, particularly to dangerous stimuli. As we will discover later, a fundamental role of ritual and ceremonial behavior appears to be to synchronize a group of people into one emotional, and therefore physiological, harmony. Obviously, when we are overwhelmed with affect, we turn to other members of our species for assistance in managing that affect. They are programmed to respond with a similar affect state and physiological pattern of responses so that we become "attuned" to each other's emotional states. Such an interaction can promote the sharing of the experience, both nonverbally and verbally. Certainly, experimental evidence indicates that people are most likely to coordinate their movements tightly with those whom they like and love. Mothers are more synchronous with their own children than with unrelated children (Hatfield, Cacioppo, and Rapson, 1994). This also explains how virtually anyone can identify two lovers, even from a distance.

Apparently, our biology dictates that we are not supposed to chide each other for our emotions, or seek to suppress our own or other people's emotional expressions. This research would seem to indicate that in fact, we are supposed to help each other manage each other's emotions, especially when we are in a highly aroused state. We are supposed to help each other contain overwhelming affect, and we are supposed to assist each other in the process of translating affect into language. This is entirely consistent with what we have observed clinically regarding the needs of people who are endeavoring to heal from trauma. They require emotional containment and support from others that enable them to reassert emotional control for themselves. Without the ability to use other people as an emotional "bridge," we resort to various forms of self-destructive and other destructive behaviors to help us reassert control through the deliberate suppression of emotions instead.

In this way, we can make a strong case for the way in which our present social norm of disavowing emotional experience is, itself, a traumatogenic force that pervades the entire cultural milieu. Our social climate right now is permeated by rampant empathic failure—the failure to respond to another's distress. Our disavowal of affect provides strong support for our assessment that we are living in a trauma-organized society. Repeated traumatic experience produces emotional numbing. Numbing is an absence of emotion, but it is more than that—it is a sense of being "benumbed" (Horowitz, 1992). Henry Krystal has intensively studied the concept of "alexithymia" (from the Greek words meaning "a lack of emotion"). People who are alexithymic cannot identify or communicate emotions. They experience the same physiological arousal associated with emotions, but they cannot put those experiences into words. Instead, they are likely to express their feelings through their bodies. In Krystal's experience, people who are alexithymic have had catastrophic experiences and are left with the inability to relate in a normal emotional way to other people (Krystal, 1988). In a study of family factors related to alexithymia, the families of adults who scored high in alexithymia had difficulty identifying feelings and problems in dealing with strong emotions within the family, as well as difficulties with behavior control, and impaired problem-solving capacities (Lumley et al., 1996).

Alexithymia has been linked to various disorders, including compulsive behaviors, anxiety disorders and panic (Friedlander et al., 1997; Parker et al., 1993; Zeitlin and McNally, 1993, as well as somatiform disorders (Bach and Bach, 1995). Alexithymia has been shown to be higher in traumatized patients who have PTSD than those without PTSD (Yehuda et al., 1997). An association between childhood abuse and the development of alexithymia is becoming increasingly clear (Berenbaum, 1996). In several studies the presence of alexithymia predicted poor outcome in alcoholic patients trying to maintain abstinence (Loas et al., 1997; Ziolkowski, Gruss, and Rybakowski, 1995). It has been associated with a number of addictive disorders including alcoholism, cocaine abuse, binge eating, and pathological gambling (Lumley and Roby, 1995). The connection between bulimia nervosa and alexithymia has also been established by a number of studies (Cochrane et al., 1993; DeGroot, Rodin, and Olmsted, 1995; Jimerson et al., 1994; Schmidt, Jiwany, and Treasure, 1993).

It has been recognized for a long time that people who have psychosomatic illness often appear to have difficulty talking about their feelings, and instead seem to express their emotions through physical symptoms.

The concept of alexithymia has provided one way of looking at this hypothetical connection. Alexithymia has been connected to impairments in the immune system that lead to cancer (Todarello et al., 1994, 1997). In a study of gastrointestinal ulcers, alexithymia was associated with more severe symptoms (Fukunishi et al., 1997) and several studies have noted the link between alexithymia and inflammatory bowel disease (Porcelli et al. 1995, 1996), as well as between alexithymia and hypertension. In a study of over 100 hypertensives, 55 percent of them were alexithymic compared to 33 percent in a psychiatric group and 16 percent in a normal group (Todarello et al. 1995). As might be expected, people with alexithymia appear to have an increased utilization of the health care system (Joukamaa et al., 1996; Lumley and Norman, 1996).

In a general population study of middle-aged men, those with the highest measure of alexithymia had a twofold greater risk of death from all causes and a threefold greater risk of death from accidents, injury, or violence relative to the men who had lower alexithymia scores (Kauhanen et al., 1996). The connection between a high incidence of alexithymia and males has been established in other studies as well (Salminen et al., 1994; Saarijarvi et al., 1993). Although it is not yet clear *why* difficulties in dealing with emotions are associated with an increased risk of illness and even death, it is increasingly clear that this certainly is the case.

Throughout most of the history of science, the scientific study of emotion has been neglected, relegated instead to the domains of philosophy, religion, the arts, and in the last century, clinical psychology and psychiatry. Now that we are learning more about the basic biological substrate of emotional behavior, we may see a burgeoning of a more sophisticated and integrated approach to humankind's emotional life. This change can come none too soon. Performance artist Julian Beck, actor and founder of The Living Theatre, once said, "We are a feelingless people. If we could really feel, the pain would be so great that we would stop all the suffering" (Beck, 1972, Meditation I, 1963). Our national numbness to the suffering of women, children, the poor, minorities, and all the rest indicates how far we have gone in our retreat from affect and from relatedness. It goes a long way toward helping to explain our national destructiveness and denial.

SEXISM

The women's movement of the past three decades produced clear gains. In challenging the issues of diminished lives and demeaning roles for women, women's liberation fundamentally altered the discourse on gender, relationships, and many other subjects. The fight against sexism has meant that young women have vistas open to them not dreamed of by their mothers.

But as society approaches the year 2000, equality for women remains a dream, despite media and conservative claims to the contrary. Nearly double the number of female workers as compared to males earn less than $20,000 (Faludi, 1991). Despite the fact that entry-level, full-time female workers might make as much as ninety-five cents to every dollar earned by males, the average working woman's salary remains as far behind the male average as it did twenty years ago. The average female college graduate earns as much as the male high school graduate; the female high school graduate earns as much as the male high school drop-out (Faludi, 1991). Nearly 80 percent of working women are in traditionally "female" jobs: secretaries, salesclerks, and administrative support workers. Less than 8 percent of all federal and state judges are women, less than 6 percent of all law partners, and less than one-half of 1 percent of top corporate managers. Only nineteen of four thousand corporate officers and directors are women. The Glass Ceiling Commission report found that 95 percent of senior management positions are held by white males (Kilborn, 1995). A Fortune poll of 1,000 chief executives reported that more than 80 percent agreed that job discrimination impeded women's progress. (Faludi, 1991).

In education at the college level, scholarships, financial aid, and athletic funding all go to men at disproportionate levels to that of women. In the secondary and elementary school levels, research by the American Association of University Women (AAUW) (AAUW, 1992) and others established how damaging the assumption of "gender-neutral" school opportunity has been for girls. Where girls and boys share a classroom, resources—whether having the floor in class discussions, teacher attention, or other privileges— invariably tilt toward the boys (Sadker and Sadker, 1994). As a consequence of this bias and the messages attendant to it, girls hit adolescence like a brick wall and exhibit marked drops in achievement and self-confidence (Orenstein, 1994). Concern over this phenomenon of a decline in early adolescent girls' self-confidence has reached the level of a social movement, with works such as Brown and Gilligan (1992) and Peipher (1994) mobilizing the attention of families and schools to support girls more effectively.

In the home, "women's" work continues to include almost all—70 percent—of the household chores. The number of families in which child care is equally shared has actually diminished in the last period (Faludi, 1991). These facts and the data on domestic violence underscore the concern of many feminists that traditional family structures and practices can actually serve to maintain women's subordinate position.

Overall, assault is the single major cause of injury to women (Attala, 1996). Studies to determine the prevalence of violence directed at women in various samples have found considerable commonality in their exposure to risk across different life circumstances. A survey of inner-city women in Philadelphia found that violence was the leading cause of injury to women age fifteen to forty-four, with 20.8 per 1,000 women affected (Grisso et al., 1991). A retrospective study of female homicides in New Mexico from 1990 to 1993 found an overall homicide rate of 4.3 per 1,000 women, with a male intimate partner responsible in 46 percent of the cases (Arbuckle et al., 1996). A cross-sectional survey conducted among the female patients of a large, diverse, primary-care practice in Baltimore found that one of every twenty women had experienced domestic violence in the previous year while one out of five had experienced violence sometime in their adult lives (McCauley et al., 1995).

As previously mentioned, sexual assault is most commonly experienced by women in intimate relationships. One study found that 14 percent of married women reported being raped by a husband or ex-husband (Browne, 1993). A recent survey of the prevalence of domestic violence against women in the United States found rates of between 8 to 22 percent (Wilt and Olson, 1996). Whether based on specific experiences or on a general sense of vulnerability to assault, the level of vigilance routinely exercised by women in relation to men suggests a society in which women have become psychologically organized in response to their exposure to violence.

Meanwhile, on the streets, at the workplace, and in schools, sexual harassment confronts women. The AAUW study, *Hostile Hallways* (AAUW, 1993), emphasized how ubiquitous sexual harassment is for girls in schools. While campuses and legal codes wrestle with the idea that "No" means "No," sexual violence remains a fear for most women who have been conditioned by experience to regard themselves as vulnerable to rape, assault, or hassle.

In polls over the last decade and a half, women's awareness of being discriminated against and their resulting unhappiness reflected steady growth. By 1990, 80 to 95 percent of women maintained that they suffered from wage and job discrimination. Overall, Roper surveys report that the number of women who felt that men were "basically kind, gentle, and thoughtful" fell from 70 percent in 1970 to 50 percent in 1990 (Faludi, 1991, p. xvi).

Reagan-era policies of the 1980s did not help matters for women, who make up the bulk of single-parent families. Budget cuts added millions of female-headed families to the poverty rolls. Program cuts targeted services primarily benefiting women. These cuts have come at a time when other sources such as support payments from divorced husbands have declined significantly.

Overall, as Congress and the President have done battle over affirmative action programs in response to the complaints of the "angry white male," the women's movement appears to have been met by a significant backlash. The manufacture of a climate in which women's liberation is blamed for deterioration of the family, rising teenage drug use, unhappy marriages, and overstressed lives represents a convergence of reaction to the challenge to men's position of privilege and power.

GENDER, MALE CONDITIONING, AND VIOLENCE

As we have seen, violence is a gendered phenomenon. The preponderance of violent acts measured in our culture are perpetrated by males, acted out against females, children, and other males. Male violence against women occurs in the form of physical, sexual, and emotional abuse, harassment, and economic and social subjugation; in 95 percent of the cases of domestic violence, the perpetrator is male (Attala, 1996). Men inflict violence on other men in overt and covert ways, through war and physical battering as well as through the economic and cultural subjugation of minority, gay, and lower-class men (Kivel, 1992). Children are victims of male violence directly through physical and sexual abuse and indirectly through exposure to family violence (Finkelhor and Dziuba-Leatherman, 1994).

Throughout history, violence has seemed to be a male prerogative. Trained for war or for economic competition, men create a Darwinian world in which might makes right in playgrounds, boardrooms, playing fields, and homes. Interpersonal violence has been so closely associated with the experience of being male, in fact, that until relatively recently it was commonly believed that male biology was an inexorable force predisposing men to be violent (Segal, 1990). Even today, books on boys continue to cite "The Big T," testosterone, as the single biggest factor driving boys' development, claiming a multitude of effects, including aggressiveness and a predisposition to dominance seeking, from its neuroendocrinologic influence (Elium and Elium, 1992; Gurian, 1996).

But it is clear that the social world through which boys must pass on the way to manhood ensures that all males in this culture absorb a healthy dose of masculine, violent conditioning. Practically all males experience interpersonal violence, directly or indirectly; boys push, pull, threaten, bully, and hurt each other normatively, usually under the noses of adults, from the time they are quite young. Regardless of social class, across many different settings, boys enact aggressive, domineering, and violent scripts at each other's expense. And as the economic polarization between haves and have-nots has grown more pronounced (Frank and Cook, 1995), youth violence in general and male-to-male violence in particular has grown dramatically worse (Sells and Blum, 1996).

Miedzian (1991) argued that it is this taken-for-granted nature of male conditioning that is primarily responsible for the prevalence of violent behavior in males. We expect and permit boys to be violent. For example, despite the fact that gender differences in a variety of health outcomes, especially in mortality and morbidity rates, have been found to be closely tied to the socialization and lifestyle choices of males, little has been done from a public health standpoint to challenge these practices (Stillion, 1995; Waldron, 1995). Risk-taking behavior and unhealthy choices reflecting a "macho" attitude end male lives prematurely without a ripple of public concern.

Given the prevalence of violence in boys' lives, we might expect concern over recent studies of children exposed to violence which found that these children, indeed, commonly display symptoms of traumatization, among which are a propensity for acting out in aggressive and antisocial ways (Osofsky, 1995; Singer et al., 1995; Spaccarelli, Coatsworth, and Bowden, 1995). Retrospective studies of the lives of male perpetrators have found that these men were more likely to have been subjected to physical or emotional abuse (Else et al., 1993). Even the witnessing of violence, when combined with the other conditioning factors in boys lives, makes male children more likely to become perpetrators of violence themselves (Davies, 1991).

Boyhood in the United States, in light of these findings, practically seems a training ground for violence in service to an ethic of proving one's manhood (Kimmel, 1995). For some time now, many academics and developmentalists (Gilligan, 1982; Chodorow, 1978; Osherson, 1986) have argued that family processes of separation/individuation are more problematic for males than females and that these set boys up for later problems. Particularly with the normative absence of fathers from the child-rearing process, boys who must renounce their intimate connections with their mothers in order to follow the prescribed passage to manhood often lose all capacity for intimacy. Power and privilege may be rewarded to those boys who complete the separation process, but this fundamental perversion of human instincts for closeness and love takes a toll on psychological health. Recent work on the psychology of male development suggests that this "traumatic abrogation" of a boy's early connections can lead to a host of relational problems, including emotional numbing, loss of empathy, and personal dissociation (Pollack, 1995).

Silverstein and Rashbaum (1994) argue that, despite Freudian beliefs that development in boys requires the suppression of the feminine, boys do not necessarily require male role models in order to define themselves as men. Silverstein argues that boys can stay close to their mothers and manage to become men, misogynist pressures notwithstanding. With women continuing to provide the bulk of child rearing, her position suggests at least one critical direction for policymakers attempting to stem the tide of male violence: offer support for single mothers that helps these women to nurture their sons adequately. Parent support and training programs represent a key element in the multidimensional approach to violence prevention recommended by recent psychological task forces (Eron, Gentry, and Schlegel, 1994).

It is, in fact, a central tenet of trauma theory that only hurt people hurt others. From this perspective, whatever the influence of gender conditioning and sociobiological factors, we must assume that some systematic hurting of boys underlies and contributes to the prevalence of violent acting out by males. Not that this bedrock of trauma sufficiently explains an individual's behavior, but that it is a necessary condition for its occurrence.

Miller (1983) had something like this in mind as she reviewed the childhood of Adolf Hitler. She argued that cruel acts have their roots in disturbed childhood development and found in Hitler's life story, as well as in that of many contemporaries whose families practiced a "poisonous pedagogy," the systematic infliction of abuse and neglect by parents and others who did not understand the nature of human development.

How we construct gender as a culture bears directly on how we treat boys. Kokopeli and Lakey (1990) make connections between culture, conditioning, traumatization, and privilege to argue that male violence is a product of social constructions of masculinity which serve the interests of the society. For many generations, we have required of boys that they be willing to fight. We have needed men to fight wars and have encouraged interpersonal battering and competition among boys as a way to prepare men for this role. Violent television, superheros, and toys all reinforce the message to boys that they must master the use of force. In his recent study of a community's complicity in the gang rape of a New Jersey retarded girl by members of the high school athletic elite, Lefkowitz (1997) makes the same point: everyone, from parents to schools to teenage peer groups, plays a part in male violence. It is this social construction of masculinity, Segal (1990) argues, that may slowly be changing under the assault of the women's movement and other social forces. But unless these changes amount to more fundamental shifts in power and status than the fine-tuning adjustments to the male role advocated by men's therapy approaches, we may not see the desired end to violence. As Connell (1995), McLean (1996) and Kaufman (1993) have all persuasively argued, the hurting of boys—men's pain, overall—is functionally related to a system of sexism and domination that fuels male violence. Not mere reform, then, but a paradigm shift in our regard for boys and in gender relations is called for.

INJUSTICE: POVERTY AND RACE

The chronic, institutional stresses of poverty and racism are examples of social forces that can be termed traumatogenic in that they breed interpersonal traumatic acts. Statistical pictures depict life in poor communities of color as among the most traumatogenic in the society. Overall, poverty affects one in ten adults and one in five children (Betson and Michael, 1997). It is not, however, an equal-opportunity condition: African-American and Latino children and children from mother-only families are disproportionately poor (Corcoran and Chaudry, 1997).

Whether we consider street violence, domestic violence, or child abuse, the incidence of trauma is higher in such communities. Difficult life conditions give rise to a constellation of cultural circumstances that make the transmission of interpersonal violence normative (Staub, 1996). Poverty has been found to have a primary influence on how well parents manage family life (Garrett, Ng'andu, and Ferron, 1994). Family poverty inhibits parental processes of family control, for example, increasing the likelihood of childhood acting out (Sampson and Laub, 1994). Under such conditions, it is not surprising that unchecked aggression is more frequently exhibited in children from impoverished families (Tolan and Henry, 1996).

Other at-risk factors for violence are also associated with economic and race stressors. High-risk adolescent behavior is most strongly predicted by early academic failure (Tuakli-Williams and Carrillo, 1995). Yet a child's chances for success in school have been found to be powerfully affected by early childhood experiences of poverty (Brooks-Gunn and Duncan, 1997). Family income, in fact, is a primary predictor of the cognitive development and behavior of children (Duncan, Brooks-Gunn, and Klebanov, 1994). The cognitive effects of poverty seem, in particular, to reflect a reduction in the brain's capacity for attentive behavior (Mirsky, 1995).

There has been a plethora of social research since the 1950s to explain this observation. Beginning with Kenneth Clark in 1954, we have been made aware that institutional segregation results in psychological damage. Public health surveys continue to report the finding that the residential segregation of poverty and the extent of income inequality are primary factors explaining rates of crime and violence (Kawachi and Kennedy, 1997). During the social consciousness of the 1960s, it was acknowledged that experiences with prejudice and discrimination contribute to alienation (Cobb and Grier, 1968). Today, following the Vietnam War and a growing understanding of trauma and PTSD, there is new appreciation for the transgenerational transmission of hurt in families that live in conditions that foster violence and trauma.

Nightingale (1993) describes in equally compelling detail from ethnographic observation the embeddedness of the harshness and abuse of racism and poverty in the family and community systems of poor, urban African Americans. Similarly, Anderson (1990) has observed about inner-city communities that alienation and violence spring naturally from the living conditions of poor and racial minorities.

Through the mechanisms of traumatic reenactment, for example, parents whose childhood experiences included physical punishment recreate these experiences in their parenting of their children. Nightingale makes the observation that research on family life in inner cities has been preoccupied by structural features—absence of fathers, matriarchy—and has ignored the quality of relationships possible in these families, despite the recognition that parents who can manage a "decent" family life can largely counteract the negative influences of the poor community (Anderson, 1994).

Embedded in the institutional stresses of racism and poverty, then, are personal experiences that provide explanations for increased levels of violence. Racism and poverty create a host of threats to child development that leave affected children vulnerable to violence as victims, perpetrators, and witnesses (Green, 1993). The terror of witnessing ubiquitous violence must be fully considered as we attempt to come to grips with the spiraling deterioration of urban poor communities (Holton, 1995).

Most significantly, the cumulative effect of violence in the home and on the streets impairs the establishment of interpersonal trust, a central outcome of the human attachment process that ideally endows citizens with a sense of investment in their community. The constant background of violence for poor urban youth creates, by contrast, a culture of careful detachment (Berman, 1992). When your experience has taught that you might be hurt at any moment, many find it safer to withdraw from human interaction, from sharing, and from empathic attachments to others.

Kody Scott (1993), Nathan McCall (1994), Geoffrey Canada (1995), and Joseph Marshall Jr. (1996) are African-American men whose autobiographical accounts describe the temptation to act out in retaliatory violence the rage, humiliation, and powerlessness resulting from racism. At this point in the culture, with black males threatened from a convergence of powerful trends, the manner in which a child internalizes the content of negative messages through distorting self-image provides additional explanation for the culture of violence swirling through urban communities. Indeed, the resentment felt by black males about stereotypes that greet them today has led to cultural forms—such as gangster rap—that embody a powerful and defiant celebration of their anger. The culture of urban street life becomes so dominated by these adaptations that a child faces enormous pressure to conform to such "protest masculinity," refusing only at the risk of his own banishment. Some researchers even argue that anger and acting out can be considered reasonable and resilient reactions to the atmosphere of hostility that African-American males encounter (Stevenson, 1997).

Twin economic trends of exclusion and inclusion have compounded the effects of racism and poverty in inner-city neighborhoods. Arguing against those who maintain that poor people's alienation results from their marginalization in the culture, Nightingale (1993) suggests that the impact of technology and media have included the poor in norms of affluence in ways that have heightened the humiliations and frustrations of economic exclusion. He illustrates how innovations in marketing have fashioned a culture of desire among poor people who can compensate for the shame of job failure with consumption. Such refinements in marketing techniques have compounded family difficulties by questioning black parents' abilities to satisfy their children's material desires.

At the same time, the rich have become richer while the poor—most often women and children—have become poorer. In the 1980s, income for the poorest 40 percent of families declined while income for the top 20 percent rose by almost 30 percent, and income for the top 1 percent rose by 75 percent. In the last decade the proportion of families moving out of poverty declined by 40 percent. Meanwhile, the increase in total salaries of people earning more than $1 million per year went up by 2,184 percent while the total dollars in wages that went to the middle class increased only an average of 4 percent a year. The result is that the top 4 percent collectively of the population earns as much as the total of the bottom 51 percent (Bartlett and Steele, 1992). Women are the fastest growing class of impoverished people, heading 24 percent of all poor households in 1960 and 48 percent of all poor households in 1984 (Katz,

1989), while 40 percent of the people living below the poverty line are children (Freedman, 1993).

SOCIAL STRESS

To give due consideration to those social forces that foster traumatic interpersonal acts, we must look at the ways in which society has changed in the last several decades. In some revealing statistics, we can see pressures that create a context for life today and that influence behavior in particular directions. According to the 1993 U.S. Advisory Board Report on Child Abuse and Neglect, since 1960 there has been a fourfold increase in births outside of marriage, a fourfold increase in the divorce rate, and a nearly threefold increase in the proportion of working mothers of young children (U.S. Advisory Board, 1993). Although there is some cultural variation, these trends can be noted in every developed country.

One effect of these demographic trends has been that American families are more mobile than ever before. One in four children lives in a different home from the one the family occupied a year earlier. The implication of this for extrafamilial support from the community is obvious: American families are more than ever on their own. This decline in informal community support has in no way been compensated for by additional services from the social service system, which has been impacted by a shrinking tax base and stunning increase in need.

Stress levels for Americans, meanwhile, are rising in other ways. By 1985, we were working 20 percent more hours than a decade before and enjoying 32 percent less leisure time, down from twenty-six hours a week in 1973 to eighteen in 1985. In her popular book, Schor (1992) cited the surprising finding that working hours over the past twenty years have increased by the equivalent of one month per year. As maintaining the economic standard has demanded two incomes, the stresses on individuals and relationships have multiplied. Eighty-nine percent of adults experience what they consider high levels of stress, 59 percent at least once or twice a week, 30 percent nearly every day. Fifty percent say that their lives have become significantly more stressful in the past ten years.

Broad macroeconomic alterations help explain these changes in the lives of families. America has gone from the world's wealthiest profit center to one among many competitors, with an enormous national debt. Companies have responded to heightened international competition with drastic restructurings, which have included massive layoffs affecting thirty million people as of 1989. In this period of retrenchment, contract givebacks have become the norm, further reducing income and benefits for the majority of Americans.

At the lowest end of the economic ladder, Reagan-era cutbacks in social services have left the safety net for poor, homeless, and unemployed Americans frayed and torn. AIDS, homelessness, factory shutdowns, bank closures, and a faltering farm industry have all affected the national consciousness.

On a broader social and psychosocial level, the breakup of the Soviet Union, which gave us a strong sense of our national identity and purpose throughout the last half-century, has left us without an enemy upon whom we can project all our national angst, rage, and fear. A common enemy helps a people "form and maintain a cohesive sense of self and, later, the sense of a group self in ethnic or national terms" (Volkan, 1988, p. 4). In 1987, Soviet policy advisor, Georgy Arbatov, threatened that his government would "do something terrible to us"—it would deprive us of our enemy (Barash, 1994, p. 17). It is not entirely a coincidence that since the breakup of the Soviet system and the consequent breakdown in our enemy system, we seem to be turning on ourselves, waging civil war on our own people, vastly increasing the social stress for everyone. In deconstructing the health care delivery system, disassembling the social safety net for the poor, scapegoating minorities, women, and the underprivileged for all the society's social problems, we see the desperate search for the enemy. Such a national self-destructive attack affects everyone in the culture as we all participate in an orgy of self-mutilative behaviors.

The overwhelming theme in all these historic economic and social changes has been an individual sense of powerlessness. People feel robbed of control over important aspects of their lives. Polls have depicted Americans as frightened, cynical, and pessimistic about the future. Movies and television portray and model a singular response to that helplessness—buy a gun and shoot it. Not surprisingly, one outcome has been a surge in hate crime violence: as the Oklahoma City bombing of a federal building brought to light, there are numerous citizen militia and other assorted collections of individuals who are persuaded that violence targeted against representative members of groups constitutes a legitimate protest against changing social conditions (Hutson et al. 1997).

EXISTENTIAL CONFUSION AND THE PROBLEMS OF EVIL

If only there were evil people somewhere, insidiously committing evil deeds, and it were necessary only to separate them from the rest of us and destroy them. But the line dividing good and evil cuts through the heart of every human being. And who is willing to destroy a piece of his own heart?

Aleksandr Solzhenitsyn

Exposure to acts of violence has many effects on the body and mind of the individuals involved, regardless of whether they are victims, perpetrators, or bystanders. People can overcome vulnerabilities, even disabilities inflicted on the body, and they can frequently rise above the traumatic effects on the mind. But this does not guarantee that they are able to integrate the effects of violence of the *soul*. All traumatic events affect the way people make sense of the world, their place in it, and the role of other people. The need to find meaning is fundamental to human existence at the individual and the social level. In facing up to the effects of violence we are really focusing on "the problem of evil" (Noddings, 1989, p. 6), humankind's age-old effort to reckon with violence done to us and violence done by us. It is a very difficult concept to grasp, not the least because there has always been so much disagreement about what evil is and what causes evil (Bloom, 1996).

For the ancient Hebrews, evil meant primarily worthlessness and uselessness, and by extension it came to mean bad, ugly, or even sad. Thus originally it meant simply bad as opposed to good (Taylor, 1985). Later words were used to refer to the breaking of the covenant with God and referred to such notions as "falling short of a target," "breaking of a relationship or rebelliousness," and "twisting, making crooked or wrong." The word for evil in Hindu texts refers to inert and benighted lethargy, to something not properly alive and yet capable of being activated as evil (Parkin, 1985). Neither the Japanese nor the Chinese make any contrast between "bad" and "evil." The Chinese character used to express "badness" connotes "disgust" rather than "wrong." In Shinto thought, good and evil are connected with purity and impurity, with life and death (Moeran, 1985). In English the word for evil has a folk usage that derives in part from Teutonic tradition and in common with the German *übel* and the Dutch *euvel,* derived from the Teutonic *ubiloz,* which refers to the root *up, over;* primarily meaning "exceeding due measure," or "overstepping proper limits" (Pocock, 1985). In English there appears to be a strong and a weak meaning of the word *evil* (Macfarlane, 1985). The strong meaning refers to the antithesis of good, which usage, interestingly enough, the *Oxford English Dictionary* declares is obsolete when referring to persons. The strong sense carries the implication of moral depravity and thorough wickedness. The weak meaning is the one usually used nowadays, meaning to cause discomfort and/or pain, to be unpleasant, offensive, and disagreeable, to be "not good" (Macfarlane, 1985, p. 57). He believes that the "disappearance of evil [in the strong sense] is one of the most extraordinary features of modern society" (p. 57). Likewise, suffering that occurs as a result of forces of nature is described as natural evil, whereas, suffering that occurs as the result of deliberate or negligent human agency is at least a partial definition of moral evil (Noddings, 1989). Metaphysical evil is a term used for the necessary lack of perfection that exists in a created cosmos, since no cosmos can be perfect as God is perfect (Russell, 1988a). Radical evil has been used to describe a "fundamental warping of the will that underlies individual actions . . . people who have allowed their wills and personalities and lives to be swallowed up by Radical Evil" (Russell, 1988b, p. 48).

Our present definitions of evil incorporate a number of different meanings: 1a: not good morally: WICKED; 1b: arising from actual or imputed bad character or conduct archaic; 2a: INFERIOR; 2b: causing discomfort or repulsion: OFFENSIVE; 2c: DISAGREEABLE; 3a: causing harm: PERNICIOUS; 3b: marked by misfortune: UNLUCKY archaic—evil. 2. evil *n.* 1: something that brings sorrow, distress, or calamity; 2a: the fact of suffering and misfortune; 2b: a cosmic evil force *n.* (*Webster's,* 1983). This brief, and albeit incomplete, look at word origins tells us something about the enormous variability of human thought and perception about the nature of evil across time and cultures. But in every culture, evil has been associated with calamity, misfortune, sorrow, and suffering and therefore with traumatic experience.

The variability in the definition of evil is important to understand because so much of the way we deal with others, about the assumptions we automatically make, as well as the structure of our institutions, is based on what we believe constitutes evil, evil acts, and evil people. We believe that these definitions of what is and is not evil play a fundamental role in helping to create a society within which traumatic events are supported and encouraged and healing from trauma is therefore made much more difficult. In Western culture, the powerful doctrine of a world divided into good and evil dates back to the Persian prophet Zoroaster, who lived around 1500 B.C. He proposed that God is wholly good and that all evil, suffering, misery, and death come from the devil. With evil trapped in a world full of life, the battle between the forces of good and evil had begun and would last through the course of history. The soul could achieve salvation but only by moving the locus of happiness from this world to the next, and if there was to be salvation it depended on one authority whose representatives were the clergy. These seeds powerfully influenced Judaism and later Christianity and are still with us today, particularly in the powerful Christian fundamentalist movement (Messadié, 1996). These ideas influence every aspect of our social milieu, from our criminal justice system to the way we view the poor to what we believe about the nature of children and childhood. If we believe that there is an eternal battle between good and evil and that good must win, then these beliefs can—and have been—used to justify any act of violence.

This structural support for violence through our deep philosophical and religious assumptions manifests in a number of ways that we can only touch upon here. In a century of incomparable bloodshed, violence, brutality, destructiveness, and under the threat of total annihilation, many authors have searched for keys to understanding evil behavior in the sanctions of the social system. Most of their efforts have been directed to the glaring evils of the twentieth century that have produced collective, state-organized acts of enormous evil. In doing so, they search for the answers to what one author cites as four distinguishable questions (1) How is evil legitimized?; (2) What kinds of shared values or beliefs or sentiments are appealed to in order to render the prosecution of evil permissible or desirable?; (3) How are people mobilized for evil actions?; and (4) How is evil rationalized? (Smelser, 1971). Evil is legitimized first by demonizing the other, while holding oneself or one's group as morally superior. The more the demonization of the other fits preconceived social stereotypes, religious beliefs, and social traditions, the easier it is to view them as evil. Rampages of destructiveness are much more likely when some person or agency in a position of power authorizes or encourages or fails to discourage the behavior. When combined with the failure of any countervailing forces of restraint, the behavior can become completely unrestrained. Rationalization of all kinds then serves to justify and excuse the perpetrators, turning their evil behavior into good. "All's fair in love and war," and "Done in the line of duty" are two such socially condoned rationalizations which assure the perpetrator that guilt is unnecessary, perhaps even unpatriotic or sick (Smelser, 1971).

Another author, prompted by the My Lai massacre in the early 1970s during the Vietnam War, wrote a chapter in which he described the eight conditions for a guilt-free massacre: (1) The person must be seen as a symbol of something totally contrary to what others in the community regard as the communal good—the humanity of the victims must be denied; (2) there must be a connection between faith in the well-being of a society and faith in its organizational arm of violence and citizens must conclude that their organizational arm of violence can do no wrong; (3) the organizational arm of violence must believe that organizational grounds for action are superior to individual grounds for action; (4) loyalty to the organization must take precedence over every other consideration, every other loyalty, every other morality and individuals who violate this standard must be ostracized; (5) individuals in the army or police or gang must begin to believe that their actions are satisfactory only to the extent that they relate to organizational rules; (6) organizations must find ways to avoid blame as well, often through secrecy and isolation that is considered vital to such aims as "national security"; (7) there must be a target population, a vulnerable population that cannot adequately fight back; and (8) there must be a motivation to commit massacre or any other evil act now defined as good or at least necessary (Duster, 1971).

Important research on the nature of authoritarianism was published in the 1950s and reviewed again in 1971. In this study, 2,500 Americans from all walks of life were interviewed about their attitudes toward Jews. The term ethnocentrism was used to describe prejudice against an out-group and bias in favor of the subject's own group. The hypothesis was that high ethnocentrism would be associated with other traits that could predispose people to act against members of an out-group, particularly within the demand of an established and authoritarian system. What they discovered was that there is a close association between ethnocentrism and the following tendencies: rigid adherence to conventional values; submissive attitudes toward moral authorities in the in-group; readiness to punish the slightest violation of conventional values; opposition to the subjective, imaginative, or tender-minded; belief in primitive hereditarian theories and in mystical determination of the individual's fate; inability or unwillingness to deal with the indefinite, the ambiguous, or the probable; preoccupation with the dominance-submission aspect of human relationships and exaggerated exertions of strength and toughness; cynicism with respect to human nature; and disposition to ascribe evil motives to people. They called this pattern of traits "authoritarianism" (Sanford, 1971). Such recent authors as Ervin Staub (1989) have taken these sociological analyses even further and include the critical role of the bystander in determining the behavior of perpetrators, a subject we explore in more depth later. Many other authors and researchers explore the various destructive roles played by the economic, scientific, psychological, sociological, and political paradigms in creating the situations that are the breeding grounds for the perpetration of evil acts.

James Gilligan, former director of the Bridgewater State Hospital for the criminally insane, and director of mental health for the Massachusetts prison system, has taken a broad view of the relationship between trauma and the perpetration of evil and takes a much more tragic view of evil behavior than has traditionally been voiced in psychological circles. "Human violence is much more complicated, ambiguous and, most of all, tragic, than is commonly realized or acknowledged" (Gilligan, 1996, p. 5). In his view, "all violence is an attempt to achieve justice" (p. 11). Even murderers believe that they are performing an act of "righteous slaughter" (p. 77). It is his belief, after years of experience in working with rapists, murderers, sadists, and the most brutal of men, that shame is the primary and ultimate cause of violence, whether it is self- or other-directed. Take shame, with the utter mortification of feeling ashamed that is equivalent to a disintegration of identity, combine it with: (1) a belief that nonviolent means cannot ward off the shame, (2) a lack of emotional capacity for normal inhibition of violence, especially love and guilt toward others; and (3) fear for the self, and you have a prescription for violence.

Carl Goldberg (1996) has studied and worked with perpetrators of evil acts. He discusses the formation of the malevolent personality and he too concurs that the cycle of malevolence begins with shame. For such people, their habitual experience of being shamed themselves pushes them to project their noxious feelings onto others, resulting in a sense of contempt for other people that helps to reverse their own underlying feeling of self-contempt. But then, efforts must be made not to see that you are doing to others what was done to you, hence rationalization plays an important role in justifying one's cruel and contemptuous acts, and taken further, you search for justifications for the malevolent actions. Regardless of whether we are discussing a parent's explanation for hitting his child, or a murderer's justifications for his acts, the same pattern emerges. For the malevolence to continue to escalate it is necessary that the malevolent person be unable or unwilling to examine his actions, motivations, and purposes for himself and magical thinking substitutes for a logical, reasoning, honest appraisal of the situation. This is the pattern of malevolence that occurs in the life of the criminal and is a pattern that can be seen even at the level of the group.

The dominant paradigm in this period of our history insists on an implicit belief system about evil and how to deal with it, a belief system that appears often, from a humanistic point of view, to be a prescription for evil itself. In this paradigm, unquestioning obedience to power is important and rebellion is evil. Women, children, the poor, and people of color are inferior, soft, indulgent, and fail to understand the importance of strength and pitilessness. To be a man means always being tough and strong, never crying, being prepared to fight. In the medieval era—and in some cultural groups today—there was (is) a preoccupation with the devil and hell. Now we are preoccupied with the atmosphere of hell—violence, sexuality divorced from intimacy, criminality, and unrelenting punishment. People get what they deserve; human nature is basically evil and requires constant restraint, and once judged evil, there is no use for confession or atonement, no pity or compassion—nothing can help the damned. This paradigm continues to serve those who have wealth and power, but we must consider that it may no longer serves the human race as a whole. At the dawn of the twenty-first century, it may be time for us to leave ancient theology behind and envision a different way of being while continuing to pursue other discourses on how to make meaning out of trauma, how to transform the effects of violence into acts of peace.

Chapter 3

Where Violence Occurs

VIOLENCE IN THE FAMILY

Cultural norms determine our reactions to violence. In U.S. society, the recent upsurge in street violence has been noticeable and widely lamented by contrast with earlier, more civil periods. Most acts of violence take place in homes, however, not in public places. The hidden nature and historic acceptance of family violence has meant that our society is only just beginning to face this phenomenon and to react to it.

How violent are American families? As Gelles and Straus (1988) found there is probably some hitting in almost every household at some time. American parents feel overwhelmingly that physical punishment of children is necessary and, consequently, practically all children in U.S. homes experience some hitting by their parents (Straus, 1994).

Sibling to sibling violence is also the norm in our homes: Finkelhor and Dzuiba-Leatherman (1994) found that 80 percent of children in various surveys reported experiencing some peer violence. Gelles and Straus (1988) found that sibling violence can be quite severe and estimate that "more than a hundred thousand children annually face brothers and sisters with guns or knives in their hands" (p. 60).

Perhaps half of all husbands and wives engage in physical fighting during their marriages. Minor acts of violence—slapping, pushing—occur equally with males and females, although when females are violent it is almost always defensive and protective. Severe acts of violence are almost entirely committed by males and are estimated to affect as many as 4 million women annually (Browne, 1992). Marital rape and other forms of sexual victimization between husbands and wives have been excluded from most state rape statutes and consequently have been hard to assess. Estimates suggest an incidence of between 10 to 15 percent of married women. And overt physical violence is not the only kind of violence in marriages. The threat of violence, often combined with acts of terrorism directed at pieces of personal property or pets, is often sufficient to dominate the women, given the fundamental physical power imbalance that exists in most relationships.

It is the impact of these numbers and the growing evidence that links a child's witnessing violence with traumatization which have led social scientists recently to refer to children in violent families as the unacknowledged victims of domestic violence (Rhea et al., 1996). How children relate to others, how they develop their sense of self and self-control and how they will interact with later intimate partners are all critically impacted by exposure to family violence (Wolfe and Korsch, 1994). In addition, recent epidemiological studies have discovered that children who live in violent families are at risk themselves for inadvertent physical injury (Christian et al., 1997).

Elder abuse is the other prevalent form of family violence. Estimates of its extent are conservative due to the isolation of elders, their dependence upon their caretakers, and their mental and physical infirmities. Including verbal abuse, various studies place the incidence of elder abuse at 500,000—1.5 million Americans. Most commonly, these victims are abused by their caretakers (Goldstein, 1989).

Implicit in these numbers are definitional problems in the use of the terms "violence" and "abuse." Gelles and Straus (1988, p. 54) have defined violence as any "act carried out with the intention, or perceived intention, of causing physical pain or injury to another person." But, in general, cultural norms determine when the use of force is deviant and thereby earns the labels "abuse" or "violence." As our understanding of the human mind and behavior have grown, we have developed a greater awareness of the nature of child development, for example, and a clearer understanding of what constitutes child abuse.

Cultural norms regarding family violence, in fact, have a great deal to do with the incidence of violent behaviors. Generally, it appears that most violence in homes occurs in an unequal power exchange. People commit violent acts because they can. They can because structural features of family life—isolation, dependence of women and children on men, laws that shield family privacy—minimize social controls. Cultural influences may also rationalize the use of violent strategies for solving problems, managing marital conflicts or childrearing, reducing guilt or cognitive dissonance.

Relational dimensions to violence also suggest that power dynamics constitute a critical component to the act. Children in abusive families have little recourse when a parent is neglectful or harmful. Women in violent relationships often feel helpless, and lose initiative and a sense of options. Compounding learned helplessness are other effects of trauma, including what has been called the "battered wife syndrome" of low self-esteem, self-blame, fear, and guilt.

On an individual level, the reasons why some people resort to violent strategies in relationships have been exhaustively studied. There is disagreement in the research as to control: whether resorting to violence reflects a loss of control or a deliberate effort to assert control. This disagreement relates to broader questions of the relative contributions of instrumental and impulsive, or emotional, motivations to relational violence. Very likely violence can be a manifestation of either, depending on the physiological and psychological conditioning of the particular person. Certainly, one of the most revealing characteristics of the battering man is a feeling of inadequacy and a belief that violence is an acceptable avenue for achieving dominance and power, frequently accompanied by childhood experiences as either victim or witness to family violence.

VIOLENCE IN THE WORKPLACE

Government agencies including the U.S. Department of Justice, the Bureau of Labor Statistics, the National Institute of Occupational Safety and Health (NIOSH) and private organizations including the Society for Human Resource Management and the Northwestern National Life Insurance Company (NWNL) all agree that workplace violence has become a major social and economic problem.

Workplace violence has tripled in the last decade. Where workplace homicide is a major cause of death among workers, its impact is considerably outweighed by the largely unreported prevalence of near-misses, physical assaults, abusive confrontations, and threats, which follow a different set of risk factors, particularly affecting women (Nelson and Kaufman, 1996; Warshaw and Messite, 1996).

Workplace homicide is one of the fastest growing types of homicide, accounting for twenty workplace deaths each week (Jenkins, 1996a). According to NIOSH it was the third leading cause of workplace death from 1980 to 1985 for men and the leading cause of workplace death for women (Duncan, 1995), accounting for 39 percent of all fatal injuries for women at work (Levin, Hewitt, and Misner, 1996). A recent report found that workplace homicide was the second leading cause of fatal occupational injuries overall (Hewitt and Levin, 1997). Following data from the National Traumatic Occupational Fatalities system from 1980 to 1992, a recent study found that 2,001 women and 7,935 men were victimized at their workplaces, producing rates of .32 per 100,000 for male workers and 1.01 for female workers (Jenkins, 1996b).

The Bureau of Labor Statistics counted 1,063 workplace homicides in 1993. Three-quarters of these deaths occurred during commission of robberies or other crimes, 11 percent involved police or security guards, and 4 percent involved personal acquaintances (Barrier 1995b; Toscano, 1996).

In 1994 there were 1,071 workplace homicides, 75 percent of which were robbery related or crimes of opportunity (McMurry, 1995). The highest risk group for workplace homicide were men, the self-employed, and those employed in grocery stores, restaurants, gas stations, taxicab services, and government service (Hewitt and Levin, 1997).

Gunshot wounds accounted for the deaths in 80 percent of the workplace homicides (Windau and Toscano, 1994), but in 97 percent of the cases of nonstranger workplace homicide the assailant was armed, reflecting careful planning in these cases (Duncan, 1995). The average number of deaths per incident, including offender suicide, was 2.5, demonstrating the typical quality of overkill in these cases. Only in 39 percent of the cases did the assailant kill one person. In 36 percent of the cases, the assailant committed suicide, indicating the extremely high risk in these cases since the assailant often has no desire other than that of revenge (Duncan, 1995).

Workplace homicides that are not related to robbery fall into three categories: (1) acts of domestic violence or stalking, (2) acts by disgruntled current or former employees, and (3) acts by customers or clients (McMurry, 1995). Particularly high-risk occupations are police officers and firefighters, but people who work in bars and banks are at high risk as well as social workers, particularly those in public agencies. The highest number of homicides occurred in the retail trade—36 percent—with sales workers in the highest category; 17 percent were among human service workers, 14 percent among executives, administrators, and managers. (Baron, 1993; Jenkins et al., 1992; Wheeler and Baron, 1994).

The U.S. Department of Justice reports that nearly a million people each year become victims of violent crime on the job. This means that one in six violent crimes happens at work (Yarborough, 1994). These acts account for about 15 percent of all acts of violence experienced by people age twelve years or older (McMurry, 1995). In addition, people experience over two million personal thefts and 200,000 car thefts while they are at work. Over 30 percent of workplace victims faced armed attackers. Over half of the victimizations were not reported to the police because the victim believed the incident to be personal or because they had reported it to someone at the company (Dilworth, 1994).

According to the NWNL survey, between July 1992 and July 1993, 2.2 million full-time workers were physically attacked on the job, 6.3 million were threatened with violence, and 16.1 million were harassed (Anfuso, 1994). Threats were made by current or former employees 43 percent of the time, by customers or clients 36 percent, and by strangers only in 16 percent of the cases (Duncan, 1995). According to Joseph Kinney, executive director of the National Safe Workplace Institute that studies work-place crime, this means that "One out of every four employees was harassed, threatened, or attacked between July 1992 and July 1993" (Yarborough, 1994, p. 1).

The Society for Human Resource Management (SHRM), an organization of human resource professionals, conducted a survey in 1993 of their members. Almost one-third of the 479 members reported acts of violence at their workplaces in the previous five years, more than half of them involving assaults by one employee on another (Barrier, 1995b). Half of those surveyed said they had observed anger or aggressive behavior in an individual who later perpetrated a violent incident (Smith, 1994). Thirty percent of workplace attacks are committed by co-workers, bosses, or former employees, as well as 43 percent of threats of violence against workers and 88 percent of harassment episodes (Anfuso, 1994). A TIME/CNN poll in 1994 said 18 percent of surveyed people had witnessed assaults at work, and another 18 percent worry about becoming victims themselves (Toufexis, 1994).

The Department of Labor and Industries received reports for sixty-three rapes in the workplace in Washington State alone from 1980 to 1989. Eighty-five percent happened to women working alone, 86 percent by strangers. This works out to be about 1.5 per 100,000 full-time female workers, but this figure represents only the reported cases, and rape crimes are notoriously underreported (Alexander, Franklin, and Wolf, 1994). The U.S. Justice Department reports that boyfriends and husbands—current and former—commit more than 13,000 acts of violence against women in the workplace every year (Anfuso, 1994). According to the Labor Department, employee disputes with personal acquaintances led to at least 39 workplace homicides in 1992 (Hellwege, 1995). A woman can change her residence to get away from men, but she cannot as easily change the address of her workplace.

Violence in hospitals has also grown apace with the violence in society. A National Institute for Occupational Safety and Health study shows that between 1980 to 1990, a total of 522 deaths occurred among health care workers on the job, with 106 of these workers murdered (Mainellis, 1996). According to a 1992 survey of 103 California hospitals, 58 percent of the staff had suffered injuries from visitors or patients, usually from guns and knives (Keep and Gilbert, 1992). Prolonged waits were the major trigger for the assaults, and were generally caused by drunken, drugged, or mentally disordered patients. Half of the assaults take place in emergency rooms. In a University of Louisville study conducted in 1988, of 127 emergency rooms where staff were surveyed, forty-one reported at least one verbal threat a day, twenty-three reported at least one armed threat per month, and fifty-five emergency room staffs sustained at least one physical assault per month. In a study of teaching hospitals, 43 percent reported that their medical staff were physically attacked on an average of once a month; 7 percent of these attacks resulted in death (Wheeler and Baron, 1994).

According to a survey sponsored by the Emergency Nurses Association (1995), of emergency department nurse managers (4,600 surveyed, 1,400 respondents), 97 percent reported staff were exposed to verbal abuse more than twenty times per year, 87 percent indicated staff were exposed to physical assault without weapons one to five times per year, and 24 percent indicated that staff were exposed to physical violence with weapons one to five times per year.

The numbers are even higher for mental health professionals. Back in 1978 a study showed that 24 percent of psychiatrists, psychologists, and social workers in a metropolitan area reported being assaulted by one or more patients during a one-year period (Edelman, 1978). A study published in 1992 surveying both a private psychiatric facility with an outpatient community mental health center in a middle-class urban area and a state hospital in a lower-middle class inner-city area showed that 62 percent of the 224 clinical staff surveyed reported experiencing a critical incident involving a serious threat to life or physical safety or witnessing a serious injury or death (Caldwell, 1992).

Incidents of workplace violence are often years in the making. Baron has noted that there are indicators of potential trouble brewing and definite red flags about who is most likely to pursue a violent course of action (Baron, 1993). After reviewing many cases of workplace violence, researchers noted the following warning signs for the violent individual: a previous history of violence, psychosis, romantic obsession, chemical dependence, depression (one in seven will commit a violent act on themselves or others), pathological blaming, impaired neurological functioning, elevated frustration with the environment, an interest in weapons, personality disorders, and a gut feeling that someone is dangerous.

There are also work-related behaviors that are cause for concern: attendance problems, increased demands for supervisor's or manager's time, decreased productivity, inconsistent work patterns, poor on-the-job relationships, concentration problems, safety issues, poor health and hygiene, unusual or changed behavior, preoccupation with weapons, evidence of serious stress in personal life that is brought into work, substance abuse on the job, and continual excuses or blaming of others.

The typical profile picture of a workplace killer is a male, aged twenty-five to forty, who has a history of violence. He owns several guns and is a loner. In the past, he has requested some type of assistance at work, but was not satisfied with the outcome. He is an angry person with little outlet for that anger and has a history of interpersonal conflict. He is often socially withdrawn and is likely to have family or marital problems. After a while, he stops expressing himself verbally and becomes increasingly introverted and isolated, moving from many complaints about work and management to silence. He becomes increasingly paranoid about others and often exhibits self-destructive behavior such as taking drugs or drinking excessively. This picture, however, is simply a guide. Many people who do not fit this profile also engage in workplace violence.

As we have mentioned earlier, the costs of this orgy of violence in the workplace are enormous. A significant proportion of the cost to industry comes out as health care costs directly or indirectly related to the violence. One of these costs will manifest through the short and long-term effects of post-traumatic stress. We are beginning to learn something about the incidence of PTSD in various populations. The incidence of post-traumatic stress disorder among workers in the medical field is high. In the mental health professional study (Caldwell, 1992), of the 224 clinical staff, 61 percent reported symptoms of PTSD such as intrusive thoughts or increased emotional reactivity. Of those reporting, 10 percent would have been given a DSM-III diagnosis of PTSD. Of the 138 clinicians who reported experiencing traumatic incidents on the job, only 15 percent reported any later external review of the experience. Of thirty-seven police officers involved in serious shooting incidents between 1977 to 1984, 46 percent fulfilled DSM-III criteria for PTSD, seventeen others showed impressive patterns of PTSD, and only three showed no PTSD (Gersons, 1989). A study of the San Ysidro Massacre showed that 50 percent of law enforcement personnel developed PTSD (Sewell, 1993).

Violence in the workplace does not just affect the victimized worker but their colleagues and families as well. In one study of young adults in the Midwest, life threat, seeing others killed or badly injured, and physical assault all produced lifetime PTSD rates of around 25 percent (Breslau et al., 1991). Rape victims report a PTSD lifetime prevalence of 80 percent. In a national sample of women who had experienced aggravated assault, 39 percent developed PTSD (Kilpatrick and Resnick, 1993). Of those who experienced traumatic bereavement, 25 percent developed PTSD. In the same study, crime victims showed current PTSD rates of 12 percent from sexual assault, 13 percent from rape, and 5 percent from traumatic bereavement. PTSD, of course, is rarely found alone, even in community samples. The most common coexisting diagnoses are major depression and substance abuse, as well as a panoply of other psychiatric and medical disorders (Green, 1994). Koss used a sample of 5,000 women enrolled in a large HMO and found 400 who admitted to being crime victims. Crime victimization was associated with significantly worse health status and reported symptoms across a wide variety of types of medical symptoms with a dramatically increased utilization of medical services (Koss, Koss, and Woodruff, 1991). In a study of 200 postmen in Northern Ireland who had been exposed to robberies on the job, absence for sickness increased by fourfold following the attacks (Jenkinson, 1993).

VIOLENCE IN THE SCHOOL

"America 'Tis of Thee, 1990s Version"

Land where the bullets fly
Land where my brothers die
From every street and countryside
Let us run and hide. (p. 52)

This grimly sardonic verse from one of today's teenagers (Brendtro and Long, 1995) indicates the current insanity that has been unleashed in this country. From *Time*, January 25, 1993, some statistics for every school day: at least 100,000 students tote guns in school, 160,000 skip classes because they fear physical harm, forty are hurt or killed, 6,250 teachers are threatened with bodily injury, and 260 are physically assaulted (p. 23). These statistics were provided by the National Education Association. Every day 160,000 students miss classes because they are afraid to go to school and a recent CDC report shows that the murder rate for fifteen- to nineteen-year-olds jumped 154 percent between 1985 and 1991, mostly attributable to guns (Arbetter, 1995). The attitudes of children may be just as frightening as the numbers of actual incidents. Twenty percent of suburban high school students endorsed shooting someone "who has stolen something from you" and 8 percent believed it is all right to shoot a person "who had done something to offend or insult you" (Toch and Silver, 1993, p. 32). In a 1993 national study of 1,700 sixth to ninth graders, a majority of the boys considered rape "acceptable" under certain conditions and many of the girls agreed (Wallis, 1995).

It is not just primary and secondary schools that have a problem. Violence on college campuses has continued to increase. One study indicated that nearly 25 percent of 2,016 college women surveyed had been raped, according to strict legal standards. Another survey revealed that 1,000 rapes were reported on college campuses during 1991 to 1992 academic year. Approximately 7,500 violent crimes occurred on 2,400 campuses from 1991 to 1992. The most lethal influences are alcohol and firearms. Ninety-five percent of violent crimes on campuses involved drugs or alcohol. Eighty-six percent of college students under legal age consumed alcohol and nearly 18 percent of this group reported experiencing alcohol-related trouble with police (Nichols, 1995).

In a recent New York Times and CBS News survey, 40 percent of teenagers said that they knew someone who had been shot in the last five years, and most of them said that the victim and the attacker were other teenagers. Thirteen percent said that at least half the students in their schools carried weapons such as knives and guns, and another 16 percent said some students were armed. Among white teenagers, 36 percent worry about being the victim of a crime much or some of the time, as compared to 54 percent of black teenagers (Chira, 1994).

They have good reason to be worried. Teenagers were much more likely than adults to be victims of crimes of violence. And they cannot expect to be safe on the streets or at school. About half of all violent crimes and 63 percent of crimes of theft against teens aged twelve to nineteen took place on the street, in a school building, or on school property. Adolescents aged twelve to fifteen were about twice as likely as older teens to experience crimes in a school building or property (Wheeler and Baron, 1994). Between 1981 and 1990, all categories of violent crime increased substantially for youths under age eighteen; murder and non-negligent manslaughter (60.1 percent), forcible rape (28.2 percent), and aggravated assault (56.5 percent). One out of every ten American youngsters who died in 1987 was killed with a gun. Teenagers in America were, at a minimum, at least four times as likely to be murdered than their counterparts in twenty-one other industrialized countries (Goldstein, Harootunian, and Conoley, 1994).

Going to school in a rural area is not protection against violence. A study done on twenty-three small rural Texas communities showed that 34 percent of students reported having been threatened with bodily harm, 15 percent claimed they had something taken from them by force or threat, 14 percent said they had been physically attacked, and 6 percent admitted that someone tried to force them to have sex. More than half said they had not received instruction in school on ways to avoid fighting and violence and 53 to 78 percent believed that they should fight if someone hits them, hurts someone they care about, insults their family, or breaks something they own (Wheeler and Baron, 1994).

Violence in school is not just a "guy thing." According to the FBI, since 1988 the number of violent crimes committed by girls has increased

63 percent. They carry blades in their cheeks, knives in their ponytails, guns in their bras, and they use them often with more force than needed (Pagnozzi, 1994).

But students are not the only victims at school. Nearly 5,200 of the nation's million secondary schoolteachers are physically attacked at school each month and about 1,000 are hurt seriously enough to require medical attention. Theft is reported by 130,000 teachers in a month's time. Teachers say that about 7 percent of the students were habitual behavior problems and that they could not keep order because of lack of alternative placement and lack of student interest. Many of them fear being sued as do their administrators and see this fear as another limitation on their ability to maintain order (Wheeler and Baron, 1994). Teaching has recently been described as a "dehumanizing experience," a situation which bodes poorly for the retention of high-quality and dedicated teachers (Calabrese, 1986). Unquestionably, teaching, particularly in the inner cities, has become a high-risk profession.

Many administrators do not report the crimes to the police, fearing that they will look incompetent. A report of the New York City schools in November 1993 stated that the Board of Education had minimized the extent of violence in the schools over the preceding years (Dillon, 1993). Another report of July 1994 revealed that principals have underreported violent incidents and that the actual number should be increased by about 30 percent over the previous year, "painting a picture of disorder that is more severe than the board had previously indicated" (Dillon, 1994, p. B1).

The National Center for Education Statistics reported that in 1990, 21 percent of 25,000 eighth graders from 1,000 public and private schools stated they had witnessed weapons at school. The students cited a number of reasons for why they carry guns: "because I feel threatened and intimidated," "to make people think I am a drug dealer," "because I need to have status," "to save my own life," "I feel I need protection . . . maybe I'm a cynic, but I'm a realist." The children usually obtain the guns from home. The impact of gangs and the presence of drugs are directly related to the increase in weapons in schools. Over 18 percent of all weapons incidents in schools are drug or gang related (Wheeler and Baron, 1994).

Asking why there is so much violence in schools can only be answered by determining why is there so much violence in America. Children are acting out adult fantasies and demonstrating our national insanity in the most poignant way—by dying for it. Violence begins in the home. A nationwide survey conducted in 1968 for the National Commission on the Causes and Prevention of Violence revealed that 93 percent of respondents reported having been spanked in childhood. Domestic violence and child abuse are a national epidemic. And television and movies bring violence into our homes every day and every night.

Many violence prevention programs are being offered in schools and little data is in yet to support which intervention programs work. Peace programming, conflict resolution, and peer mediation programs are necessary in the schools and necessary to prepare children for healthy adult behavior. Focusing on the children, however, will not solve the problems. Violence in the schools originates with a violent society that allows easy access to guns, that actively supports and encourages the perpetuation of violence. Until we address this at a mass social level, children will continue to mimic adult behavior as children have always done, and children will continue to kill other children, just as their parents do.

VIOLENCE IN THE CHURCH

We cannot leave a discussion of violence in our major social institutions without looking at the relationship between violence and religion. In order to do so, we have to take a look backward, to ideas that continue to influence our social climate even if they are now divorced from their original religious context. After all, violence and religion have a very long and associated history that continues even today in many parts of the world. Using a deity to justify the use of violence is as old as the history of mankind. The origins of all religious pursuit can be found drenched in blood. Many wars have been fought in the name of God, and even the mass feelings inspired by war have been compared to those normally aroused by religion (Ehrenreich, 1997). It has been suggested that religion may be rooted in the primordial encounter with predators. According to the ethnologist Konrad Lorenz, there are physiological parallels between what humans experience as religious awe and what animals experience in the face of threat, what is known in German as the "holy shiver" of awe. Certainly deities have always been objects of worship and of fear (Ehrenreich, 1997).

There is—and always has been—a close connection between religion and the notion of sacrifice. Many scholars believe that the rites of sacrifice originated in fear of the dead. In its most basic form, sacrifice involves the belief that someone can achieve prosperity or long life if someone, and later something else, is killed or destroyed (Bergmann, 1992). As Girard has pointed out in his classic work *Violence and the Sacred*, "If sacrifice resembles criminal violence, we may say that there is, inversely, hardly any form of violence that cannot be described in terms of sacrifice" (1972, p. 1). Historically, sacrifice has been an act of violence inflicted on a victim as a collective substitution for the community that absorbs the tensions, rivalries, and bad deeds of everyone (Girard, 1972). Violence was, well into the historical era, at the very core of what humans define as "sacred" (Ehrenreich, 1997, p. 21). Girard tells us that all religious rituals spring from surrogate victims and that all the great institutions of mankind, both secular and religious, come from ritual. In that vast evolution, we lose site of the original violence, but the violence is always there, waiting, and that is why *"violence can always stage a stunning, catastrophic comeback"* (p. 307).

In his study of Western religions, Bergman (1992) argues persuasively that the struggle against the sacrifice of children has been a driving force in the development of all Western religions, and that the fear of being sacrificed is still alive in the unconscious of men and women today. Psychohistorians have argued that the continuing need to sacrifice children is a major motivator, albeit unconsciously, for wars, economic depressions, and of course, child abuse (DeMause, 1982, 1990, 1991).

We have seen the presence of these age-old ideas in the struggles of this century. "Holocaust" in Greek means burnt offering, made to protect the sacrificer from the hostility of the deity. The participants of the war in Bosnia justified their acts in the name of religion. In the name of religious beliefs heated battles are waged every day in Israel and in other places in the Arab world. The Protestants and Catholics of Northern Ireland use religion as an excuse for their compulsive hatred and violence. As in Jonestown, religious cults justify suicide in the name of their religion. And here at home, religious fundamentalists condemn the "sacrifice" of children in abortion while condoning violence directed toward children in the name of discipline (Grasmick, Bursik, and Kimpel, 1991; Greven, 1990; Straus, 1994).

In recent times here, the most obvious connection between violence and the church can be found in the antiabortion movement in which religious beliefs can be used to justify acts of violence against property and people. Most church-related violence, however, comes about through church-supported approval for the corporal punishment of children, through ideas of sin and punishment that continue to permeate the criminal justice system, through sexual boundary violations by members of the clergy, and through the failure to take active stands against violence.

Legitimizing Violence

We have already touched upon the role religion plays in legitimizing violence against children in the earlier section on childrearing practices. Ellison and Bartkowski (1997) did a review of the ways in which current fundamentalist Protestant writers on parenting use religion to sacralize violence by linking corporal punishment with such ultimate concerns as salvation or divine will. At the same time, religious values attempt to delimit the extent of the violence that parents can use against their children.

> Religion is implicated in processes that make certain uses of coercive physical force seem natural, appropriate, and unavoidable. By sustaining "ground rules" that are frequently well understood by both perpetrator and victim as well as by others in society, religious legitimization can redefine certain acts of physical force as something other (and less serious) than "violence". . . Rather, physical punishment is considered a vital part of a child's spiritual development, communicating lessons about the essential nature of God, the centrality of scriptural guidance over human affairs, and the importance of obedience to structures of authority over the life course. (pp. 47-48)

This legitimization of violence is based on fundamentalist notions that the Bible, as interpreted by their leaders, is not liable to any error. A biblically legitimated expert must be obeyed unquestioningly in relationships between pastor and congregation and between parents and children. As a result, there is little place for democratic or egalitarian values in the family. In early Christian thought, evil entered the world because men and women wanted to be like God, and from the beginning man has been rebelling against God. This is the "original sin" as defined by Augustine, a term he first used in the fourth century A.D. Original sin means that all human beings, regardless of their individual sins, are infected with the inescapable taint of corruption and no human effort alone can erase this corruption. Man is fallen, evil, and guilty from birth (Cavendish, 1980). Children are born sinful, predisposed toward selfishness, and inclined toward rebellion against authority and it is this rebellion which must be stamped out. If children are allowed to question authority, they will grow up to be antiauthoritarians and this tendency will undermine their occupational success as well as their marital and family relationships. More important, it means that children will not accept the values of their parents and therefore will not accept the guidance and dictates of God. Challenges to parental authority are inevitable and must be dealt with forcefully, but not abusively. Physical discipline communicates a positive spiritual lesson to children that can ultimately save their souls (Ellison and Bartkowski, 1997). As a major researcher on religion states, "Religion should be called to task to the extent it has created a breeding ground in which the abuse of children is permitted" (Pargament, 1997, p. 332).

Criminal Justice and Religion

Throughout the history of penal practice religion has been a major force in shaping the ways in which offenders are dealt with (Garland, 1990). According to the famous sociologist Durkheim, in ancient and primitive social groups, the penal process was invested with a wholly religious meaning, so that punishment was understood as a necessary sacrifice to an aggrieved deity. In such cultures, crime is associated with sin, impurity, and danger and the act of punishment involves a process of expiation as well as a ritual cleansing of polluting elements in society.

There is no evidence of the use of torture in the early Christian Church. St. Bernard of Clairvaux stated, "Faith must be the result of conviction and should not be imposed by force" (Forrest, 1996, p. 21). But by the eleventh century, heretics were being subjected to torture to force them to recant, or executed cruelly if they refused to do so. By the later Middle Ages torture began to be used in secular courts as well. The use of torture to obtain strong proof of guilt or a confession or to obtain the names of co-conspirators became more widespread and relied upon in criminal trials. It was during the Papal and Spanish Inquisitions against heretics, Moors, and Jews that methods of interrogation and torture were used routinely and codified. These religious inquisitions proceeded throughout various parts of Europe from the twelfth through the early nineteenth century, when they were finally suppressed (Forrest, 1996). Sweden was the first country to outlaw the use of torture in 1734, just as it was the first country to ban corporal punishment of children.

From the Middle Ages right up to the present, religious belief has been an important force in shaping the practice and evolution of punishment. As Friedman (1993) points out,

> It would be hard to overemphasize the influence of religion—the beliefs of magistrates and leaders—in shaping the criminal codes, in framing modes of enforcement, and generally, in creating a distinctive legal culture. The criminal justice system was in many ways another arm of religious orthodoxy. (p. 32)

In the early colonies, little distinction was made between sin and crime. The criminal code was composed of the laws of God, not man-made standards. Confession and repentance were crucial aims of the criminal process in addition to punishment, often carried out through whipping, such humiliating devices as the stocks, body mutilation, or death (Friedman, 1993).

The penitentiary system, although used by the Church as far back as the ninth century, really originates with the Enlightenment reform movement and came to the United States in the nineteenth century. Philosophically, the penitentiary idea was that criminals could be reformed, could be led to become penitent and repentant, if they had time alone in solitary confinement to think about their sins and their wayward lives. These ideas came directly from religious life and religious experience. As late as the eighteenth century, the Vatican prison served as a model for prison design in both Europe and America (Garland, 1990).

The Quakers led the penitentiary movement in this country, first forming the Pennsylvania Prison Society in 1776 to begin reviewing penal reform. Out of this reform movement ultimately grew the Eastern State Penitentiary in Philadelphia, which became a model for prisons built around the world (Johnston, 1994). The Quaker penitentiaries of the early nineteenth century helped to formulate the combination of solitary confinement and productive work that was supposed to produce spiritual redemption as well as painful bodily punishment. "The Quakers were the chief promoters of this softened system," wrote Duke de la Rochefoucauld-Liancourt in the late eighteenth century. "Public labor, . . . mutilation, . . . and whipping were outlawed" (Finkel, 1994, p. 9). Probation began as a form of missionary work funded by church-based temperance societies, and evangelicals in Britain and the United States were in the vanguard of reform movements to ameliorate conditions of captivity or to aid prisoners upon their release (Garland, 1990).

Sexual Violations by the Clergy

The relationship between a clergyman and his or her parishioner is a special relationship, similar in some ways to that between psychiatrist and patient. For many reasons, too extensive to be detailed here, it lends itself to the possibility of sexual boundary violations (Gabbard, 1989). Though some estimate that up to one-third of North American ministers admit to having engaged in sexual misconduct, most work indicates that about 25 percent of pastors have had some kind of sexual involvement with a parishioner. Actual intercourse rates are said to be between 10 to 15 percent (Hood et al., 1996). Pastoral counselors are also vulnerable to boundary violations. Young and Griffith (1995) report that courts have been reluctant to hold pastoral counselors accountable for acts of sexual abuse against their clients because of concerns about religious freedom. This is particularly a problem for pastoral counselors who are practicing outside of traditional church settings and organizational structure. They report that questions of whether society does in fact value religious freedom above protection of clients sexually abused by clergy counselors remains an important policy issue. This is a form of violence that affects not only the people involved, but the entire congregation. But what is of even more concern for churches and society is the frequency of sexual abuse among members of the clergy and children. Between 1983 and 1987 more than two hundred priests or religious brothers were reported to the Vatican Embassy in Washington, DC, for sexually abusing youngsters—an average of nearly one accusation a week just during those four years. Between 1982 and 1992, approximately 400 priests were reported to civil and church authorities for the same criminal behavior, mostly accused of multiple victimizations. By 1992, the Roman Catholic Church's financial losses had reached an estimated $400 million (Berry, 1992).

Failure to Oppose Violence

With some notable exceptions, churches have often been slow to respond to violence in the community, failing to serve a powerful role of leadership. Fundamental to this failure has been the continuing support for violence that occurs when any social institution fails to face or actively supports the many forms of economic, political, social, and familial injustice and discrimination that plague women, minorities, the poor, and children in this culture. The church has often used biblical justification for this continued oppression. As Hood and his colleagues make clear, "There is little doubt that in sponsoring traditional sex roles, religion can be an impediment to female aspirations, empowerment, and mental health" (p. 432). Using data from a national survey in Canada, researchers confirmed one U.S. study showing that very high rates of spousal abuse occurred among those who were least religious, but conservative Protestant women reported even higher abuse rates, not confirmed by the men's data (Brinkerhoff, Grandin, and Lupri, 1992; Hood et al., 1996). Their rates of abuse were 37.8 percent compared with 28.1 percent for mainstream Protestants, 23.9 percent for Catholics, and 30.8 percent for nonaffiliated people. Certainly, many victims of domestic violence have told of how their clergymen advised them to stay with their batterers for "the sake of the children" and have asked them to reform their habits so their husbands would not feel compelled to beat them.

One significant example of clerical apathy in the face of violence occurred during the 1957 Little Rock school integration crisis when only five of the clergy did little to promote racial harmony, even though the majority of them supported integration. Out of twenty-nine, only two of them used the pulpit to voice support for integration. When this group was studied, factors that impeded them included fear of dissension in the church and criticism from their superiors (Pargament, 1997). The church failure to consistently promote nonviolence can be seen as a major contributor to violence, in that the church's moral authority is ceded over to other, often more violent voices.

Chapter 4

Active Support for Violence

In many ways, our society provides nonverbal consent, support, and even encouragement for violent forms of interaction. By our attitudes we condone violence as a viable method of solving problems. Here we focus on four specific areas in which we believe the society actively supports and provocates a violent agenda.

FIREARMS

Every day, our emergency rooms are filled with victims of the escalating violence plaguing the United States. Today, an American child dies of gunshot wounds every one and one-half hours; and every two days, the equivalent of a classroom of children is lost (Powell, Sheehan, and Christoffel, 1996). A recent article in the *Archives of Surgery,* using trauma center and police data sources, showed that from June 1991 to May 1992 and June 1993 to May 1994, the incidence of penetrating trauma increased from 27 percent to 35 percent of trauma center admissions. During the period from June 1985 to May 1994, assault with a deadly weapon increased by 220 percent and firearms became the most common assault mechanism (from 32 percent to 54 percent). Assailants using guns became significantly younger, with assailants aged eleven to twenty years increasing from 24 percent to 47 percent. The ages of assault victims also decreased but were more evenly distributed across age categories (Davis, Kaups, and Rhames, 1997).

Concerned health care workers meet to discuss the causes of violence and what can be done to eradicate it, much as the same groups have formulated plans to control the spread of HIV infection. Violence has many causes, some deeply rooted in the psychological and physical structure of this country. But whatever the precipitating factor that makes one person strike out against another, the common denominator that all too frequently turns the violent act into a death is the gun. Just as in HIV disease, society is infected with the metaphoric viruses of poverty, injustice, poor education, and lack of caring for children, but it is not these that, in themselves, are fatal. Just as it is toxoplasmosis or pneumocystis that actually kills the AIDS patient, the gun is the pathogen that kills in a setting ripe for violence. Although a violent act might involve a weapon other than a gun, use of a gun is far more likely to result in a fatality than a knife or other weapon (Baker, 1985; Hedeboe et al., 1985; Schwarz et al., 1994; Zimring, 1991).

Guns are not the cause of violence, but rather "people without guns injure people, guns kill them" (Baker, 1985, p. 587). In defining the relationship between guns and violence, one has to ask: What is the extent of the problem? How many guns are available? When are they used, in what situations, and who are the at-risk victims? What can be done? Do our laws prevent action? Do other countries have the same problems—if not, why not?

Over 200 million firearms are owned by U.S. civilians or one for every one-third to two-thirds of all households. Of these, approximately one-third are handguns and of the handguns, approximately 30 million are semi-automatic weapons (Schwab, 1993). The guns are not just sitting in homes awaiting the arrival of an intruder. Various reports indicate that 6 to 20 percent of high school students have carried a gun to school, and in the inner city, 20 percent have been shot at (Callahan and Rivara, 1992; Russell, 1993). A retrospective study of youth gunshot wounds between 1986 to 1995 in Philadelphia found an alarming 110 percent increase over the ten-year study (Nance, Stafford, and Schwab, 1997). In Connecticut, firearms were found to be second only to motor vehicle accidents as a cause of mortality in children and youth (Zavoski et al., 1995). In 1991, a year with 24,703 murders, almost 17,330 were committed with a firearm and in approximately 14,700 cases the weapon was a handgun (Callahan and Rivara, 1992).

In a milieu of violence, are most of these murders due to crime, or to stop a crime? Statistically, the answer is neither. In 1992, the Bureau of Justice Statistics' National Crime Victimization Survey showed that handguns were used only 262 times in a justifiable homicide. Only one-fifth of all homicides were the result of a crime. In various reports, 29 to 50 percent of homicides are precipitated by an argument (Schwab, 1993; Sugarmann et al., 1994; Prothrow-Stith, 1992; Wolfgang, 1958), and the arguments are usually among family, friends, or acquaintances. In 1992, 12 percent of victims were related to and 34 percent were acquainted with their killers (Schwab, 1993). Saltzman reported that firearm-associated family and intimate assaults were twelve times more likely to result in death than in similar assaults that were not firearm associated (Saltzman, 1992). Kellerman similarly reported that a gun kept in the home for self-defense is twenty-one times more likely to be used to kill accidentally than to be used to kill a home invader (Kellerman, 1986). Just the presence of a gun in the home is associated with increased risk of homicide in that home, and virtually all of this risk involved homicide by a family member or intimate acquaintance (Kellerman, 1993).

Homicide is only the minority side of the gun death equation. The majority of firearm deaths are due to suicide. In one study, 58 percent of those dying during a suicide attempt used a firearm (Kellerman, 1991) and of those who attempt suicide with a firearm, 92 percent are successful (Card, 1974). Kellerman has found that a gun kept in the home for self-defense is 167 times more likely to be used in a suicide than in a defensible homicide (Kellerman, 1986). Guns are twice as likely to be found in the homes of suicide victims as in those of suicide attempters (Brent et al., 1991).

The number of deaths from gunfire is only the tip of the iceberg. For every death, there are at least five nonfatal injuries (Mercy et al., 1986). Handguns are estimated to cause approximately 100,000 injuries per year and handguns terrorize far more people than they kill (Larson, 1993). Today, as we near a new millenium, availability of guns turns neighborhoods and schools into lethal battlefields in which gun-related and gun-induced violence may momentarily erupt. In parts of inner cities, carrying a gun has become normal behavior for many young men and women (Durant et al., 1995). An epidemiological study of injuries due to firearms in three cities—Memphis, Galveston, and Seattle—found that 88 percent of the firearm injuries during an eighteenth-month period from 1992 to 1994 resulted from assaults, and that handguns were used in nearly all of the cases (Kellerman et al., 1996).

Is the United States alone involved in an epidemic of gun violence? Compared to other well-developed (first world) countries such as England, France, Japan, Canada, and Germany, the answer is yes, with a sixteen to twenty-ninefold differential separating prime-risk American males, aged twenty-five to thirty-four, from their foreign counterparts (Fingerhut et al., 1990). In a comparison of the similar, nearby cities of Seattle and Vancouver, a citizen in Seattle had a 4.8 times higher risk of being murdered by a handgun than in Vancouver, while the rate of homicide by other means was similar in the two cities (Sloan et al., 1988). In 1990, 10,567 handgun homicides occurred in the United States, while in Canada, there were

68 (Russell, 1993). All of the countries mentioned have strict handgun control laws, except the United States.

Why does the United States not have strict gun control laws? The powerful gun lobby headed by the National Rifle Association continues to exert control over the issue, despite the wishes of a majority of the American public. They have accomplished this by using political means such as rallying a membership of 3 million to contact representatives to support a pro-gun agenda, contributing heavily to pro-gun campaigns (Sugarmann, 1994), and aborting legislative means to control guns. They are loud, aggressive, and intimidating and as a result, their voice is heard above others and given the most authority. The major pro-gun argument is based on an interpretation of the second amendment, which guarantees the right of citizens to bear arms. The second amendment states: "A well-regulated militia, being necessary to the security of a free state, the right of the people to keep and bear arms, shall not be infringed." When gun control laws have been brought before the Supreme Court, the constant decision is that the second amendment does not protect individual civilian ownership or use of firearms (Zimring and Gordon, 1987). Small inroads into gun control have been made with the passage of legislation similar to the Brady Bill, but most efforts are stymied by the bullying power of the NRA.

The result of gunfire is a medical problem but the control of guns is political. It is not enough for physicians and others to be concerned with the medical effects of violence. They must also discuss the problem of guns and gun ownership with their patients and must also be involved in community antiviolence efforts, such as those implemented in schools around the country. Health and mental health professionals can also play a key role in informing legislators about the need to reduce the numbers of firearms, helping them to realize that the very presence of a gun, especially a handgun, can have fatal consequences.

There is great danger here. The catastrophe that has already descended on the urban young is bad enough, but there is worse ahead. We have prepared a breeding ground for levels of violence that most Americans have never imagined.

Bob Herbert
"Call to Arms," 1994

SUBSTANCE ABUSE

The relationships between substance abuse, violence, and crime are complex and in some cases, controversial. No one, however, doubts that there is a relationship, at least as a risk factor. In a classic study done by Shupe in 1954 and cited in Volavka (1995, p. 191), 87 percent of 882 persons arrested shortly after committing a crime had measurable levels of alcohol in the urine. A recent reanalysis showed that higher alcohol levels were more correlated with perpetrators of violent than nonviolent crimes (Volavka, 1995). Clearly alcohol is a risk factor for interpersonal aggression. In Murdoch's words, the probability of aggression between two people is "greatest when both are intoxicated, intermediate when one person is intoxicated, and least probable when both are sober" (Murdoch et al. as cited in Volavka, 1995, p. 191). Overall, the extensive literature on assault and homicide indicates that assailants were under the influence of alcohol in over half of the violent crimes (Volavka, 1995).

In violence against women and children, alcohol can serve a number of purposes in the service of male aggression: as a disinhibitor for male aggressive behavior, as an excuse for his behavior after the fact, as a strategy to reduce victim resistance (Koss et al., 1994). One- to two-thirds of college student rapists and approximately half of victims had consumed alcohol prior to the rape (Koss et al., 1994). Numerous studies have shown a relationship between substance abuse and child abuse, spouse abuse, and elder abuse (Lystad, 1986). Sixty to seventy percent of incest victims say their fathers had been drinking at the time the incest first occurred (Crewdson, 1988). There is controversy, however, about whether individuals drink, lose control, and then become violent, or whether they drink because they want to become violent and need alcohol or another drug as a release.

Regardless of the mechanism, it is estimated that one out of every seven people in the United States abuses or is dependent on alcohol and an additional one in twenty individuals abuses or is dependent on other drugs (Fialkov, 1992). We know that there is a connection between violence and substance abuse. We also know that there is a connection between substance abuse and trauma. Although the demographic data is still in the process of being collected, it is clear from studies done thus far that a significant proportion of the substance abuse population suffers from trauma-related syndromes. Approximately 50 to 60 percent of women and 20 percent of men in chemical dependency recovery programs report having been victims of childhood sexual abuse. Approximately 69 percent of women and 80 percent of men in such programs report being victims of childhood physical abuse (Matsakis, 1994). In a study of fifty patients in an inpatient chemical withdrawal unit and fifty patients assessed for an outpatient chemical dependency program, 39 percent had a dissociative disorder and forty-three reported childhood abuse (Ross et al., 1992). In another study of 265 men being treated in an inpatient substance abuse unit, 41.5 percent scored high on tests that assessed histories with traumatic childhood events (Dunn et al., 1993). Yandow estimates that as many as 75 percent of women in treatment for alcoholism have a history of sexual abuse (Bollerud, 1990).

Likewise, patients with a history of exposure to trauma are at significant risk for substance abuse. War trauma has been associated with very high rates of substance abuse with 60 to 80 percent having concurrent diagnoses of alcohol abuse or drug abuse or dependency. Vietnam veterans with higher levels of war zone stress were more likely to exhibit chemical abuse or dependency than those with lower levels of stress, indicating that the neurobiological alterations associated with PTSD may make affected individuals more susceptible to substance abuse (Friedman, 1990). Chemical dependency is a complicating feature of multiple personality disorder in 31.4 percent of a series of 236 cases and 50 percent in a series of 102 cases (Ross et al., 1992). Battered women are fifteen times more likely to abuse alcohol (Salasin and Rich, 1993). Briere reported that 27 percent of sexual abuse victims had a history of alcohol abuse and 21 percent a history of drug abuse, while Herman found that 35 percent of female incest victims abused drugs and alcohol (Green, 1993). The numbers rose to 80 percent in a group of female incest survivors who had been inpatients (Green, 1993). Substance problems have been shown to increase over time in several studies of disaster victims (Grace et al., 1993). Of a sample of 2,300 police officers, 23 percent reported drinking problems and another 10 percent said they abused other drugs (Mitchell and Dyregrov, 1993).

The connection between dissociation and substance abuse disorders is just beginning to be investigated. One hypothesis about the strong correlation between the dissociative disorders and substance abuse is that patients are using drugs and alcohol to block out their more severe abuse histories and to suppress some of their dissociative symptoms. Substance abuse may sometimes cause dissociative symptoms, it may sometimes be secondary to a primary dissociative disorder, or it may sometimes involve a bidirectional causality (Ross et al., 1992). Whatever the etiology, there is a strong suspicion that these patients could account for a sizable segment of chronic relapsers (Dunn et al., 1993).

There is good reason to believe that substance abusers who are also trauma survivors are initially attempting to self-medicate themselves in an effort to "treat" the underlying neuroregulatory problems associated with acute and complex post-traumatic stress disorder (Kosten and Krystal, 1988). The recognition of this connection goes at least back to the last century when Weir Mitchell noted that Civil War veterans and female civilians self-medicated with alcohol and opiates to relieve their symptoms (Sutherland and Davidson, 1994). The continuing use of the substance then becomes a problem of its own.

Biochemical support is beginning to accumulate about the relationship between trauma syndromes and substance abuse. It appears that the enzyme that breaks down neurotransmitters such as norepinephrine—MAO—is low in PTSD and in abstinent alcoholics, according to one study, thus perhaps providing a biological link for the two disorders (Kosten and Krystal, 1988). Alcohol, barbiturates, and opiates acutely decrease the hyperarousal caused by the alarm reaction and therefore reduce PTSD symptoms, although this effect is lost rapidly with chronic use and replaced by dysphoria. Then, when the person begins to withdraw from the alcohol or the opiates, the PTSD symptoms and accompanying hyperarousal become much worse, often leading to a further increase in substance abuse. There is growing reason to think that patients with PTSD may have an endorphin deficiency, not unlike some surgical patients who have been studied and who require far more post-surgical analgesia than patients with normal endorphin levels. Opiate abuse, then, would be their own attempt to increase their endorphin level to what it should normally be but the drug necessary for them to do that—heroin—produces other side effects including euphoria. In Part II we will look at what substance abusers may be trying to "treat" when they use drugs, and how this relates to what happens to a child's brain as a result of early childhood exposure to overwhelming experiences.

Whatever the complex network of causes and effects, it is clear that trauma, violence, and substance abuse are linked and that involvement in a culture of drug and alcohol abuse increases the risk for violent perpetration. In our cultural support and acceptance of excessive drinking, in our willingness to hold people under the influence less accountable for their behavior, and in our refusal to properly fund substance abuse treatment, we provide active support for the continuation of this connection.

PORNOGRAPHY

Taking a stance on pornography puts us at risk for being called uptight prudes, regardless of whether we are men or women. But what gets confused in this subject is the difference between erotica, referring to "sexually suggestive or arousing material that is free of sexism, racism, and homophobia, and respectful of all the human beings and animals portrayed" (Russell, p. 4) and pornography. Diana Russell defines pornography as "material that combines sex and/or the exposure of genitals with abuse or degradation in a manner that appears to endorse, condone, or encourage such behavior" (1993, p. 3). Unless you have actually seen what Russell is talking about, you may just think that pornography is about people having consensual sex. But it is not about sex—it is about violence, terrorization, and domination. It is sex in service of the abuse of power.

> While the sexual objectification of women is common to all pornography, women are the recipients of even worse treatment in violent pornography, in which women characters are killed, tortured, gang-raped, mutilated, bound, and otherwise abused, as a means of providing sexual stimulation or pleasure to the male characters. (Longino as quoted in Russell, 1993, p. 5).

Photographs, books, and movies detail murder, torture, and mutilation in every imaginable combination—but virtually always of men against women. To give an even clearer idea, according to the definition written by Catharine A. MacKinnon and Andrea Dworkin,

> Pornography is defined as the graphic, sexually explicit subordination of women whether in pictures or words that also includes one or more of the following: women are presented dehumanized as sexual objects, things or commodities; or women are presented as sexual objects who enjoy pain or humiliation; or women are presented as sexual objects who experience sexual pleasure in being raped; or women are presented as sexual objects tied up or cut up or mutilated or bruised or physically hurt; or women are presented in postures of sexual submission; or women's body parts are exhibited such that women are reduced to those parts; or women are presented being penetrated by objects or animals; or women are presented in scenarios of degradation, injury, abasement, torture, shown as filthy, or inferior, bleeding, bruised, or hurt in a context that makes these conditions sexual. (Dworkin, 1992, pp. 525-526)

Pornography is big business. In 1984, 200 million issues of 800 hard and soft-porn magazines were sold in the United States, totaling $750 million (Kimmel, 1990). Readership of major pornographic magazines is estimated at 52 million (Russell, 1993). Paid subscribers to *Penthouse* and *Playboy*, the two largest-selling magazines, totaled 8 million in 1992, exceeding the circulation of *Time* and *Newsweek*. Adding in sales and rentals of movies, videos, and pictures, the pornography industry has developed a market presence that generated about $8 billion in 1984 in the United States alone (Itzen, 1992).

Who consumes pornography? In 1970, the first President's Commission on Obscenity and Pornography found that 90 percent of pornography was geared to male heterosexuals and 10 percent to male homosexuals and that consumers were mainly white middle-aged, middle-class men who were married (Kimmel, 1990). A telephone survey of 600 respondents in 1985, however, found pornography to be quite accessible to teenagers and younger males (Russell, in Itzen, 1992):

• The average age at which males saw their first pornographic magazine was eleven years old.
• All of the high school male respondents had read or looked at some pornographic magazine.
• High school males reported having seen an average of sixteen issues; junior high school males reported an average of 2.5 issues.
• The average age for viewing sexually oriented films was 12.5 years.

The content of mass consumption pornography has been established through several content analysis studies. According to Russell (1993), a survey of "adults only" paperbacks available to general public readers published between 1968 and 1974 revealed:

• One-fifth of all sex scenes involved completed rapes.
• The number of rapes increased each year of the study.

A survey of the content of sexual cartoons in *Playboy* and *Penthouse* from 1973 to 1977 revealed:

• About 5 to 10 percent of the materials depicted sexual violence.
• The amount of violence increased markedly over the period studied.

In a Canadian study of 150 adult home videos, 19 percent of all the scenes involved aggression and 13 percent involved sexual aggression. Rape is one of the most prevalent forms of sexual violence depicted, although bondage, hitting, spanking, sadomasochism, and sexual mutilation all get a great deal of film time (Russell, 1993). Consistent with other aspects of violence in society, sexual violence as depicted in pornography has also increased over the years.

In addition to increases in themes of aggression and violence in pornographic materials, there has also been an increase in child pornography.

Department of Justice figures estimate the child pornography "cottage" industry to be worth between 2 to 3 billion dollars a year (Itzen, 1992). The largest geographic source of child pornography has been Denmark, which temporarily relaxed laws banning it in the 1960s and 1970s. The result was the commercial birth of child pornography.

It is easiest to see the links between pornography and violence in child pornography. Most obviously, every sexual act filmed or depicted in such materials is an illegal act of child abuse: the children pictured are being coaxed or coerced by adults to participate in sexual acts. Who are these children? Overwhelmingly poor, they are desperately trying to find ways to ensure their own survival. Increasingly they are from poor, often black, countries. A study in 1990 in Britain found that 70 to 80 percent of children contacting a child welfare agency had been involved in some form of child pornography (Itzen, 1992). Abusers recording their own abuse produce the bulk of child pornography.

The second observation that can be made about child pornography and violence is the link to pedophilia. While perhaps not causal, the association of child pornography with child abusers is well established. The U.S. Postal Service found that 80 percent of those it identified as purchasers of child pornography were active abusers (Itzen, 1992). In Chicago police found that in 100 percent of cases of arrest for child pornography, photos and other evidence documented the actual abuse of children by these pornography purchasers (Itzen, 1992).

For the larger domain of adult pornography, there has been a long-standing controversy over the impact of these materials on individuals and the culture. Two presidential commissions—under two separate conservative presidents—targeted pornography as an example of crumbling family values. Civil libertarians responded in a defense of pornography under the banner of freedom of speech and press. The women's movement shifted the debate from family values to women's rights, seeing a fundamental insult to women in the existence of a big business based on images of the sexual subjugation of women.

Feminists, while not all agreeing on the solution, generally agree that pornography is harmful to women. The Minneapolis ordinance, which outlawed pornography and was passed and then revoked in Minneapolis and several other U.S. municipalities, was crafted by feminists Dworkin and MacKinnon, and the latter has summarized much of the research of the harm pornography does to women:

> Recent experimental research on pornography shows that the materials covered by our definition cause measurable harm to women through increasing men's attitudes and behaviors of discrimination in

both violent and non-violent forms. Exposure to some of the pornogra-phy in our definition increases normal men's immediately subsequent willingness to aggress against women under laboratory conditions. It makes normal men more closely resemble convicted rapists attitudi-nally, although as a group they don't look all that different from them to start with. It also significantly increases attitudinal measures known to correlate with rape and self-reports of aggressive acts, measures such as hostility towards women, propensity to rape, condoning rape, and pre-dicting that one would rape or force sex on a woman if one knew one would not get caught. This latter measure, by the way, begins with rape at about a third of all men and moves to half with "forced sex." (MacKinnon, 1992, p. 477)

Pornography promotes violence toward women: it makes sexism "sexy." "The point about pornography is that it changes men. It increases their aggression toward women. It changes their responses" (Dworkin, in Kimmel, 1990). Like the link between child pornography and pedophilia, this relationship has been associational: rapists have been found to be pornography consumers. Russell (1993) makes the case that pornography lays a psychosocial foundation for rape through eroding inhibitions and creating desire. Further, pornography symbolizes and maintains the sub-ordination of women by men. It socializes young men into their misogy-nist roles. In playing this lynchpin role in the system of sexism, pornogra-phy encourages all of the violence men perpetrate against women. And while the connection between pornography and rape is nonlinear and complex (Kutchinsky, 1991), a study of the association between pornogra-phy and relational violence found strong correlations in families of bat-tered women (Cramer and McFarlane, 1994).

Pornography desensitizes men to the abuse of women. Evidence from repeated exposure to these materials suggests that desensitization occurs where men take such images for granted. From a feminist perspective this desensitization represents an accommodation to a culture in which it is normal to treat women abusively.

From a cultural perspective, it is argued that the chief impact of pornog-raphy is in reifying the social construction of sexism. The inequality of women is represented visually in powerful images that have persuasive effect on nearly all men. In linking sex discrimination to eroticism, the culture has fashioned a way to socialize young males into their roles in relation to women. Denied any real information about bodies or sexuality, young men are able to satisfy this natural and necessary curiosity only through images that communicate these distorted messages about women and sex. Use of pornography becomes institutionalized, a rite of passage to manhood. The modeling effect of older brothers and male parents teaches boys how integral pornography is to sexuality and to manhood.

In this sense, pornography hurts males as well as females. As a primary source of instruction in sexuality, the use of pornography as practice materials for a detached, mechanical, phallocentric eroticism inducts boys into a performance mentality absent any relational dimension. When studies of well-being and life satisfaction point to the crucial part played by intimate partnerships for adult men, pornography reifies the tradition of men operating like the Lone Ranger.

There are other reasons why men may use pornography, suggesting further concern for the effect of pornography on men. In an age of shifting sex roles and advances by women in all spheres of life, men can reaffirm their sense of control through the traditional emphasis in pornography on women's "place" as men's sexual servants. Pornography bolsters the fragile egos of those men who feel threatened by strong women through the illusion that self-esteem can be established at the expense of another group in the population. In so doing, it can also numb men to the potential for personal and social change.

Increasing evidence indicates that attraction to the themes of violence and humiliation found in pornography represents the pull of traumatic reenactment. As work in the area of child sexual abuse proceeds, society is discovering that many men have also been sexually abused as children (Hunter, 1990; Lew, 1988). Sexual fantasies generated by such child abuse represent the effort by the mind to process these experiences and can be a force propelling men into activities many feel are shameful or degrading. In line with the notion of traumatic addiction, the finding that many men feel compulsively "pulled" toward pornography tells us something about the lives of these men as boys.

MEDIA VIOLENCE

Formula-driven media violence is not an expression of crime statistics, popularity or freedom. It is de facto censorship that chills originality and extends the dynamics of domination, intimidation and repression domestically and globally. The violence overkill is an ingredient in a global marketing scheme imposed on media professionals and foisted on the children of the world.

George Gerbner
University of Pennsylvania, 1996

Socialization, a process once centered in the stories of a child's family, teachers, neighbors, and friends, is now based primarily on the messages of television. Today, stories about life, the world, and the values we seek are largely mass produced and mass marketed by a small number of commercial conglomerates. For them, success is measured by the size of the audience that they sell to advertisers and not by the content or quality of the programming (Gerbner, 1993). As a consequence, ten-year-old children can name more brands of beer than presidents (Carton, 1991).

The world that television presents is a homogenized, narrow, and violent place. Women, minorities, and those portrayed as mentally ill are underrepresented and overvictimized. Older people and the disabled are rarely seen. The number and nature of violent acts and violent murders on television exceed and distort reality. Sixty percent of men are involved in violence and 11 percent are killers. Prime time television has four to five violent acts hourly and two entertaining murders a night. Unlike actual rates, in the media the majority of homicide victims are women (Gerbner, 1994).

Gerbner and his colleagues studied the local news on Philadelphia television stations in the summer of 1995. Acts of crime and violence were consistently the lead stories and preempted balanced coverage of the city. Only 20 percent of crime and violence on the local news was local to the city and only 40 percent was local to the area. Lending support to our continuing problem with racism, whites are more likely to be reported when they are victims and African Americans when they are perpetrators. Other research has shown that this racial bias is consistent in other cities as well (Gerbner, 1996).

It is odd, given the commercial incentives of television, that they should be paying so little attention to their own ratings. Gerbner and his colleagues compared the ratings of more than 100 violent shows with the same number of nonviolent shows aired at the same time on network television. The average Nielsen rating of the violent sample was 11.1; the rating for the nonviolent sample was 13.8. The share of viewing households in the violent sample was 18.9 while for the nonviolent sample it was 22.5. The nonviolent sample was more highly rated than the violent sample for each of the five seasons from 1989 through 1993. So the usual rationalization that media violence "gives the public what it wants" is simply untrue. The public rarely gets a fair choice (Gerbner, 1996).

Violence also dominates what we export to the rest of the world. Gerbner and his colleagues compared 250 U. S. programs exported to ten countries with 111 programs shown in the United States during the same year. Violence was the main theme of 40 percent of the homeshown and

49 percent of the exported programs. Crime/action series ("action" is the code word for "violence") comprised 17 percent of what was shown at home and 46 percent of what was exported (1996).

TV-viewing adults see the world as a dark and sinister place. Gerbner has shown that heavy viewers are more likely than comparable groups of light viewers to overestimate their chances of involvement in violence, to believe that their neighborhoods are unsafe, to state that fear of crime is a very serious personal problem and to assume that crime is rising, regardless of the facts of the case. Heavy viewers are also more likely to buy new locks, watchdogs, and guns "for protection" (Gerbner, 1996). Broadly, the media sets social standards that become implicit, and not necessarily attributed to media influence. "Violence is a demonstration of power. It shows who can get away with what against whom. That exercise defines majority might and minority risk, one's place in the societal 'pecking order'" (Gerbner, 1996, p. 11).

The significance of television in shaping the beliefs, attitudes, and behavior of children, however, is more striking. Often children watch TV violence as two- and three-year-olds, years before they will be able to distinguish fantasy from reality. Furthermore, because of the pervasive nature of television, young children are not shielded from the adult world. And, as noted, the adult world that is portrayed is inaccurate. Surveys have found, for example, that sex in TV programming relates largely to prostitution and extramarital affairs, and is often linked to violence. In contrast to actual homicide statistics, the majority of victims on television are women.

Since 1967, George Gerbner and his associates have been measuring TV violence using an index that includes: (1) the percentage of programs that contain any violence, (2) the rate of violent scenes/programs, and (3) the percentage of major characters involved in violence (Gerbner, 1993). Although a recent small decline has occurred in violence in adult programs as measured by the index, in recent years children's programs have been more violent than the average for the twenty-five-year period of study.

Children's programs are fifty to sixty times more violent than prime time shows. Some cartoons have averaged more than eighty violent acts per hour. By age eighteen, the typical American child, in watching twenty-eight hours of television a week, will have witnessed 40,000 simulated murders and 200,000 acts of violence. By age eighteen a child's view of the world, its composition, and the role and characteristics of women, minorities, the disabled, and other groups and individuals will be most profoundly influenced by the content of television programs (Gerbner, 1993, 1994). Media characterizations of interpersonal relations, in particular, have been found to have an influence on young people's perception of normative behavior that snowballs: the more they view certain interpersonal patterns, the more likely they are to see these as "normal" (Schooler and Flora, 1996).

Violence, in both "entertainment" and news programs, is increasingly portrayed in blood-spattered graphic detail. Despite this detail, television misrepresents the violence; the physical and emotional consequences are omitted. The perpetrator's remorse, the victim's rage, pain, and injury or the family's loss are unseen and children witness only fast-paced, violent action without consequence—happy violence. On television, where the heroes are frequently the murderers, the message is clear: violence is appropriate; it solves problems.

Although the overall incidence of violence and crime does not appear to be increasing, violence and antisocial behavior among adolescents and young adults, as measured by homicide and arrest rates, has increased sharply in recent years. A body of evidence links viewing of TV violence with aggressive behavior and, overwhelmingly, these studies do not support the concept of "catharsis," the contention that viewing violence rids children of violent, antisocial tendencies (Wood and Wong, 1991). However, given the number of risk factors that contribute to violence, including drugs and alcohol, availability of guns, poverty and limited economic opportunity, family disintegration, and declining educational objectives, the significance of TV violence has been questioned.

Nonetheless, while TV viewing will not turn the class valedictorian into a cold-blooded killer, hundreds of studies have confirmed that media violence, both short and long term, is an important piece of the complex puzzle of risk factors that underlie abusive and violent behavior. Most experiments and short-term field studies have demonstrated that media violence increases children's aggressive behavior as demonstrated by their spontaneous, natural behavior following exposure (Centerwall, 1992). Children's play is consistently more aggressive, with more hitting and punching following viewing of violent TV shows (Huesman, 1986). In a Canadian town in which TV was first introduced in 1973, a 160 percent increase in aggression, hitting, shoving, and biting was documented in first and second grade students after exposure, with no change in behavior in children in two control communities (Centerwall, 1992).

Long-term field studies with exposure to media violence in naturalistic settings were also associated with increased aggressive behavior in boys. The findings were less consistent for girls (Turner, Hess, and Peterson-Lewis, 1986). In these studies, behavior was probably also influenced by several variables including academic performance, family viewing habits, socioeconomic status, and family patterns of punishment. Other studies of long-term exposure support a correlation between viewing TV violence and contact with the criminal justice system even after controlling for the effects of socioeconomic class, education, and race. In men, a strong correlation was found between conviction of a crime and two of the following: physical abuse by the mother, physical abuse by the father, and exposure to TV violence (Heath, Bresolin, and Rinaldi, 1989).

A striking association between the introduction of TV nationwide in 1974 and an increased homicide rate was demonstrated in South Africa, independent of other confounding variables including alcohol, firearms, economic conditions, and civil unrest (Centerwall, 1992). The homicide rate, as it had in the United States and Canada in the 1940s and 1950s, doubled thirteen years after the introduction of TV. This lag time is consistent with the impression that TV has its greatest impact on children. Based upon this fact, violence would be expected to increase progressively first in children, then in adolescents and finally in adults, as, indeed, was the case in South Africa after 1974.

Although experiments demonstrate that TV's aggression-enhancing effect is long term and extends into adulthood, in general the critical period of exposure is in preadolescent childhood. Infants imitate observed human behavior, including that which is destructive and antisocial. Up to age three or four, children see TV as a source of entirely factual information on the nature of things. Over time, media violence many distort a child's perception of how the world works. The tendency toward violent behavior after viewing violence may be enhanced by identification with aggressive media characters, belief in the reality of the programs, and violence in the home (Heath, Bresolin, and Rinaldi, 1989).

Processes that account for immediate aggression after viewing violence include imitative learning, physiological arousal, and a cognitive process, i.e., the perception that violence is normal and acceptable (Green and Thomas, 1986). Huesmann (1986) attributes "delayed" violent behavior that follows long-term exposure to media violence to a cyclical learning process in childhood. According to this concept, over time, children acquire aggressive "scripts" for behavior as they observe media violence, and this aggressive behavior, incidentally, includes further observation of media violence. Subsequently, in both childhood and adulthood, various cues seen on television may activate the aggressive scripts acquired through TV, or scripts acquired by other matters, and lead to aggressive behavior. This continues as a cumulative learning process which, if not modified or dampened, can establish permanent patterns of behavior that persist into adulthood.

This concept is consistent with a study that found that those children who were rated by their peers as most aggressive at age eight were more likely to have been convicted of a crime by age thirty (Huesmann et al., 1984). In comparison to the control group, those with criminal records had heavy exposure to violent TV programming as children, based on content analysis of self-reported viewing. The significance of TV as a variable in violent behavior in this cohort was independent of measured intelligence or socioeconomic status (Huesmann, 1986).

Since the cumulative effect of TV on long-term behavior is "encoded" during early childhood (Huesman, 1986), the issue of TV violence must be addressed in the preadolescent years. In addition to modifying content and exposure time, any response must consider the conditions under which programs are viewed. This includes the attitudes of others in the room, the psychological characteristics of the targets of aggression, the viewers perception of the situations' reality (Berkowitz, 1986), and the accepted norms for aggression in the home and the community (Heath, Bresolin, and Rinaldi, 1989).

The influence of media violence is enormous, leading not only to overt displays of aggression but also to the more pernicious effects of a decrease in sensitivity, concern, and revulsion toward violence (Goldstein, Harootunian, and Conoley, 1994). Among the scientific community there is a general consensus that television can cause aggressive behavior and that there is a cause and effect relationship between exposure to media violence and aggressive attitudes and behavior. The American Academy of Child and Adolescent Psychiatry, The American Academy of Pediatrics, the American Medical Association, the American Psychiatric Association, the American Psychological Association, the Centers for Disease Control and Prevention, the National Institutes of Mental Health, and the Surgeon General's Office have all gone on record saying that there is overwhelming scientific evidence that media violence is a causal factor in the promotion of violent attitudes and behaviors (American Medical Association, 1996). It is clear that there are, indeed, vulnerable viewers who are more impressionable, less likely to critically examine violent programming, and more likely to be deleteriously affected by it (Lande, 1993).

Major change in program content is unlikely given commercial near-monopolies, yet it is important that the entertainment industry recognize its social responsibility because of the potential impact of media violence on children. A number of studies suggest that prosocial messages on television can have a greater effect on behavior than antisocial messages (Friedlander, 1993) and the industry can respond to this need without concern of control or censorship.

At the same time, parents must understand the role that television plays in shaping children's attitudes and behavior. Parents need to monitor and discuss programs and modify viewing patterns when necessary. This process can be guided by available violence rating systems and aided by television sets with built-in time-channel lock circuitry. In addition, children, as viewers, need to be educated in regard to the lack of reality of the characters and the importance of responsibility for individual behavior. Finally, the Committee on Communication of the American Academy of Pediatrics has recommended that pediatricians advise parents to limit children's viewing to one to two hours a day (American Academy of Pediatrics, 1990). We will have more to say later about medical recommendations for television viewing.

Chapter 5

Our Response to Violence

For every action there is a reaction. Violence occurs and we respond in any number of ways. Our reaction then continues the chain of action onward in a cascade of effects that determines events far beyond what we can see in the present. In this section we will look at some of the fundamental ways that we respond to violence. We will focus first on the most obvious—crime and punishment. Our spontaneous reaction to any disobedience is to seek retribution. The criminal justice system is based on this basic human desire. Sadly, it is this intrinsic desire for retribution that contributes so greatly to the spiral of trauma within which we are all presently trapped. But revenge is not our only reaction. In any situation, there are bystanders—people who know what is going on, who could act to change a situation, but do not. We consider this extremely important variable under the rubric of a "failure to protect." We will also look at the larger social picture to get some idea about what our present climate of hatred and violence is doing to all of us, turning us into "robopaths." Finally, we will look at alternative responses—what goes into helping a child or adult develop resiliency, the capacity to bounce back after stress.

CRIME AND PUNISHMENT

In New Jersey in mid-summer 1994, a young girl was sexually abused and killed by a man from her neighborhood. It was learned upon his arrest that this man was a convicted pedophile, recently released from prison. Just prior to his release, the man and those providing treatment to him had each expressed misgivings about his readiness to be released from a secure setting. Neighbors, following the girl's funeral, began to lobby for a new "right to know" law, which would require officials to notify neighborhoods when a sex offender is released to the community. Such laws have grown in popularity during the last decade and are on the books in many other states.

At this point in the history of criminal rehabilitation, communities have all but given up hope that anything can be done for those who perpetrate acts of violence. Conservatives are rivaled by liberals in the outcry for more cops and more prisons. Safety from perpetrators is to be achieved through incarceration. More and more men and women, especially those who have experienced poverty, a violent childhood, or other trauma, are behind bars.

Crime and punishment are central to our society's effort to deal with violence, in several ways. Social controls have long been regarded as essential to moderate antisocial impulses and it is through the enactment of laws and their enforcement that we effectuate these controls. Civilization, it is reasoned, requires limits on the individual's ability to act out in harmful ways. We define harm and attempt to deter such acts through a system of crime and punishment that, in essence, raises the "cost" of the behavior.

The delineation of crimes and the establishment of a criminal justice system to enforce criminal behaviors serve the additional social purpose of establishing a public morality, marking the boundaries of right and wrong. Parents teach their children "a lesson" when they punish behavior; so society teaches a lesson not just to the criminal but to all when it punishes crime.

Beyond its deterrent and teaching effect, though, enlightened society hoped that its criminal justice system might also rehabilitate "the soul" of the criminal (Foucault, 1973). The complex psychology of the antisocial personality was scrutinized in an effort to program a restorative process. The myriad contributing factors of poverty, childhood deprivation, inadequate socialization, and so forth were incorporated into a host of strategies for resocializing criminals. It is the bankruptcy of this rehabilitative philosophy that has led communities to lobby for "right to know" laws. A part of this bankrupt vision can be accounted for by ignorance. Until recently, we knew very little about the long-term consequences of exposure to violence and the role that such consequences have in the evolution of the individual who ends up committing criminal acts. As a result, treatment for these effects within the prison settings has been minimal.

As the penal system swells with unimagined numbers of perpetrators—rising 170 percent to 1.3 million between 1980 and 1992—society has grown cynical about the efficacy of its rehabilitative treatments. It is a cynicism born from failure and fear. In 1990, 51 percent of respondents in a Gallup poll reported that there was more crime in their area than a year ago. In 1990, 2.3 million Americans were victims of violent crime. Signs of a fortress mentality abound.

On February 18, 1993, *The New York Times* reported that sales of Mace in December 1992 were ten times higher than one year before; that burglar alarm companies were flourishing; that self-defense seminars were springing up like weeds; and that thousands of people were buying car phones so they could dial 911 in case of sudden predation (Friedman, 1993).

Other evidence of feeling embattled has been the building of prisons and the emphasis on punishment over rehabilitation. We wish to "put people away" with little real faith that they will be improved by the process. In fact, as conventional wisdom would suggest and a recent report confirms, many inmates leave prison in worse shape than when they entered (Irwin and Austin, 1994). Prison conditions exacerbate problems of impulse control, social attachment, and conscience.

Add to these problems the observation that the criminal justice system, perceived by most to be full of holes, fails to deter. Calculated criminals can gamble with the odds on their side that they can escape detection, arrest, conviction, or jail. And because so many crimes are impulsive in nature, it is dubious whether stiff penalties can deter behaviors anyway.

From the perspective of trauma theory, the failure of the criminal justice system is both predictable and lamentable. To retraumatize a perpetrator who is in the grips of a traumatic reenactment will do little to resolve the repetition compulsion. Spanking, while perhaps satisfying in perverse ways to the parent, adds complex layers of shame, fear, and anger onto the existing misbehavior. The child does not "learn his lesson," though he may learn to hide and calculate more carefully. Children gain control through healing, not fear. Antisocial behavior, however repugnant, will not be resolved through blame or punishment. The criminal can be rehabilitated only in programs that are based on sound principles of trauma treatment. Until this has been thoroughly attempted we have no idea who is and is not treatable. Some may have permanent damage and require permanent incarceration to protect others from their destructive behavior. If so, it is vital that we find ways to prevent them from harming others without retraumatizing them. This is as important for us as for them. Inflicting brutal punishment, even on the brutal, is damaging to the punishers and the punished.

FAILURE TO PROTECT: THE BYSTANDER EFFECT

Not everyone has the experience of being either victim or perpetrator of the more severe forms of violence. All of us, though, have the experience of witnessing violent acts in this age of electronic community. We have become a nation of bystanders and carry within the burden of vicarious traumatization. Understanding the import of this cultural development can help us recover sensitivity and efficacy in dealing with violence.

Who is a bystander? Bystanders are the audience. They are all those present at the scene of an incident who provide or deny support for a behavior. The victim and perpetrator form a linked figure and the bystanders form the ground against which the perpetration is carried out or prevented. It is useful to note that among acts of perpetration which have been studied, it is the behavior of the bystanders that determines how far the perpetrator will go in carrying out the act of violence (Fogelman, 1994; Staub, 1989, 1992). In Stanley Milgram's famous studies of obedience, the powerful influence of the group was found to determine whether otherwise healthy people could be persuaded to become abusive (Milgram, 1974).

From this perspective, it can be said that bystanders share elements of both victimization and perpetration in the dynamics of violence. Healthy attachment generates empathic connections among people: we cannot observe abuse and violence without being affected. We identify at one end or the other and through this identification are inducted into the traumatic event. The phenomenon of "secondary traumatization" refers to the toxic effects of a violent act upon the community of bystanders. Failure to act to prevent harm undermines our sense of efficacy, reinforces powerlessness, and often results in profound feelings of guilt and shame.

How do we cope with our considerable exposure to violence as witnesses? Many of the same psychological processes we will discuss for victims of trauma come into play with secondary trauma. The human mind can handle only so much before primitive defensive strategies are activated. As tests have proven in studies of secondhand cigarette smoke, passive exposure to noxious agents can be debilitating.

Attribution theory teaches us that one's psychological state influences perception of responsibility and agency in acts of violence. Many, for example, upon learning of an instance of rape, find themselves driven by personal distaste and powerlessness to discounting the crime in an effort to feel less uncomfortable. We find ourselves wondering "if she brought it on herself."

Coates and colleagues (Harber and Pennebaker, 1992) explored other people's willingness to listen to and support a victim's need to disclose information about his or her experience. It was quite clear in their research that the bearers of disturbing information and negative emotions are suppressed in various ways. Listeners switch the topic away from trauma. They attempt to press their own, less upsetting perspective of the trauma upon the victim. Listeners tend to exaggerate the victim's personal responsibility in the traumatic situation. If these strategies do not work to get the victim to stop talking, then the listener will avoid contact with the victim altogether. The reasons for this behavior are fairly clear. The suffering of victims can threaten the listener's assumptions about a "just world" in which people get what they deserve. The feelings of a trauma victim can be so relentless in intensity and negativity that even the most empathic person becomes overwhelmed. Victims are usually quite aware of the reluctance of listeners to hear and will often cease talking in order to protect their social connections. "Victims may be trapped in a complicated dilemma in which they can maximize their social acceptance only at the expense of their personal adjustment" (Harber and Pennebaker, 1992, p. 367).

Devaluation is another example of distorted perception. The murder of a person with high status will evoke a much stronger reaction than the murder of a person with low status. Revelations about sexual abuse were not remarkably startling to the public as long as sexual abuse was thought to occur only among the poor and disenfranchised. When reports began surfacing about sexual abuse in the middle class, in the clergy, and among other members of the community who have a higher status, sexual abuse became topical and more controversial. Countries in which anti-Semitism was strongest were those in which Nazis executed the largest number of Jews.

Denial is another delusional mechanism vital to the bystander's effort to cope with violence. In all of its forms—minimization, rationalization, projection—denial assists the uncomfortable bystander to manage the painful observation by bending and twisting reality into a more digestible form. That "bad things happen to bad people" is a rationalization we are conditioned to believe through a childhood of messages that we deserve what we get. But, a key finding with respect to research on the bystander effect is this: we cannot detach ourselves from another's suffering and hurt without paying a high price. Lessons from soldiers in wartime teach us that traumatization occurs when we participate in the infliction of harm, particularly when there is no cause or sense of a higher purpose to help us rationalize the act. Even where we can momentarily persuade ourselves that we are unaffected, we find haunting images and memories become a part of our psychological baggage, persisting until we resolve them.

The body social can become infected just as can the body physical, and the metaphor of an infection is useful in understanding this phenomenon. The infectious agent can be seen as the perpetrator, the immune system as the potential victim, and the other resources in the body as the bystanders. The state of nutrition, fitness, and overall well-being of the body determines the state of the immune system that determines how far the infection can spread. In a deteriorating body, the capacity of the immune system is overwhelmed and death easily occurs. Once the body has become overwhelmed by a pathogen, no amount of attention to diet, stress management, or fitness will help determine the outcome.

Similarly, in social behavior, early intervention and prevention works best. As bystanders become increasingly passive in the face of abusive behavior, action becomes increasingly difficult. Just as there is a deteriorating spiral of perpetration in which each act of violence becomes increasingly easy to accomplish, so too is there a deteriorating cycle of passivity. As the perpetrators actively assume control over a system without any resistance on the part of bystanders, their power increases to the point that resistance on the part of bystanders becomes extremely difficult if not useless, except to the extent that such behavior serves as an example for others.

However, all it takes is for one bystander in a group to take some sort of positive action against perpetration and others will follow. Resistance to perpetration on the part of bystanders, both in words and in actions, influences others to become active instead of passive. There is much to be learned from the behavior of bystanders who DO help because in any situation of perpetration, they define a different reality. Their actions provide an alternative way of relating, another example to the perpetrators and would-be perpetrators, and victims, all of whom become locked into the cycle of violence and abuse (Staub, 1989, 1992).

Latane and Darley have outlined a five-stage process by which bystanders turn into helpers (Fogelman, 1994; Latane and Darley, 1970). First bystanders notice that something is amiss and then they interpret the situation as one in which people need help. In the next critical stage, they assume responsibility to offer that help, then choose a form of help, and finally implement that help. Helpful behavior can be derailed at any of these stages. But what increases the likelihood that helpful bystander behavior will not be derailed?

First, there is the intrinsic nature of the bystander. Helpful bystanders have many characteristics in common that tell us a great deal about how we need to raise our children and how we must behave in situations that confront us. Helpers have strong moral concerns that are transmitted by their parents and among those values are a fundamental sense of empathy for others, standards that are applied to people in different social, ethnic, and religious groups. Bystanders who become rescuers often have experience with being marginalized or victimized themselves, but have been able to sustain connections with others rather than disconnect from human bonds. Helpful behavior falls along a very long continuum and evolves gradually over time. Each successful attempt to help leads to more helping behavior that becomes self-reinforcing. This implies that helping behavior can be modeled, learned, taught, reinforced—that it is not a given in any situation but can and must be constantly recreated.

But even willing helpers can be derailed by social propaganda, by coercion, and by the influence of others who want to deny the perpetrator behavior and who offer an alternative with such explanations as "He deserves what he gets," "People can always find a job if they look hard enough," "The problem is not guns; it's the people who use them," "People just want to blame their parents," "Welfare recipients are just lazy and don't want to work," "There's more crime because we've gotten too soft on criminals."

If helpers can get past the propaganda and see the flaws in thinking, they still have to feel that they have some responsibility for solving the problem and that they are able to choose something to do to help and put their plan into action. This sense of mutual responsibility can be taught later in life but is mostly easily modeled within the family systems by what the children see in the behavior of their own parents toward other people. Finding effective ways to help often requires larger scale organization and the participation of others. It is the reverse of the downward spiral of perpetration.

The fundamental question is whether witnesses to the mistreatment of other people have an obligation to act. What is our moral responsibility to each other? Are we, in fact, "our brother's keeper?" Until quite recently in human history, the family group or the tribe were the only groups to which we felt the kind of loyalty that demands protective action. In the last two centuries, our sense of loyalty has expanded to our national groups. More recently, global ethnicity has been commanding fealty. But we have entered an age of such intense global interdependency that perpetration against one can be seen increasingly to affect the whole in an escalating cycle of violence and destruction. We may never be able to eliminate the forces that produce violence, but it is not too late to contain them. This containment can happen, however, only if bystanders choose to become witnesses and rescuers, instead of silently colluding with the perpetrators.

ROBOPATHOLOGY

The culture responds in certain subtle but typical ways to violence. Such responses can serve to escalate or decrease the amount and nature of violence. These factors, however, are difficult to quantify, although everyone recognizes them when they are present. As we will discuss in more detail later, when an individual is traumatized, one of the typical responses is a progressive emotional numbing that seriously impairs the capacity to relate to self and others. Over twenty years ago, the psychologist and psychodramatist Lewis Yablonsky coined the word *robopathology* (Yablonsky, 1972, 1992), a useful way of talking about similar effects on a larger social scale. Robopaths are people who are socially dead, who behave more like robots than human beings. Yablonsky identified eight interrelated characteristics that defined a robopath. He said, "In a society of robopaths, violence reaches monstrous proportions, wars are standard accepted practice, and conflict abounds" (Yablonsky, 1992, p. 250). In examining "robopathology" we can see some of the accepted social norms and practices that provide the setting within which violence, and our reaction to violence, supports its continuation and extension.

Ritualism is the first characteristic of robopathology. Robopaths respond in ways that are socially defined, free of spontaneity and creativity. Sex, violence, hostility, and recreation are all preplanned, programmed, predictable activities. Social interaction is ritualized as well; little relief is seen from dull routine with little attached meaning. Robopaths are oriented to the past, often responding to situations with past solutions that are no longer relevant in the present, and appear unable to respond to changing demands or future emergencies. One example Yablonsky uses is our refusal to move away from gasoline-powered forms of transportation, even though we know that the fuel supplies are running out. Other examples from our perspective would include our present insistence on addressing violence through punishment rather than prevention, blaming the poor for the lack of jobs, scapegoating single mothers for poor childrearing, and blaming teenage incest victims for pregnancy.

Robopaths emphasize the need to conform and maintain obedience to authority. They ask no questions about the ultimate outcome of conforming to norms established by someone else in an earlier period. Creativity is seen as strange and bizarre. They automatically obey authority without questioning the grounds on which this authority is based or the goals of established authority. Stanley Milgram's experiments in obedience graphically portrayed this situation, as 65 percent of experimental subjects conformed to the demands of authority to the point at which they supposedly inflicted severe pain or possible death on another human being (Milgram, 1974; Yablonsky, 1992). This was the "I was only following orders" defense of the Nazi leaders.

For robopaths, the sense of self is determined by presenting the image that is expected by other people. There is little inner sense of direction or purpose. For them the focus is on recognition from outside of themselves, playing to an audience, or cultivating a cult-like following as celebrity status substitutes for character. Fame is determined not by actual accomplishments but by the level of media attention. What is most important is projecting the right image, not actually being a defined and internally consistent human being.

More ominous signs of robopathology are hostility, alienation, and lack of compassion. Robopaths are arrogant about their own rights and well-being but remain unconcerned about the welfare of others unless they are directly affected. They cannot show empathy and have great difficulty in "walking in the other person's moccasins." They are so cut off from the creative wellsprings of life and feeling that they often express venomous hostility. The particular nature of this hostility depends on other factors, including the extent to which they have power over others. Members of government can show hostility by enacting legislation that cuts off basic services to the poor. The director of benefits in a corporation can vent hostility by reducing medical benefits to his workers. The manager of a health insurance company can discharge hostility by turning over management to a ruthless intermediary who will obtain profit by depriving people of health care. The father of a poor family can vent his hostility by beating his wife and children. Regardless of the economic circumstances or role in the society, such enmity and lack of compassion is related to robopathology.

Robopathology culminates in a deep and pervasive sense of alienation—from self, others, and the natural environment. To the robopath, all living things, including self, are objects for which no compassion or care is demanded. Values are grounded in material possessions, rather than in feelings, social welfare, mercy, love, or peace. Established ways of doing things, institutions, and processes must be maintained at all costs, regardless of their cost/benefit ratio. Robopaths have limited capacity for humor, joy, creative expression, or vision and they seek to cut off these capacities when they see them in other people. Any reference to emotional expression, higher spiritual values, the emotional necessity of artistic expression, or the need for human compassion and interconnection are likely to be met with a fiercely and well-defended cynicism that ridicules and seeks to humiliate any inclination toward the creation of a better society.

The concept of robopathology illustrates the effects of an entire cultural attitude that permeates our social climate. Our response to escalating violence is often robopathological—ritualized, stuck in the past, conforming to an image of change rather than change itself, characterized by a lack of compassion, overt hostility to the powerless, and ultimately by a profound social alienation. When too many people turn into robopaths the social climate becomes pervaded by hostility, hatred, and cynicism. A resistance is felt to expressions of love, hope, creativity, and humor.

RESILIENCY: PROTECTIVE FACTORS

Resiliency is the term used to describe the phenomenon of individual difference in people's response to stress and adversity. In simple terms it is the capacity to "bounce back" or recover from a disappointment, obstacle, or setback (Demos, 1989). It is not just a matter of constitutional strength but a reflection of what the individual does in a particular stressful situation. Resilience is the ability to maintain adaptive functioning in spite of serious risk hazards (Rutter, 1990). Defined broadly, resiliency refers to the ability to function psychologically at a level far greater than expected given a person's earlier developmental experiences (Higgins, 1994). Each individual response is profoundly affected by other people. It is this person-environment interaction that is so important in determining a person's coping responses.

We know far more about pathology than we know about what makes someone mentally healthy. Likewise, we know far more about people who suffer the extreme negative consequences of trauma than we do about people who are traumatized and yet manage to transcend their traumatic experiences, living lives characterized by the capacity to love, to work, and to be creative. In studies of resilience it appears that in most samples, resilience is a noteworthy factor in about 10 percent of the populations that have been studied.

Gina O'Connell Higgins has studied resilient adults, all of whom suffered extreme traumatic events in childhood. Resilient adults tend to have above-average intelligence, demonstrate exceptional talents, have obtained higher economic levels than their families of origin; demonstrate high levels of ego development; have sustained empathic relationships with others over extended periods of time; frequently have very disturbed siblings; and maintain strong political and social activism. They are committed to continuing growth and change, tend to turn negative experiences into positive challenges, and demonstrate a profound form of faith and hope in a better vision for themselves and for humanity. They are optimists, a pleasure to be with, hard workers, and determined not to repeat the mistakes of the past (Higgins, 1994).

Wolin and Wolin (1993) have listed seven lasting strengths or aspects of the resilient person:

- *Insight:* the habit of asking tough questions and giving honest answers.
- *Independence:* drawing boundaries between self and troubled parents; keeping emotional and physical distance while satisfying the demand of conscience.

- *Relationships:* intimate and fulfilling ties to other people that balance a mature regard for one's own needs with empathy and the capacity to give to someone else.
- *Initiative:* taking charge of problems; exerting control; a taste for stretching and testing oneself in demanding tasks.
- *Creativity:* imposing order, beauty, and purpose on the chaos of one's troubling experiences and painful feelings.
- *Humor:* finding the comic in the tragic.
- *Morality:* an informed conscience that extends the wish for a good personal life to all of humankind.

We can guess at what resilient people look like and how they behave. But how do they get that way? Is it just genetics and luck or are there ways that the environment can be influenced to increase the odds in favor of resiliency? In research on stress-resistant children, Garmezy has concluded that there are three broad sets of variables that serve as protective factors: (1) personality factors of the individual such as autonomy, self-esteem, and positive social orientation; (2) family cohesion, warmth, and absence of discord; and (3) the availability of external support systems that encourage a coping response for the child (Rutter, 1990).

What abilities of the child are necessary to produce resilience? At the very least, resilience requires that the child take an active stance toward an obstacle or difficulty, seeing the problem as a challenge that can be worked on, overcome, changed, endured, or resolved in some way. This persistence must be combined with the ability to know when to stop. Resilient children have the ability to try a number of different problem solutions and demonstrate a wide range of interests and goals. They also show the flexibility to know when to use a particular coping skill. And they have sufficient experience with discovering that their efforts are successful or gratifying in some way. Young children who will become resilient experience "I can do things"; "I can solve problems"; "I can endure frustration and discouragement because I know things will get better"; "bad things don't last forever" (Demos, 1989, p. 17).

Family factors also influence the development of resilience. Children do best when their caregivers are able to respond to their particular innate temperament with empathy, adjusting themselves to the needs of their child. Sadly, many parents are able to extend empathy only to children who are like themselves and have similar responses and behaviors; this is called "selective empathy." To the extent that the child is constitutionally like the parent, this empathic regard can be helpful. But when conflict occurs between the child and his/her caregivers, the empathic connection breaks down, often leaving the child exposed to stress. Another important family characteristic is the degree of resilience in the family system. Children need parents who are role models for resiliency, who solve parent-child problems with more empathic responses than spanking, angry commands, isolation, and threats of abandonment and banishment. Since one of the key ingredients to resiliency is flexibility in trying many different options to problems, resilience is lowered when the caregiver makes a minimum investment in the child. Without parental guidance and support, a child tends to constrict activities and skills and thus lowers possibilities for resilient problem solving. For the same reasons, such a child often turns away from others, thus reducing even further the opportunities for self-efficacy. Children also need protection from overwhelming stress. Children and families who are resilient show better than average ability to manage negative emotional states (Demos, 1989).

Finally, to understand resiliency we must look at the seventh aspect of the resilient person that Wolin and Wolin referred to—morality. Fogelman (1994) has studied aspects of resilience among people who were rescuers during World War II, often risking their own lives and the lives of loved ones. Apparently it was their strong sense of moral integrity that appeared to play such a significant role in their refusal to submit to coercive authority. Norma Haan (1989) has stated that certain forms of moral interchange build children's resiliency while other forms may leave children vulnerable to life stress. Haan speaks of practical morality—the morality people use and cherish in their everyday life. She sees this morality as being interactional, motivated by three common human desires: first, the need to feel that one is moral; second, the need to feel that others think one is moral; third, the need to feel that one's world is just.

One way of testing practical morality is to put children in a situation where a moral choice must be made and see how they perform. Haan put four-year-olds in a situation where they could not "win" without hurting their partner and their attempts at "winning" could be stalemated by their partner—thus providing for a balance of power and the opportunity for choice. Children had five options: *equalization* in which both children received one penny, *stalemate* in which neither child received any money, *default* in which one child got two pennies and the other got none, *reparation* in which both children agreed that the child who was behind could catch up, and *betrayal* in which one child deliberately broke an explicit agreement to equalize. She considered equalization and reparative acts as evidence of children's general moral concern for others as well as their ability to recognize their fate and that of their fellow as being of mutual concern. A naturally selfish child would not be expected to either equalize or repair. In 85 percent of the dyads, four-year-olds acted to equalize at some point in the play and overall, 32 percent of their plays were equalizations compared to 29 percent for university students. Only 27 percent *never* verbalized moral ideas, explaining the choices they had made. Sixty percent of the "winners" made reparations at some point. She reached the following conclusion from the study:

> The major conclusion to be drawn from these observations is that these four-year-olds did not act as they should if they are cognitively unable to understand and coordinate their views with another's or if they are morally selfish. . . . . Their incidence of equalization and reparation . . . was not radically different from . . . the university students that we had previously tested with this same situation. . . . A second finding is that these four-year-olds acted . . . as if they were having the same kind of experiences as the adolescents and young adults we studied earlier—in the kind of problems they generated, solutions they developed, and emotions that accompanied their acting. In other words, they experienced the same moral impulses, uncertainties, outrages, and stresses. . . . The clearest difference between the age groups is that the four-year-olds were not often verbally articulate or sophisticated about their positions and emotions. . . . I suggest then that young children's understanding of basic human reciprocity is much the same as adults', but children lack knowledge, cognitive skills, objective power, responsibility, and material resources to empower their negotiations. Because children are readily stressed, moral violations only intensify the helplessness they already feel. (Haan, 1989, pp. 34-38)

To understand this work, we must point out that it is based on a different view of very young children's morality. As we discussed earlier, according to the religious doctrine of original sin, children are born sinful, predisposed toward selfishness, and inevitably rebellious. These ideas, even though no longer necessarily connected with a religious viewpoint, have contaminated our entire social milieu concerning our view of basic human nature and our expectations for children. What science is demonstrating is that these impressions are far from the whole truth. Young children have the same basic moral understandings and concerns as adolescents and young adults. The tendency to intuitively grasp the principles of reciprocity appears to be innate, a naturally evolved strategy for a socially interacting species (Wright, 1994). Young children, however, have fewer skills to deal with moral dilemmas and are more susceptible to stress. Additionally, they are relatively powerless and are vulnerable to the parental position that they are selfish—a position that operates as a self-fulfilling prophecy.

In fact, Haan proposes that observed deficiencies in all people's moral functioning can be understood as failures to cope with conflict and the stressful processes of its resolution. Moral performance improves with age because ego skills and skills for resolving conflict improve with age.

If children have moral understanding, then they must be involved in moral negotiations even when they are in error. This means that they must be involved in preserving their moral honor and participation rather than just being manipulated—or beaten—into compliance. If they have moral understanding, then their attempts to protect their own self-interests must be taken seriously rather than cast off as evidence of their selfishness. Being ignored as a moral being produces a great sense of helplessness—a main component of human stress. The idea that children are morally ignorant gives rise to repeated experience of being morally ignored or used (Haan, 1989).

Haan believes that childhood resiliency and vulnerability have specific relationships to the moral climate of families that build children's expectancies about the nature of moral interchanges:

> Resilient children will have reason to be optimistic that moral difficulties can usually be worked out: They will be heard; they will usually be able to protect their legitimate self-interests; they will understand that no human is faultless, that even adults morally violate, so they will "speak truth to power" and be able to forgive themselves. Resilient children may be those who are confident that most human interchanges make moral sense and those who understand why some interchanges do not. (Haan, 1989, p. 40)

It is clear that if we want to produce children and adults who can bounce back from stress then the response of the other people in their environment is critical. Given what we know about feelings and coping responses, we must do much more to enhance positive feelings and decrease negative feelings, particularly during times of overwhelming stress. Using this data, we must also reevaluate all situations in which adults take actions against children that are morally inconsistent and even reprehensible and then expect children to respond in a healthy way. For instance, we must consider whether we can continue to teach children that violence is wrong, that hitting other people is wrong, while assaulting children in the name of justice.

SUMMARY: A TRAUMA-ORGANIZED SYSTEM

What has been destroyed for children traumatized by community violence is the idea of home, school, and community as a safe place. . . . Danger replaces safety as the organizing principle.

Garbarino et al., 1992

On the news, in the newspapers, in the course of conversation, on television shows and in the movies, we hear about these sources of violence every day. But we hear about them separately. A murder here, a case of child abandonment there. A wife is brutally battered. A homeless Vietnam vet is caught robbing a bank. An African-American family has a cross burned on their lawn. A thousand more workers are laid off in another industry downsizing. Gunshots ring out from a schoolyard. An obstetrician is killed in the bombing of an abortion clinic. A basement full of dogs are found starving to death. Another riot breaks out in a prison. Children are brought over from China to make child pornography. Another health care mogul becomes a billionaire. The ozone layer is going. These incidents are overwhelming for most of us. The age-old solution to this is to attribute the problem to fundamental, probably hormonal and genetic, flaws in human nature. Such flaws, it is postulated, can never be remedied; they can only be contained. With such an oddly comforting assumption we do not really have to *do* anything except individually sit back and get the most we can get out of life.

It is true that within every aspect of reality there are constraints. But in the case of what is commonly known as "human nature" it is our hypothesis that we do not even know yet what human nature *is* and therefore we cannot yet safely evaluate the extent of our natural constraints. We fail to see that the exposure to individual, social, and structural violence has predictable, cumulative effects on all of us—on the ideas we promulgate, the beliefs we cherish, the way we feel, the way we treat each other, the implicit assumptions we make and the kind of society we create. We fail to see that all violence is interconnected and that there are identifiable cycles of violence that could be avoided, prevented, or circumvented. Having reviewed the sociology of violence, we believe we have made a strong case that our society has become organized around unresolved, multigenerational traumatic experience. The impact is so insidious that we no longer see it for what it is. Much like an individual victim of repetitive abuse, violence has become a way of life—the rule not the exception. We have become desensitized to it, conditioned to accept it, even addicted to it. Many of us have come to expect certain forms of violence.

The anthropologist Colin Turnbull witnessed what rapidly happened to a previously stable, moral, family-oriented, ecologically fit hunter-gatherer tribe of people who were displaced from their ecological niche in such a way that their entire social structure was disrupted and destroyed. Under such conditions, the Ik became so cruel that their behavior could easily be described as "evil"—children older than three were abandoned to fend for themselves, the very old were abandoned and left to die, the dead were left unburied, the sick were uncared for, and the level of cruelty and sadism was unsurpassed in their history. They had become, as Turnbull described them, "the loveless people" witnessing the "end of goodness" (Turnbull, 1972). The Ik have a powerful lesson to teach all of us, as we socially condone some of the same behavior.

We cannot begin to formulate effective strategies to deal with violence unless we have a common knowledge base that explains to us what violence actually does to the body, mind, and soul of the individual and how that affects the group. Trauma theory provides just such a knowledge base. In a way, trauma theory allows for the possibility of a "unified field theory" of human behavior, serving as the anchor for the integration of various psychological theories, techniques, and opinions. In this next section we will summarize the findings available thus far.

PART II:
TRAUMA THEORY

In the last twenty-five years, the field of traumatic stress studies has exploded. Researchers and clinicians, confronted with the serious adjustment problems of the returning Vietnam veterans, reached back to research initiated during and after World War I and II on combat soldiers, prisoners of war, refugees, and Holocaust survivors. They began developing new hypotheses for explaining what had happened to produce such psychological damage to the men—and some women—they were trying to treat. The development of these hypotheses and the synchronistic efforts of others working with battered women, abused children, rape victims, survivors of disaster and terrorism, and others has led to the development of a biopsychosocial model for understanding the profound impact of severe stress on the body, mind, and soul of the survivors. In this section we will examine the information that has been gathered thus far that can help provide us with an empirically based and systematic way of beginning to solve some of the problems that face us as a society.

Chapter 6

Normal Reactions
to Abnormal Stress

Problems with memory and a tendency to compulsively repeat the past are the hallmarks of trauma. The history of the study of trauma illustrates these same problems. The effects of trauma have been noted and then forgotten several times over the last century and a half. Freud originally stated that the patients he saw who suffered from hysterical symptoms had been traumatized as children. At the same time Freud was formulating his ideas, Pierre Janet developed a rigorous psychological theory centering on the effects of psychological trauma, much of which has been "rediscovered" in the past few decades. But Janet's work was largely ignored in this century until quite recently, while Freud's later theories, which largely avoided the full impact of trauma, were embraced and expanded (Van der Kolk, Brown, and Van der Hart, 1989; Van der Kolk and Van der Hart, 1989).

Warfare has played a significant role in helping us to come to terms with the fact that human beings are vulnerable to the effects of overwhelming stress. But it has taken years of advocacy to bring about an understanding that this vulnerability could not be understood in the context of individual weakness. During the Civil War, a wide variety of acute and delayed stress disorders existed in soldiers, doctors, nurses, and exposed citizens. Many combatants were diagnosed as insane and the cause was listed as "exposure to the army," the "shock of battle," "shell explosions," or simply "The War." Another major diagnostic category was "homesickness" or "nostalgia," a medical term in use since the seventeenth century to describe the mental deterioration suffered by soldiers stationed far from home. A third Civil War diagnostic category was "soldier's heart," "irritable heart," or DaCosta's Syndrome, characterized by attacks of dizziness, palpitations, a sense of smothering, vertigo, nervousness, and sleeplessness, first observed by British physicians during the Crimean War (Dean, 1997). In World War II the same syndrome was called "battle fatigue" and there was finally a recognition that anyone could succumb to the effects of stress with extensive exposure (Herman, 1992). In 1952, the DSM-I was released as the official classification scheme of the American Psychiatric Association and "gross stress reaction" was the category that included exposure to overwhelming stressors such as combat (American Psychiatric Association, 1952). But the first revision, DSM-II, released in 1968 at the same time as the TET offensive, removed "gross stress reaction" and substituted "adult adjustment disorder," with little mention of the consequences of trauma (American Psychiatric Association, 1968). When men and women veterans began returning from Vietnam with symptoms clearly attributable to combat exposure, there was no way to diagnose their disorders adequately, no way to justify veterans benefits or insurance coverage. As a result, it took the combined activist efforts of veterans, clergy, and mental health professionals who protested publicly and testified before Congress, for "post-traumatic stress disorder" to be included as a diagnostic category in 1980 (Scott, 1993; Shatan, 1985).

During the 1970s and 1980s, other researchers who were working with different survivor groups began talking about various clinical syndromes they were identifying. Clinicians and researchers working with women identified "rape trauma syndrome" (Burgess and Holmstrom, 1974) and "battered woman syndrome" (Walker, 1979). Even earlier, Eitinger and others had described the effects of internment in the concentration camps on survivors of the Holocaust (1961). Studies of disaster victims began to be published discussing the typical reactions of people subsequent to a disaster (Green, 1982; Raphael, 1986). In 1974 the granddaughter of William Randolph Hearst and heiress to the Hearst fortune, Patty Hearst, age nineteen, was kidnapped by a terrorist group while sitting at home with her boyfriend. Until September 1975, she was a captive of the group and was physically, sexually, and emotionally tortured. She developed a new persona and a new name, "Tanya," and was caught by the FBI while participating in a bank robbery with the group. In 1976 she was convicted and sentenced to seven years in jail, three of which she served (Hearst, 1981). In the same year, a bank robber in Stockholm, Sweden, took a bank teller hostage. They fell in love and had sex during a long siege in the bank vault (Ochlberg, 1996). This powerful bonding between kidnapper and victim was later recognized in other types of captivity situations and came to be known as the "Stockholm Syndrome" (Strenz, 1982). Kempe and his colleagues, Green, and others published data on child abuse and out of the increased recognition of this phenomenon arose the clinical descriptions of child physical abuse and child sexual abuse (Green, 1993; Kempe and

Kempe, 1978). In 1985, the founding meeting of the Society for Traumatic Stress Studies, now the International Society for Traumatic Stress Studies (ISTSS) brought together clinicians, researchers, advocates, victims, clergy, and others who were studying the effects of overwhelming stress. The recognition grew, promulgated by members of this group and supported by what became the first journal devoted to the study of trauma, the *Journal of Traumatic Stress,* that there is a universal reaction to overwhelming stress, a reaction that is largely biologically determined but that affects every aspect of human function. Victor Frankl was a psychiatrist who survived the Nazi concentration camps and he frequently pointed out that one's standard for expectable behavior changes depending on the circumstances, so that under extreme conditions people frequently develop abnormal reactions that must then be considered normal behavior under those circumstances (Frankl, 1959).

It became increasingly clear that a substantial number of traumatized people do not just "get over" the traumatic experience. Unable to process the experience, the mind becomes preoccupied. Janet, an early trauma theoretician, referred to this preoccupation as an "idée fixe." The human organism appears to work through trauma with a repetitive recreation of the traumatic experience through flashbacks, dreams, and compulsive behaviors. As the mind defends its integrity by fighting in this way to stay whole, unwilling to move on in the present while unable to completely digest the past, we can see the roots of behaviors that have confused observers of human behavior for centuries. The repetition compulsion, although sometimes representing a positive force for health and integrity for the individual, can lead to behavior for the individual and society that can be highly problematic.

Perhaps this can best be observed in survivors of such catastrophes as floods or nuclear power plant malfunctions. Studies have demonstrated the persistence of feelings of victimization among significant portions of the traumatized population for long periods following such events. Baum (1991) followed a population affected by the Three Mile Island Nuclear Power Plant accident of 1980 and discovered many who continued to display measurable hyperarousal reactions as late as six years after the event. Although the catastrophe was averted, the populations exposed to the threat of disaster were not so quick to forget. Frederick (1991) likewise observed chronic reactions in victims of terrorism, including severe psychic disturbance. Profound and long-term disturbances have been found now in every survivor group and may even affect subsequent generations (Danieli, 1997; Egeland and Susman-Stillman, 1996; Rosenheck, 1986).

Trauma in childhood appears to be particularly disruptive because not only is the individual forced to deal with the symptoms that relate directly to post-traumatic stress, but he or she must also contend with the extremely detrimental effects of trauma and its aftermath on normal development (James, 1989; 1994; Terr, 1990, 1994)

PSYCHOLOGICAL TRAUMA DEFINED

To understand what trauma does we have to understand what it is. We need an adequate definition of psychological trauma. The DSM-IV states, "The person has been exposed to a traumatic event in which both of the following were present: (1) An event or events that involved actual or threatened death or serious injury or a threat to the physical integrity of self or others; (2) The person's response involved intense fear, helplessness, or horror. In children, this may be expressed instead by disorganized or agitated behavior" (American Psychiatric Association, 1994, p. 427). This is a more stringent definition than the previous DSM-III and DSM-IV-R criteria of an "event that is outside the range of usual human experience that would be markedly distressing to almost anyone" (American Psychiatric Association, 1980, 1987). Unfortunately, this current definition does not always encompass events that are, indeed, traumatic, most particularly the prolonged effects of chronic and repetitive exposure to physical and sexual violence in the family (Herman, 1992; Wilson, 1995).

Lenore Terr writes, " 'Psychic trauma' occurs when a sudden, unexpected, overwhelming intense emotional blow or a series of blows assaults the person from outside. Traumatic events are external, but they quickly become incorporated into the mind" (Terr, 1990, p. 8). Van der Kolk makes a similar point about the complicated nature of trauma when he says, "Traumatization occurs when both internal and external resources are inadequate to cope with external threat" (Van der Kolk, 1989, p. 393). Both clinicians make the point that it is not the trauma itself that does the damage. It is how the individual's mind and body reacts in its own unique way to the traumatic experience in combination with the unique response of the individual's social group.

Consider the example of Bob and Harry, both trapped in the rubble of a shattered building after an earthquake, both physically unharmed. Bob manages to extricate himself, and hearing a cry for help nearby, is able to pull another survivor out of danger. As he stumbles out of the building, cradling the person he has rescued, flashbulbs capture his moment of triumph and he figures largely in the evening news broadcast and the next day's papers. It is possible that for Bob, the experience will turn out to be the source of a positive mastery experience as well as social approval and he may feel that the earthquake was the best thing that ever happened to him. Harry is less fortunate than Bob. He cannot get out because he is pinned beneath a steel girder. He is forced to wait for rescuers, helpless to aid himself or anyone else. During the time that he waits, he does not know whether he is going to live or die and he exists in a state of terror. For those hours or days, Harry is confronted by his utter helplessness and dependency. He is far more likely to experience the long-term consequences of overwhelming stress.

Or consider four young girls, Sally, Fran, Joy, and Betty, each of whom is sexually abused by her father. Here are four possible scenarios for what is, essentially, the same traumatic event. Sally is so terrified that she tells no one, blocks out the experience, and later, as an adolescent begins to mutilate herself with razor blades, uses alcohol excessively, cannot maintain stable relationships, and ends up psychiatrically hospitalized as a young adult. Fran tells her family about the abuse, but they tell her she is lying and that whatever happened, she has no one but herself to blame. As a teenager she starts stealing, engages in progressive lying, spends most of her time with friends who are involved with a gang, drops out of school, and ends up at age twenty participating in an armed robbery and serves her first of many jail terms. Joy tells her mother about the abuse and the mother believes her and leaves the marriage. The family suffers extreme economic hardship as a result and the girl never sees her father again. As a young adult she experiences her first episode of major depressive disorder, makes a suicide attempt, and is treated with some degree of success with an antidepressant. Betty tells her family about the abuse, the family responds with outrage, horror, denial, and blaming but ultimately gets some help. The abuse stops, the family breaks up temporarily but comes back together. The father and daughter make an uneasy reconciliation that they continue to work on in the present. To the outside world, Betty is a successful career woman, although she avoids contact with men. In each example we can see how the original event combines with the unique characteristics of individuals interacting with their social support system and resulting in many different possible outcomes.

Children are traumatized whenever they fear for their lives or for the lives of someone they love. We must always look at this experience through the eyes of the child, for a child can be terrified by events that are of little significance to an adult. It is the experience of overwhelming, helpless terror, rage, loss, and shame that is so disabling. A traumatic experience affects the entire person. The way we think, the way we learn, the way we remember things, the way we feel about ourselves, the way we feel about other people, and the way we make sense of the world are all profoundly altered by traumatic experience. Let us more thoroughly explore the inner resources of the child, what the child brings into the traumatic situation, and what happens to the mind and body after the traumatic experience.

THE FIGHT-OR-FLIGHT RESPONSE

We are animals and like other animals, we are biologically equipped to protect ourselves from harm as best we can. The basic internal protective mechanism is called the *fight-or-flight* reaction (Horowitz, 1986). Whenever we perceive that we are in danger, our bodies make a massive response that affects all of our organic systems. This change in every area of basic function is so dramatic that in many ways we are not the same people when we are terrified as when we are calm. Our heart rate increases, as does our blood pressure and respiration. Blood moves away from our digestive tract and into our muscles. Our pupils dilate and our hair stands on end. Hearing and seeing become more acute. Our emotions are heightened to make sure that we pay attention and we enter states of fear, terror, and panic that urge us to get away from the danger. Our thought processes narrow so that we can think only of actions that will relieve the danger. Our memory shifts to recalling other experiences when we were in danger and were successful in protecting ourselves. When under this kind of stress it is as if we become another person, no longer able to respond to others as we would under less threatening circumstances.

Each episode of danger connects to every other episode of danger in our minds, so that the more danger we are exposed to, the more sensitive we are to danger. With each experience of fight-or-flight, our mind forms a network of connections that get triggered with every new threatening experience. Because we are so intelligent, these connections can be very widely linked to the dangerous experience. Delores is a child who was sexually abused in a yellow room between the ages of five and seven. In third grade, her classroom is painted blue and Delores is a model student. But something goes wrong when Delores hits fourth grade. From the very first day of school, she has problems. She acts out in class, asks to go to the nurse's office frequently, and does not appear to be able to concentrate. Her teachers and her mother are puzzled by her behavior. Her mother wonders if it could have something to do with the sexual abuse of years before, but no one is likely to realize that every time Delores walks into her yellow classroom, she feels panic, and an urge to run away. Delores herself is not aware that it is the color of the room that is triggering the response, nor can she put her terror into words. The perception and association to previous danger occur completely out of awareness. This entire complex series of responses is totally beyond her control. Tommy is beaten regularly—"whether he needs it or not"—while his father is screaming at him. Whenever he hears a male voice, even a voice raised in excitement on the sports field, he becomes terrified. This association between physical pain, male aggression, and masculine behavior haunts him throughout his life and continues to radically alter his perception of and reactions to other men, dramatically altering his experience of himself as a man as well.

If children are exposed to danger repeatedly, their bodies become unusually sensitive so that even minor threats can trigger this sequence of physical, emotional, and cognitive responses. They can do nothing to control this reaction—it is a biological, built-in response, a protective device that only goes wrong if we are exposed to too much danger and too little protection in childhood or as adults. If trauma occurs in adult life, the same sequence of events takes place but is far less likely to skew normal development since the character traits are already established. It has also become clear that prolonged exposure to combat, torture, captivity, death, and destruction can bring about long-lasting changes in personality (Southwick, Yehuda, and Giller, 1993). In the psychiatric classification scheme of the World Health Organization, the ICD-10, it has been recognized that if trauma is sufficiently disruptive to the continuity of the personality, it can lead to enduring changes in character structure. This recognition is signaled by the development of a new category of personality change following exposure to catastrophic stress (Silove, 1996).

LEARNED HELPLESSNESS

If a person is able to master the situation of danger by successfully running away, winning the fight or getting help, the risk of long-term physical changes is lessened. But in many situations considered to be traumatic, the victim is helpless and it is this helplessness that is such a problem for human beings. As a species, we cannot tolerate helplessness—it goes against our instinct for survival. We *must* respond to danger by trying to the best of our ability to protect ourselves and the people and things we love. Children are especially prone to post-traumatic stress because they are helpless in most situations.

It is not just humans who respond to helplessness so negatively. In animal experiments, animals who are repeatedly shocked and who are able to escape from their cages obviously will do so. Then, when the cage doors are closed and the animal is repeatedly shocked, the animal becomes extremely disturbed, distressed, depressed, frightened, unable to get along with other animals, unable to function properly in social situations, unable to learn, with impaired immunity as demonstrated by an increased incidence of tumors and infections. Interestingly, when the experimental conditions are changed and the animals are shocked again but allowed to leave their cages, they do not do so—they have "learned" to be helpless. Apparently, there are detrimental changes in the basic neurochemistry that allows them to self-motivate out of dangerous situations. Instead they just huddle in their cages, the doors wide open, suffering shock after shock. Change only occurs when the experimenter actively intervenes and pulls the animal out of the cage. At first, the animal runs back in, but after sufficient trials, it finally catches on and learns how to escape from the terror once again. The animals' behavior improves significantly, but they remain vulnerable to stress. As in human experience, animals show individual variation in their responses. Some animals are very resistant to developing "learned helplessness" and others are very vulnerable (Seligman, 1992; Van der Kolk et al., 1985).

There are hints about what may be going on at a biochemical level in the brain as a result of learned helplessness, and as with everything to do with behavior and the brain, the answers are going to turn out to be complex. Basic research indicates that the important neurotransmitter, serotonin, is increased with helpless behavior, supporting the hypothesis that brain serotonin excess may be causally related to the development of learned helplessness (Petty et al., 1994b). There is also some recent information from animal experiments that the effects of learned helplessness may be related to the endorphins. Our bodies make these substances normally, and they are chemically related to morphine and heroin, which we will discuss later (Besson et al., 1996; Tejedor-Real et al., 1995). Other studies on rats have demonstrated that handling in infancy improves behavioral adaptation to the environment, including enhanced adaptive response to stress and the effects of learned helplessness (Costela et al., 1995). Yet another group of researchers examined the effects of learned helplessness on the hippocampus, a part of the brain integrally involved in the processing of verbal memory. They found that inescapable stress appears to sensitize the hippocampus to increases in norepinephrine release in response to a subsequent smaller stressor. They hypothesized that this hypersensitivity could underlie learned helplessness and can play a role in the development of some of the symptoms of human post-traumatic stress disorder (PTSD), such as the poor coping associated with seemingly mild stress (Petty et al., 1994a).

LOSS OF "VOLUME CONTROL"

If you are sitting in your living room and you hear a loud noise in the hallway, you will automatically have a startle response; your attention will be focused on discovering the source of the sound. You will not calm down until you have discovered that your cat has simply knocked over a vase. But then, you will calm down and rapidly be able to return to reading your book. Your response will be very different if you hear a loud noise in the hallway and discover an intruder holding a weapon. Your initial startle response will escalate and your body and mind will make the dramatic shifts that we discussed as the "fight-or-flight" response. And even if the intruder suddenly leaves without harming you, you will not rest easily that night, nor maybe for several nights. For the next few days, weeks, or even months, you may find yourself edgy, overly reactive, irritable, unfocused, and even depressed.

The experience of overwhelming terror destabilizes our internal system of arousal—the internal "volume control" dial that we normally have over all our emotions, but especially fear (Van der Kolk, 1988). Usually, we respond to a stimulus based on the level of threat that the stimulus represents. A clumsy cat should evoke less arousal than an armed gunman. People who have been traumatized lose this capacity to "modulate arousal." Anyone who has been in a car accident can testify to the subsequent irritability, aggressiveness, and impulsivity that follow for days to weeks, before finally settling down. This is a sign of altered physiology, not psychology. Instead of being able to adjust their "volume control," the person is reduced to only an "on-or-off" switch, losing all control over the amount of arousal they experience to any stimulus, even one as unthreatening as a crying child.

Children are born with only an on-or-off switch. Gradually, over the course of development and with the responsive and protective care of adults, the child's brain develops the ability to modulate the level of arousal based on the importance or relevance of the stimulus. This is part of the reason why the capacity of adults to soothe frightened children is so essential to their development. They cannot soothe themselves until they have been soothed by adults. Johnny, at five, is easily frightened and when he is, his father comforts him and then shows him how to cope with the danger. Gradually, Johnny learns to tell the difference between what is truly dangerous and what is an opportunity for learning. Catherine is three and becomes very upset whenever her mother leaves home. Her mother spends time talking to her and prepares her for any departure by telling her what to expect. She buys Catherine a special toy lion to keep her company whenever Mom is going away. In time, Catherine learns that although Mom goes away, she will return and Catherine learns to tolerate separation without being overwhelmed by feelings of abandonment. In calming a child, the adults around them are playing a vital role in the child's brain development. Through the complex and subtle negotiations between parent and child, the brain "learns" how to manage emotions.

Children who are exposed to repeated experiences of overwhelming arousal do not have the kind of safety and protection that they need for normal brain development. They may never develop normal modulation of arousal. Children who are raised in homes where violence is part of the routine of existence, often dosed out erratically and unpredictably, fail to develop "volume control." As a result they are chronically irritable, angry, unable to manage aggression, impulsive, and anxious. Under such circumstances, children will understandably do anything they can to establish some level of self-soothing and self-control (Van der Kolk and Greenberg, 1987). Often they have learned that they cannot depend on the soothing of other people, since other people are the source of the danger. Under such circumstances, children frequently turn to substances, such as drugs or alcohol, or behaviors like sex or eating, all of which help them to calm down, at least temporarily. If you have never been able to really control your feelings, and you discover that alcohol gives you some sense of control over your internal states, it is only logical that you will turn to alcohol for comfort. The experience of control over helplessness will count for much more than anyone's warnings about the long-term consequences of alcohol abuse.

THINKING UNDER STRESS—ACTION NOT THOUGHT

Our capacity to think clearly is also severely impaired when we are under stress (Janis, 1982; Fish-Murray et al., 1987). When we perceive that we are in danger, we are geared to take action, not to ponder and deliberate. This tendency to act, not think, makes sense from an evolutionary point of view. Verbal thinking about the logical alternatives and long-range consequences of our decisions takes a great deal of time. Anyone who has sat through a committee meeting can testify to that. In many situations of acute danger it is better that we respond immediately without taking the time for complicated mental processing, that we respond almost reflexively to save our lives or to protect those we love. The problem, of course, is that modern life provides us with multiple situations that induce acute stress that are not, in fact, life-threatening situations, but our bodies and minds still respond as if they were. As a consequence, whenever we are stressed, we are unable to problem-solve well.

For children who are exposed to repeatedly stressful environments, this is an overwhelming problem. These children have not even had time to learn good problem-solving skills under calm circumstances, much less how to protect themselves from stress. When stressed, we cannot think clearly, we cannot consider the long-range consequences of our behavior, we cannot weigh all of the possible options before making a decision, we cannot take the time to obtain all the necessary information that goes into making good decisions. Our decisions tend to be based on impulse and are based on an experienced need to self-protect. As a consequence these decisions are inflexible, oversimplified, directed toward action, and often are very poorly constructed (Janis, 1982).

Many children and adults can do far better under situations when they are calm. During such a period, they may even be able to sit with a teacher or other adult and strategize how they can best alter their behavior, with sincere good intentions to do so. But then, when stress occurs and their body takes over, they are thrown into the fight-or-flight state. At this point their brain functioning shifts toward an action mode and they cannot control it. Once that shift occurs, it is as if their normal brain function has switched off and it is not that they *won't* take the time to think, it is that they *can't* think. This can happen under conditions of immediate and real threat or it can happen as a result of anything that reminds the person of a previous threat, even though the child or adult may not have any idea of what it was that triggered off such a reminder. In such situations people demonstrate poor judgment and poor impulse control. The mind is geared toward action and often the action taken will be violent.

If you have been subjected to experiences of threat repeatedly, then you will learn how to adapt, how to survive, in a threatening environment. But once such an adaptation has taken place, it may not be so easy to stop those automatic ways of thinking and behaving simply because the threat has been removed. A combat veteran whose behavioral responses were appropriate in the jungle are maladaptive when the soldier returns to civilized life and finds himself responding to the normal activities and stimulation of daily life as if they were threats to his life. His brain has been reset, so that even mild threats activate a full-scale response that is unnecessary and in many cases, overtly harmful (Chemtob et al., 1988).

As a result, many victims have long-term problems with various aspects of thinking. It has been described that Vietnam veterans have difficulties making healthy decisions and solving problems (Richards and Handy, 1995). An intolerance of mistakes, denial of personal difficulties, anger as a problem-solving strategy, hypervigilance, and absolutistic thinking are other problematic thought patterns that have been identified (Alford, Mahone, and Fielstein, 1988). When tested, veterans with chronic PTSD show wide-ranging cognitive performance deficits when compared to other military troops judged to be free of stress-related psychopathology. These results are consistent with the veterans' complaints of concentration and memory problems (Uddo et al., 1993).

Problems with cognitive functioning are not limited to combat veterans. Abused children have lowered verbal and full scale IQ's correlated with the degree of abuse (Carrey et al., 1995). In his longitudinal study of sexually abused girls, Dr. Frank Putnam reports that only 2 percent of the children have a normal school trajectory (Putnam, 1996). Children who are abused learn trauma-related behaviors that shape the way the child thinks (Burgess, Hartman, and Clements, 1995).

REMEMBERING UNDER STRESS

Our way of remembering things, processing new memories, and accessing old memories is also dramatically changed when we are under stress. The subject of memory and traumatic memory is a complex one and we are learning new things about memory every day. Still, there is a growing body of evidence indicating that there are actually two different memory systems in the brain—one for normal learning and remembering that is based on words and another that is largely nonverbal (Southwick et al., 1994; Squire, 1987; Van der Kolk, 1994, 1996b). Our verbally based memory system is vulnerable to high levels of stress. Under normal conditions, the two kinds of memory function in an integrated way. As a result, we can drive a car and think about where we are going, or follow explicit directions, while at the same time our foot is working the accelerator and brake pedals and our hands and eyes are coordinating the steering. Our verbal and nonverbal memories are thus usually intertwined and complexly interrelated.

What we consider our "normal" memory is based on words. From the time we are born we develop new categories of information, and all new information gets placed into an established category, like a filing cabinet in our minds. We talk in words, of course, but we also think with words. When we need to recall something, we go into the appropriate category and retrieve the information we need. But this superb skill came about very late in evolution. Speech is what dramatically sets us apart from our primate relatives. Under conditions of extreme stress, our memory works in a different way. When we are overwhelmed with fear, we lose the capacity for speech, and we lose the capacity to put words to our experience. Maybe this happens because it is a flaw in our evolutionary development, or maybe it happens because falling back on a faster form of mental processing than thinking in words is better for emergency situations. Whatever the case, there is some indication that at least one of the substances released during stress, cortisol, may have toxic effects on the part of the brain that categorizes information (Bremner et al., 1995; Nadel, 1995; Van der Kolk, 1996b). This leads to the experience of "speechless terror" that writers, poets, and commentators have recognized for many years.

Without words, the mind shifts to a way of thinking that is characterized by visual, auditory, olfactory, and kinesthetic images; physical sensations; and strong feelings. It is much more like the kind of mental processing that is characteristic of our animal relatives. After all, if you are in a forest and you hear a growling noise behind you, it is far better for your brain to flash up an image of a threatening beast, or just a feeling of intense fear that impels you to run for your life, than it is for your brain to stop and ponder in words a series of alternative explanations or actions. Our evolutionary ancestors may have lacked verbal capacities, but their survival depended on remembering danger. Just as this memory system developed earlier in evolution than our more recently evolved verbal memory system, it may also be operational far earlier in our development than the verbal system, which does not become available until later in development. Children may, in fact, have nonverbal memories long before they have memories that can be given any kind of verbal form. These memories may then linger as vague physical sensations and images and not as verbal messages.

This system of processing information may be adequate under conditions of serious danger. But the powerful images, feelings, and sensations do not just "go away." They are deeply imprinted, more strongly in fact, than normal everyday memories. The neuroscientist Joseph LeDoux has called this "emotional memory" and has shown that this kind of memory can be difficult or impossible to erase, although we can learn to override some of our responses (LeDoux, 1992; 1994). This "engraving" of trauma has been noted by many researchers studying various survivor groups (Van der Kolk, 1994; Van der Kolk and Van der Hart, 1991). Problems may arise later because the memories of the events that occurred under severe stress are not put into words and are not remembered in the normal way we remember other things. Instead, the memories remain "frozen in time" in the form of images, body sensations such as smells, touch, tastes, and even pain, and strong emotions.

A flashback is a sudden intrusive reexperiencing of a fragment of one of those traumatic, unverbalized memories. Sometimes a flashback is experienced like a flashback in a movie—an immersion in the entire memory of the event on the stage of consciousness. But more commonly, a flashback appears as a fragment of a traumatic memory, unconnected to any sense of time, place, person, or meaning. It may be an image, or a smell, a feeling in the body, or a taste. During a flashback, people become overwhelmed with the same emotions that they felt at the time of the trauma. Flashbacks are likely to occur when people are upset, stressed, frightened, or aroused or when triggered by any association to the traumatic event (Van der Kolk, 1994, 1996b). Their minds can become flooded with the images, emotions, and physical sensations associated with the trauma once again. But the verbal memory system may be turned off because of the arousal of fear, so they cannot articulate their experience and the nonverbal memory may be the only memory a person has of the traumatic event. In a study by Van der Kolk and Fisler (1995), all subjects, regardless of the age at which the trauma occurred, reported that their initial memory was not in the form of a narrative, but was instead a somatosensory or emotional flashback experience. Seventy-five percent of the subjects with childhood trauma had external confirmation of the traumatic experience.

At the time of the trauma they had become trapped in "speechless terror" and their capacity for speech and memory were separated. As a result, they developed what has become known as "amnesia" for the traumatic event—the memory is there, but there are no words attached to it so it cannot be either talked about or even thought about. Instead, the memory presents itself as some form of nonverbal behavior and sometimes as a behavioral reenactment of a previous event. Ted is a Vietnam veteran who works at an office job. He is terribly ashamed one day when he finds himself "coming out of it," huddled under his desk with tears running down his cheeks. The last thing he remembers is pouring a cup of coffee. His co-workers report that he seemed fine until a helicopter flew loud and low over their building. When he heard the sound of the helicopter, Ted seemed to go into some kind of altered state, looked terrified, appeared to be carrying an object that was not actually there, and ran for his desk where he huddled, cradling something in his arms. Only when Ted is told what his colleagues had observed does he begin to remember an episode in the jungle when his company was under siege from helicopters overhead, and recalls that the object he was cradling was the head of his best friend.

It is common for a flashback to emerge as a "body memory." The body often remembers what the mind forgets. Thus, a trauma victim may present to a physician with many different symptoms that are actually memories. Paula suffers from chronic pelvic pain. She has been to a number of gynecologists, has had repeated gynecological procedures and testing. Now she is scheduled for surgery because her specialists do not know what else to do but go into her pelvis and see what they can find that might be causing her pain. She has been having problems for the last four years, but gradually the pain has gotten worse and she has become increasingly unable to function. Her disability has put a strain on her relationship with her teenage daughter who has had to assume many of the family responsibilities. Although Paula remembers being raped when she was sixteen, she tries never to think about it because it is too disturbing. She has never told anyone in her present life about the rape, and her gynecologist has never asked. She is admitted in the evening for surgery the next day and meets the young resident who comes to take her history. In the course of taking a history, he notices that she avoids questions about her previous sexual experience and so he asks her directly if she has ever been raped or molested. At this point, Paula, to her own surprise, breaks into tears, and begins talking about the rape and the fact that she lives in fear that the same thing could happen to her own daughter who soon will turn sixteen. The resident wonders to himself and suggests to her that maybe the chronic pelvic pain could have something to do with unresolved memories of and feelings about her own rape. Paula has never considered this could even be possible, and decides not to go ahead with the surgery. A referral to a therapist who is able to deal with trauma-related issues results in the nonsurgical resolution of the pain, a return to normal function, an improvement in the relationship with her daughter, and the ability to finally leave the past in the past. But Paula was one of those rare cases in which a medical provider had the insight, training, and skill to recognize how closely interconnected are the mind and body. All too often, "body memories"—the physical sensation in the present of what is an unresolved past pain—are misdiagnosed as physical disease with all the attendant risks of medical and surgical treatment.

Even thinking of flashbacks as "memories" is inaccurate and misleading. When someone experiences a flashback, they do not *remember* the experience, they *relive* it. Often the flashback is forgotten as quickly as it is happens because the two memory systems are so disconnected from each other. This is not at all like remembering things as you can right now remember what you wore to work yesterday or what you had for dinner last night. When people are put in situations that "remind" them of these stored away traumatic memories, a series of brain events occur culminating in the intrusive review of these traumatic experiences, a review they do not wish for and cannot control (Schwarz and Perry, 1994; Van der Kolk, 1988; Van der Kolk, 1993; Van der Kolk and Saporta, 1993).

Sometimes flashbacks come at night in the form of post-traumatic nightmares that plunge the sleeper into a state of terror, pain, or rage. Vietnam veterans have been known to wake up beating their wives in the bed next to them, believing that she is the enemy. Some nightmares are the exact replay of the actual traumatic event and some are disguised behind frightening symbols. Some nightmares decrease in frequency over time and just seem to fade away until triggered by a new stress. Others appear to become incorporated into other thematic experiences of life, often of earlier trauma or symbolized conflicts (Lansky and Bley, 1995).

These intrusions, whether flashbacks or nightmares, do not necessarily go away spontaneously. The past can become a haunting presence that dramatically interferes with normal functioning. When people have flashbacks, before they understand what is happening to them, they frequently become convinced that they are losing their minds. These experiences are so noxious that the traumatized person is likely to seek out any behavior that affords them some sense of control over overwhelming emotions, even if that control is only temporary. They will often do anything they can to make the flashbacks stop and to not let other people know what is happening to them. Increasingly they will avoid situations that trigger any kind of disturbing response, avoid people who trigger the response, and find any external behavior or substance that at least temporarily reduces the anxiety—and even terror—that is associated with the response. Consequently, it is quite easy for the untreated traumatized person to develop such secondary symptoms as alcohol abuse, drug abuse, eating disorders, sexual addictions, workaholism, and other forms of self-destructive behaviors, that serve in the short term to help them control the flashbacks and the bad feelings but which in the long run create a downward spiral of problems.

Some data are now available from positron emission tomography that provides more information about how these intrusive phenomena may occur. Traumatic memories appear to "happen" principally in the emotional centers of the brain's right hemisphere, and are accompanied by an increase in activity in the visual areas of the brain. This indicates that people with PTSD actually "see" their flashbacks while there is a decrease in the area of the brain in charge of the translation of emotional states into language (Rauch et al., 1996; Van der Kolk, Burbridge, and Suzuki, 1997; Van der Kolk and Fisler, 1995).

Over time, as people try to limit situations that promote hyperarousal and flashbacks, limit relationships that trigger emotions, and employ behaviors designed to control emotional responses, they may become progressively numb to all emotions, and feel depressed, alienated, empty, even dead. In this state, it takes greater and greater stimulation to feel a sense of being alive. They will often engage in all kinds of risk-taking behaviors since that is the only time they feel "inside" themselves once again. *Fearless,* a movie that came out a few years ago about the victim of a plane crash, provides a good example of how dramatically, automatically, and unwittingly these events can conspire to alter a person's life for the worst. Since this entire syndrome, now called post-traumatic stress disorder, was first recognized as a long-term complication of combat, many of the Vietnam era movies also provide illustrations of how this happens.

If we cannot remember an experience, we cannot learn from it. This is one of the most devastating aspects of prolonged stress. The implicit functioning of the brain, life saving under the immediate conditions of danger, becomes life threatening when the internal fragmentation that is the normal response to overwhelming trauma is not healed. The picture becomes even more complicated for children who are exposed to repeated experiences of unprotected stress. Their bodies, brains, and minds are still developing. We are only beginning to understand memory, traumatic memory, and how these memory systems develop and influence each other (Perry, 1993; Schwarz and Perry, 1994). We do know that children who are traumatized also experience flashbacks that have no words. For healing to occur, we know that people often need to put the experience into a narrative, give it words, and share it with themselves and others. Words allow us to put things into a time sequence—past, present, future.

Without words, the traumatic past is experienced as being in the ever-present *Now.* Words allow us to put the past more safely in the past where it belongs. Since a child's capacity for verbalization is just developing, his or her ability to put traumatic experience into words is particularly difficult. In cases of childhood terror, language functions are often compromised. Instead, children frequently act out their memories in behavior instead of using words (James, 1989; Van der Kolk, 1989). They show us what happened even when they cannot tell us. This is automatic behavior. It is not planned, or conscious, and if asked, children cannot give words for anything they are doing, although they may attempt to do so to please the listening adult or simply to try and understand it themselves. We call this automatic behavioral reliving of trauma, "traumatic reenactment." Much of the most disturbing behavior that children enact in the classroom and at home can be seen as forms of traumatic reenactment. There is another meaning in the message besides bad behavior and unless we hear the message, the behavior will continue unaltered, and regardless of discipline, the child is unlikely to be able to control it. It is as if the body keeps trying to tell us what the mind has forgotten (Van der Kolk, 1994).

It would not be responsible to leave this discussion of traumatic memory without mentioning the phenomenon known as "false memory syndrome." Although the word "syndrome" generally connotes a medical consensus, "false memory syndrome" is actually an unproven and highly politicized lay diagnosis in which therapists are said to implant false memories of childhood abuse—usually sexual abuse—in the unwitting and suggestible heads of their adult patients, usually women. This "syndrome" now serves as a useful defense for accused sexual offenders and began to be actively employed in the forensic arena when adult survivors of abuse began suing their alleged perpetrators.

Once we understand more about the way the brain works, the simplistic argument about "false" versus "true" memories becomes a bit ludicrous. Amnesia has been found in every survivor group ever studied and our study of trauma and the brain is beginning to illuminate how much stress impacts on memory processes in a number of different and dramatic ways (Bremner et al., 1995, 1996; Brown, Scheflin, and Hammond, 1998; ISTSS, 1998; Van der Kolk, 1996b). Just as true is the fact that memory is subject to a variety of distortions, some of which can be induced by other people under laboratory conditions. People who suffer from post-traumatic stress disorders typically suffer from too much or too little memory in the form of flashbacks, nightmares, and amnesias.

Given this information, one might be led to wonder why there has been so much public debate about the so-called "false memory syndrome," so much in fact, that vast numbers of the public believe that this syndrome is real and scientifically validated, which it is not. Part of the problem has been the misuse of words. The term "memory" is used to describe a wide variety of events. It is clearly not the same to watch a movie of a car accident and to watch your child being killed in the seat next to you during a car accident. And yet some authorities on memory have used the results of laboratory stressors as "proof" that people in traumatic circumstances can be suggestible and develop false memories. This is highly dubious scientific criteria. We can safely say that post-traumatic memory impairment is very common, both forgetting and difficulty remembering despite repeated efforts to do so. A minority of people—about 20 percent—are highly suggestible, and under certain circumstances can come to believe that events that never happened did occur or that actual events never occurred. But that means that most people are resistant to this "implantation." As Baars and McGovern point out, "Adult survivors of abuse may show both more false memories and more false forgetting than the normal population" (Baars and McGovern, 1995, p. 68). On the positive side of the ledger, the controversy has sparked a renewed interest in memory research and how we come to "know" things about our past, and has opened up a wider discourse between disciplines including broadening the discussion between psychiatry and the law (Brown, Scheflin, and Hammond, 1998; ISTSS, 1998).

We must remember that people who have committed criminal offenses against others are highly motivated to avoid taking responsibility for their acts and that blaming the victim and denying the reality of criminal acts directed at women and children has a very long history. It is more difficult to discern the motivation for falsely accusing someone you love of a crime. Nonetheless, the public has come to believe that many of the sexual abuse accusations are false and malicious. Similar to the strategies employed in the anti-abortion movement, the false memory attack is directed not at the adult child who makes the accusations against a former caregiver, but at the therapist who is blamed for starting the whole thing. This entire debate presents an excellent example of how political and social forces can influence scientific debate as well as judicial decisions with little regard for the complex nature of reality (Bloom, 1995b; Kristiansen, Felton, and Hovdestad, 1996; McFarlane and Van der Kolk, 1996).

LEARNING AND TRAUMA— STATE-DEPENDENT LEARNING

Our learning is dependent on the state of consciousness we are in when the learning occurs (Van der Kolk, 1989; Van der Kolk and Van der Hart, 1989). We think in categories and all new learning gets immediately put into a category. The learning curve for children is steep because they are in the process of creating all the new categories that exposure to life requires. However, we can only create new categories in a state of calm contemplation. Children who are repeatedly exposed to overwhelming stress cannot create new categories and cannot learn as well as children with more protected functioning.

Each category of material is connected to our emotional experience as well, so whatever is learned when we are frightened gets attached to that fear "file drawer" in our minds that we mentioned earlier. Whenever fear is triggered again, the file drawer is accessed and no other file drawers can necessarily be opened. As a result, these children's repertoire of responses to any fearful situation, even a mildly frightening one, will be quite limited and will be characterized by the on-or-off response that we focused on earlier. If they have learned that lashing out physically toward a threatening person helps to protect them, then whenever they feel threatened a sequence of automatic learned behavior will take hold and they will lash out aggressively. If they have learned that they cannot do anything to protect themselves except lie there and take it while separating themselves from the abuse emotionally, then when they are afraid, they will be incapable of protecting themselves, even in situations where they could if they tried. In nonthreatening situations, however, these same children may be quite capable of normal learning and behavior. Understanding this sequence of events can help the parent or teacher understand the apparently erratic behavior of many children who could do better but who constantly seem to sabotage themselves.

Learning for adults is state dependent as well and this can have profound effects on treatment. Mary is a forty-five-year-old woman who goes to see her family physician with vague complaints of recurrent headaches. Her physician has had training in evaluating women for signs of domestic violence and when he asks her some questions about her home life, Mary breaks into tears and admits to him that her husband batters her regularly. She feels safe with her doctor, appreciates that he cares enough to get this information from her, and together they develop a safety plan. She leaves the office determined to change her life and finally get out of this abusive situation. Then she goes home. She is in her apartment; it is 6:30 in the evening and her husband still has not arrived home. She knows that this means he has been drinking for three hours since work let out and that he will come home ready to fight. Her anxiety begins to increase as she waits. She hears his footsteps on the stairs. The third stair from the top has a loud creak when it is stepped on, and the moment she hears the sound of that stair, terror seizes her. Her body and mind enter the fight-or-flight response, and in this state, she can recall nothing of her conversation earlier in the day with her doctor. The only information she can access is whatever she has done in the past to survive, because after all, she is still alive. So when her surly husband enters the room, she tries to appease him, and when it does not work—as it never does—and he starts hitting her, she covers her head and waits for him to pass out. With any luck, he passes out before he kills her, and over the next few hours, she calms down. But when she does, she remembers that her physician cared enough to take the time to talk to her, that she had the information available to her to help herself, and that she failed to do anything. At this point she feels overwhelmed with shame. Everything she has ever heard about battered wives comes back to her, about how she could get out if she really wanted to, about how she asks for what she gets. Her shame and embarrassment prevent her from keeping her next appointment with her doctor, and he never sees her again. Her learning was "state dependent," meaning her access to what she had learned in the past depended entirely on the state of mind she was in at the time the learning occurred.

Most helping professionals can give examples of the many times they have sat in their office with someone seeking advice as to how to get out of, or protect themselves from, a dangerous situation. Together they carefully formulated a strategy for self-protection. In the calm circumstances of such an interchange, the victim is in a state of mind that is conducive to learning. Unfortunately, however, once the patient returns to the threatening situation, he or she becomes quickly hyperaroused. In that very different state of consciousness, the previous learning with the helping professional is not available and the individual reverts to behavior that was learned in states of danger before—strategies that often lead to more violence rather than less. As a result, both doctor and patient feel like failures; both give in to the hopelessness so frequently associated with chronic trauma. In Mary's case, if her physician had warned her that this could happen, if he had been able to predict the possibility, then perhaps it would not have changed the outcome this time, but at least Mary would be more likely to come back and see him again. Very often, those small steps are what really matter in the long run.

Just consider what a child learns growing up in a violent home, on violent streets. He or she learns that attachment is paid for with the price of personal safety, that the person who abuses others is the person least likely to get abused, that violence works—at least to keep people afraid of you, and that violence is the way problems are solved. This kind of learning does not go away because the child grows up or the environment changes. For such a child, violence becomes normal and the child grown up will recreate the violence simply because it *is* normal. This is not the kind of learning that is conducive to the creation of safe homes, safe streets, or a safe society. Instead, we have thousands of adults walking the streets and filling our prisons who are still behaving like angry, hurting, six-year-olds.

EMOTIONS AND TRAUMA—DISSOCIATION

We do not usually think about it, but it is possible to die of fright or to die of a broken heart. Every vital organ system is closely tied through the autonomic nervous system to our emotional system. "I'm sick at heart," "My bowels are in an uproar," "Stop your bellyaching," "You are a pain in the a—," are all colloquial expressions for this very real connection. This is the reason why emotional health and physical health are so interconnected, although this interconnectedness is still largely ignored by modern medicine.

Given the helpless and undefended state of children, the young are especially vulnerable to the effects of severe fright. The psychohistorian, deMause, recounts the story of an American two-year-old in 1882 whose nurse wanted to spend an evening undisturbed by the child while the parents were out. So she told the child that a

> horrible Black Man . . . was hidden in the room to catch her the moment she left her bed or made the slightest noise . . . to make double sure that she should not be interrupted during the evening's enjoyment. She made a huge figure of a black man with frightful staring eyes and an enormous mouth and placed it at the foot of the bed where the little innocent child was fast asleep. As soon as the evening was over in the servant's hall, the nurse went back to her charge. Opening the door quietly, she beheld the little girl sitting up in her bed, staring in an agony of terror at the fearful monster before her, and both hands convulsively grasping her fair hair. She was stone dead! (DeMause, 1982, p. 13)

In fact, however, such stories are relatively rare. A fundamental reason for such rarity, despite the extent of fearful circumstances that children face, is the built-in "safety valve" that we call "dissociation" (Putnam, 1991; Van der Kolk, 1987b). Dissociation is defined as "a disruption in the usually integrated functions of consciousness, memory, identity, or perception of the environment" (American Psychiatric Association, 1994, DSM-IV, p. 477). We often hear people substitute "disassociated" for "dissociated" probably because the former word is actually more accurate—there is a disassociation between various mental functions that are usually well integrated and impossible to separate. Under normal conditions, we are functioning "on all six cylinders." We are conscious of what we are doing; we can remember what we just did as well as related things that happened years ago; we know who we are; and, using our various senses, we are perceiving what is going on in our environment and interacting with it. However, there are many occasions when this is not the case. If you have ever driven to work, successfully navigated busy roads, stopped appropriately at red lights, avoided hitting other cars, and arrived at work having no memory of actually driving that route because you were preoccupied with thinking about something else, you were in a trance—you were dissociated. Dissociation helps us do more than one thing at once. We can go on autopilot and automatically complete tasks that we have previously learned well, while we are focused on something else. This increase in efficiency may help explain why we evolved the ability.

Children are very good at dissociating. This is at least part of the reason why children are so good at make-believe and at creating imaginary playmates and imaginary places. They can lose themselves in a make-believe reality, while remaining grounded in the real world. Traumatized children make special use of this capacity. If you are little and helpless in the power of large and frightening adults, you cannot run away, and if you try to fight back you will only be hurt more. But, with your mind, you can "go away." And that is precisely what traumatized children do.

Political prisoners and victims of torture teach themselves to do the same thing (Herman, 1992). Judy Herman tells us about Elaine Mohamed, a South African political prisoner describing the psychological alterations of her captivity:

> I started hallucinating in prison, presumably to try to combat loneliness. . . . And I started talking to myself. My second name is Rose, and I've always hated the name. Sometimes I was Rose speaking to Elaine, and sometimes I was Elaine speaking to Rose. I felt that the Elaine part of me was the stronger part, while Rose was the person I despised. She was the weak one who cried and got upset and couldn't handle detention and was going to break down. Elaine could handle it. (Herman, 1992, p. 88)

By intensely focusing attention elsewhere it is possible to not feel pain, to put your consciousness in a nearby object or on the ceiling while you watch yourself be hurt and not even feel it—at least consciously. The former Miss America and incest victim, Marilyn Van Derbur, talks about how she coped with her father's abuse by creating a "day child" and a "night child." During the day she would be a well-liked successful student, apple of her father's eye, an apparently well-adjusted child, while the "night child" would deal with the horror and pain of her father's abuse.

When these kinds of adaptations in adults happen acutely we call this "being in shock." On a recent TV show, after an earthquake, a woman wrapped in furs in the middle of summer walks into the emergency room looking for someone to fix her broken necklace. As viewers, we know that her husband has just been killed. The ER nurse says, "She's in shock, someone needs to talk with her and stay with her." This seems perfectly commonplace under the circumstances of an acute disaster. But we have more difficulty recognizing this phenomenon in children or adults when it comes as a result of repetitive trauma. Children raised in violent homes or who must face violence every day on their sidewalks may be "in shock" a great deal of their waking lives. This is, after all, a normal human reaction to a highly stressful situation. But prolonged "shock"—prolonged dissociation—can have detrimental effects on a person's capacity to cope in many other ways.

There are different ways that people dissociate. Fainting is an extreme form of simply stopping consciousness. Psychogenic fainting is the brain's way of saying, "I can't handle this." But we can also split off memories from consciousness awareness, as we have already discussed, and develop "amnesia." Rarely, someone can develop amnesia for their entire identity and begin a separate life—a fugue state. More commonly people develop amnesia for parts of their lives or just for parts of certain overwhelming experiences. Hollywood has been repeatedly fascinated by the themes of fugue and amnesia so that from Charlie Chaplin's 1940 production of *The Great Dictator* to Kenneth Branagh's *Dead Again* the themes of over thirty-two movies focus on the subject of amnesia.

Less understood has been what happens to children's growing sense of identity when they are exposed to repeated, sadistic, and overwhelming stress. In such cases, children can do nothing to cope with the pain and terror except to dissociate, to split off fragments of their being to deal with every different horrific experience, each different perpetrator, every new onslaught to the self. In these cases, children's identity does not have an opportunity to solidify around a solid core and there are also indications that their brain function develops in a way quite different from other children as well (James, 1989; Putnam, 1990). Instead of establishing one clear identity, it remains fragmented and the fragments are separated from, and inaccessible to, each other.

A child who has come to depend upon dissociation as a means of coping with overwhelming stress is likely to resort to the same means of coping even under conditions of normal stress. In this way, dissociation can become habitual. Such a child may fail to learn how to use other coping skills within himself or herself and may also fail to learn how to develop relationships with others in efforts to modulate emotional arousal. Instead, the child's personality fragments even further and each new stressor, even the normal stressors of growing up, will trigger further dissociation. Based on past experiences under conditions of trauma, the child will now relegate a new stressful experience to a fragmented aspect of his or her personality to manage, and each aspect of the personality may develop somewhat differently over time.

In the end, the most extreme cases of such a process are diagnosed as what was formerly called "multiple personality disorder," and is now called "dissociative identity disorder." These children use whatever abilities they have in service of survival under the most desperate conditions a child can face. Their abilities raise serious questions about the mind/body dichotomy, about our latent psychic abilities, about what we are truly capable of accomplishing when we really put our minds to it. While in different personality states, people suffering from multiple personality disorder have been known to accomplish amazing intellectual and physical feats that cannot be explained with our present models of the mind. Researchers report cases of different allergies, different responses to drugs, different physical disorders, different eyeglass prescriptions and ophthalmological measures, different handedness, and different autonomic system responses to various stimuli (Kluft, 1996; Zahn, Moraga, and Ray, 1996).

Our present model of the connection between mind and body cannot explain these phenomena. This lack of an adequate model for understanding such apparently strange phenomena helps us to understand why there would still be people in the professional community declaring that multiple personalities cannot exist or that therapists are creating a nonexistent disorder. Human beings tend to be frightened of and reject what they cannot understand, and without a clear understanding of how children must cope with overwhelming terror, the development of multiple personalities is indeed difficult to understand. But refusing to believe in something fails to prove that it does not exist. In fact, there are clear clinical records for the reality of multiple personalities going back several centuries, long before there were mental health professionals.

Psychogenic fainting, traumatic amnesia, fugue states, and multiple personalities all represent ways that the mind copes with overwhelming experience through the use of the capacity for dissociation. But there is another way we can dissociate that is so common that almost everyone does it—splitting off experience from our feelings about that experience. In its most extreme form, this is called "emotional numbing." So commonly do human beings cut off feelings about what happened to them while still remembering everything, that often we have to look closely at the person before we see something is wrong—they do not feel the emotions that would normally be expected under the circumstances. In such cases, instead of seeing the emotional numbing that has occurred to the person, we will make comments about "how well Sheila is coping with her loss" or "how extraordinary it is that John never seems to get ruffled, even if someone is yelling at him." But Sheila and John are not necessarily "coping well"—they may be dissociated from their feelings and their capacity for normal emotional interaction may be consequently diminished.

We are able to cut off all our emotions but that usually happens only in extreme cases of repetitive and almost unendurable trauma. More commonly we cut off or diminish specific emotional responses, based on the danger the emotion may present to continued functioning. Our emotions are intimately tied to the expression of emotion through our facial expressions, our tone of voice, our gestures, so that we easily give away what we may be consciously trying to hide. Actors spend years training themselves to mask their emotional responses and generate other emotions that are relevant to the text. Most of us are not so talented that we can easily do that. But if you grow up in a violent home, where every time you express anger you get beaten, it is best that you never show anger. If you grow up in a home—or a culture—that says that little boys who cry are wimps who should be taught a "lesson," then it is a good idea to learn to never feel sadness, therefore minimizing the danger of tears. If any sign of pleasure or laughter is met with hostility and abuse, then it is best that you never feel joy. In this way, children from destructive situations learn how not to feel, they learn to dissociate their emotions from their conscious experience and their nonverbal expression of that emotion and in doing so, they can possibly stay safer than if they show what they feel. That does not mean that the emotion actually goes away. It does not. Emotions are built in, part of our evolutionary, biological heritage and we cannot eliminate them, we can only transmute them. There is an abundance of evidence from various sources that unexpressed emotions may be very damaging to one's mental and physical health (Pennebaker, 1995, 1997b).

It is certainly clear that emotional numbing is damaging to relationships. We need all of our emotions available to us if we are to create and sustain healthy relationships with other people. If we cannot feel anger, we cannot adequately protect others and ourselves. If we cannot feel sadness, we cannot complete the work of mourning that helps us recover from losses so that we can form new attachments. If we cannot feel joy, life seems not worth living. This is yet another example of how a coping skill, which is useful for survival under conditions of traumatic stress, can become a serious liability over time.

Let's explore a bit further how useful the capacity of dissociation can be under situations of acute danger, but how damaging it is for long-term adjustment. We function best when we can function in an integrated way, with our consciousness, memory, identity, and perceptual skills all interacting fully, providing information and allowing for carefully considered decisions that inform our behavior. Dissociation does not appear to spontaneously resolve under most circumstances. In fact, it often continues to increase its scope long after the need for it has evaporated. There is a good reason for this. The dissociative splitting occurs in the first place because of a perceived threat to life. It occurs because of the implicit dangers involved in the prolonged experience of overwhelming fear. The mind perceives that knowing this information is simply too dangerous for existence to continue and therefore it is better not to know. Once that "decision" has been made (it is, after all, automatic and not carefully considered thought), then anything that may lead to remembering that information is *also* automatically dangerous and must also be dissociated. And it is not just direct information to which this injunction is extended. It is also feeling states that are similar to the original trauma and might lead back to it, sensory perceptions that may do the same, and information from our bodies that could remind us of the original, life-threatening experience.

As this process continues over time, we gradually may shut off more and more of our normal functioning (Herman, 1992; Schetky, 1990; Southwick, Yehuda, and Giller, 1993). We may dampen any emotional experience that could lead back to the traumatic memory. We may withdraw from relationships that could trigger memories. We may curtail sensory and physical experiences that could remind us of the trauma. We may avoid engaging in any situations that could lead to remembering the trauma. At the same time, we may be compelled, completely outside of our awareness, to reenact the traumatic experience through our behavior. This increases the likelihood that instead of managing to avoid repeated trauma, we are likely to become traumatized again. As this process happens, our sense of who we are, how we fit into the world, how we relate to other people, and what the point of it all is, can become significantly limited in scope. As this occurs, we are likely to become increasingly depressed. These *avoidance* symptoms, along with the *intrusive* symptoms, such as flashbacks and nightmares, make up two of the interacting and escalating aspects of post-traumatic stress syndrome, set in the context of a more generalized physical hyperarousal. As these alternating symptoms come to dominate traumatized people's lives, people feel more and more alienated from everything that gives our lives meaning—themselves, other people, a sense of direction and purpose, a sense of community. It is not surprising, then, that slow self-destruction through addictions, or fast self-destruction through suicide, is often the final outcome of these syndromes. For others, rage dominates the picture and these are the individuals who become significant threats to the well-being of others.

Adult-onset trauma can be devastating, but formerly well-adjusted adults usually fare better than children who have been traumatized. Traumatized adults at least have some idea of normality, of what they were like, other people were like, and how they felt before the trauma. They may never completely recapture their pre-trauma lives, but they can, at least, approximate normal because they retain the same personal and interpersonal coping skills that they have always had. This situation is very different for traumatized children (James, 1994). Children who are traumatized do not possess developed coping skills, a developed sense of self, or self in relation to others. Their schemas for meaning, hope, faith, and purpose are not yet fully formed. They are in the process of developing a sense of right and wrong, of mercy balanced against justice. All of their cognitive processes, such as their ability to make decisions, their problem-solving capacities, and their learning skills are all still being acquired. As a consequence, the responses to trauma are amplified because they interfere with the processes of normal development. For many children, in fact, traumatic experience becomes the norm rather than the exception and they fail to develop a concept of what is normal or healthy. They do not learn how to think in a careful, quiet, and deliberate way. They do not learn how to have mutual, compassionate, and satisfying relationships. They do not learn how to listen carefully to the messages of their body and their senses. Their sense of self becomes determined by the experiences they have had with caretaking adults and the trauma they have experienced teaches them that they are bad, worthless, a nuisance, or worse. Living in a system of contradictory and hypocritical values impairs the development of conscious, of a faith in justice, of a belief in the pursuit of truth. It should come as no surprise then, that these children often end up as the maladjusted troublemakers who pose so many problems for teachers, schools, other children, and ultimately all of us.

HEALTH AND TRAUMA

The connection between exposure to stress and physical problems has been long noted. Many disorders are known to be related to stress, including gastrointestinal disorders (gastrointestinal physiology, peptic ulcers, ulcerative colitis, irritable bowel syndrome, esophageal reflux); cardiovascular disorders (cardiovascular physiology, essential hypertension); respiratory disorders (allergy, bronchial asthma, hyperventilation); musculoskeletal disorders; skin disorders, and others (Everly, 1989). But it is perhaps the work emerging in the field of psychoneuroimmunology that is the most interesting.

A growing body of evidence supports a relationship between impairment in the immune system and exposure to stress. In a 1989 review of the literature, one group of investigators found considerable evidence for an association between a variety of stressful events and lowered immunity and between severe depression and lowered immunity (Evans et al., 1989). Since then, others have looked at specific groups and traumatic incidents in attempts to develop our understanding of these complex phenomena.

One group of researchers looked at schoolchildren who had a high incidence of recurrent colds and flu and compared them to healthy children. Several dimensions of psychosocial stress, including exposure to stressful experiences, stress-prone personality traits, and signs of emotional disturbance were elevated in children with a history of recurrent colds and flu and a deficiency of measures of immunity was present in the children's nasal and oral mucosa (Drummond and Hewson-Bower, 1997). Another study indicated that when individuals undergoing chronic life stress are confronted with an acute psychological challenge, an exaggerated psychological and central nervous system reactivity occurs that is associated with decreases in individual natural killer cell function and is protracted beyond the termination of the stressor (Pike et al., 1997). Baby monkeys separated from their mothers at birth show impairments in their immune systems, as noted below, but in recent studies, this reaction to loss can be somewhat attenuated if the monkeys have other monkeys with whom they have developed a relationship (Boccia et al., 1997). Ironson and colleagues explored what happened to survivors after the losses they experienced secondary to Hurricane Andrew. They noted changes in immune function which were correlated with loss and with post-traumatic symptoms (1997). In a longitudinal study of sexually abused girls, abnormal immune function is suggested (DeBellis et al., 1996).

James Pennebaker and his colleagues have been engaged in a number of experiments looking at the relationship between traumatic exposure, talking about the traumatic event, writing about the traumatic event, and later health problems. Their results from recent surveys and experiments indicate: (a) childhood traumatic experiences, particularly those never discussed, are highly correlated with current health problems; (b) recent traumas that are not discussed are linked with increased health problems and ruminations about the traumas; (c) requiring individuals to confront earlier traumas in writing improves health and immune system functioning; and (d) actively talking about upsetting experiences is associated with immediate reductions in selected autonomic activity (Pennebaker 1989, 1995, 1997b; Pennebaker and Susman, 1988).

Earlier we discussed the concept of "alexithymia" and the negative impact that the inability to express and communicate emotion seems to have on health. Interest has also grown in looking at the connection between women's experience of violence and subsequent health problems. In a recent study, one group of researchers documented the negative health effects of experiences of sexual violence for women with abusive partners (Eby et al., 1995). Salmon and Calderbank (1996) studied 275 British undergraduates and surveyed their history of sexual and physical abuse in childhood and their health care utilization, somatization, and hypochondriasis as adults. Physical and sexual abuses were recalled by largely separate groups, with physical abuse predominating in males and sexual abuse in females. Both types of abuse were followed by a greater number of hospital admissions and surgical procedures, somatization, and hypochondriasis in adulthood.

Internists specializing in gastrointestinal disorders have been noticing the connection between chronic disorders and a past history of childhood abuse. One study viewed 239 patients presenting to a gastroenterology clinic and found that 66.5 percent of the women had experienced physical and/or sexual abuse. The women with a sexual abuse history had more pain, other somatic symptoms, bed disability days, lifetime surgeries, and functional disabilities than those without sexual abuse. Women with physical abuse also had poorer health outcome on most indicators, while rape victims and life-threatening physical abuse seem to have worse health effects than less serious physical violence and milder forms of sexual abuse (Leserman et al., 1996). Fukudo and colleagues studied irritable bowel syndrome and observed that the IBS patients have an exaggerated responsivity of the gastrointestinal tract to mental stress (Fukudo et al., 1993). Walker and colleagues examined the comorbidity between chronic pelvic pain, irritable bowel syndrome, and a past history of abuse. They found that compared to women with irritable bowel syndrome alone, those with both irritable bowel syndrome and chronic pelvic pain were significantly more likely to have a lifetime history of dysthymic disorder, current and lifetime panic disorder, somatization disorder, childhood sexual abuse, and hysterectomy (1996). In an randomized survey of 1,599 women, 31.5 percent of participants reported a diagnosis of gynecologic problems in the past five years. Those with problems were more likely to report childhood abuse, violent crime victimization, and spouse abuse (Plichta and Abraham, 1996).

Another study explored the connection between chronic intractable pain and histories of childhood sexual abuse in 112 women sampled from a large university campus health center. A sample of fifty-nine women with chronic back pain were compared with fifty-three control subjects obtained simultaneously from the same clinical population. The women with chronic intractable back pain had a significantly higher percentage of childhood sexual abuse experiences than controls (Pecukonis, 1996). Koss and her associates looked at the long-term physical health consequences of criminal victimization. Among a population of almost 400 adult women, they found that compared with nonvictims, victimized women reported more distress, less well-being, visited the doctor twice as frequently, and had outpatient costs that were 2.5 times greater (Koss, Koss, and Woodruff, 1991). They also studied almost

2,300 women in a health maintenance organization. A 45 percent response rate to their survey showed 57 percent of the women had been victims of crime. Rape incidence was approximately 15 times higher than the National Crime Survey estimates for women. Medical care had been sought by 92 percent of crime victims during the first year following the crime, and by 100 percent during the second year (Koss, Woodruff, and Koss, 1990).

Finally, in a recent review article, Biondi and Zannino (1997) conclude that after one hundred years of research on man and animals, psychological stress is a potential cofactor in the pathogenesis of infectious disease. Psychological stress seems able to alter the susceptibility of animals and man to infectious agents, influencing the onset, course, and outcome of certain infectious pathologies. As Heninger (1995) has argued, the data suggests that many of the adverse health consequences of stress may be mediated through the immune system.

CHARACTER CHANGE AND TRAUMA

If trauma is sufficiently disruptive to the continuity of the personality, then it can lead to enduring changes in character structure, a hypothesis that challenges long-standing psychiatric assumptions about the immutability of established personality (Silove, 1996). Veterans of World War II, Korea, Vietnam, and the Gulf War have all described how their families have told them that the men they sent off to war were not the same men who returned. Researchers studying POWs from Vietnam noticed the predominance of a heightened drive to achieve, character rigidity, and decreased interpersonal relatedness (Ursano, 1985). Women who have been battered can vividly describe the changes in their personality as a result of living in a captive situation with an abusive man. Researchers studying victims of disaster noted character changes included psychic constriction, denial, somatization, and survivor guilt (Lindy and Titchener, 1983).

If the impact of trauma is so powerful that it changes character in adults, it gives us some idea of the impact that repetitive trauma has on children. Dr. Judith Herman described the changes that happen to a person who is subjected to totalitarian control over a prolonged period and she termed it complex PTSD. This term serves to adequately describe the living situation of many victims of childhood abuse, prisoners of war, victims of torture, and domestic violence survivors. The changes include alterations in affect regulation, consciousness, self-perception, perception of the perpetrator, relations with others, and systems of meaning (Herman, 1992).

Van der Kolk (1996a) also has described the results of extensive field trials that were done for the DSM-IV supporting similar extensive changes that result from prolonged and repetitive trauma. These chronic character changes include alterations in self-perception, chronic guilt and shame, feelings of self-blame and ineffectiveness, and of being permanently damaged as well as distorted beliefs about and idealization of the perpetrator, an inability to trust or maintain relationships with others, a tendency to be revictimized, a tendency to victimize others, feelings of despair and hopelessness, and a loss of previously sustaining beliefs (Van der Kolk, 1996a).

Given these findings, we must ask ourselves about the social consequences of a nation comprised of large numbers of people who have undergone such personality change, particularly since such changes are usually characterized by serious difficulties in managing chronic and unmitigated anger. The evidence for such changes is so persuasive that in the World Health Organization psychiatric classification scheme, the ICD-10, a new category was devised describing personality change following exposure to catastrophic stress.

LOOKING FOR AN ANTIDOTE

We pointed out earlier that traumatization requires both internal *and* external resources that are inadequate to cope with external threat. We now have a better understanding of what traumatized people are endeavoring to cope with within themselves. It is vital to recognize how difficult or impossible it is for traumatized people to "pull themselves together." They are, in fact, "doing it themselves"—they are caught in a recursive loop that informs them that they must continue to fight for their lives, long after the original threat is over. They cannot control how their bodies automatically respond. They cannot command that their memories be properly restored. They are trapped in the tragedy of human existence. The only real antidote to all this is the healing power of other people. It is time to understand more about the profound way in which other people determine the ultimate outcome of the traumatic experience. Other people are the external resources—our family, friends, neighbors, co-workers, bosses, schoolmates, teachers, administrators, clergymen, and anyone who represents our social group. These external resources can either be the source of the problems or the source of the solutions. We all can become the antidotes to the poisonous experiences of other people.

ATTACHMENT BEHAVIOR

As we now recognize, "the sudden, uncontrollable loss of attachment bonds is an essential element in the development of post-traumatic stress syndromes" (Van der Kolk, 1989, p. 393). But what is this thing called "attachment"? Attachment is defined as a reciprocal, enduring, emotional, and physical affiliation between a child and a caregiver (James, 1994). John Bowlby was one of the most important voices in the field of attachment behavior. He noted that our need to attach to other people follows us from cradle to grave. We always need others and this normal need of a social species has been called such pejorative names as "dependency" and "neediness" because of our overburdened notions of individuality and independence (Bowlby, 1982, 1984, 1988).

Human beings are utterly unable to develop normally without loving and protective attachments. Through our relationship with the mothering person, we as infants develop a working model of ourselves and our parents (Bowlby, 1988) that forms the basis of our personality and gives us a model for how we treat each other and ourselves. This model determines what information is attended to, which memories are evoked, what behaviors are employable. It is the basis for our sense of self and other. Patterns of attachment developed between mother and infant appear to carry over into our adult behaviors and these patterns are transmitted from generation to generation (Main and Hess, 1990).

FAILURE OF ATTACHMENT

We know how damaging the failure of attachment is, both from human and animal studies. World War II provided the opportunity to study babies who had been orphaned and through these studies, the human separation response was documented (Spitz, 1945). When children are first separated from their primary caretaker, they respond loudly and vocally in an attempt to get the caretaker to return. This is called "protest." If the caretaker fails to return, the child sinks into the next phase called "despair." At this point, the child may just die from failure to thrive. In the wild, these children would be unlikely to survive, vulnerable to dangers in the environment and helpless to fend for themselves. If they do survive, these children become "detached." If they have entered this phase, they are relatively unresponsive to human contact, tend to use other people in instrumental ways, as objects to meet their needs rather than as whole people with needs of their own, and continue to prefer things over relationships with people. It is well established that early attachment problems produce all kinds of problems for children including impaired social relationships, learning problems, problems with sleeping, eating, walking, and talking (Alexander, 1992; Cole and Putnam, 1992; Fisher and Ayoub, 1994; James, 1994). A child's emotional system and ability to self-control is also largely determined by primary attachment experiences.

Primate data supports and extends these observations (Reite and Boccia, 1994; Van der Kolk, 1987b). Monkeys who are isolated from their mothers and other animals from birth become severely disturbed. They demonstrate many different kinds of abnormal behaviors including withdrawal and hyperactivity. They are aggressive toward themselves and others. They ignore normal monkey social cues and therefore are frequently the target of aggression from others. They have difficulty with sexual functioning but if they do mate, they are aggressive toward their own offspring. They are also medically compromised, showing a higher rate of tumors and infections. If these monkeys are placed in living situations with normal monkey peers for an extended period of time, they do learn more normal behavior, so that an outside observer can no longer tell the difference between them. However, if these previously isolated monkeys are stressed, they regress to more abnormal behavior. If these same monkeys are given amphetamines, they will often turn into killers while normal monkeys remain unaffected. If given access to alcohol, they will drink to excess, unlike normal monkeys. It is believed that the early maternal deprivation may cause permanent brain damage to the centers associated with bonding and attachment.

ENDORPHINS AND ATTACHMENT

For normal brain development, children need to be cared for by adults who are safe, who allow them to explore and satisfy their curiosity while protecting them from overstimulation. They need adults who can adequately comfort them when they are frightened and who can resonate with their emotional experience enough to provide the containment for those feelings that are too overwhelming to handle alone. This need is not just a psychological requirement. We are beginning to understand some of the brain chemistry that underlies our need for other people (Reite and Boccia, 1994; Van der Kolk and Greenberg, 1987). This description is probably very oversimplified and remains a mixture of theory and research, but nonetheless, it does point us in some interesting directions with important implications. In developing children, there is some reason to believe that exploration and curiosity trigger the release of norepinephrine, a stimulating neurochemical. When this substance gets too high in the brain, the child goes from experiencing interest and excitement to feeling terror. The child then runs back to mother for comfort. It may be that the smell of her skin, the touch of her hand, the sound of her voice, triggers the release of opposing chemical substances—endorphins—which counteract the effects of norepinephrine and are calming, soothing, and make us feel good. Once calm, the cycle repeats itself. In the months and years of this repetition during a child's early years, the brain "learns" the proper balance of these various brain chemicals. We can only begin to hypothesize what happens when the environment is too dangerous for the child to be allowed to explore, or what happens when the child returns to mother for comfort and there is a stranger there, or the mother hits the child instead of providing comfort.

It is entirely likely that a normal endorphin response—and probably other biochemical changes as well—is related to our relationships with other people throughout our lifetimes. If you think about it, other people affect our internal states every day. Contrast the difference for yourself between going home from a bad day and having your significant other comfort you and cater to your needs versus having your significant other criticize your bad mood and insist that you "pull yourself together." In the first example, you will feel better, your muscles will become less tense, laughter will help put your day in perspective, a good meal will relax you further, and you will be able to sleep that night. In the second example, you are likely to feel angry, hurt, and resentful. Muscles tighten, the stomach aches, appetite wanes, laughter is impossible, sleep becomes impossible. There is a wish to lash out and hurt the one who has hurt you. In both cases, nothing changed about the events of your day—the difference was in how your mind and body responded to the behavior of the other person. Our effect on one another—even at the level of basic biochemistry—is profound.

ENDORPHINS AND STRESS—
ADDICTION TO TRAUMA

These magical substances called endorphins are a part of normal, everyday functioning, but they are especially important during times of stress (Bremner et al., 1993; Van der Kolk and Greenberg, 1987). Again, if we look at evolution, this makes sense. Not only do endorphins calm anxiety, improve our mood, and decrease aggression, but they also are great analgesics since they are related to morphine and heroin. Therefore, in times of stress, they provide enough pain relief that we are not disabled by injuries that would otherwise prevent us from escaping the danger. If people are only exposed to rare episodes of overwhelming stress, then they are less likely to show alterations in this biochemical system. Far more problematic are those people who are exposed to repeated experiences of prolonged stress. These people, often children, are exposed to repeatedly high levels of circulating endorphins. One hypothesis is that people can become "addicted" to their own internal endorphins and as a result only feel calm when they are under stress while feeling fearful, irritable, and hyperaroused when the stress is relieved, much like someone who is withdrawing from heroin (Van der Kolk et al., 1985; Van der Kolk and Greenberg, 1987).

If this cycle is in place, then it helps us to understand many of the perplexing symptoms that have been incomprehensible without this information. Stress-addicted children will be those children in the classroom who cannot tolerate a calm atmosphere but must keep antagonizing everyone else until the stress level is high enough for them to achieve some degree of internal equilibrium again. Violence is exciting and stressful and repeated violent acting out, gang behavior, fighting, bullying, and many forms of criminal activity have the additional side effect of producing high levels of stress in people who have grown addicted to such risk-taking behavior. This also helps to explain self-mutilation in its many forms—these children and adults have learned that inflicting harm on the body will induce the release of endorphins that will provide some comfort, at least temporarily. These are children, who grow to be adults, unable to trust or be comforted by other people—in fact other people have been the fundamental source of the stress. Instead, they must fall back on whatever resources they can muster within themselves, resources that they can control, to achieve any kind of equilibrium. As adults, under stress, people who have been brutalized as children may again resort to behaviors that help induce some kind of alteration in the opioid system. These behaviors can include self-mutilation, risk-taking behavior, compulsive sexuality, involvement in violent activity, binging and purging, and of course, drug addiction.

But, at the level of the brain, the situation may be even more complicated. It has been reported that plasma beta-endorphin levels are low in patients with PTSD (Hoffman et al., 1989). Acute opiate use seems to diminish PTSD symptoms while chronic opiate abuse and withdrawal appear to make such symptoms worse. There have been clinical reports of lowered pain thresholds in PTSD patients and of links between PTSD and chronic pain (Stine and Kosten, 1995). Pitman and colleagues studied Vietnam veterans and found that the arousal of trauma-related memories as a result of watching a movie produced a 30 percent decrease in pain responses that was reversible by opiate antagonists, drugs that can counteract the effects of morphine, heroin, and the endorphins (Pitman et al., 1990). There is evidence that the avoidance and numbing that is associated with PTSD is related to a dysregulation of the opioid systems. The endorphins may serve to dampen the hyperarousal that accompanies PTSD (Southwick, Yehuda, and Morgan, 1995).

Clinical reports have helped to clarify some of the implications of the relationship between the endogenous opioids and stress (Glover, 1992). Glover (1993) reported on the use of opiate antagonists to treat the emotional numbing associated with combat trauma. Bills and Kreisler (1993) reported on the use of opiate antagonists to stop flashbacks. There have been reports on the use of opiate antagonists in the treatment of people who self-mutilate indicating that the self-mutilation is evoking an endorphin response and that the opiate antagonist counters that response so that the self-destructive behavior stops, possibly because a more normal response to pain is restored. But most of this work has been done in small populations of severely mentally retarded individuals (Crews et al., 1993; Herman et al., 1989; Kars et al., 1990). Thus far, few studies have attempted the use of opiate antagonists for adult psychiatric patients who self-mutilate. One study found that the treatment with naltrexone was very effective in six out of seven cases (Roth, Ostroff, Hoffman, 1996). In the clinical experience of an inpatient program specializing in treating adult victims of trauma, clinicians report positive gains in stopping self-mutilation if the patient usually experiences some relief from dysphoria and analgesia as a result of the self-mutilation. In such cases the use of an opiate antagonist appears to restore pain sensitivity, reducing the "rush" that usually accompanies the cutting, and this change helps the motivated patient regain control over the behavior (Bills, 1997).

Regardless of how complicated the biochemical picture turns out to be, the opioid system appears to be intimately involved with the development and maintenance of PTSD and with the attachment system in subhuman primates and human beings. Professionally and socially, we can no longer afford to avoid the implications of this work. It means that relationships have a profound capacity to alter the internal bodily states—and the development of the brain—for good or for ill.

TRAUMA-BONDING

Even more ominous for repeatedly traumatized people is their pronounced tendency to use highly abnormal and dangerous relationships as their normal idea of what relationships are supposed to be (Herman, 1992; James, 1994; Van der Kolk, 1989). Trauma-bonding is a relationship based on terror and the twisting of normal attachment behavior into something perverse and cruel. People who are terrorized, whether as adult victims of torture, or domestic violence or child victims of family abuse, experience their abuser as being in total control of life and death. The perpetrator is the source of the pain and terror, but is also the source of relief from that pain. The perpetrator is the source of threat but is also the source of hope. George Orwell described the creation of a trauma-bond in his classic book, *1984,* in which his main character, Winston Smith, is being tortured and brainwashed by Big Brother. The process has taken many years, and finally, it is working. The torturer, O'Brien, tells Smith that he is improving, meaning he is finally coming around to appreciating the benefits of Big Brother. But he notes that he still has not made sufficient progress emotionally because he does not yet *love* Big Brother. Smith concurs and admits to O'Brien that he hates Big Brother and O'Brien insists that the time has come for Smith to learn not just to obey Big Brother, but now he must love him.

O'Brien manipulates Smith into betraying the woman he loves by using the most horrific threat he can imagine, and in his act of betrayal, what remains of Smith's will gives way. By the closing sentences of the book, the final betrayal of the self, the "soul murder" is accomplished (Shengold, 1989). Smith looks at the enormous face of Big Brother and chides himself for all the years and all the misunderstanding, "[b]ut it was all right, everything was all right, the struggle was finished. He had won the victory over himself. He loved Big Brother" (Orwell, 1981, p. 245).

If it is your own mother and father who have been the source of danger, then you are going to persist in believing that attachment = danger. This is particularly true when the occasions of danger have been intermittently supplanted by more rewarding aspects of a relationship. This is complicated by the fact that on a very basic, perhaps even biological level, danger enhances attachment behavior. Again, from an evolutionary point of view, this is sensible. Our best protection against danger is the help of other people. So danger calls us together as a highly adaptive coping strategy under circumstances of external threat.

Unfortunately, when the danger is not external to the social group, but instead comes from within the immediate family circle, the body reacts in exactly the same way. This produces the apparently paradoxical situation in which the abuser is the very person that the battered child or spouse turns to for safety. The primary caretakers have total control over children's lives and if abusive they become the source not just of the abuse, but also of the relief from this abuse. The children end up unable to imagine survival without their abusers, since it was their abusers who repeatedly granted them their life by not killing them. The relief they feel for this is expressed as gratitude toward the perpetrator (James, 1994). Children thus affected may never develop the capacity to attach normally and receive love, nurturance, and protection, respect for themselves or for others, self-mastery, or autonomy. They internalize the image of their own helplessness and the role of the perpetrator and go on as adolescents and as adults, reenacting one or both of those roles.

TRAUMATIC REENACTMENT

It has long been recognized that "history repeats itself," but never before have we so clearly understood *why* history does so. Children who have been traumatized cannot heal themselves alone. It is one of the tragedies of human existence, that what begins as life-saving coping skills, ends up delivering us into the hands of compulsive repetition. We are destined to reenact what we cannot remember. Freud called it the *repetition compulsion* and he said, "He reproduces it not as a memory but as an action; he repeats it, without, of course, knowing that he is repeating. . . . He cannot escape from this compulsion to repeat; and in the end we understand that this is his way of remembering" (Van der Kolk and Ducey, 1989, p. 271).

It has become clear that the very nature of traumatic processing determines the reenactment behavior (Van der Kolk, 1989). We must assume that as human beings, we are meant to function at our maximum level of integration and that any barrier to this integration will produce some innate compensatory mechanism that allows us to overcome it. Splitting traumatic memories and feelings off into nonverbal images and sensations is life-saving in the short term, but prevents full integration in the long term.

The field of traumatic stress studies could say that it received an initial stimulus to growth from a dramatic reenactment. On May 6, 1972, the Op-ed page of *The New York Times* published an essay written by Chaim Shatan titled, "The Post-Vietnam Syndrome." In the piece, Shatan described the tragedy of Dwight Johnson and that article attracted widespread attention from Vietnam vets involved in rap groups around the country and helped to mobilize a response that eventually led to important changes in legislation.

Dwight Johnson was a Medal of Honor hero who was haunted by the face of a Vietnamese soldier who he had killed after coming face to face with the man who was aiming a gun point blank at him—a gun that misfired. On April 30, 1971, Johnson, now married and the father of a little boy, left the Valley Forge Veterans Administration medical center on a three-day pass and went home to Detroit. In an incident eerily similar, in reverse to his Vietnam experience, he was shot and killed while attempting an armed robbery of a grocery store. The store owner told the police, "I first hit him with two bullets but he just stood there, with the gun in his hand, and said, 'I'm going to kill you . . .' I kept pulling the trigger until my gun was empty." In the exchange, Dwight Johnson, an experienced combat soldier, never fired a shot (Nordheimer, 1971).

Lenore Terr brought the subject of childhood traumatic reenactment to center stage in her book that detailed the results of the 1976 Chowchilla school bus kidnapping. One of the many examples she gives of a behavioral reenactment was that of young Bob Barklay, the children's hero who had helped them to escape. As Terr tells it,

> One Sunday afternoon eighteen months after the kidnapping, the adult Barklays noticed a car parked on the road edging their property. The hood of the strange car was up. "Go see what's going on, Bob," one of the Barklays suggested. The fifteen-year-old boy banged the door and went outside. A few minutes later shouts and screams in an Oriental language broke the calm of the afternoon. Cookie and Hal Barklay ran out. A tourist from Japan had stopped his rented automobile outside the Barklay's property. It had been overheating. The tourist had lifted his hood in order to check the radiator. Just then Bob had come charging out of his house. He shot the tourist with his BB gun. It hurt. Stung the man badly. The tourist was both confused and outraged. What was wrong with this boy? These country people must be crazy.
>
> We know what was wrong with Bob Barklay. The Chowchilla kidnapping had started, as far as Bob was concerned, with a van "in trouble" at the side of the road. As Bob's school bus had slowed down to pass the van, three masked men had jumped onto the bus. Eighteen months after that, Bob spotted another vehicle seemingly in trouble at the side of the road. The start signal for a kidnapping popped off in Bob's mind. The kidnapping was to take place at Bob's own house. Everybody, his parents, his sister, and himself, were in danger.
>
> Bob came out shooting. Nobody was going to kidnap him again. If Bob had to be a hero, he'd be a hero fast, not after hours of mental anguish. So Bob Barklay shot first and thought later. That's what I mean by a single behavioral reenactment. It's dangerous. Crazy. But it makes perfect sense when you think about it. (Terr, 1990, p. 275)

The study of criminal behavior has much to gain from an understanding of traumatic reenactment. For instance, in 1988 Burgess and her colleagues released a study of serial rapists. In this study they noted that the rapists had a substantially higher rate of sexual abuse as children, other forced sexual encounters as children, and sexual abuse by family members. Their first reenactments of their own abuse began when they forced sex on other neighborhood children or family members as preadolescents.

Explanations for traumatic reenactment behavior vary widely. Some believe that the re-experience of traumatic memories is the way the mind tries to make sense out of what happened. Others hypothesize that trauma causes people to revert to a more primitive form of information processing and memory retrieval, so that the memories return in the form of images, sensations, and motor reenactments. Others believe that the victimized may identify with the perpetrator in an attempt to overcome the helplessness involved in a traumatic experience. Alternately, the inability to self-protect may leave the victim a target for subsequent victimization (Saporta and Van der Kolk, 1992).

Based on what we know about the split between verbal and nonverbal thought, it may be that the most useful way of understanding traumatic reenactment is through the language of drama. Shakespeare told us that the whole world is our stage, and with behavioral reenactments we see this doctrine in action. The only way that the nonverbal brain can "speak" is through behavior, since it has no words. If we examine reenactment behavior we can see that the traumatized person is trying to repeatedly "tell his or her story" in very overt, or highly disguised ways. If only we could still interpret nonverbal messages, perhaps we could respond more adequately to this "call for help." For healing to occur, we must give words to our overwhelming experiences. In *Macbeth,* Shakespeare urges us to "Give sorrow words; the grief that does not speak whispers the o'er fraught heart and bids it break." But we cannot find the words by ourselves. That is the whole point—the traumatized person is cut off from language, deprived of the power of words, trapped in speechless terror. We need the help, the words, the signals, of caring others, but to get their attention we must find some way to signal them about our distress in a language that has no words. This is the language of behavior, the language of the mime, of the stage. Unfortunately, we have largely lost the capacity for nonverbal interpretation, and so most of these cries fall on deaf ears.

Traumatized children are playing the role of their damaged selves. On the stage that is the school, they enact their pain, distress, fear, and rage. We are the audience and rarely do we make a meaningful interpretation of their play. We are far more likely to condemn them for trying to get attention, blame them for their negative behavior, and attribute it to effects rather than to causes, because the causes cannot be spoken but can only be seen in their symbolic, disguised behavior. In fact, all of our social systems, including our schools, have become so "trauma-organized" (Bentovim, 1992), that we do not even recognize it when we see it. It has become too much a part of our expectations, of all our reality, that we fail to perceive how truly abnormal our systems are, how unresponsive to fundamental human needs. People are constantly reenacting past experiences, often in very destructive ways, but we do not recognize this behavior for what it is. The victim of child sexual abuse becomes a prostitute, the boy who is anally raped becomes a serial rapist, the child punched in the head for a bad report card grows up to beat his son to death. These are the headlines of our daily newspapers, but we only are willing to hear these as "excuses" that need to be fought against, rather than the explanations for behavior that could be prevented.

The challenge for systems of treatment, and for all systems within which human beings strive to learn and grow, is to change our approach. How do we develop a technology in which traumatic reenactment is understood as a fundamental mechanism within all groups and that part of our social responsibility is to help each other break the cycles of traumatic reenactment, the cycles of violence? How do we redesign or alter systems so that they allow for opportunities to *redirect* the individual's traumatic reenactment? The traumatized child or adult cannot be expected to be able to do that alone, or even without resistance. Remember that the traumatized person perceives that remembering, feeling, and knowing the truth of his or her own reality is a threat to survival. Hurt children need to be repeatedly convinced that human beings *can* be trusted, that relationships *can* be safe, that they *can* direct their own lives down less self-destructive paths. This can only be done in the context of safe relationships with other people.

ISSUES OF MEANING AND SPIRITUALITY

As Ronnie Janoff-Bulman has shown (1992), the experience of trauma shatters—often irrevocably—some very basic assumptions about our world, our relationship to others, and our basic sense of identity and place in the world. A sense of meaning and purpose for being alive is shaken. For people who are traumatized as children, systems of meaning have not even been firmly established before they are torn asunder. Somehow, the survivor must re-establish a sense of meaning and this cannot happen alone. Our view of reality is a shared perception, as are all our systems of meaning-making.

The literature that describes traumatic experience has much in common with many of the discourses about the nature of evil that we have briefly reviewed. Sickness has traditionally been one of the great evils that plague mankind, and sickness has traditionally been represented as a loss of intactness, a separation into parts, a fragmentation. An old expression for mental illness described someone as having "lost their balance." The original therapists, the Greek *therapeutes*, were the attendants of the cult of Asclepius, the god of healing. According to Plato, it was Asclepius who was able to bring about "love and reconciliation between the most antithetic elements in the body" (Meier, 1989, p. i). The connection between illness and social harmony has long been recognized by tribal cultures. For the Navahos:

> illness is the symptoms that somewhere on whatever level or levels—the ecological unit is disturbed. To be sick is to be fragmented. To be healed is to become whole, and to become whole one must be in harmony with family, friends and nature. (Van der Hart, 1983, p. 57)

Pain is another of humankind's great evils and we now have a much clearer idea of what the overwhelming stress of suffering does to the human organism. As Elaine Scarry (1985, p. 23) has poetically put it, "What is literally at stake in the body in pain is the making and unmaking of the world." Pain and fear rob us of language, split us off from our innate need to share our experience with others of our kind. A growing body of evidence supports the recognition that traumatic experience may, indeed, generate a separate consciousness, which, although absent language, may still carry with it memory, emotions, images, sensations, and a frustrated plan of action (Galin, 1974).

Separation and the loss of relationship is yet another great human evil. The Devil's loss is that he is separated from God. According to the story, once seated in a place of honor, through his own pride and disobedience he is now a fallen and unredeemable angel. To the extent that traumatic experience shatters the bonds that keep the victims connected to others, they are cut adrift, alone in a sea of pain, anger, guilt, despair, hopelessness, and meaninglessness. Other people avoid them because they are tainted, defiled, bad, crooked, ugly, and impure. They are infected with evil and must be shunned. As bearers of troubling thoughts and feelings, victims are suppressed; listeners change the topic away from their tales of woe; they attempt to press their own interpretation of events upon the victims; they blame them for their pain, and finally shun them altogether (Coates, Wartman, and Abben, 1979). The effects of trauma are catching, and the listener is always in danger of empathetically resonating with the victim and thus converging emotionally within the same traumatic envelope (Harber and Pennebaker, 1992; Hatfield, Cacioppo, and Rapson, 1994). As Euripedes said several thousand years ago, "Where there are two, one cannot be wretched and one not."

Throughout the history of the human species, helplessness has been another great evil. Helplessness evokes shame, a feeling so overwhelming, so paralyzing and disabling, that it must be defended against. One reaction to helplessness is to the loss of agency, a perpetual dependent turning toward external authority for rescue, a pervasive sense of powerlessness.

But another reaction is anger, a willingness to seize power, an escalation of anger to rage, fury, and a profound desire to seek revenge and defeat the shame. The greater the loss, separation, helplessness, shame, and suffering, the greater will be the temptation to avenge oneself and at least preserve even a fragmentary sense of pride. The "problem of evil" and the role of God is fundamentally a struggle to make meaning out of a universe that appears cruel and wicked, experientially overlying an intuitive awareness of goodness. The experience of trauma shatters our fundamental assumptions of security in the world. One of the most striking metaphors for what trauma does to the victim is that of the "black hole" (Pitman and Orr, 1990), also a metaphor for hell, the dark, speechless, empty, meaningless, suffering void of evil. Like characters reenacting the tragedies of Greek drama, victims of trauma wrestle to pull some meaning out of war, plague, earthquakes, fires, floods, incest, betrayal, accidents, torture, rape, assault, suicide, murder, and genocide. But like Prometheus, they are often chained to the rock of traumatic reenactment, while an eagle eats their immortal liver that continually replenishes itself.

Most of the work that has thus far been done on survivors of trauma comes from the perspective of the victim. But if we are going to study the enactment of evil, if we are ever going to be able to prevent such enactment, then we will be better served by shifting our focus to the perpetrator. Ervin Staub (1989) has pointed out that perpetrators often disguise their true intentions, unaware of their own unconscious hostility and scapegoating, frequently hurting others in the service of a "higher good" and justifying their behavior on the basis of the victims' "evil" nature. The sociologist, James Aho (1994) takes this idea even a step farther, "My violation of you grows from my yearning to rectify the wrong I sense that you have done me. Violence emerges from my quest for good and my experience of you as the opponent of good" (p. 11).

According to a survey published by Patterson and Kim (1991), 90 percent of Americans questioned said that they truly believe in God, but they do not turn to God or religion to help them decide about the seminal or moral issues of the day, issues of right and wrong. For most people, religion plays virtually no role in shaping their opinions on public questions. Most people do not even know their church's position on important issues. Only one American in five ever consults a minister, priest, or rabbi on everyday issues. Although 58 percent of people went to services regularly growing up, only 27 percent go regularly today. Only one in ten believe in all of the Ten Commandments; 40 percent believe in five or fewer.

Such information is disturbing, less for what it says about the state of organized religion than for what it says about the national sense of trying to make meaning out of shared experience. A growing body of evidence supports a long-held belief that religious or spiritual beliefs play an important role in individual and social health. Marian Wright Edelman has talked about the importance to African-American children of growing up within a community of faith. "We black children were wrapped up and rocked in a cradle of faith, song, prayer, ritual, and worship which immunized our spirits against some of the meanness and unfairness . . . in our segregated South and acquiescent nation" and she attributes the success in her life as being in part related to a deep spirituality she developed as a traumatized child (Clinton, 1996, p. 181). People who have studied altruism under particularly dangerous conditions have noted that it is religious faith that is a major determinant for someone's decision to risk themselves for the sake of others (Oliner and Oliner, 1988). In a review of over two hundred studies relating faith and health, researchers conclude that the two tend to go together, even to the extent that those with faith may live longer (Hood et al., 1996). What does it mean that 90 percent of Americans say they believe in a Higher Power, but that this belief is disconnected from the way they make decisions and the way they live their lives?

Making sense out of violence, transcending its effects, and transforming the energy of violence into something powerfully good for oneself and the community describes what Judith Herman has called a "survivor mission" (1992, p. 207). It is often a mission that encompasses the remainder of one's life. Confrontation with the spiritual, philosophical, and/or religious context—and conflicts—of human experience is impossible to avoid if recovery is to be assured.

TRAUMA-ORGANIZED SYSTEMS

Why are our children killing each other?
Because we are teaching them to.
Our society glamorizes violence.

Deborah Prothrow-Stith, 1992
Harvard University School of Public Health

We can find common ground only by moving to higher ground.

Jim Wallis
The Soul of Politics

As the twentieth century draws to a close, we find ourselves, as an entire civilization, at a critical turning point. As a species, we are Nature's biggest anomaly. Our bodies are evolutionarily adjusted to an environment that no longer exists, an environment in which bands of humans could live apart from one another, battling together against the forces of nature. Fiercely territorial and protective of those to whom we are attached, our capacity for violence was adaptive in the very different circumstances of our evolutionary history. But our big brains and the fluke of language guaranteed that evolution would take an interesting turn. Thanks to our unique brains we have achieved a level of species success unparalleled by any other living creature. But our brains and our bodies did not keep pace with each other and we still react to danger as we did millions of years ago, disabling our higher powers, at least temporarily.

We have gone a long way toward taming the forces of nature that presented such a threat to us throughout our long evolution. But we have yet to learn how to live successfully with each other in balance with nature under the circumstances that we have created. At this point, humanity is in grave danger of outstripping the resources that sustain our lives. Like the sword of Damocles, annihilation hangs poised over us in many different forms—nuclear disaster, environmental pollution, biological or chemical warfare, biological disaster, economic disaster, global warfare. The road to annihilation could come to an abrupt and rapid end, as it does for so many individuals, at the barrel of someone's gun, or it could be a slow deterioration in the quality of life so damaging that it amounts to cultural suicide. Whatever the course, we do not have to be prophets to look down the road toward the future and see where the present paths are taking us. Although we look at these threats and decry their inherent irrationality, we appear helpless to stop the self-destructiveness that characterizes so much of our modern behavior. In fact, for the most part we dwell in denial.

Violence in America is the number one public health problem that faces us. Despite our apparent economic prosperity, serious injuries to children at the hands of their caretakers have quadrupled between 1986 and 1993. A species that intentionally kills, wounds, or handicaps its young is a species dooming itself to destruction.

Child murder, of course, is a relatively small proportion of the toll caused by child abuse. Most abused children grow up to become parents themselves. It is becoming increasingly clear that the transgenerational transmission of the effects of trauma is also a serious problem. Although only a certain proportion of abused children will grow up to abuse their own children, they have suffered damage nonetheless. An accumulating body of research indicates that even when one generation refuses to abuse the next, the abuse at the hands of the previous generation is so destructive of attachment bonds that the disturbed patterns of attachment are passed on, even though the abuse is not (Main and Hess, 1990). And it is not just abuse that poses a problem. Trauma of any sort can disrupt normal attachment bonds between people, particularly interpersonal trauma, and can therefore interfere with the capacity for healthy parenting. Once disturbed patterns of relating are established, they are difficult to alter without conscious and deliberate effort.

Sadly, trauma is not a unique occurrence. As we discussed earlier, recent studies confirm clinical impressions that a substantial proportion of Americans—about three-quarters—have experienced some significant traumatic experience in their lives. We know because of the dynamic of traumatic reenactment, people who are traumatized in childhood tend to have repetitive traumatic experiences. On a very broad scale, there is not a single American family that is absent a history of what for many was a wrenching experience—immigration. By definition, immigration is founded on broken attachment bonds. For many, the migratory experience itself was preceded by persecution, wartime flight, extremes of poverty that necessitated the abandonment of home, or forced enslavement. Given what we are beginning to understand about intergenerational trauma, it should not surprise us that we have become a "trauma-organized society."

What does it mean that we are "trauma-organized"?

> We live in a culture of violence—The United States has strong laws against violence, but they are inconsistently applied and compete with pervasive proviolence messages. Most violence is a private affair, in abusive homes ruled by petty tyrants. But America's infatuation with violence extends to the media, sports, politics, the military, and even church and school. (Brendtro and Long, 1995, p. 52)

To be a society organized around traumatic experience means that the effects of trauma are ever present, playing an enormous role in our current social problems, but unseen, misinterpreted, or misunderstood, just like the blind men and the elephant. In that fable, each blind man held and carefully described the separate parts of an elephant—the trunk, the tail, the leg, and the side—believing and insisting that each separate part *was* the elephant, completely unaware that they were mistaking a part for the whole. We do the same when we insist that one thing is the cause of a problem—and that changing that one thing would solve it. The problem of violence is *not* due to family breakdown, racism, poverty, male hormones, female hormones, violence genes, sexism, intolerance, bigotry, hatred, lack of leadership, conflicting values, personal narcissism, greed, weaponry, media violence, pornography. *All* of these factors interact to produce a climate in which violence is tolerated, supported, encouraged, and condoned. Regardless of what we *say* about violence, it is what we *do* that tells a different story. Everyone participates in creating this climate. Many of us say, "But I don't do these things; I don't carry weapons; I am not a violent person. I don't beat my kids or my spouse." As true as these facts may be, what we are beginning to realize in a heartfelt way is that old and worn aphorism, "It you're not part of the solution, then you are part of the problem." Or, put another way, it is as wrong to fail to protect, as it is to do harm. Claiming to be innocent bystanders, uninvolved, minding our own business, or just following orders is no longer a sufficient excuse for failing to take action. Our world has become far too interconnected and interdependent to accommodate such rationalizations.

We are beginning to understand that we are all part of a vast ecological system that encompasses *all* life on earth. The global network of communications brings the violence from around the country and around the world into our homes every night. At an intellectual level, we know that we are interdependent, that we can no longer function as isolated individuals or isolated communities, or isolated countries in a fragile world that has become preciously small and dangerously overcrowded. The more we destroy life around us, the more we destroy our children's future and ourselves. And yet, we have not yet made the shift in our thinking, feeling, or practice that will enable us to cope with this unique and evolutionary change in perspective. If we are to envision, create, and sustain a new world, we will have to make a *major* shift in perspective.

Therapy can help a lucky few, but therapy is not the answer. There will never be enough therapists, time, or money to treat any except the most severe cases of the growing number of traumatized children in society. We have become such an expert-dependent society, that many otherwise well-intentioned and socially motivated people believe that they have nothing to offer because they do not have the proper credentials. The increasing level of violence in our society is spreading the traumatic "infection" at geometrical rates, since we know that the effects of trauma spread across and down through the generations. There is no answer except to dramatically change the way we deal with hurt children and with each other within our social systems. The present stresses on the family, particularly families-at-risk, are so toxic and require such fundamental long-term structural changes, that entire generations will be wasted unless we respond with some more immediate interventions. Children are at school for at least nine months of the year, five days a week, six to eight hours a day. Is it possible that the school can play a major rehabilitative role for children, become a more welcoming environment for teachers and administrators, and still serve in its fundamental capacity as the main instrument of educating children? Can workplaces become truly safe environments within which people are offered the opportunity for corrective emotional experiences as well as salaries? Can the justice system alter to reflect a concern with restoration and restitution, not just retribution?

Such a change is called a "paradigm shift," meaning that it is not a change in technique or policy but a change in essential thought, a shift in the assumptions upon which we base our knowledge. Right now, we are on the verge of this shift, individually and socially hovering on the edge, not entirely sure whether to go ahead into the unknown or to continue to look backward for salvation. As the social activist and minister Jim Wallis has said:

> The truth is that we are in a time of transition, an in-between period when the old is dying and the new has yet to be born. The values, assumptions, and structures that have governed us for so long have come to their logical end, and we now find ourselves at a dead end. But new values, patterns, and institutions have not yet emerged. We are caught in the middle, stranded between paradigms . . . . America today lacks any coherent or compelling social vision. (Wallis, 1994, p. 5)

CHANGING PATTERNS OF THOUGHT

> A civilization generally refuses to accept a cultural innovation that calls in question one of its own structural elements. Such refusals or unspoken enmities are relatively rare: but they always point to the heart of a civilization.
>
> Braudel
> *A History of Civilizations*, 1994

There are frequent references made these days to something called a "paradigm shift." But what *is* a paradigm and what does it means when it shifts? Paradigms are the underlying assumptions upon which we base our thought and our behavior (Kuhn, 1970). They are the things we just take for granted and never really think about until they are challenged. A few centuries ago, people in Europe made a very basic assumption that Earth was at the center of the universe, while the sun and all the other planets revolved around it. Such basic assumptions do not just affect the one area of study that pertain to them, but instead serve as a model for all other areas as well. Earth at the center of the universe was perfectly in accord with the view that as God had ordered all this for the good of Man, the Church was the institution around which all others were to revolve, and the Pope, God's representative on Earth, was to have unchallenged authority. The social, political, and economic implications of such a well-ordered system were widespread, unchallenged, and accepted by everyone. For learned people of the fourteenth century, this was reality, not a theory. It was a basic paradigm (Capra, 1982; Schwartz, 1992).

Then, as technology progressed and astronomical discoveries were made thanks to such inventions as the telescope, certain anomalies were noted that could not be explained by using the basic assumption that the Earth was the center of the universe. Copernicus had the temerity to suggest that the Sun, instead of the Earth, was at the centerpoint and that the Earth revolved around it. Other men of science such as Bruno and Galileo began adding their own careful observations in support of a very different model of the universe. Taken by itself, from the point of view of our space-age century, it would seem to be of little but scientific importance whether the Sun or Earth was central. Yet Bruno was burned at the stake and Galileo had to pursue much of his most important work in secret because the church authorities were so opposed to their work. In those days, to study science was to endanger your own life and the lives of people you loved. One author has even suggested with good supporting evidence, that the reason science gave up any serious study of the mind, the spirit, and the soul, was because men like Galileo realized that dividing mind from body was the only way that they would be able to pursue science in peace, without persecution by the Church (Schwartz, 1992).

Ultimately, as we know, this was a battle that the Church lost, as the new "paradigm" served to explain much more about the known universe than could be explained by the old model. These new explanations paved the way for enormous technological advances that produced progress for all humankind. But when Galileo and his colleagues made their compromise with the Church in order to be able to pursue their work, they ended up splitting much of importance off from the whole that is human nature and human life. Although our advances with this paradigm have been great, we have ended up in the late twentieth century with an enormous technology largely divorced from values, emotion, compassion, intuition, creativity, and human needs. The problem is not the technology—the problem is that we are fragmented and so are all our basic studies. The right hand, quite literally, does not know what the left hand is doing. And sometimes one or both of the hands is doing something that is extremely destructive.

Just as the previous paradigm shift began with astronomy and basic physics, so too does the paradigm that is presently emerging. We can date this new paradigm to the insights that derive from quantum physics that were developed in the first half of this century. Among other insights, quantum physics implies that the universe is actually very different from the way we presently perceive it. On the level of quantum mechanics, everything is interconnected, not in a hierarchy but in a vast, interconnected and far-reaching network. Events at a great distance appear to have effects that cannot be explained by conventional explanatory systems. Modern physicists have even been speculating about the possibility of God, the Soul, life after death and other such topics that have been banned from science since before Copernicus (Margenau and Varghese, 1992). This shift in basic assumptions, just as the one before it, is having a profound effect on all areas of modern knowledge, even though those changes are just now being articulated. Regardless of where we look, the most progressive leaders in every field are talking the language of virtual reality, neural networks, systems theory, cybernetics, the global village, cyberspace.

Trauma theory represents a parallel shift in paradigm for the specific area of mental health studies. Consistent with the basic assumption that is representative of this shift in paradigm, the underlying premise of trauma theory is the interconnectedness of mind and body, self and other, the personal and the political. The knowledge base that forms the basis of trauma theory has been discovered, forgotten, and then rediscovered several times in the past century. It appears that there is a cultural resistance to this material. This certainly is consistent with the assertion that trauma theory represents a shift in paradigm. A new paradigm is always resisted by those who are strongly committed to the old paradigm. But why should there be such a cultural resistance to gaining an understanding about trauma in what is, arguably, the most violent century in all history? What basic paradigmatic structures does trauma theory challenge?

One of our basic social structures is that of *deviance.* In our society deviants fill the ranks of either the mentally ill or the criminal. Whatever the problem, deviance as presently defined locates the problem firmly within the deviant person. Regardless of the cause of their problems, it is their fault and their responsibility. Children are expected to grow up to be productive and responsible citizens no matter what has happened to them, barring actual physical disability or mental retardation. Trauma theory challenges our basic definitions of deviance because it places the cause of so many mental health and criminal problems in the space that connects the individual with his or her social group. If we arrive at the conclusion that many individual mental health problems have their origins in injury that the person sustained at the hands of someone else, then we move from a sickness model to an injury model. In doing so we immediately involve other people as causative agents in the individual's distress. If we arrive at the conclusion that many problems of individual social maladjustment, including much criminal behavior, likewise have their origins in injury that the person sustained as a child, then our definitions of badness and goodness need to change as well. After all, who is more wrong, the criminal who commits the act or the society that failed to protect the criminal from harm as a child? When retribution is so basic to human nature, can we fail to understand the ways in which the criminal attempts to "get even" for such a basic betrayal?

This entire line of thought strikes deeply at another fundamental social structure: our gut-level desire for retribution. When we have been hurt our first and most primitive basic desire is to get even. The leaders we hold most dear—from Jesus Christ, to Gandhi, to Buddha, to Martin Luther King Jr.—all have urged an opposite, turn-the-other-cheek approach, but when we are hurt and angry and we want to feel better, we want revenge. It makes no difference whether it achieves some longer-term goal or sabotages that goal. We just want to get even and we will not rest until we do. But who do we get even with? What exactly are we punishing? What are we trying to accomplish? When we punish, does it actually bring about positive results for the society?

These ideas about deviance are threatening to segments of both the mental health profession and the criminal justice systems whose laws, regulations, and practice are based on an established and accepted view of individual pathology and culpability. If the social group has failed to protect these people from harm as children, then how can we continue to fail them when they finally end up displaying any of the vast array of symptoms that the *Diagnostic and Statistic Manual of the American Psychiatric Association* describes? How can we so self-righteously punish them in the hell that is a modern prison and expect them to come out as anything but more barbarous, more traumatized?

And as for the mentally ill, how can we go on self-righteously pretending that their problems are largely the result of some basic biological or character flaw in the individual when we know that there is such an intimate connection between what happens to a person and how they turn out? How can we continue to legitimatize an exclusive biological emphasis on the treatment of such complex phenomena? Paying attention only to the biology or genetics of a person makes no more sense than only paying attention to their psyche and pretending that they do not have a body.

Trauma theory also challenges the fundamental split originated by Descartes and supplemented by great scientists ever since—the mind/body dichotomy. In gaining an understanding of the ways in which trauma affects us, we see a number of interfaces between behavior and biochemistry, voice and action, relationship and internal bodily changes, meaning-making and neurochemical change. It is disturbing to our existing medical model to think that the simple acts of changing the way we speak to other people, or of participating in theater or painting or dancing or ritual, or the simple act of putting feelings into words in a safe social space can bring about profound physiological changes. Likewise, it is quite disturbing to speculate about the implications of violence and to realize that violence perpetrated as domestic violence and not as acts of war, has become the major public health problem of this era, far surpassing even the devastation of AIDS.

When science split off mind/soul/spirit, it also split off feelings. Trauma theory brings our emotional life back to the forefront of interest and concern. If we are born with basic affects then they are there for very good reason. Nature does not evolve such a complex, interconnected system just to be a nuisance to us. Trauma fragments our emotional life from the rest of our existence. But in our present paradigm, emotions are at best an unavoidable annoyance, at worst the root of all our problems, dangerous and to be avoided at all costs. Without feelings we suffer from "robopathology," a syndrome characterized by social death. Without feelings, we cannot feel for other people, and therefore we can do anything in the service of some ideology or another, even if it means torturing another. The necessity of confronting the emotional nature of our basic identity is threatening to a system grounded in the objectivity and unemotional nature of science.

Another deeply troubling structure that trauma theory attacks is our definitions of what is "rational" and what is "irrational." As we have discussed at length, we know that there are many forces in our society that are traumatogenic, meaning they produce an environment within which the chances of being traumatized are greatly enhanced. Climates of poverty, racism, sexism, and injustice provide a fertile ground for traumatic experiences. Our culture actively encourages violence through our addictive preoccupation with violence on TV and in the movies and violence toward women through pornography. And we promote violent acting out through our refusal to deal with gun control. Yet, all of these activities are considered "rational" and are a "rational" way to make money, to support the economy, and to protect civil rights. Meanwhile, people who question this, people who complain about victimization, remember abuse, or confront perpetrators are often labeled "irrational."

Coming to grips with the reality of child abuse is a difficult task for our society, not only because we are genuinely horrified at the treatment of children, but also because we participate in a culture that has a deep ambivalence about those very children. In fact, the entire history of mankind demonstrates an ambivalence even more profound than ours today. One of our deep social presumptions is that children do not remember, that you can do almost anything to a child and that child should still be able to make responsible choices as an adult. Only gross insanity is an unargued legal defense. But we know now—not just in a literary but in a scientific sense—that the "child is father to the man." Early childhood development determines adult behavior. There is some plasticity up to the age of twenty, but after that, changes in biologically based developmental schemas are virtually impossible.

All of this leads to a redefinition of individual rights and responsibilities and social rights and responsibilities. We know now that our unitary and individualistic sense of self is a socially and cognitively structured illusion. We do not have any control over our lives as long as we are tied to the unmetabolized events of a personal and transgenerational past. We know that in any interaction with another person we have the potential to heal or to harm, and that our intervention or lack thereof, may be a major determinant of the other person's behavior. Given this, what is our responsibility? Is it as wrong to fail to protect, to fail to act to help as it is to actively hurt? If so, then we are all victims AND we are all perpetrators, and another deep structure crumbles under our feet.

Trauma theory changes not just the details, but the *patterns* of our thoughts. We are compelled to wrestle with our deeply ingrained patterns of blaming, scapegoating, and empathic failure. We are pushed and pulled into the repeated encounter with the suffering other who rightfully demands our compassion rather than our condemnation, and who asks us for a healing and integrating, rather than a fragmenting, response. Up until now, the deviant person has had to accept the full weight of responsibility for his or her problems. In this model we are forced to share the burden and this is the source of our powerful resistance to this material. It is exceedingly hard work.

In real terms, what does this mean? It means developing a social process and practice in which compassion for children is expressed through a true understanding of children's developmental needs and a willingness to make sure those needs are met for every child. It means developing a society characterized by *true* integration of the sexes and the races so that no one suffers as a result of the simple fact of their gender or color. It means developing a society in which none of us can rest easily until all of us have full bellies, a roof to sleep under, and a sense of self-respect. It means developing a society in which universal health care is a source of pride and comfort for everyone. It means developing a society in which our elderly citizens are valued, cherished, and protected. It means developing a society in which we can all feel biologically, psychologically, and socially safe with each other. These goals have always been the sacred goals of humankind. But it has lately become unfashionable, even naive, to talk about them, to imagine them as possibilities, to at least attempt to reach them. Yet, what is it all for if not for that reaching?

We desperately need such a coherent social vision, but it is probably impossible to engage in such a creative effort until we have begun the process of healing ourselves. We are still far too self-destructive to think creatively. We cannot heal until a proper assessment has been performed and an appropriate diagnosis has been made. The sources of this self-destructiveness are complex, and yet there is a common thread that can be traced throughout human history and that thread is a failure to recover from the long-term effects of overwhelming traumatic stress. The results of this failure are passed on from generation to generation until even the definitions of normality and health are profoundly skewed and represent a post-traumatic adjustment. There has been relatively little ongoing social discourse about what full humanness is or what a society would look like, feel like, and be like that truly reflected the possibilities for humanity rather than its limitations.

Thus far in this book, we have put together a great deal of information that helps us assess the problem of violence. We have calculated the numbers of traumatized people presently in our cultural milieu. We have looked at the forces that are implicit in the society that are the fertile ground upon which the infection of trauma takes hold and spreads—corporal punishment, inadequate parenting, poverty, sexism, racism, and other forms of social stress, and deep questions of meaningless and spiritual alienation. We have looked at the source sites for the violence infection in the most important places where human beings live their lives—our homes, our schools, our workplaces, and our churches. We have reviewed the cultural activities that are jointly a reaction *to* the traumatic infection and carriers *of* the infection—firearms, pornography, and media violence. We have discussed our varying reactions to the infection—our attempts to isolate it through imprisonment, to ignore it through our failure to protect, and our individually unique ways of bouncing back from it that we call resiliency. And finally, we have described the infection itself—how it affects our various organ systems and functions in such a way as to make us both victims of and carriers of the infection of violence as its effects spread across and down through the generations.

In the next section we will look at the basic assumptions, values, goals, and processes that go into turning an environment into a truly safe place for children and adults. Out of these principles we can begin to understand that everyone has a role to play, that no one has to be an expert in order to play a beneficial role in another person's life. Now it is time to think about how this information has to change us, how we are to break out of the old and useless molds of the past, the patterns that determine traumatic re-enactment, and launch ourselves into a new and unpredictable future. Unpredictability is frightening for human beings, and yet the present pre-dictability of our behavior is—literally—killing us.

Given the complex nature of the problem of violence, it is understand-able that anyone would feel overwhelmed upon facing up to the question "What can I do?" Jim Wallis in his book, *The Soul of Politics* (1994) has pointed out that "America lacks a social vision" (p. 5). When Martin Luther King Jr. said, "I have a dream . . . " he was describing a process that is essential for change to begin in a nonviolent way. One of the far-reaching implications of quantum physics is that through our thoughts we play a significant role in creating reality. We must not leave this essential envision-ing up to prophets, geniuses, or fascist ideologues any longer. Each of us must begin to envision a world that is better, more humane, more livable and sustainable. Change for the better begins with a dream.

Implicit in the material we will present in the next section is a different vision of society. That vision is not so radically different that it would necessitate a violent revolution. Such an outcome, as so vividly demon-strated in the twentieth century, can only lead to more violence. To the extent that what we are describing is different, it differs most dramatically in terms of "attitude," most important, the attitude we hold when we face the other, the fellow members of our own—and other—species. And it differs in terms of consistency. The values we hold most dear must be the construction blocks for any different approach, but they must be consis-tently applied. And it differs in terms of balance or integration. As William James said, almost a century ago, "If the balance exists, no one faculty can possibly be too strong—we only get the stronger all-round character" (1902, p. 333). An individual is strengthened by integrating the various aspects of the self and so is a society.

In creating this vision of a better world, and in making that vision a reality, we all have a role to play. It cannot be accomplished without the massive human investment of time, love, and resources. And then there is an even more radical notion: creating and fulfilling this vision could be a great deal of fun. We can, if we choose, celebrate diversity, celebrate change, celebrate health, and celebrate life—together.

PART III:
A PUBLIC HEALTH APPROACH

DEFINING A PUBLIC HEALTH APPROACH

As health care providers, a significant motivation for writing this book is to convey to both the professional and the public community that there are no adequate medical solutions to the problems of violence. A public health approach makes much more sense and is far more likely to be effective. A public health approach focuses on prevention activities that generally occur at three levels: primary, secondary, and tertiary. Tertiary prevention directs services at reducing the negative consequences of whatever disease has already occurred and is presently taking a toll. Secondary prevention targets at-risk populations to alleviate conditions that are associated with the problem or disease. Primary prevention activities are directed at the general population with the goal of stopping the problem or disease before it starts. Prevention activities attempt to accomplish three major goals: to deter predictable problems, to protect existing states of health, and to promote desired life objectives (Bloom, M., 1996). A public health approach means thinking broadly, synthetically, and collaboratively. A public health approach necessitates mobilizing all of society's institutions to manage the problem. Let's look at some ideas, plans, suggestions, and programs that make sense from a public health perspective if we really want to do something about violence.

Chapter 7

Tertiary Prevention:
Fixing What Is Already Broken

Tertiary prevention focuses efforts on trying to treat whatever the problem is that is already established. So, in the case of infectious disease, it means treating the illness in those already infected and trying to prevent the spread of the disease by those infected. In the case of individual instances of family violence it can mean establishing programs such as intensive family interventions with counselors on a twenty-four hour basis, parent mentoring programs, and direct mental health services for children and families. If we apply tertiary level prevention ideas to an entire society, then we need some principles that will carry across the entire society.

TRAUMA-BASED PRINCIPLES FOR INTERVENTION

Regardless of what emergency measures we take, we must agree on a common knowledge base. Without a set of shared and articulated assumptions, as well as shared goals, our interventions are likely to be poorly planned, incoherent, and ultimately destructive. Trauma theory provides us with a shared theoretical base as a starting point for discussion about any possible intervention. Here are some basic assumptions that need to be shared implicitly if adequate, encompassing, and successful interventions are to be planned and implemented.

Shared Assumptions

- No child is born bad. Work with victims of trauma, in fact, convincingly demonstrates how hard children struggle against hostile environments and traumatizing experiences. It takes a great deal of mistreatment to channel a naturally cooperative and creative child toward destructive behaviors. When children act bad, that does not mean that they have *become* bad. Within every traumatic reenactment is a child who can be saved. Posttraumatic stress reactions are the reactions of normal people to abnormal stress. The key observation from clinical work with trauma survivors is that the human mind can be overwhelmed and that traumatization can affect behavior in persistent and pernicious ways. Generally speaking, the more severe the stressor, the earlier the age, the more impaired the social support system, the greater the degree of prior traumatization—the greater will be the posttraumatic effect.

• When people are traumatized, the effects of trauma interfere with normal functioning. Symptoms are usually adaptations that might once have been useful coping strategies but which, outside of the traumatizing experience, limit functioning. In this sense, victims of trauma become trapped in time, repetitively re-experiencing trauma.

• The systematic misuse and abuse of power creates both victims and perpetrators. Perpetrators are people who have learned to abuse power rather than be abused by it. Hurt people hurt people. Many victims will identify with the aggressor in a confused effort to overcome a sense of helplessness and to avoid feeling victimized. To the extent that the culture encourages certain groups to assume dominance over other groups and to exercise physical control over them, there is a higher likelihood that traumatized members of this group will perpetrate aggression and violence.

• In general, most trauma survivors wrestle with the issue of healing and forgiveness versus perpetration and revenge. Many victims fail to recognize the more subtle ways that victimization can turn into perpetration through the emotional abuse of others, extreme dependency, or self-destructive behaviors.

• People who are traumatized dissociate in order to cope with overwhelming feelings. The nature of the unhealed trauma is such that many can not recall having been hurt and have little idea of the connection between the original hurt and later problematic symptoms. Recovery and the re-establishment of control over behavior necessitate the integration of memory with awareness.

• Trauma survivors can become caught up in a prison of traumatic reenactment. Through the phenomenon of traumatic addiction and the unconscious compulsion to cycle through the traumatic memory in dreams, relationships, and other life choices, individuals who have dissociated from the injury are at risk for a repetitive spiral of exposure to new trauma.

- The need to relate to others, to attach, follows us from cradle to grave and provides the impetus for a natural healing capability that resides within every person. Disrupted attachment, abandonment and other betrayals of a child's trust can interfere with the working of this ability. But practically everyone can be said to have the capability to recover from trauma through a natural process of relating to others. A key factor in mitigating the effects of traumatic experience, in fact, is the availability of trusted relationships.

Shared Goals

Utopia may be unrealistic, but there really is no reason we have to settle for what we have now. It will take time to create a better society, but change always starts with a dream. We must share a vision of a society capable of creating and sustaining an atmosphere of kindness, respect, mutual regard, tolerance, and nonviolence rather than one of hostility, humiliation, exploitation, fear, disrespect, shame, or intolerance. To accomplish this we need to commit ourselves to make conscious what is unconscious, to make peace and eschew violence and to work toward alleviating the suffering and improving the level of functioning for everyone. We need to commit ourselves to the creation of both a civilized and a decent society. The philosopher Margalit describes a civilized society as one whose members do not humiliate one another, while a decent society is one in which the institutions do not humiliate people (1996). With these assumptions and goals as starting points, we can begin to formulate a public health strategy to restore health to the system. But we must start with some emergency measures if we are to get some control of a situation that is dangerously out of control.

EMERGENCY PRESCRIPTION
FOR THE BODY POLITIC

We must admit, as an entire society, that we do have a public health emergency, that violence is out of control and spreading its effects throughout the population at a rate far faster than any clinical measures can subdue. Such a situation, as in any public health emergency, calls for strident emergency measures. For a temporary period, when public health is at stake, dramatic steps must be taken in service of the public good. In

1985, the surgeon general convened a task force to study what measures need to be taken immediately if we were to alter the course of violence spreading throughout the country (Benedek, 1989). These were the recommendations of that task force:

Surgeon General's Recommendations

- There should be a complete and universal federal ban on the sale, manufacture, importation, and possession of handguns except for authorized police and military personnel; and regulations on the manufacture, sale, and distribution of other lethal weapons such as martial arts items (for example, numb chuck stars and knives).
- There should be criminal penalties associated with possession of any weapon where alcohol is sold or served.
- There should be development and implementation of a full employment policy for the nation with immediate attention aimed at the creation of jobs for those at high risk as either abusers or victims.
- There should be an aggressive government policy to reduce racial discrimination and sexism.
- There should be a decrease in the cultural acceptance of violence by discouraging corporal punishment in the home, forbidding corporal punishment in the school, and abolishing capital punishment by the state because all are models and sanctions of violence.
- There should be a decrease in the portrayal of violence on television and discouragement of the presentation of violent role models in all media forms with encouragement of the presentation of positive, nonviolent role models.
- The public should be made aware that alcohol consumption may be hazardous to health because of its association with violence.

Yes, these measures may, on the surface, sound drastic. Yes, it is true that the country appears to be moving in a direction that is diametrically opposed to such an approach. And yet, thirteen years have gone by since the recommendations were first made and in these thirteen years, our social welfare has decreased enormously. It was perfectly obvious thirteen years ago that these were the steps that needed to be taken to decrease the violence in our society. We lack courageous leadership. Making these necessary changes has significant implications for individual rights, but then who determines whose individual rights are cherished? Why is it that your right to carry a gun repeatedly overrides my right to walk the streets in safety? Particularly if I have demonstrated that I can responsibly walk the streets, while the rate of gun violence must lead us to seriously question whether Americans—as a whole—can safely be responsible for managing guns. Why must we go on protecting the right to kill more strenuously than we protect the right to live?

It is time for a wider dialogue about these issues that concern basic, fundamental safety. *The establishment of safety is the starting point for all efforts at healing.* To establish safety, there must be a social will to vehemently defend the rights of women, children, and minorities to be protected from those who abuse power. Community leaders have been meeting nationally and locally to address the problem of basic safety. Here are two examples, one from a major national think-tank conference, another from a local urban task force effort.

National Conference on Family Violence

In March 1994, an important three-day meeting of over 400 hundred professionals was held in Washington, DC. This was the National Conference on Family Violence: Health and Justice. The conference was organized by the American Medical Association and funded by the National Institute of Justice, the Centers for Disease Control and Prevention, and others. Cosponsored by over eighty-three organizations within health, social services, and justice systems, it grew out of an earlier AMA initiative to train physicians in identifying and responding appropriately to victims of family violence. Out of a series of working groups that met throughout the conference, recommendations were made in the areas of assessment, interventions, media, prevention, and professional education. In emphasis, all of the recommendations reflect the importance of interdisciplinary collaboration, empowerment of victims, perpetrator accountability, violence prevention, and the strengthening of families and communities.

Their recommendations, made almost ten years after those of the surgeon general, reflect the same critical concerns (Witwer and Crawford, 1995). Among many concerns that we will touch on later, they recommend that the problem of firearms be firmly dealt with in quite specific ways:

- Control the manufacture and sale of ammunition and its components.
- Tax weapons, ammunition, and ammunition components sufficient to pay for the results of firearm violence.
- Mandate recurring licensing and training owners of firearms.
- Ban assault weapons and the ammunition that supports them.

The Safe Neighborhood Network

We each have to pause and ask how long we are going to let this insane arms race within our own borders continue. Communities around the country are struggling with the reality that although gun control could go a long way toward reducing the problem of violence, the political situation is such that the bullying tactics of the National Rifle Association and their supporters are not soon to be overcome. As a consequence, we have to look for ways around such obstacles if we are to save the lives of young people. There is much that can be done to enhance the quality of life for these kids, to improve other opportunities for them besides selling drugs, and to get them the kinds of social service interventions that they need. Philadelphia Physicians for Social Responsibility is administering a five-year, multidisciplinary community-based project called the Safe Neighborhood Network. The goal of the project is to reduce youth violence and the risk of firearm injury and death in several of the ethnically mixed, impoverished, and dangerous neighborhoods in the city, including "The Badlands," so named because it is the center of the street drug trade. Coalition partners in the project include the Temple University Department of Health Studies, the Temple Law Education and Participation program and the Children's Hospital of Philadelphia. Organizational meetings were held with representatives from the District Attorney's Office, the Bureau of Alcohol, Tobacco, and Firearms, the Philadelphia School District, the Philadelphia Police Department, the Juvenile Defenders Office, the Juvenile Law Center, Family Court, the Department of Recreation, several area health centers and hospitals, and the Office of Housing.

Needs assessment is still underway but it is intended that assessment, training, and technical assistance within the participating communities will support area health care personnel in the following ways:

- Anticipatory guidance in health care settings in firearm safety and violence prevention
- Screen and interventions for aggressive/antisocial behaviors
- Family violence interventions
- Counseling of adolescents on weapons, substance abuse, anger management, and conflict resolution
- Counseling of young people exposed to violence
- Emergency room responses, including education and referral for intentional injury victims
- Interdisciplinary youth education collaborations
- Participation in community response teams that intervene in the community following episodes of violence.

HEALING AS INTEGRATION

What *is* healing? For our purposes here we define healing as "integration," the ability of any system to function harmoniously as a whole without attempting to destroy any parts of the whole. This concept can be used as a metaphor for the individual or for a group as large as a nation. The hallmark of trauma is fragmentation. That is what a traumatic experience does—it fragments—or dissociates—functions so that they lose their interconnectedness and each fragment then takes on an autonomy of its own that will be in conflict with the whole. Dissociated memories are split off from consciousness but continue to play a role in determining behavior at a level at which the individual can exert little control. Children "dissociated" from a family begin to function in opposition to the family with a subsequent loss of basic integrity of the family system. A group of people dissociated from the whole are forced to develop ways of being, thinking, and behaving that are often in serious, sometimes destructive conflict with the whole. The entire principle of democracy rests on a conceptualization that envisions every person, every group as being an essential part of the whole cloth that comprises the nation. Oppression toward any of the parts will cause traumatic dissociation and result in any of the forms of destructive behavior on the large group level that we can see readily occurring on the individual level.

Judith Herman has identified stages in healing from individual trauma: the establishment of safety, remembering and grieving for past losses, and reconnection (Herman, 1992). Regardless of the particular trauma, people who are fragmented need to experience all of these stages if healing is to occur. We believe it is possible to make some important generalizations to larger groups from work with individuals and we believe these principles of intervention have far-ranging implications for social institutions as well.

ESTABLISHING SAFETY

Since its inception, America has been a place of sanctuary for groups of people who have been forced to flee from some form of personal or political oppression in their native land. As a people, we are getting stingier and stingier about providing that sanctuary for others, and perhaps most important, at providing it for ourselves. America is not a safe place. Not if you are a woman, a child, an old person, a sick person, a poor person, or anything but a white person. And it is no longer a particularly safe place for white men either.

Safety is where healing must begin. No healing can take place until the person is physically safe. The establishment of safety is precisely why measures such as gun control are so essential if we are to heal as a nation. Healing cannot even begin until we all feel safer just walking down the street. Now let's look at what else goes into healing from trauma.

Whether in the case of an abused child, a battered spouse, a car crash victim, or a disaster victim, safety comes first. No further work of integration can occur until the person's physiological well-being has been stabilized. Any attempts at understanding, remembering, discussing, or contemplating the past experience of trauma is useless unless the person is calm, feels some degree of security, and is no longer in a physically hyperaroused state. But a sense of safety does not just rely on physical safety, but also on harder-to-define "psychological," "social," and "moral" safety as well (Bloom, 1997). We can feel psychologically safe when our selfhood is respected and when we are in environments in which our own separate identity is affirmed and reinforced. We can feel socially safe when we are in environments with other people, all of whom agree on basic rules of how to behave with each other and who are willing and able to contain and help modulate each other's overwhelming emotional experiences. We are in an environment of moral safety when there is an agreed upon, compassionate way of making sense of the world, a process for working through hypocrisy, and a shared vision of future possibilities.

Creating Sanctuary

For a car crash victim who comes from a loving and compassionate family who spontaneously knows how to help someone in distress, the provision of psychological, social, and moral safety is likely to occur naturally. For victims of interpersonal trauma however, particularly if the violence is experienced at the hands of family members, it is unlikely that the victim's sense of safety will be easily restored because the family, having failed to protect one of its members, is *not* psychologically, socially, or morally safe. As a result, such victims often need a "corrective emotional environment" which allows them multiple opportunities to experience all levels of safety at once. We call the process of creating and maintaining such an environment "creating sanctuary" (Bloom, 1994; 1995a; 1997).

"Creating sanctuary" refers to the shared experience of creating and maintaining safety within any social environment. Within such a social space, people can stabilize their internal physiology, begin to let down their guard, rest, and laugh in the comforting presence of other human beings, learn and share important information that can assist with complex decision making, experiment with new ways of being and relating, grieve over past losses, and avail themselves of opportunities to expand their context of meaning. None of these gifts of our higher intelligence are possible until violence to self and others has stopped. As long as the threat of violence is present, our minds and bodies cannot rest, we cannot think clearly, we cannot resolve emotional conflicts, and we cannot find meaning in our lives. Sanctuary is what we find through the shared, contained, and compassionate experience of other human souls.

Establishing social environments in which sanctuary can be created is essential if we are to heal from the wounds that we already have and if we are to begin truly protecting our children. But how do we create social safety? What goes into creating and maintaining an environment in which people feel safe enough to explore the past while opening themselves up to positive change for the future? Relatively little attention has been paid to this question. We seem to take it for granted that we know how to create environments of social safety and yet most people can recount experiences in social settings in which they felt threatened, frightened, or overtly abused. We have discussed the physical dangers that are so evident today in our schools, workplaces, hospitals, and homes. But it is not just physical danger that is a problem. Overt violence is the endpoint of a continuum of behaviors that originates in the more common and routine neglect and bruising of many relationships. The study of disturbed family systems has taught us a great deal about how human relationships go wrong. Before we can figure out how to do it right, it is often useful to look at what it is like when something goes wrong. Let's look at some characteristics of a "dysfunctional" system.

Sick Systems

Unhealthy systems are those in which members are frequently hurt in both psychological and physical ways. Some of the characteristics of such systems are known. Typically such systems are riddled by collective denial of problems and shared and shameful secrets. A lack of honesty exists between system members—a web of lies that is difficult to penetrate. The system tends to stay isolated from other systems so that information is not easily shared. The isolation helps maintain the atmosphere of secrecy and ignorance. The leaders of the system control information and manipulate the information that is available to other members of the system and in doing so, they define reality for everyone. Often unclear and shifting roles among members of the system result in diffuse and confusing personal boundaries. Differences are poorly tolerated among members of the system and no good mechanism for conflict resolution exists.

Instead of being resolved, conflicts are kept submerged for as long as possible. If they finally rise to the surface they are dealt with in a highly moralistic, and usually hypocritical way. The open expression of emotions, especially the positive emotions that lead to joy, laughter, play, relaxation, friendship, affection, tolerance, forgiveness, and mutual self-regard, are discouraged or actively inhibited. Negative emotions such as anger, shaming, ridicule, cynicism, and humiliation are far better tolerated or even encouraged in such systems. Violence or the threat of violence is permitted, supported, and used as an ongoing method to control the behavior and experience of others (Courtois, 1988).

If you are trying to function within such a system—be it family, school, workplace, congregation, organization, or nation—then you know exactly what it feels like to be in one. It does not feel good. If you are a child in a family or classroom such as this, you will end up having to spend most of your time and energy just trying to protect yourself and there will be little stamina left over for growth, exploration, curiosity, or creativity. Thus you will get blamed for underachieving. If you think that perhaps you or someone you know is receiving unfair treatment in such a system, you will be punished for protesting and bullied back into conformity. If you continue to protest, you will be punished into silence by coercion, threats, abuse, ridicule, or the loss of personal freedom. If you are smart enough, rather than be silenced, you will either learn how to be a bully yourself or you will figure out ways to protest that are so obtuse that no one in a position of authority will recognize that you are protesting. And, if you are really smart, you will figure out a way to subtly protest and still have some fun without making those in power so angry or threatened that they hurt you or silence you. Regardless of the path you choose, the oppressions that are inherent in such systems will change and deform your character. Those deformations may end up doing you and everyone a great deal of good or they may end up with you spending your life in prison or going to the electric chair, but you will never have the opportunity to find out who you would have been had those system forces not been coercing you to grow and twist yourself into the shapes they wanted.

This is worth thinking about because our historical systems have been so repetitively oppressive to so many aspects of the human spirit that we really have no way of knowing the extent of human potential for good. This century, however, has provided us with a very clear idea of our potential for evil. What would human society be like if we were raised and lived in less oppressive systems that were truly responsive to human emotional, intellectual, and spiritual needs? All our concepts about human beings are fundamentally skewed by our immersion in dysfunctional systems from the moment of birth, and that has been true throughout most of recorded history. Maybe all men would be aggressive killers without a complex system of punishment that begins at birth. Maybe war is inevitable and all we can do is search for ways to contain it. Maybe the suffering of women is the inevitable price of the forced dependency of childbearing. Or maybe these and other underlying assumptions about the basic nature of humankind are dreadfully biased, unbalanced, and self-fulfilling. We really do not know.

Group Safety

We do, however, have the beginnings of some insights from people who have been the most victimized by oppressive systems—soldiers, refugees, concentration camp survivors, child abuse victims, victims of torture and kidnapping. And we know something about the alternative systems designed to help them begin the process of healing. After World War II many POWs and combat veterans needed hospital treatment for their psychological problems that were secondary to combat stress or imprisonment. Some innovative psychiatrists in the United States and Britain experimented with a new kind of hospital-based treatment termed the "therapeutic community." The therapeutic community was designed to provide a microcosm of the real world, an experimental laboratory for behavior change. Much of what we now understand about human social behavior derives from work accomplished in such therapeutic communities (Bloom, 1997; Clark, 1975; Jones et al., 1953; Jones 1968; Wilmer, 1958, 1964).

In principle, when people get together in a group, the group takes on a life of its own that transcends the individuals within the group. As a consequence, groups are an extremely powerful influence on human behavior. Such power can be exercised to bring about great destruction as in wartime on the battlefield, or as in Nazi Germany. But group energy can also be harnessed for the good—witness the civil rights movement, the women's movement, and the antinuclear movement—all examples of a group process experience of change. However, to promote a positive outcome to a group experience, certain rules of structure and function must be adhered to by the entire group.

The first requirement for any group to function effectively is physical safety. This is a factor that we can no longer take for granted in any institutional setting and must be the starting point for any group intervention. Establishing safety requires the active participation of the entire group. It is also a process that must be continually maintained. No group can afford to be ambivalent about violence. The starting point must be the absolute unacceptability of violence in *any* form. This includes violence against the self. In a working group, violence to one is violence to all.

When there has been a breach in physical safety and a dangerous, threatening, or violent situation has occurred, then active efforts must be made to reestablish the sense of safety, and everyone must participate. This means that safety must be openly and honestly addressed on a regular basis within any group or community. All too often the approach to violence within groups is to hush it up afterward, to pretend that nothing has happened, and to try to keep the effects confined. This is impossible. When violence has broken out, everyone knows it. They can actually feel the results in the atmosphere around them even if they remain ignorant of the details of the event. In fact, the emotional contagion of violent events is more likely to provoke further violent acting out if a wall of silence is maintained because people react to and feel the violent emotions without knowing why. It is important, therefore, that everyone participate in understanding the situation that bred the violence, analyze the reactions to the violence when it occurred and immediately afterward, and learn important lessons from the experience that can help promote better prevention.

Episodes of violence must always be perceived as a failure of the group to contain and modulate overwhelming emotions. If violence breaks out in a classroom, then the entire class must participate in analyzing the situation, breaking it down into its parts, and planning for ways to prevent such outbreaks in the future. If violence occurs in the workplace, the same process must occur. And, unlike our usual way of doing things, the entire group must be involved. *Violence is a group phenomenon. The violent person is the weak link in a complex chain of interaction that culminates in violence after a cascade of previous, apparently nonviolent, events. When violence has occurred, the entire group has failed to prevent it, not just the individuals immediately involved.*

Occasions of uncontrollable violence may necessitate the loss of group members in order to preserve the integrity of the group. We are a long way from overcoming the need for prisons. The well-being of the whole must not be threatened by the disease of the part. There are times when an individual's leg or arm is so diseased that a limb must be amputated. The same holds true for the group. However, every effort should be made short of "amputation," to save the limb, or save the group member, because an amputation means a serious and permanent loss to the function of the whole that may only be recognized long after the limb has been severed. This is basic ecological thinking. A child whose arm has been cut off may not recognize the full cost to autonomy until he or she is sixteen and ready—but not able—to drive without assistance. So too, each member of a group has an inherent potential for the well-being of the group that may not be realized until some time in the distant future, and the loss of that member may impair the group function long after there is any remedy.

Controlling violence in any group is vital because trauma theory has convinced us of the importance of emotions in determining human behavior. We understand now that our reactions to each other are often the most critical determinant of whether someone feels comforted and becomes calmer, or feels hurt and frightened and escalates from outrage to violence. Therefore, one of the main goals of any successful group must be to provide predictable and reliable opportunities for modulation of affect—for helping people feel better when they are distressed. We know that humans can only think well when they are calm, and therefore the outcome of any group process will be determined not just by the intellectual abilities of the group members, but also by their emotional states.

This being the case, under what circumstances does a group of people feel most emotionally safe? One critical factor is the authority structure of the group. Democracy, thus far, has proven to be the most effective form of national government. But the same can be said of small groups as well, including a group as small and central as the family. Democratic principles work best to afford people within a group a sense of fair play, equity, and voice. In a democratic process, change occurs most constructively through consensus. And the best decisions come about through diversity of opinion, knowledge, and experience. Decisions that are made by arriving at a consensus often take longer to reach than decisions made in an authoritarian system, but in the long run they tend to cause far fewer problems because the opposition has been worked through ahead of time rather than after the fact.

Group process works, but requires more time and energy in the beginning while trust is forming between the group members. The group must be safe enough to support dissent so that "groupthink" does not occur. When a group has caught the "disease" of groupthink, members try so hard to agree with one another that they commit serious errors that could easily have been avoided. Consensus appears to emerge out of the group process but it is a false consensus because all of the members of the group are simply focusing on the way they agree and refusing to look at divergent or contradictory information. All group members share a sense of invulnerability conveyed by nothing except that they are in this group together and therefore such intelligent people could not be mistaken. This kind of thinking leads to decisions that spell disaster (Forsyth, 1990; Janis, 1972).

In any group, there may be times when it is absolutely necessary for group leaders to resort to authoritarian practices, i.e., when there is an immediate need for quick decisions and leadership. However, the practice of consensus should be restored as quickly as possible. Group leaders have an essential task in their ability to articulate the group vision and goals, the group expectations, values, and norms. They must also be willing and able to reassert these same norms when there have been aberrations from the usual group standards. The ongoing challenge for leaders is to promote interdependency without promoting hierarchical dependency on the leaders. Group leaders should see themselves as facilitators rather than authority figures.

Conflicts must be resolved. Unresolved conflicts are like splinters lodged in the group skin. Left to fester, they can easily become open sores threatening the integrity and the very life of the group. Conflict resolution is a skill and an art that must be learned and practiced. A method for resolving conflicts must be a fundamental part of any group function and the expectation of conflict resolution should be part of the group's standard behavior. Conflict should be resolved at the level at which it occurs and resort to a higher level of authority should only happen if the immediate conflict appears irresolvable by the parties involved.

In the early stages of group work, conflicts often present threats to stability. However, conflict provokes change and growth. Dissent is absolutely essential to group process if a group is to develop as a living being, and therefore such dissent must be welcomed. For this to happen, the group must move away from competition and "getting the best" of the other guy, and instead move toward a model of interaction in which the entire group values the integration of dissenting viewpoints as a true test of group viability. This requires a shift away from our typical mode of individualistic thinking and toward a position in which each individual is a valued part of a larger whole.

The Buddhist Practice of Conflict Resolution

Thich Nhat Hanh is a Buddhist monk from Vietnam, who has been instrumental in bringing Buddhist practices to the attention of the West. In his writing he has shared the 2,500-year-old Buddhist system of seven practices of reconciliation, originally formulated to settle disputes within a circle of monks (1987). The first practice is *Face-to-Face Sitting* in which everyone involved sits together, mindfully, breathing and smiling with a willingness to help and an unwillingness to fight. Where there are two conflicting people, they should be sitting facing each other and surrounded by others of the community who expect them to make peace. Everything that is to be said is said to all, and within the community, not outside and not as rumor.

The second practice is *Remembrance.* Both individuals who are party to the conflict try to remember and recount the entire history of the conflict and every surrounding detail of the life having to do with the conflict, while everyone else patiently sits and listens. The more detail the community has, the easier it is to help.

The third principle is *Non-stubbornness.* Everyone in the community sets an expectation that the people involved in the conflict will not be stubborn, that they will work toward reconciliation.

The fourth practice is *Covering Mud with Straw.* One respected, usually senior member of the community is appointed to represent each side of the conflict. These two advisors then address the assembly, trying to say something to de-escalate the feelings of the people concerned. In the course of this dialogue, each advisor is "laying down straw across the mud"—soothing the feelings of both parties in the conflict. The mud is the dispute and the straw is the loving-kindness that is applied.

The next stage is *Voluntary Confession.* Each party to the dispute reveals his or her own shortcomings, without waiting for others to voice them. As one makes a small confession, it gives the other permission and encouragement to do the same. The atmosphere is encouraging. Everyone is supportive, expecting that de-escalation will be realized. In such an atmosphere, the capacity for mutual understanding and acceptance can be born. The senior advisors make it clear to both parties in the conflict that they must consider the well-being of the community.

The sixth and seventh practices are *Decision by Consensus* and *Accepting the Verdict.* It is agreed in advance that both conflicting parties will accept whatever verdict is pronounced by the whole assembly, or they will have to leave the community. After exploring every detail of the conflict, after realizing the maximum of reconciliation, a committee presents a verdict. It is announced three times. The head of the community reads the decision in this way: "After meditation, after exploration, after discussion, after all efforts have been made, it is suggested that this person will do so and so, that person will do so and so, this should be repaired in this way, that should be repaired in that way. Does the assembly accept this verdict?" Silence means "okay." The leader makes this announcement three times. If silence remains, he pronounces that the community has accepted the verdict, and instructs both parties to carry out the decision.

For the individual, there is a price to pay with such an approach and that price is responsibility for the well-being and growth of the group. Each individual is responsible for the whole. Scapegoating and blaming are seen as inadequate, naive, and stupid pseudosolutions to complex group problems. They represent a failure of group process, even though the group often experiences them as an enormous relief of pressure. We regularly use other people as "poison containers" (DeMause, 1974; 1982) for our own unwanted feelings. This is behavior that originates in childhood when parents take out their unresolved feelings on their children. "Dumping" on other people becomes a way of life, a preferred method for dealing with others.

The group must unashamedly and unabashedly articulate group norms for how people are to treat each other, fearlessly using such words as kindness, respect, tolerance, and mutual regard. Robert Fulghum (1989, p. 29) has pointed out that the most important things that we need to know about how to deal with each other, we learned in kindergarten—"share everything, play fair, don't hit people, say you're sorry when you hurt feelings." Sadly, we seem to forget many of these things on the way to becoming adults, even though we may go on behaving as if we were still five years old. It is time to go back to these early and essential lessons and reassert them as standards for getting along with other people. These norms must then be applied with particular emphasis on the ways in which ideas and attitudes are conveyed as much as to the ideas and attitudes themselves. Trauma theory has taught us the value of nonverbal communication and the role it plays as the heart of human interactions. Group members must be held accountable for their nonverbal as well as their verbal behavior.

Whenever two or more people get together, traumatic reenactment may be a potential problem. We must all develop a better understanding about how this very basic principle of human interaction works and how to manage it when it appears. As we have already pointed out earlier, people unconsciously reenact the experience of their earlier lives. If those experiences have been traumatic, then they will compulsively draw other people into their drama, cueing others in a way that will compel them to repeat the pain of the past. This is the core of human interaction that we must learn to resist. We must begin to see this behavior on the part of the Other as a "cry for help." In acting out their painful experiences they are signaling their distress in the only way they can—nonverbally and through behavior. As a responsible part of the whole it is our social and moral obligation to respond to that cry for help. We must learn to respond not by giving in to the cues for reenactment but by reflecting back to the injured person what we are being cued to do and refusing to do it—openly, consciously, deliberately, and meaningfully. In their approach to violence this is the essential lesson of Jesus Christ, Gandhi, and Martin Luther King Jr.—refuse to play the game. It is a case of the old, still rhetorical question: "What if they gave a war and nobody came?"

FORGETTING THE PAST MEANS REPEATING IT

What do we know about memory and healing? Why can we not just leave the past in the past? Why do past traumas haunt people? The answers to these questions lie in understanding what trauma does to the vital function of memory. As we explained earlier, states of extreme emotional arousal seem to shut down the normal verbal system of memory processing. Instead, the experience of trauma is recorded in the form of nonverbal images, emotions, and body sensations. These nonverbal forms then keep intruding into consciousness in all kinds of thinly disguised or highly symbolized forms, compelling reenactments of the traumatic experience. Early in the history of understanding the effects of trauma both Freud and Janet "claimed that the crucial factor that determines the repetition of trauma is the presence of mute, unsymbolized and unintegrated experiences" (Van der Kolk and Ducey, 1989, p. 271). Freud said,

> He reproduces it not as a memory but as an action; he repeats it without, of course, knowing that he is repeating . . . he cannot escape from this compulsion to repeat; and in the end we understand that this is his way of remembering. (Van der Kolk and Ducey, 1989, p. 270)

Janet described the ways in which people became attached to the trauma, unable to move ahead with their own development because they had not assimilated the memories, meaning they had not put the memories into a narrative form that could then assign the memories to the past. The traumatic memories had never been categorized and given meaning so that they remained unattached fragments, continuing to intrude into consciousness as terrifying perceptions, overwhelming feelings, and painful bodily experiences. Janet said it is "as if their personality development has stopped at a certain point and cannot be expanded any more by the addition or assimilation of new elements" (Van der Kolk and Ducey, 1989, p. 270).

As Van der Kolk and Ducey (1989) have so clearly articulated, "A sudden and passively endured trauma is relived repetitively until the person learns to remember simultaneously the affect and the cognition associated with trauma through access to language" (p. 270). It is *integration* that is the vital goal of remembering the past. We function best when we function as a whole and as long as we are fragmented, our function will be compromised. When we remember what has happened to us and reexperience the dissociated emotion, then and only then can we put the experience into a meaningful perspective and fit it into some category requiring language that allows us to put it aside. Only when a memory is put into language can it be shared with other people. After all, we must remember that the "sudden and uncontrollable loss of attachment bonds is an essential element in the development of post-traumatic stress syndromes" (Van der Kolk, 1989, p. 393). The capacity to relate and to trust other people must also be restored after trauma and it can only happen if the traumatized person can share this experience with others through language.

Collective Remembering

The philosopher George Santayana said, "Those who cannot remember the past are condemned to repeat it." We know that this is true among populations of traumatized individuals. But what about groups of people? The subject of collective remembering and forgetting is relatively new and little has been written about it until recently (Pennebaker, Paez, and Rimé, 1997). As in the lives of our patients, the past plays a large role in determining the present and the future, so we are wise to gain an understanding of the critical role that collective memory plays in our group life.

Pennebaker (1997a, p. 17) has summarized some important findings thus far in the study of collective memory. Collective memories are most likely to be formed and maintained about events that represent significant long-term changes in people's lives and social institutions. When this change does not occur, the events are far less likely to become part of a society's collective memory, even if that event was a major upheaval at the time it took place. Memories are more likely to be formed if people actively talk and think about events a great deal and this social sharing helps shape the perceptions of the event so that a shared narrative forms. But if the event does not change the course of history, talking about it appears to help people assimilate it and ultimately, forget it. Emotionally charged events that people avoid discussing will continue to affect them through increased thinking and dreaming about the events. As a consequence, political repression of speech is more likely to keep the memory alive. Events that have a collective psychological impact result in collective individual behaviors so that following significant cultural events, changes in crime, suicide, physical health, and even prosocial behaviors can be expected. Major national events affect people of different ages in different ways so that in general, people between the ages of twelve and twenty-five at the time of the event will be most affected by it and those events will have the greatest impact on the collective memories of that generation. People tend to look back and commemorate the past in cyclic patterns that appear to occur every twenty to thirty years in the form of movies, monuments, and books.

It has been noted that it is usually the victors in any struggle who write the history books and the voice of those who have been oppressed by the superior power—and often violence—of the victors is lost. According to the philosopher Halbwachs, the function of socially shared images of the past is to allow the group to foster social cohesion, to develop and defend social identification, and to justify current attitudes and needs (Paez, Basabe, and Gonzalez, 1997). But there are also memories of traumatic political events that are "silent memories," usually repressed, which although forgotten continue to divide a society, much as the same kind of "forgetting" divides an individual. Research being conducted on this subject is beginning to demonstrate that one of the purposes of collective memory, in fact, is to forget (Paez, Basabe, and Gonzalez, 1997).

> Because of the normative nature of collective memory aimed at defending social identity, a common response to a traumatic past event is silence and inhibition. Groups organize informal forgetting, reconstruction, and positive distortion of the past in order to defend group values and their own image. . . . Social history studies suggest that forgetting and silence is a very common reaction. (p. 161)

Although in the short term, such forgetting may serve useful social purposes, research is beginning to demonstrate that inhibiting the social sharing of traumatic events impedes the cognitive assimilation of the experience. Neglecting to work through trauma can lead to rumination, increased individual physiological arousal, as well as collective distress. This distress can then manifest through increases in aggression and illness (Paez, Basabe, and Gonzalez, 1997; Pennebaker, 1990). As we have seen in individual victims of trauma, failing to assimilate the memories of the traumatic experience often leads to physical, emotional, and behavioral symptoms, most of which are destructive to self and others. According to clinical wisdom, the most difficult memories to assimilate are those connected with one's own acts of perpetration. In treatment, these are typically the last to surface, and the most difficult to work through. If that is the case for individuals, it is also possible that it is the case for nations as well. People who have deliberately perpetrated acts of cruelty and violence against others have a vested interest in denying guilt and avoiding the consequences of their act. And since we identify part of our sense of self with the groups we belong to, we all collude with this denial to avoid the unpleasant consequences of our social acts, not just our individual acts. But this denial will make us sick as a nation, just as individual denial of traumatic reality leads to sickness.

There is a growing understanding of this reality. Certainly, since World War II there have been numerous individual and collective attempts to hold Germany accountable for the Nazi era. More recently, in Chile, the National Commission for Truth and Reconciliation was established in 1990 to address gross violations of human rights during the military dictatorship that stretched from 1973 to 1990. The commission was created because it was generally felt that the past was "an open wound," affecting all of Chilean society that had to be healed if the past were not to be repeated. But there has been enormous resistance to remembering the past and to date, most of the perpetrators have not been held accountable (Lira, 1997; Paez, Basabe, and Gonzalez, 1997).

South Africa is wrestling with a similar issue, creating the Truth and Reconciliation Commission. The Commission recognized that it must deal with three major questions, questions that bear a striking resemblance to the fundamental questions of individual survivors: (1) How do emerging democracies deal with past violations of human rights? (2) How do new democratic governments deal with leaders and individuals who were responsible for disappearances, death squads, psychological and physical torture, and other violations of human rights? and (3) How does a new democracy deal with the fact that some of the perpetrators remain part of the new government and/or security forces or hold important positions in public life? (Boraine, 1996). As the Minister of Justice, Dullah Omar has said, "We recognized that we could not forgive perpetrators unless we attempt also to restore the honor and dignity of the victims and give effect to reparation . . . we need to heal our country if we are to build a nation which will guarantee peace and stability" (Omar, 1996).

These questions are not that different from those of individual victims of trauma who ask (1) How do I deal with the people who have harmed me? (2) Shouldn't my perpetrators be held accountable for what they did to me? and (3) What do I do about the fact that my perpetrator is still a member of the family or workplace or community?

That is true of Chile and South Africa—but what about the United States? How effective are we at collective remembering when it comes to our participation in events that involved perpetration against others? According to Tina Rosenberg, "Nations, like individuals, need to face up to and understand traumatic past events before they can put them aside and move on to normal life" (p. xviii, 1995). As a nation, we are in the process of occasionally "remembering," our past, although we have difficulty remembering a past that challenges the assumptions of the established order. The Vietnam era monuments and the Holocaust museum are part of this remembering and commemorating. But the Vietnam monuments commemorate the sacrifice of America's children in battle and we do not feel responsible for the Holocaust. What about the memory of events for which we as a nation bear significant responsibility? Opportunities for remembering periodically crop up in the social environment. On the fiftieth anniversary of the dropping of the bombs over Hiroshima and Nagasaki, the Smithsonian decided to mount an exhibit that came under strong criticism before it was even opened. The criticism centered on the fact that the exhibit was attempting to show the United States in less than the golden light of pure intentions from a historical point of view. But the forces of suppression were more powerful than the need to remember, and the exhibit was cleansed of any essence of our shared guilt. According to a visitor to the monument in Hiroshima dedicated to the victims of the bomb, the comments from the international community that are placed there share in the tragedy of the victims—except for many of the comments from the United States, which focus on denying responsibility and placing blame on the Japanese.

The issue of slavery is recurrently in the news: an elementary school wants to change its name from George Washington because he was a slaveowner; a CNBC show focuses on whether the United States should apologize for slavery and make restitution to African Americans; Spielberg launches a new movie to remind us of what slavery was really like. We wrestle with remembering and forgetting. Every now and then, some news item or motion picture reminds us of the first people we "ethnically cleansed"—the Native Americans—those we keep isolated in faraway places, much as our patients keep parts of themselves isolated and separated in their minds. Then some book appears to remind us that we owe a powerful and positive legacy to these people who now we largely ignore (Johansen, 1982). We hear—and deny—and forget—and then hear again —stories of our government's illegal involvement in atrocities committed around the world, all in the name of freedom and democracy, and we shut it out, we forget. We pretend that it is not us, it does not mean anything, it did not really happen, or if it did, it was for a good reason that we cannot really be expected to understand. These kinds of rationalizations on a national scale are reminiscent of the same rationalizations you can hear every day should you visit a criminal court proceeding: "I didn't do it, but if I did do it I didn't really mean it, because I didn't know what I was doing, and besides he/she/it deserved it, and everyone knows that it didn't happen anyway."

These are all questionable actions of the past, sins of the fathers back to the third generation and beyond. What about acts of perpetration in the present? We even have difficulties with our short-term memory. How else to explain cutting off welfare without designing systems to save impoverished families? We forget as quickly as we hear it that: children constitute 38 percent of nation's poor; that one in every five children lives below the federal poverty line; that one in ten lives in extreme poverty which is defined as living at less than 50 percent of the federal poverty level; that 43 percent of black children and 41 percent of Hispanic children live below the poverty line; and that families who make less than $15,000 per year are twenty-two times more likely to maltreat their children (Gallo, 1997). It goes right in and out of our heads that the incidence of serious injuries to children quadrupled between 1986 and 1993; that one in five pediatricians have treated a gun injury in the last twelve months (Olson, Christoffel, and O'Connor, 1997); that one in eight American women will be raped (Kilpatrick, Edmunds, and Seymour, 1992); that over 50 percent of women will be battered (National Victim Center, 1993); that one out of every four employees will be harassed, threatened, or attacked at work (Yarborough, 1994); and that 83 percent of Americans will be victims of violent crime.

The price for forgetting acts of perpetration in the life of an individual is more perpetration, either against the self or against others—or more usually, both. We must consider that the price we are paying for our national forgotten and denied perpetration is also more perpetration in the form of self and other destructiveness. If we are to heal as a nation, if we are to stop the violence as we say we want to do, then we are going to have to remember even the ugly, awful things we have done to others. We need some national Twelve Steps that include "taking a fearless moral inventory" and "making amends."

How can a society heal? Once an individual is willing to confront problems, he or she can go to a therapist. But who are the "therapists" for a society? The therapists that we have to count on, the only ones who are in a position to do the job, are the media and our artists.

The Media and Remembering

At present, counting on the media to help us heal as a nation is a bit like going to a therapist who has problems worse than your own. We have already noted what an important role the media immersion in violence has to play in contributing to the violence in society. We are addicts and they are pushers. But it does not have to be that way. The national public knows what the national television networks continue to deny. In a Harris poll of 1985, 78 percent of the public disapproved of media violence, and in a Times Mirror poll in 1993, 80 percent said entertainment violence was harmful to society. When Electronic Media took a survey of its own 100 general managers, 75 percent said that there is too much needless violence on television, and a *U.S. News and World Report* survey in 1994 found that 59 percent of Hollywood media workers saw media violence as a serious problem (Gerbner, 1996). We know the addiction is wrong; we just do not have the will to detoxify.

There are signs that a growing number of journalists, both out in the field and in academia, are turning away from the rampant promulgation of violence and toward more thoughtful, balanced, and constructive reporting, even if there are few signs yet that this is affecting commercial television or print media. In 1996, the Nieman Report devoted an issue to "Violence: Do the Media Understand It? Do the Media Abet It?" One of the journalists, Michael Kirkhorn wrote,

> The direction American journalism must take, and in some places already is taking, is to report the extent and consequences of violence by doing what the media is supposed to do, apply careful observation and intelligent explanation to the issues in combination with a careful examination of its causes and a refined sensitivity to its circumstances and effects. If there are social and political reasons for the widespread prevalence of violence they should be explained to the American people. . . . In an age when violence is an issue that cannot be evaded, journalism's moral responsibility is intellectual. It is, simply, to be as smart as possible, therefore resourceful, therefore imaginative, comprehensive and interesting, in its reporting on the topic . . . a journalistic equivalent of moral purpose could be found in a determined—indeed a crusading—desire to bring to bear the powers of observation needed to allow us to explain to ourselves the wilderness of American violence. The keystone of this effort would be, not empathy or sensitivity or compassion, though these have always been ingredients of great reporting, but intelligence. (1996, p. 7)

Frank Ochberg is a psychiatrist and adjunct professor in journalism. As a hostage negotiator and advisor to the FBI, U.S. Secret Service, U.S. Air Force, and the National Security Council, he had many opportunities to interface with the media. In 1991, he and faculty member, Bill Coté, founded the Michigan State University's School of Journalism's "Victims and the Media Program" with funding from the Dart Foundation of Mason, Michigan. The purpose of the program is to enhance understanding of the effects of violence on victims and to improve the interpersonal skills required to approach and interview victims. The program holds seminars and workshops both on and off campus, conducts specialized classroom instruction, publishes literature, produces videotapes, maintains a Web site, and sponsors the Dart Award. This is a $10,000 award funded by the Dart Foundation and given annually to the newspaper demonstrating the best team effort in coverage of victims and their experiences. A similar effort, the "Journalism and Trauma" program, has also been started by Roger Simpson at the University of Washington School of Communication.

As these ideas spread, we may yet see some change in the quality of media reporting in print and even in television. We need to remember that our awareness of the problems that exist is largely due to the influence of the media. We know as much as we do about domestic violence, child abuse, and related social stresses because our newspapers and our television shows have intensively reported on these subjects. But that is not enough. This is like going to a therapist every week, week after week, and having the therapist diagnose your problems without offering treatment— necessary but not sufficient. We need to know about solutions as much as we need to identify the problems. But perhaps what is most important, we need role models; we need to know how to intelligently and comprehensively *think* about the problems if we are to develop effective solutions. And the less educated the populace the more critical becomes the role of the media in education. We need an informed, thoughtful, and intelligent media to help us deal with the entire issue of perpetration, holding the perpetrators accountable while placing them in an overall social context that seeks explanation, not blame. We need some good therapy.

Remembering Through the Arts

It may be politically incorrect to talk about a purpose for the arts, since they are supposed to be a purpose unto themselves. Nonetheless, the current marginalization, attack on, and underfunding of the arts seems to justify a possible explanation of the utility of artistic expression. Particularly since we are discussing "remembering." As we know from the study of trauma, overwhelming experience is largely stored in the form of nonverbal memories and experiences. To heal, we must retrieve our split-off past. Somehow the nonverbal images, sensations, and emotions associated with trauma have to be "translated" into language. But how can this happen when the forces associated with trauma are bent on keeping the nonverbal and verbal forms of information apart? For answers to this dilemma we must turn to the more creative, metaphorical, often nonverbal forms of human expression: drawing, painting, sculpting, poetry, myth-making, dance, storytelling, music, ritual, ceremony, and drama.

Before language there was another form of human communication: *mimesis*. Mimesis is the ability to produce conscious, self-initiated representational acts that are intentional but not linguistic (Donald, 1991). It derives from our primate ancestry and arose much earlier in evolution than the development of language. Mimetic representation is a central factor in human society and communication and is also at the very center of the arts. Mimesis underlies all modern culture and forms the most basic medium of human communication. The emotional information that is carried through facial expression, gesture, tone of voice, and posture are all aspects of mimesis. Language and the mimetic function carry on in parallel, but whereas language is widely variable across cultures, mimetic functions show far more similarity demonstrating the core of a root culture that is distinctly human (Donald, 1991).

Mimesis is the basis of ritual behavior—the ancient and traditional human way of going from the inexpressible to the expressible. As Driver (1991) has pointed out, "In [ritual] performance we come upon something quite basic about human beings—that we constitute ourselves through our actions" (p. 80). Traditionally, it was through the use of ritual that major life transitions and traumas were worked through as social drama: "Rituals are not merely another form of art or play, although they are surely artful and playful. . . . Their business in society is to effect transformations that cannot otherwise be brought about" (Driver, 1991, p. 91). Ritual behavior brings about these transformations by uniting a group in common action, in part by producing states of consciousness in which the participants in a ritual all share the same emotional states and therefore share the same states of physiological arousal (D'Aquili, Laughlin, and McManus, 1979; Lex, 1979).

As we have seen, the response to trauma, so useful under conditions of acute stress but so detrimental when maintained over the long haul, is a biologically adapted physiological mechanism. In service of the preservation of life it cuts the traumatized person off from overwhelming emotions and memories. The subsequent walling off of the traumatic memories, images, and feelings results in a cutoff from self-identity and from other people as well as prolonged and disturbing physiological states. These split-off complexes then propel the person—outside of conscious awareness—to reenact the story of the traumatic experience through his or her behavior. This reenactment frequently results in disastrous consequences as the person experiences repeated trauma, apparently self-initiated.

Just as this is a biologically evolved pattern of behavior, likewise, the capacity to perform and express ourselves nonverbally through all of the mediums that we now call "the arts" has simultaneously evolved (Dissanayake, 1992). Evidence for the evolutionary nature of the arts is that they are ubiquitous—they are present in every culture throughout all human history as far as we know. They are sources of pleasure as are most important functions that are necessary for survival—eating, sleeping, reproducing. They are integral to many basic human activities and not to be omitted. From an evolutionary point of view, anything that is granted that much importance has to have significant survival value, and for more than the entertainment or investment value that are now virtually our sole requisites for the arts.

We have good reason to believe that this simultaneous evolutionary occurrence is probably not a coincidence. Performance—in all its aspects—appears to be the bridge across the "black hole of trauma" (Pitman and Or, 1990). When we perform a ritual or a rite; act out a psychodrama; draw a picture that elicits our emotion; sculpt a three-dimensional expression of a profound feeling or experience; use the voice of poetry to convey image and affect; dance, sing, write, or play a piece of music that stirs the soul; create a story that embodies some emotion—then we are bridging the gap between our uniquely human nonverbal and verbal worlds. Through creative artistic and performance efforts we are able to take what is inexpressible and therefore solitary and turn it into the expressible and the shared.

Performance is the key to health and healing for individuals and for an entire culture. Evidence abounds supporting this notion if we look at the literature related to the necessity of creative therapies for healing individual victims of trauma. If victims of trauma lack a structured and guided way of using the creative arts, they frequently find it themselves by spontaneously drawing, writing, painting, sculpting, versifying, dancing, playing, or composing as a way of groping their way toward integration. Certainly, ideologues have long been aware of the overwhelming power of the nonverbal. Hitler was a genius at organizing massive, highly ceremonial rituals with all the attendant music, color, costume, and symbols that appeal so strongly to the nonrational, nonverbal side of human beings. He carefully studied gesture, intonation, and facial expression in order to convey his messages nonverbally in parallel with his speeches (Rosenbaum, 1995).

Victims of trauma spontaneously evoke nonverbal mimetic functions not only through the creative arts, but universally through the enactment—or reenactment—of their traumatic experience. Robert Lifton, who has intensively studied various trauma groups including victims of Hiroshima and Nagasaki, has identified a phenomenon he calls "failed enactment" (Lifton, 1993, p. 12). He has found that at the time of the trauma, there is some beginning, abortive image toward acting in a way more positive than can actually happen at the time. This schema for enactment is never completed, and was in most instances impossible to achieve in the first place. Nonetheless, the person feels guilty about not having completed the successful act, even though it was impossible in reality. It is this failed enactment that probably helps to propel the reenactment behavior, as the person unconsciously attempts repetitively to do the situation differently, unwittingly becoming traumatized over and over again.

This reenactment behavior, therefore, seems to also be biologically based, part of the innate and programmed behavioral repertoire of the traumatized person. We can look at the trauma victim as someone who is—in mime—trying to tell the story of indescribable pain, the pain from which all language has been violently disengaged. From this point of view, then, posttraumatic symptoms, and perhaps most psychiatric and socially disruptive symptoms, are actually nonverbal messages from the fragmented and hurt individual to his or her social group. In the past, and all too often in the present, we have pejoratively called this behavior "attention-seeking," "hysterical," "manipulative" behavior. Actually, it would appear that the individual is trying to do exactly what he or she is biologically programmed to do—to engage the social group in the shared experience of tragedy, the collective experience of pain.

The traumatized person is asking us to help him or her integrate the experience, to offer words where there is only silence, to provide soothing safety where there is only terror, to suggest meaning where there is only chaos. When we fail to hear the meaning in the message—a message that is usually first sent in childhood—it is the not the victim who has failed but the corporate body. It is the social and moral responsibility of the social group to reintegrate its traumatized members back into the whole. The fragmented part tells exactly what it needs—it is the whole that refuses to listen or respond.

Just as the individual victim of trauma uses creative expression to reassemble the split-off parts of experience, the arts play a major role in helping a society remember, reconstruct, and assimilate collective traumatic events. The artistic reconstruction of social memory appears in cycles of twenty to thirty years after the events. This effect has been demonstrated for the Spanish Civil War and the French Algerian War by looking at the changing themes of film versions of the events over time (Igartua and Paez, 1997). It has been suggested that art, in its broadest sense, has as one of its functions helping cognitive development while entertaining. In studying the effects of the mass media, especially those using a narrative format such as films and series, researchers believe that such "cultural artifacts [may] exercise an influence in maintaining collective memory and contributing toward the cultivation and reinforcement of certain beliefs on events that have had a great affective impact on specific collectivities or social groups" (Igartua and Paez, 1997, p. 92). These authors point out that *Schindler's List* has played a significant role in alerting the public to the dangers of the Nazi revival and recovering the memory of the collective trauma of the Holocaust. They believe substantial evidence exists that works of art stressing individual participation while ignoring sociopolitical context help us distance ourselves from collective events and foster forgetting. Exactly the opposite happens when the work of art insists on depicting the suffering and sociopolitical causes of a collective catastrophe.

It is no wonder we want to marginalize and silence the artist. The artist gives voice to the part of us that cannot adequately communicate in words. Language often fails us, not the least because language allows us to lie. Orwell (1981) knew that language may be used to exert virtual control over an entire population:

> The purpose of Newspeak was not only to provide a medium of expression for the worldview and mental habits proper to the devotees of Ingsoc, but to make all other modes of thought impossible. It was intended that when Newspeak had been adopted once and for all and Oldspeak forgotten, a heretical thought—that is, a thought diverging from the principles of Ingsoc—should be literally unthinkable, at least so far as thought is dependent on words. (p. 246)

But this deception will only work if the culture does not get too much disturbing input from the other reality—from the artists and those considered by society to be mad. The arts challenge the established order, the status quo, and are therefore political. As Elaine Scarry tells us, physical pain initially has no voice; it is a speechless surrender to suffering. But eventually, that pain can be expressed verbally, and when it does finally find a voice, it begins to tell a story that is simultaneously personal and political (Scarry, 1985). "All drama is a political event: it either reasserts or undermines the code of conduct of a given society" (Eslin, 1976, p. 29).

Since art, traditionally is meant to be an "investigation," meant to tell us something about our inner contradictions, to illuminate what is in darkness, to assist us to integrate the fractured parts of our socially constructed consciousness (Becker, 1994), it should not surprise us that the role of the arts in our society is criticized, marginalized, and censored. In discussing this censorship, Becker has observed that:

> The art that has been targeted for attack in each case reflected social concerns. It was work that would never allow us to believe that

we all lived in the same America, shared similar desires, or were equally committed to maintaining the elaborate psychological, philosophical, economic, and sexual repression necessary to sustain Western Civilization as we have known it. . . . Those who spend their time analyzing such events understood that if the national/international art police were to have their way, art would be forced to lose its uniqueness and social value to become innocuous entertainment or else run the risk of losing its often minimal government support. (p. xiv)

Through plays, movies, books, stories, songs, poems, dance productions, photographs, sculpture, and painting we are constantly reminded of post and current events that we are trying to forget. This is precisely why the arts are so critical to our present social situation of escalating violence and deteriorating community. As long as society fails to provide nonverbal means of expression and integration to its wounded members, it remains vulnerable to other forms of exploitation of this profound need. Cults, religious fanatics, gangs, and political ideologues will continue to provide a disturbing fascination because they instinctively know how to exploit our very basic human need for ritual, ceremony, and performance. If we are to become healthier as a society then we must recognize this need and supply it, particularly for our most damaged members. Instead of decreasing funding for the arts, particularly in inner-city communities and schools, we should be massively increasing such funding. We should be encouraging community theater, creative writing classes, dance and music programs, video projects, public art projects and more, all as part of an extensive social commitment to finally hear, rather than deny, the pain of our fellow countrymen and women as well as our own.

Under the oppressive rule of Communism, the hope—and memory—of freedom was kept alive through art. In some countries, the Czech Republic being the most obvious, the artist led the way, making sure that his or her compatriots would not forget a vision of a better world. As Vaclav Havel, ex-political prisoner, playwright, and now president of the Czech Republic has said:

Every work of art points somewhere beyond itself; it transcends itself and its author; it creates a special force field around itself that moves the human mind and the human nervous system. . . . One way of helping people is by reminding them that the time is getting late, that the situation is grave, that it can't be ignored. Seeing the outlines of horror induces the will to face up to it. (Havel, 1990)

THE GRIEF THAT DOES NOT SPEAK . . .

As we have seen, victims of trauma live with ghosts. They are haunted by the past. Over time, the present gradually disappears, the future fails to exist, and the past dominates existence. These are the symptoms of unresolved grief. Victims of unresolved trauma live with tragedy without having yet achieved a state of communal tragic consciousness. George Steiner, in describing the nature of tragedy has said,

> I believe that any realistic notion of tragic drama must start from the fact of catastrophe. Tragedies end badly. The tragic personage is broken by forces which can neither by fully understood, nor overcome by rational prudence. . . . This again is crucial. Where the causes of disaster are temporal, where the conflict can be resolved through technical or social means, we may have serious drama, but not tragedy. Tragedy is irreparable. (Steiner, 1961, p. 8)

Victims of trauma are tragic figures. Their loss cannot be repaired. They cannot turn back the clock and make the drama of their lives unfold differently, regardless of how many times they reenact it. To complete mourning, they must stop reenacting and start acting for themselves. They must let go of their attachment to and involvement in the past. Tragedy as an art form arose out of ancient rituals of mourning. Mourning rituals have always been a communal and shared response to loss. In his book, *Plays of the Holocaust,* Fuchs (1987) describes our present situation:

> In the world after the Holocaust, we live daily with the dark companion of extinction—by famine, plague, force, and above all, by the fire of nuclear holocaust. We live in a time of tragic consciousness. For us, tragic loss is measured in groups, peoples, species. The theatre, above all other forms of artistic practice insists on the life of the community; it cannot be made without it. . . . In the very act of representing the annihilation of the human community, then, the theatre itself offers a certain fragile potentiality for recreation. (p. xxii)

As Americans, we have difficulty coming to terms with this irreparable nature of tragedy. We like to believe in the inevitability of progress. One of the downsides of our psychotherapeutic culture is that we have comforted ourselves with the myth of reversibility, or curability. The solution to any interpersonal problem is always therapy. We behave as if damage done in childhood can readily be reversed in adulthood. This is a myth. Childhood damage can be *transformed* and *transcended* but it cannot be undone. Once safety has been established and the process of remembering is progressing well, victims must wrestle with a profound sense of grief and loss for what can never be and for what is forever lost.

Trauma theory leads us to a direct confrontation with the tragic nature of human existence. Our bodies and minds respond to overwhelming stress in ways we cannot control despite our enormous technology. It was the Greeks who brought us the sense of the tragic, that "necessity is blind" that there is no "just and material compensation for past suffering" (Steiner, 1961, p. 9):

> Call it what you will: a hidden or malevolent God, blind fate, the solicitations of hell, or the brute fury of our animal blood. It waits for us in ambush at the crossroads. It mocks us and destroys us. In certain rare instances, it leads us after destruction to some incomprehensible repose. . . . There is no use asking for rational explanation or mercy. Things are as they are, unrelenting and absurd. We are punished far in excess of our guilt. (p. 9)

Tragedy, Grieving, and Spiritual Passage

When our patients cannot grieve, they cannot heal. Shakespeare advises us to "give sorrow words; the grief that does not speak whispers the o'er fraught heart and bids it break" (*Macbeth*, Act IV, Scene 3). When people cannot grieve, they become psychologically, physically, and socially sick. One of the common outcomes of pathological grief is an increase in hostility toward oneself and others. Other outcomes include hatred, disgust, inertia, hypochondriasis, numbness, irritability, feelings of worthlessness, and apathy, avoidance with an increase in substance abuse, intrusive symptoms with nightmares, flashbacks, compulsive reenactments, depression, somatic symptoms, anxiety, rage, guilt—you name it—failing to complete the process of grieving is seriously bad for one's health.

Victims who fail to complete the process of mourning can become trapped in seeking revenge. As a society, we appear to be trapped in trying to "get even" as our criminal justice system gears up for increasingly punitive sentences and the creation of traumatogenic prison environments, despite the fact that we know these do not work to stop crime. What is it that we cannot bear? What loss, as a nation, might we be avoiding? America is built on several premises: that there will always be a frontier, that there will always be progress; that if we work hard we will succeed and be prosperous, that we always are on the side of the angels; that our system is the best system in the world. The late twentieth century is presenting a number of challenges to our fundamental assumptions that we are having difficulty changing, not the least of which is our place in a global economy. Perhaps we are grieving for a time past, a lost "innocence" which, although an illusion, was a sustaining illusion. We do not yet have a vision of a future in which America is but a part of an interconnected, and potentially joyful, larger whole. Without such a vision of future health, we seem to be hostilely engaged in trying to recapture a flawed but predictable past. This is a sign of failed bereavement. Instead of moving ahead into a sustainable and nonviolent future, we are hell-bent on punishing— criminals, the poor, women, children, workers, the sick, as if battering our family members could restore our sense of wholeness and integrity. This strategy does not work in the American family and it will not work for American society. It simply delays the moment of reckoning and creates more and more wounds to be healed. Unchecked, it could lead to social suicide.

There are two social institutions available to us, through which we could help ourselves to grieve: the arts and religion, both with common origins in the human need for shared meaning and performative acts. "The grave is the birthplace of tragic drama and ghosts are its procreators" (Cole, 1985, p. 9). Tragedy, in particular, has played a vital role in the evolution of human social experience. Death is humankind's greatest mystery and our awareness of our own mortality is our greatest burden. Our profound and innate need to bond to others of our kind makes the unvarnished inevitability of loss unbearable unless we can alter the reality in some way, unless we can transform the tragic into some kind of shared meaning on an intellectual, but more important, an emotional level. For many religious people, the shared rituals of the church provide a transformation that enables them to make sense of the experiences that are beyond human understanding. Grief must be shared and there must be a pathway through the stages of grieving that are safe.

Twelve Steps to Recovery

The twelve-step programs are so useful for people because they provide a clear and structured pathway through the stages of establishing safety, remembering, and grieving in a social context that leads to meaningfulness. This method has been found beneficial for the treatment of substance abuse problems and other addictions, probably because it encompasses keys to healing from violence that are psychologically sound and spiritually informed. Based on structure, safety, social support, grieving, and reconnection, Brende (1993) has outlined twelve themes that are important for trauma survivors to reckon with and twelve steps in a process of recovery that can be of use to individuals, to groups, and even to an entire culture. The twelve steps as Brende describes them are: power versus victimization, seeking meaning, trust versus shame and doubt, taking a self-inventory, dealing with anger, managing fear, managing guilt, dealing with grief, choosing life over death, searching for justice instead of revenge, finding a purpose in life, and discovering nonabusive relationships and love. To accompany the twelve steps, Brende has established twelve principles of recovery and twelve themes. He urges survivors to follow the twelve steps to help break the cycle of victimization (and perpetration). The strength of this program is that it is a graded, gradual, self-help program that incorporates many of the fundamental, time-tested ingredients that go into psychological healing—comfort, confession, repentance, grieving, affect modulation, reformulation, reconnection with others and with a higher purpose. One of its strengths, however, is also its weakness. The emphasis on a relationship with God, usually perceived as a male deity, puts off many trauma survivors, particularly those who have been traumatized by a member of the clergy, or who have had religion included in some way in their abuse. Nonetheless, the twelve-step programs have become a powerful resource for people recovering from the tragedies of life.

The Question of Forgiveness

Grieving for partial losses, for lost opportunities, for lost childhood, for lost innocence, for losses of long ago and far away is quite difficult. Within every religious tradition there are defined, ritualized pathways to mourning that serve the living as well as the dead, but for traumatic losses that do not involve immediate death, grieving is often an uncharted and socially unsupported wilderness. Many victims become trapped in a stage of mourning that results in anger, resentment, even hatred. In doing so, they remain attached to those who have perpetrated against them. And yet, it is natural for human beings to experience these feelings as a result of being mistreated. Increasingly, the process of transforming these feelings is being examined, questioned, and researched. What is forgiveness? Can people really forgive? Is forgiveness good for the health or is it simply a way of denying the problem? Does forgiving let the perpetrator "off the hook"? Here we have one of the many crossover points between science, medicine, religion, psychology, and philosophy. It may be that the present resurgence in spiritual concerns, in and outside of traditional religious frameworks, is related to a powerful social need to find a way out of the trap of traumatic bereavement so that we can move on, as individuals and as a society.

RECONNECTION

As the grieving process begins to resolve, the individual victim of trauma begins to feel a sense of coming alive, of returning to the world from a long and arduous trip to the underworld. They begin to create a new life for themselves, reconnecting to others, drawing upon all they have learned, transforming their experience with trauma into a renewed sense of commitment to self and others. For many, part of this transformation involves the development of a "survivor mission."

> These survivors recognize a political or religious dimension in their misfortune and discover that they can transform the meaning of their personal tragedy by making it the basis for social action. While there is no way to compensate for an atrocity, there is a way to transcend it, by making it a gift to others. (Herman, 1992, p. 207)

Reconnection is simultaneously a physical, psychological, social, and spiritual task. Signs of reconnection abound throughout the social sphere and we will touch upon many of them in these next sections. At a macro-cosmic level, basic scientists are finding ways to study the soul (Davies, 1983; Margenau and Varhese, 1992), while religion is opening up to scientific study (Hood et al., 1996; Pargament, 1997). Business executives are talking about spirituality, creativity, and global responsibility (Ray and Rinzler, 1993). Ecologists are referring to the spirituality of the earth and the connection between ecology and the mind (Dyson, 1992; Roszak, Gomes, and Kanner, 1995). Larry Dossey endeavors to find ways of integrating medicine and spiritual healing (Dossey, 1993). McLaughlin and Davidson call for another reconnection:

> We feel the time has come to unite that which has been separated for so long—politics and spirituality. Politics—local, national, and global—must be lifted beyond power-tripping, deceit, manipulation and restored to its highest purpose: addressing the greatest good for the greatest number. This is the deeper meaning of politics. (1994, p. 6)

Jim Wallis reminds us that:

> Spiritual and religious values, indeed, can contribute in a time of social crisis to a renewed vision of politics. Yet, one need not be a member of a church, synagogue, or mosque to appreciate that contribution. In fact, one need not be a religious person at all. Anyone who believes that moral issues are at stake in our political choices can understand the need for renewal. Most people would probably agree that beneath the social, economic, cultural and political problems we confront lie critical questions concerning our deepest values. Our crisis is also one of the spirit—deeper than just the turns and twists of secular politics. (Wallis, 1994, p. 32)

Reconnection is our only hope for the future. Only if we can get out of the trap of endless reenactment and failed bereavement can we reconstruct a better, nonviolent society. Michael Lerner learned from his teacher, the theologican Abraham Heschel, that the quest for meaning is the central hunger in advanced industrial societies. For Lerner, this search has come to signify a life's work, "It is the desire for meaningful connection—not only to other human beings, but to transcendent purpose in the universe—that plays the central role in shaping human reality" (Lerner, 1996, p. 29). We can only create a nonviolent society with a nonviolent, persistent, integrated social movement. We believe that the groundwork for such a movement is being laid. The knowledge base is being developed in every discipline, from physics to psychology. Human evolution is no longer biological; it is social. And sometimes, evolutionary change does not come about gradually but takes a quantum leap to a new level of existence. Such a change in practice begins with thinking differently and perceiving the world in different ways.

Chapter 8

Secondary Prevention:
Containing the Traumatic Infection

We have discussed various aspects of healing from traumatic experience for those who have already been injured and touched upon aspects of healing that are relevant for the national "psyche." We have already touched on the emergency measures that are necessary for any preventive efforts to work, especially gun control, the abolition of corporal punishment, aggressive policies to rid the country of sexism and racism, a full employment policy, and decreased media violence. Secondary prevention focuses on efforts to contain any infection, to keep it from spreading, particularly among those members of the population considered to be at most risk. Those most at risk in our society are children, women, and the poor.

A BILL OF RIGHTS FOR CHILDREN

Children will not receive the rights of protection they deserve until they are no longer considered property, but instead, young citizens. In their 1993 report, the U.S. Advisory Board made a long list of recommendations. One important proposal was for the endorsement of a national child protection policy. This is a policy that we desperately need in order to provide the necessary structure for social policy change. The Board drew some of their language from the United Nations Convention on the Rights of the Child. This is their proposed declaration:

- Respect for the inherent dignity and inalienable rights of children as members of the human community requires protection of their integrity as persons.
- Children have a right to protection from all forms of physical or mental violence, injury or abuse, neglect or negligent treatment, mal-

treatment or exploitation including sexual abuse, while in the care of parent(s), legal guardian(s) or any other person who has the care of the child, including children residing in group homes and institutions.

- Children have a right to grow up in a family environment, in an atmosphere of happiness, love, and understanding.
- The several Governments of the United States share a profound responsibility to ensure that children enjoy, at a minimum, such protection of their physical, sexual, and psychological security.
- The several Governments of the United States bear a special duty to refrain from subjecting children in their care and custody to harm.
- Children have a right to be treated with respect as individuals, with due regard to cultural diversity and the need for culturally competent delivery of services in the child protection system.
- Children have a right to be provided the opportunity to be heard in any judicial and administrative proceedings affecting them, with ample opportunity for representation and for provision of procedures that comport with the child's sense of dignity.
- The duty to protect the integrity of children as persons implies a duty to prevent assaults on that integrity whenever possible.

The Convention of the Rights of the Child was adopted unanimously by the General Assembly of the United Nations on November 20, 1989, paving the way for ratification by each separate nation and the setting up of monitoring committees. Previous declarations on the rights of the child were adopted by both the League of Nations in 1924 and the United Nations in 1959. It was felt that there was a need for a comprehensive statement on children's rights that would be binding under international law. So far, as of last March, 186 countries have ratified the Convention, the end of a long process that began in the 1979 International Year of the Child (United Nations, 1996). These are the highlights of the Convention:

- Every child has the inherent right to life, and States shall ensure to the maximum child survival and development.
- Every child has the right to a name and nationality from birth.
- Children shall not be separated from their parents, except by competent authorities for their well-being.
- States shall facilitate reunification of families by permitting travel into, or out of, their territories.
- Parents have the primary responsibility for the child's upbringing, but States shall provide them with appropriate assistance and develop child-care institutions.

- States shall protect children from physical or mental harm and neglect, including sexual abuse and exploitation.
- States shall provide parentless children with suitable alternative care. The adoption process shall be carefully regulated and international agreements should be sought to provide safeguards and assure legal validity if and when adoptive parents intend to move a child from his or her country of birth.
- Disabled children shall have the right to special treatment, education, and care.
- Children are entitled to the highest attainable standard of health. States shall ensure that health care is provided to all children, placing emphasis on preventive measures, health education, and reduction of infant mortality.
- Primary education shall be free and compulsory. Discipline in schools shall respect the child's dignity. Education should prepare the child for life in a spirit of understanding, peace, and tolerance.
- Children shall have time to rest and play with equal opportunities for cultural and artistic activities.
- States shall protect children from economic exploitation and from work that may interfere with their education or be harmful to their health or well-being.
- States shall protect children from the illegal use of drugs and involvement in drug production or trafficking.
- All efforts shall be made to eliminate the abduction and trafficing of children.
- Capital punishment or life imprisonment shall not be imposed for crimes committed before the age of eighteen.
- Children in detention shall be separated from adults; they must not be tortured or suffer cruel or degrading treatment.
- No child under fifteen shall take any part in hostilities; children exposed to armed conflict shall receive special protection.
- Children of minority and indigenous populations shall freely enjoy their own culture, religion, and language.
- Children who have suffered mistreatment, neglect, or exploitation shall receive appropriate treatment or training for recovery and rehabilitation.
- Children involved in infringements of the penal law shall be treated in a way that promotes their sense of dignity and worth and aims at reintegrating them into society.
- States shall make the rights set out in the Convention widely known to both adults and children. (United Nations, 1996)

Unlike every other developed country in the world—and most underdeveloped countries as well—*the United States of America has as yet failed to ratify the Convention.* Many of the countries that have ratified it have not enforced it. We tend to create rules long before we follow them so it may take us centuries to live up to such a convention. But society can only move ahead if we have a moral vision. Establishing the rights of children is the next step in the attainment of basic human rights for all.

DAY CARE AND FAMILY SUPPORT

We must give up the pretense that, for the foreseeable future, either parent can afford to stay home to raise children. The present economy makes that a fundamental impossibility except for the very wealthy. This necessitates a basic change in the way we view the family and the social responsibility we all have for making sure that children get what they need to develop in healthy ways. Such change requires a massive shift in our attitude toward early infant and toddler care. Children require stable attachments for normal development. They need day care workers who are reliable, loving, and who will be with them steadily and predictably for the first few years of life. Day care needs to be viewed as an extremely vital profession that deserves a high educational standard and salaries to match.

Employers need to recognize that the provision of child care for working parents—which is most parents—makes good economic sense for long-term productivity and investment in the economy. Given the spread of computer-generated work, trends toward increasing numbers of workers at home should be encouraged and supported by both state and national policy.

Parent education programs located in high schools for teen mothers, substance abuse treatment programs for mothers and families with young children, respite care for families who have children with special needs, and family resource centers for families in high risk communities are all programs that could help reach out to families and children at risk.

Hawaii's Healthy Start

Single mothers require even more assistance because they are trying to do more with less income and support. It has been shown that for high-risk mothers, early infant home visitation programs, such as Hawaii's "Healthy Start" (Breakey and Pratt, 1991) are effective at reducing the incidence of child neglect and maltreatment. This program has its roots in an early study done by Kempe and his associates in Denver in the 1970s. They took at-risk families and randomly assigned them to two groups, one which had home visitation and the other that did not. After three years, the group of twenty-five families who had been part of the home visitation program had no incidents of child abuse, although three children were put up for adoption. Of the twenty-five families who did not participate in the program, five children were hospitalized for head injuries, scaldings, and fractures.

Unlike other similar programs, Hawaii Healthy Start follows the child from birth (or before) to age five with a range of services, and it assists and supports other family members. To ensure systematic enrollment, Healthy Start signs up most families right after delivery of the child, although approximately 10 percent of families are enrolled prenatally. Healthy Start has formal agreements with all hospitals in Hawaii to enable it to perform postpartum screening through a review of the mother's medical record or a brief in-person interview. Fewer than 1 percent of mothers refuse to be interviewed, 4 to 8 percent later refuse offers of services, and about 7 percent cannot be located after release from the hospital. A screening instrument was developed to assess mothers who are considered to be most at risk. Some of these factors include: single, separated, or divorced marital status; an unemployed partner; inadequate income; unstable housing; no phone; less than twelve years of education; inadequate emergency contacts; a history of substance abuse; late or no prenatal care; a history of abortions; an unsuccessful abortion; a history of psychiatric care; marital or family problems; or a history of current depression.

Paraprofessional home visitors call on families weekly for the first six to twelve months. Early in the relationship, the home visitor helps parents develop an Individual Support Plan, specifying the kinds of services they want and need and the means by which to receive them. As part of its oversight, the Maternal Child Health Branch requires completion of a series of Infant/Child Monitoring Questionnaires to identify problems in child development at four, twelve, twenty, and thirty months. If these show developmental delays, further assessments are performed and appropriate services are offered. In 1994 a confirmed child care abuse and neglect case cost the Hawaii family welfare system $25,000 for investigation, related services, and foster care. In contrast, Hawaii Healthy Start officials estimate an annual average cost of $2,800 per home visitor case. Preliminary evaluation findings indicate that Healthy Start families have lower abuse/ neglect rates and their children are developing appropriately for their ages. Between July 1987 and June 1991, 2,254 families were served by Healthy Start. Indicators of the program's success over this three-year period include: 90 percent of two-year-olds in families receiving services were fully immunized; 85 percent of the children in served families had developed appropriately for their ages; thirteen of the ninety families (4 percent) known to CPS at or prior to intake with a confirmed combined abuse/neglect report for siblings or imminent danger status, no further reports occurred during these families' program enrollment. Three cases were reported after the families left the program. No instances of domestic homicide have been recorded since the program's inception (Earle, 1995).

The U.S. Advisory Board (1991; 1992; 1993) has been urging implementation of these programs for years. Such simple, well-researched, community-oriented, and relatively low budget programs, instituted universally, could do much to prevent early childhood abuse and developmental failures, but they must be properly conducted and adequately funded.

DEALING WITH FAMILY VIOLENCE

Report Card from the AMA

Many people have joined forces to address the issue of intervening with and preventing family violence. The American Medical Association has been giving the nation a report card every year on violence and in 1996, our grade for family violence was a C, an improvement over the previous year since the grade then was C−. The improvement was attributed to a dramatic increase in public awareness and education on the issue of domestic violence over the past year. In addition, initiatives such as the Violent Crime Control and Law Enforcement Act of 1994, the largest crime bill in U.S. history, have specifically impacted domestic violence by encouraging and funding prevention measures. This law also protects women by calling for:

- Establishment of a national, twenty-four-hour, toll-free, bilingual hotline (800-799-SAFE) to provide immediate information and assistance to victims and care providers.
- Prohibition of firearm possession by, and sales to, persons subject to family violence restraining orders.
- Establishment of the Violence Against Women grant program to support police/prosecutor efforts, strengthen enforcement, and provide victim services. Twenty-six million dollars was made available to states in 1995, $774 million in formula grants, and over $200 million for related competitive grants for 1996-2000.

- Provision of $325 million to the Department of Health and Human Services for shelters for battered women and other prevention activities.
- Bans on juvenile possession of handguns and ammunition or transfer of arms to juveniles by adults, except under certain limited circumstances. Aimed at decreasing likelihood such guns may be used in family altercations or suicide attempts.
- Encouragement of a proarrest policy in domestic violence cases when police are contacted.
- Special assistance for rural efforts in domestic violence and child abuse.
- Federal prosecution of domestic violence when state lines are crossed by a perpetrator.

The AMA also reported on the improvement in the workplace of programs dealing with domestic violence. Still, actual incidence rates of domestic violence, child abuse, elder abuse, and suicide are not declining. In fact, as we know now, child abuse appears to be increasing. Their comments about elder abuse were also revealing:

> Elder abuse remains deeply shrouded by the secrecy surrounding family violence. Estimates range from 1 to 2 million cases per year, but it is believed that as few as one in every 14 victimizations are reported to a public agency. Although widely acknowledged by experts as a problem, elder abuse continues to receive little attention. Reports indicate that despite the fact that 40 percent of reported abuse involve elders, states spend less than $3 per elder for protective services. With the elderly segment of the population rapidly increasing it is expected that there will be a steady increase in the number of elder abuse cases. (American Medical Association, 1996)

Violence and the Family:
The American Psychological Association

In 1996, the American Psychological Association published an extensive report titled *Violence and the Family*. In their report, they make a number of recommendations for interventions for changing the attitudes and behavior of at-risk groups that are entirely consistent with all that we have discussed in this book.

- Volunteer visits to high-risk homes to prevent family isolation.
- Empowerment training for girls and women who have been exposed to violence in their childhood homes.

- Interventions for boys and men who have been exposed to physical or sexual abuse or maltreatment as children.
- Social and community support for isolated, young, single mothers and for families with many children or with one or more children with disabilities.
- Respite care for caretakers of those with physical disabilities and the elderly.
- Interventions for boys who repeatedly use bullying behavior on the playground or unusually high levels of aggressive behavior in the home, school, or community.
- Psychoeducational programs for children at battered women shelters or through a domestic violence court.
- Community-based recreation and care programs for the elderly.
- Restriction of possession of firearms for anyone who has been convicted of any violence or who has domestic violence charges or restraining orders pending.
- Group discussion and support programs for recent immigrants conducted in their own language to reduce isolation.
- Attention to adolescents who are being victimized by family members and schoolmates.
- Safety programs for elderly battered women whose partners are diagnosed with deteriorating physical conditions that are associated with a high risk of battering behavior.

National Conference on Family Violence

Earlier we mentioned the National Conference on Family Violence, held in Washington, DC, in1994 and co-sponsored by over eighty organizations including the American Medical Association and the American Bar Association. The recommendations of this conference were wide in scope, interdisciplinary, and applicable to the entire community. This is the only kind of approach that can be effective for a problem as widespread and interconnected as family violence.

We decided to include a detailed description of the recommendations from the Conference because there is a prevailing attitude in the wider community that we do not know what to do about family violence, that somehow it is all too big a problem. The material below provides evidence that we *do* know what to do—we just lack the social commitment to do so.

Assessment

Develop an effective, multidisciplinary, communitywide assessment process that maximizes safety for all family members.

Strategies

All communities should:

- Form multidisciplinary family violence coordinating councils.
- Develop and distribute an interdisciplinary glossary of terms and resources.
- Establish standards for minimum community resources necessary to ensure the safety of all family members.
- Develop community intervention referrals available to frontline screeners. These should include mental health services and social services.
- Investigate appropriate case-tracking systems by computer to enhance civil tracking and medical tracking of survivors.
- Evaluate the effectiveness of the assessment process from the perspective of survivors and health and justice professionals.
- Provide feedback on outcomes of interventions to screeners.
- Promote research on the effectiveness of universal screening and the benefits and the risks of mandatory reporting.
- Develop a mechanism for the confidential sharing of appropriate and relevant information both between and within the health and justice systems.
- Develop routine procedures for assessment that will preserve information that may be necessary for intervention by other systems.
- Promote early self-identification through public education about health, legal, and community services.

Conduct early universal screening emphasizing safety of the family, which is sensitive to different racial, cultural, and socioeconomic characteristics of the family, and with an awareness that multiple forms of abuse/violence may occur within the same family.

Strategies

- Develop a form/protocol for screening that includes risk assessment.
- Utilize health, social, and justice groups to develop and distribute guidelines and protocols to be used by first-line screeners.

- Develop a mobile twenty-four-hour crisis intervention team available to the community.
- Develop curricula and continuing education/training for all professionals including cross-disciplinary training for health care providers, social services, police, judges, and others.
- Consider linking training to licensure requirements. Implement training through impaired provider programs to reach professionals who are survivors or abusers.
- Fund studies to analyze the impact of universal screening including forms and protocols for outcomes-based research.
- Encourage self-assessment and community assessment through public education.

Interventions

In the area of interventions, the goal of health, justice, and social service systems is to stop violence and abuse. In accomplishing this goal, communities must:

- protect and support victims;
- empower victims to protect themselves;
- hold offenders accountable for past and future behaviors; and
- demand that abusers change their behaviors so that their membership in our community engenders no fear.

Therefore, each community should create a family violence coordinating council to coordinate these efforts at the local level.

Philosophy and Rationale

Individual communities are in the best position to understand the needs and resources of that community and that the efforts of family violence councils should therefore be community driven. Communities are also in the best position to prioritize community needs with respect to family violence and to allocating increasingly scarce resources. Interventions for family violence must be tailored to all specific forms of family violence under consideration, including, but not limited to child abuse and neglect, child sexual abuse, partner abuse, emotional abuse, abuse of physically and mentally handicapped adults and children, and elder abuse, neglect, and exploitation. Furthermore, specific approaches to family violence must be sensitive to the cultural, linguistic, and other diverse populations in which family violence occurs as interventions are contemplated.

The council should be composed of representatives of all persons and agencies who deal with family violence. There should be no barriers to membership and the full spectrum of all interested parties in the community should be encouraged to join. These may include: physicians, nurses, nurse practitioners, clinical nurses, midwives, medical administrators, legislators, judges, victims, victims advocates, law enforcement officers, educators, social workers, clergy, pharmacists, school nurses, substance abuse counselors, prosecutors, attorneys, probation and parole officials, corrections officials, mental health providers, researchers, community-based organizations, rehabilitated offenders of family violence, and concerned community members.

The general purpose of the Council shall be:

- To effectuate coordination between hospitals, service agencies, police departments, and the courts with victims of family violence and abuse. Such coordination occurs at the systems level in which the broad implementation of programs and efforts must be integrated as well as at the service/case level, in which services delivered to any individual victim of family violence must be organized. The council should also facilitate communication by members of the health, justice, and other systems between the systems level and the service level.
- To provide opportunities for the various disciplines to educate each other and to facilitate cross-training for all health care providers.
- To promote and evaluate interventions that have been found to be effective.
- To improve the response to family violence and abuse so as to reduce its incidence.
- To identify and enumerate areas where interventions are known to work and need only to be coordinated; to elucidate areas lacking effective programs wherein new interventions must be developed for health, justice, and social services.
- To promote the development and support of hospitals and health care system-based intervention programs.
- To promote the development and replication of family-centered community-based intervention programs.

Besides providing leadership on interventions and rehabilitation, family violence councils also will be in an ideal and unique position to address prevention, community education, assessment, media, and the integration of these functions. Strategies of the Council should include:

- Developing and/or revising more policies and procedures for inter-agency coordination and cooperation at both the system and service /case levels.
- Convening conferences that focus upon family violence in the community.
- Promoting educational programs in primary and secondary schools.
- Providing professional education.
- Identifying health and justice intervention and rehabilitation methods that have been shown to be effective in other disciplines (e.g., substance abuse) that can be applied to the family violence area.
- Searching for cross-disciplinary approaches.

As a part of any family violence coordinating council there shall be a health care systems committee. The purpose of the health care systems committee shall be as follows:

- Develop cross-system intervention protocols for health care providers dealing with individuals who might be victims of child abuse, domestic violence, or elder abuse.
- Develop and provide training for all members of the health care community in these intervention protocols.
- Provide a forum for the resolution of problems common to the health care and legal communities as they relate to areas such as evidence, reporting, and confidentiality.

The American Medical Association should assume a major leadership role in identifying, pursuing, and obtaining long-term funding for interventions so that the victims of family violence are adequately protected and assisted. Funding priorities should include:

- Trained advocates who have flexibility in their roles. Advocates should be accessible at all sites in the health and justice systems. Ideally, advocates should be recruited from the communities in which they serve.
- Improved access/outreach services directed at victims, as well as novel approaches/programs to reach underserved communities.
- Shelters and other protected environments for all victims.
- Mental health and substance abuse services.
- Rehabilitation needed to provide offenders with the knowledge, attitudes, and behavioral skills to develop nonviolent, parenting partnerships and caregiving choices in their relationships.

In addition, the American Medical Association should convene meetings with other national health care associations to assist in securing necessary funds and in the long-term development process for family violence intervention programs.

Every community should have a comprehensive culturally sensitive and accessible intervention system for family violence that links health, justice, mental health, social service, and educational systems. It is essential to respect and preserve the dignity, legal rights, and safety of the affected individuals. This intervention system must include:

- A family violence advocate/specialist in all practice settings who serves as a bridge to and among all community resources. This professional must be knowledgeable in health, justice, social services, mental health, education, and all forms of family violence throughout the life cycle.
- Better training and sensitization for health, social service, mental health, justice, and educational intervenors, coordinated over time and across systems to enhance the ability to provide appropriate, long-term assistance in cases of abuse, battering, and neglect.
- Comprehensive management information systems and technologies to link health care, justice, social services, mental health, and educational systems consistent with confidentiality guidelines.
- Identification, evaluation, and replication of existing model family violence intervention programs, e.g., a Unified Court model, hospital-based models, etc.
- Appropriate short-term and long-term follow-up services for all affected individuals.

Training the Health Care Community—RADAR

One example of a family violence training program is the RADAR program, created by the Philadelphia Family Violence Working Group (PFVWG) under the direction of Philadelphia Physicians for Social Responsibility (PSR). In 1994, Philadelphia PSR convened all the parties in the city who had a concern for the well-being of domestic violence victims and asked what needed to be done. The consensus was clear—medical providers were not asking the questions and were failing to ask women about family violence. After receiving funding from a local organization, the William Penn Foundation, the Family Violence Working Group developed the RADAR Training Project. Over the three years of the funding grant, the entire staff of sixteen community health centers providing health care to the underserved in Philadelphia received training and follow-up support. The evaluation and breadth of the project demonstrated positive results on outcome measures. Over 140 trainings have been provided, reaching about 5,000 field workers. Three citywide medical student conferences on family violence issues were held reaching over 850 medical and health professional students. The RADAR materials, which include Pocket Cards, Where to Turn for Help cards, a RADAR slide show, RADAR Abuse Assessment form, RADAR stamp, all developed by the PFVWG, have been distributed regionally and across the United States, Canada, and the Netherlands. The first citywide conference on "The Impact of Domestic Violence on Children" was held with over 350 people attending from a cross section of disciplines including child welfare, HIV risk reduction, maternal and child health, domestic violence, and law enforcement. One of the area domestic violence agencies, Women Against Abuse, gave Philadelphia PSR its "Peace Begins at Home" award for the training program. The Society of Behavioral Pediatrics gave Philadelphia PSR a special award for activities promoting the health and well-being of children and their families. Along with three other Philadelphia organizations, Philadelphia PSR was invited to the White House to hear a special presentation by Vice President Gore on Domestic Violence in the Workplace. The RADAR Training Project was selected as one of ten state-of-the-art domestic violence training models in the nation. And in 1998, the RADAR Training Project was selected by the Health Resources and Services Administration of the U.S. Department of Health and Human Services as one of the six award winners in their "Models That Work Campaign," a program dedicated to increasing access to primary and preventive health care for underserved populations.

SANCTUARY IN THE CLASSROOM

Schools provide society with an excellent opportunity to engage in all three levels of prevention. They can diagnose, refer, and provide support for children who are already in trouble, they can tailor programs to meet the needs of high-risk children, and they can improve the general health and well-being of all children. With some relatively minor changes, classrooms across the country could be turned into opportunities for children to learn democratic principles, necessary social skills, and affect modulation, all of which enhance the ability to concentrate, assimilate, and learn (Bloom, 1995a). The schools have an extraordinary role to play in providing a hub of services to parents as well as children. Classrooms provide a wealth of opportunities for the children to have corrective emotional experiences that can counteract many of the deficiencies or absences that the children experience at home. This requires, however, that nonparental adults see it as a social responsibility to get involved with other people's children and that parents see this involvement as a help, not a criticism of their own parenting abilities. The African proverb, "It takes a village to raise a child," could become an American slogan as well. At this point in time, however it is not. Schools are not performing as the effective and powerful institutions that they could be. Instead, as we have seen, the schools have increasingly become subcultures of violence.

As in all of our social systems, reductionism continues to interfere with progress in making our children safe. Lindquist and Molnar pointed out our long-standing cultural tradition of calling a troublesome child a "bad seed."

> As adults, we need to acknowledge the nature of this world more frequently in our discussions of youth violence. These discussions [of youth violence] have been mired in grand oversimplifications and hard-edged absolutes. Complexity and tentativeness seem to have little place either in the body politic or on talk radio. (1995, p. 50)

After all, children have not created this present situation. Children do not produce the guns. Children are not in charge of alcohol and drug distribution.

> Considering the scale of violence in our culture, it is surprising that citizens are so ill-informed about its causes and cures. Perhaps this is because those who shout the loudest know the least, particularly politicians who exploit the public fear of crime. Trapped in survival-mode mentality, the public wastes resources fighting delinquents instead of delinquency. (Brendtro and Long, 1995, p. 53)

The school setting naturally lends itself to the creation of sanctuary-type environments (Bloom, 1995a; 1997). But to turn a system around, a great deal of preparatory work has to be accomplished first. A consensus must be reached by all the concerned parties in the school setting, using an agreed-upon theoretical base for planning strategy. In every school, only a small proportion of the student body creates most of the problems. These are the conduct-disordered children who can be identified in grade school, but who tend just to be moved on from one grade to the next. Schools in the past have not been successful at managing these children.

Some of the problems schools encounter are similar to problems in the psychiatric system. In 1975, Congress passed the Education for All Handicapped Children Act. Schools were given strict guidelines requiring them to provide education for all students. Although well-intentioned and of benefit to many students, these measures did not provide adequate provisions that would help schools manage the more disruptive students. Schools coped as best they could, but as the numbers and degree of violence of these students increased, some schools resorted to punishment and expulsion to get rid of the most troublesome children. Obviously, this did not turn out to be a good solution. "Excluding violent students from an education is no more moral than forcing the most critical patients from an emergency room. These students need to belong somewhere" (Brendtro and Long, 1995).

It is clear that the violent and disruptive students in high school were usually the behaviorally problematic children in grade school, and that most of these problems originated in abuse and neglect at home, often exacerbated by punitive measures in school. These are the most traumatized children, and they can only be understood and managed by having a cognitive framework that helps organize our thinking so that we can plan coherent strategies. Victims of trauma require a balanced approach—nurturing, compassion, and care, balanced with a strong emphasis on self-discipline, personal accountability, and social responsibility. It is not a "hard" approach versus a "soft" approach, but an integrated approach that makes a difference. But to accomplish the development of an integrated approach, all of the members of the school community who are devising a violence prevention strategy for the school must share a knowledge base and a set of fundamental assumptions similar to the ones we have outlined earlier.

Any school that takes on this challenge will find that success requires a much broader understanding and wider goals than providing violence prevention programs or conflict resolution courses. It requires system change. Creating safe schools requires change from everyone—teachers, administrators, school boards, and the wider community. In many ways, our schools are as archaic and unresponsive to human needs as are our hospitals, prisons, work settings, media, and government.

The goal of the school is to prepare children to become healthy and useful, contributing citizens. In the world we now live in, learning the three Rs, though necessary, is not sufficient. Just as important is the development of what Brendtro and Long (1995) have called the four As: attachment, achievement, autonomy, and altruism. "The best ... programs seek to do more than change individual students. Instead, they try to transform the total school environment into a learning community in which students live by a credo of nonviolence" (Johnson and Johnson 1995, p. 64). Peter Senge, author of *The Fifth Discipline,* takes this even further in his description of a learning organization as "an organization in which people at all levels are, collectively, continually enhancing their capacity to create things they really want to create" (O'Neil, 1995, p. 21). The schools can only change for the better if the administrators and teachers have an environment that is as physically, emotionally, socially, and morally safe as the one they must create for their students. Blaming the schools for all of the problems, while refusing to take responsibility as an entire social group for the welfare of our children is unforgivable. Schools now must provide far more extensive services than in the past and we can and should expect that this is going to cost more. We get what we pay for.

Violence prevention programs that are successful take this wide approach. "The public schools don't work worth a damn," declared Joseph P. Alibrandi, CEO of the Whittaker Corporation, Los Angeles, after years of trying to assist schools in the 1980s. "Band-Aids won't work anymore. We need a total restructuring" (Wallis, 1995). To implement this change, schools seek consensus, organize centrally, attain central office support, include all elements of the community, study the problem carefully, look at various curriculum approaches, review existing policies and procedures and change whatever is necessary, devise intervention strategies based on this wide assessment, provide for evaluation of these strategies, develop a crisis response and crisis teams, evaluate and modify security measures, carefully train staff and students for crises, and implement changes in policy that will make the school safer for everyone (Watson, 1995). In the process of this intensive and protracted conversation between all vital school elements, the system changes. In such a setting a "group consciousness" can arise that in itself begins the process of creating an environment of safety for the students. This becomes the basis of the shared assumptions, shared goals, and shared practice that is so essential for system change (Bloom, 1997).

The change in the system really needs to begin with the adults who run it. Senge has made observations about the educational system that is just as true for the professionals working in the psychiatric, medical, prison system, and child protection systems,

A large percentage of people enter this profession with a high sense of personal purpose. It is converted into a liability, because within a few years they become extraordinarily cynical . . . if you dig down deep enough you'll find that sense of purpose and deep caring in the most hardened cynic . . . [But how do you harvest this gold mine?]. The process always involves two dimensions. One is creating a reflective environment and a degree of safety where individuals can rediscover what they really care about. And the second dimension is to bring those people together in such a way that their individual visions can start to interact. (O'Neil, 1995)

As in any system, strong leadership is necessary for effective change, as is a movement from a vertical hierarchy to a more weblike organizational structure. Bernie Hoffman, retired Deputy Superintendent of the award-winning Neshaminy, Pennsylvania, School District, has emphasized how vital central office support is for any program implementation. Bernie calls himself a "benevolent dictator" and before his retirement, he took charge of all violence prevention efforts in the district. He saw his job as constantly "running interference" between the larger social sphere and the programs in the school. He put himself in charge of the crisis intervention team, he wrangled for money for the program, and dealt with the press whenever an incident occurred. Under his leadership, strong and creative team interventions became the norm, a wide circle of connections with community members and agencies were established, and he mobilized an exceptionally dedicated staff to often radically alter their schedules to bring about changes in the school.

Establishing Safety in the Schools

The first goal in establishing a school as a sanctuary is reclaiming the sense of safety that is so vital if any learning is to occur. There has to be a "zero tolerance" for violence of any kind. A variety of different measures may have to be instituted in order for the adults in the system to regain sufficient control of the physical environment for the children and faculty to feel safe once again. Most schools have increased security and many have installed security cameras, have requested extra police, and have even installed metal detectors to try to screen out weapons. One administrator has utilized breathalyzers to test for alcohol use on school grounds, requiring parents of disruptive students to accompany their children to classes, having disruptive students pay for the time lost, rewriting and instituting stricter disciplinary codes, contacting police immediately upon suspicion of illegal drug use (Wallis, 1995).

Chicago school officials hired security staffs composed of parents and other community members and found that the conspicuous presence of more adults, particularly parents, was the most successful deterrent to school violence. In Buffalo and Memphis, telephone tip lines were established for students to report weapon possession and Memphis even paid children for reporting weapons on school grounds. Baltimore held several "safe school summits" and found that students needed the creation of "safe corridors" so they could safely get to school and get home. Community members, churches, and other agencies responded by providing children with "safe havens" on their school routes (Crouch and Williams, 1995).

Safety on college and university campuses has posed problems as well. In 1990, Congress enacted the Campus Security Act mandating that all post-secondary institutions receiving Federal aid must report specific crime statistics on an annual basis. It also required them to develop educational programs for safety and security and to establish policies and procedures for notifying the proper authorities when a crime occurs. They were also mandated, as a later amendment, to provide programs aimed at reducing sexual assault (Nichols, 1995).

The University of Washington responded to an outbreak of violence on campus with a firm resolve. They convened a task force that was comprised of students, faculty, staff, administration, police, fire officials, liquor control board officials, and representatives from the community. Unregulated alcohol consumption with subsequent rowdyism, sometimes escalating to violence, was focused on the fraternities and sororities, particularly during their scheduled parties. These clubs were located off-campus as separate corporations and therefore not under the university regulations. However, the charter of the clubs was dependent on the continuing approval of the university. The task force agreed that the fraternity or sorority would be required to get a permit from the university in order to have a party, and a banquet permit from the liquor control board. Such a permit required the clubs to post the permit. Alcohol could be served only to guests of legal age, and the premises could be inspected on an announcement basis only. Also, sorority and fraternity leaders had to sign the permits, thus incurring civil and criminal liability. The police were to be notified in advance of any party and any police incidents would be forwarded to the University President for Student Affairs. The result was that 1993 produced the lowest arrest and expulsion level in the previous two decades (Shanahan, 1995).

Actions such as these are tremendously powerful in conveying to the school community that responsible adults are taking charge and are serious about the problem of violence. It is an absolutely essential first step about which there can be no ambivalence. The entire community must join together to change what in many schools has become normal behavior. The specific actions taken may not be as critical as the consistency and coherence of the message. In the beginning of change, these methods alone can be of enormous benefit in reclaiming a sense of safety. They are the "hard" options that are absolutely necessary in order to restore order to a system in chaos. But they are not enough.

Reconstructing the School System

The safety measures are necessary but will not hold without reinforcing change in the entire context that has until now supported a culture of violence. These aspects of violence prevention within the schools can be broken down into primary, secondary, and tertiary prevention (Brendtro and Long, 1995). Secondary and tertiary prevention efforts focus on identifying and treating children at risk beginning in the elementary schools. The Neshaminy School District has been awarded local, state, regional, and national awards for their programs designed to target these children and guarantee that their needs will be met and their life course altered. Neshaminy is an interesting example because it is a school district that is responsible for 10,500 children of a mixed socioeconomic group. Part of the district extends into very wealthy areas of Bucks County, an area of large country estates, expansive lawns, and country clubs. The other part of the district extends through solidly middle-class and working-class neighborhoods.

Their oldest program is the NEST—Neshaminy Educational Support Team, an outgrowth of the Student Assistance Programs that were instituted throughout the state of Pennsylvania in the 1980s. The NEST program has twice won the Safe and Drug Free School Recognition Program awarded by Presidents Bush and Clinton. Originally focused on substance abuse problems, these teams of faculty and staff operating at the elementary, middle, and high school levels found many kinds of problems so interrelated and connected that they had to be prepared to deal with anything. At the elementary and middle schools most of their work focuses on preventive maintenance functions, while the high school teams function more as a crisis intervention program. When a child gets into some kind of trouble, the team acts to evaluate the situation, involve the parents, refer to treatment, and make any connections that need to be made for the child to show improvement. Neshaminy developed one of the first crisis response teams in the East and responds to any emergency that involves a school student—accidents, severe or fatal illnesses, shootings, attempted suicides, suicides, and murders. They institute debriefing for the students directly involved and also target the at-risk children who could be negatively influenced by whatever tragedy has occurred. When the team intervenes, 75 percent of the parents and children are willing to go for help. The parents consistently perceive that the team members are offering a caring rather than a punitive response, and take the recommendations seriously.

Over time, the district administrators realized that they were spending 92 to 95 percent of their time at the secondary level, on 2 to 4 percent of the students. Security measures such as searching lockers, patroling lunchrooms, and monitoring discipline was simply not doing the job and in addition, the other children were being neglected. They decided that the disruptive child would not continue to take the vast majority of the instructional day resisting measures that were not working anyway.

Their response was to create three other programs directly targeted at the children at risk for long-term problems. One program, called PASS, for Planned Actions Stimulating Success, takes children who are guaranteed to fail, who have identifiable factors at middle school that escalate as they move into high school. These are children who have had discipline problems, multiple suspensions, particularly for fighting, have failed at least one full grade prior to grade nine, are sixteen years or older, are at-risk for mental health and substance abuse problems, and have family problems. This program pairs each student with a faculty member who provides ongoing support—at least twice as much as for other students. The faculty members serves as the "gluon," the person who connects the child up with whatever services are necessary that will help him become more successful. The objective is to break the "cycle of failure."

The school-based probation program is geared for youngsters who are on probation for any offense and are obviously heading toward repeat offending. An arrangement was worked out with the county probation office to have probation officers—three staff members—on the school campus. The probation officers provide preventive maintenance for the younger children and can be called in to talk to kids who appear to be taking a wrong turn. For the older children on probation, the probation officer checks on them regularly; if they are absent from school he calls to find out where they are. If the child has a disciplinary suspension, he does not get to sit at home watching television or playing with his friends, but instead reports to the probation officer for whatever county work duty he is assigned to do. The on-site presence of law enforcement officers on the school grounds gives a very positive message of concern and vigilance to the children on probation but also says to the other children that breaking the law is not as much fun as it appears to be on TV. The result has been lowered absenteeism and lowered discipline occurrences.

The alternative school program is for children who are conduct disordered in ninth to twelfth grade. It combines a regular educational program with intensive therapy and indoor Outward Bound activities. The program is housed in a huge barn facility away from the main school campus. Children who are repeatedly in trouble, disruptive in the classroom, and interfere with the learning of others are sent to this school for a forty-five-day cycle. If they are successful but not quite ready to go, then they can attend the alternative school for up to ninety days, but rarely any longer. During that time they are expected to keep up with their normal classroom activities but intensive attention is given to addressing their special therapeutic needs and providing them with a corrective emotional and social experience. If they do well in the program, they return to their regular class with a clean disciplinary slate. When this information was obtained, the alternative school was operating in its second year and out of forty students, thirty-eight appeared to have been successful. One student had dropped out of school and the other continued to pose serious disciplinary problems and at the time, expulsion was considered a possibility. But the rest of the kids were showing definite improvement. All of these programs are voluntary and admission is dependent on the approval of the student and the parents.

And the price tag? Thirty-three dollars per student in the district per year. For the price of a double CD, six pairs of socks, or a cheap dinner for two, a school can provide for the needs of the most disturbed kids while continuing to provide high-quality educational services to all of the children in a safe school environment.

Innovative programs and a strong commitment to addressing the needs of the most troubled youngsters can go a long way toward restoring order to the school systems. But restoring order is not sufficient. Just because overt violence has been decreased, does not mean that the problems have been solved. We have to learn other ways of resolving conflicts together that encourage and support human growth and connection.

Reconnection and Primary Prevention

The schools are an essential part of our socialization system, and these days the schools often are forced to compensate for lessons and experience that children cannot get at home. This deficit certainly is due to the loss of structure and viability of the nuclear family, but is also related to the very real possibility that there is something seriously wrong with the "nuclear" family in the first place. We currently tend to romanticize the idealized Ozzie-and-Harriet family of the 1950s. But it is quite likely that many of our present problems stem from the postwar widespread loss of extended family networks and community attachments, huge social changes that have effected all of us and over which we have had little control.

The human species is designed to live in groups. Group living is a part of our evolutionary makeup. Children function best in situations that provide a wide variety of attachments to people of different gender, interest, and age which they can freely choose according to their own particular needs. Obviously, living in a nuclear family is not necessarily the best way to learn about functioning in groups. Such a situation severely limits the repertoire of behavior and responses that a child is able to learn. Under the best of circumstances, the school compensates for this deficit. The school environment provides a child with a wider experience with other people in a group setting. Unfortunately, our present schools are largely divorced from the broader community and children have little access to adults outside of the school system and often have relatively little contact with other children outside of their specific age group. But all of that could be altered if we have the will to do so.

Can we expect the schools to solve all of our social problems? Certainly not without a great deal of help from the rest of us. But yes, the schools could solve—or rather prevent—many of our future problems but it does mean some rather dramatic changes in the way we currently think of schools. After all, the schools need to change just as every aspect of our social system needs to change, "What is it that keeps us from beginning to recognize that, just as in the realm of medicine, the way schools treat children is so very often cause of the supposed problem?" (Mercogliano 1995, p. 10). If we can change the structure of the way the schools work, it may be possible to provide an environment that is therapeutic and preventative, by using the natural resources that are already available in the schools but that remain relatively untapped.

The School as Therapeutic Community

Human beings thrive in environments that are safe, structured, and relatively ordered but within which the maximal amount of freedom and creativity is encouraged and supported. We are a species that has strong emotional reactions but we only learn over time and experience how to manage those emotions in ways that are life-enhancing and nonviolent, and we only learn in the context of our relationships with others of our kind. We innately mimic the behaviors of those around us and therefore, we do best when there is a great variety of responses to choose from and more experienced members of the community who are able to help direct and guide us when we are lost or confused. We are innately empathic to the distress of others but easily learn to protect ourselves from this connection by developing ways of coping that can become quite cruel. We are leaders and followers and these abilities appear also to be at least partially innate. We must create. Our tendencies to create art, music, performance, and dance are evolved and innate capacities that must have expression if we are to be healthy and whole. Our propensity to seek knowledge, to experiment, and to satisfy our curiosity is innate and any curbing of that propensity without redirection will lead to pathology. As one innovative educator puts it,

> Our systems of conventional schools, both public and private, with all of their fear- and control-driven practices, have consistently failed to take into account the fact that human children—and all animal young, for that matter—are inexorably programmed to learn. (Mercogliano, 1995, p. 4)

Children need to learn the process of practicing democracy from the moment they set foot in a school. The classroom needs to be children's first experience in learning how to do group process while preserving individual integrity. This means creating classrooms that are therapeutic communities. This is not a new concept. In the psychiatric literature, Maxwell Jones envisioned schools as therapeutic communities, "My own experience working as a facilitator in a classroom setting has convinced me that social learning could, with advantage, be added to the formal curriculum from elementary school onwards" (Hinshelwood and Manning 1979, p. 8). David Clark pointed out that "Some of the most famous experimental schools have been very like therapeutic communities . . . . At A.S. Neill's Summerhill School there is a School Council that makes all the rules, where teachers and children have equal votes" (Clark, 1975, p. 96). John Dewey, A.S. Neill, Ivan Illich, Paolo Friere, Jonathan Kozol, and others have argued for years about the need for school reform. But now, the needs are urgent. On the one hand, schools do need to take the "hard" line approaches if order and safety are to be restored to the school setting. But simultaneously, the schools need to provide environments within which troubled children who are not appropriate for alternative settings can still be managed without causing a deterioration in the educational opportunities for the healthier children. "We must redesign schools to restore the sense of tribe . . . and prevent 'broken belongings'" observe educators Larry Brendtro and Nicholas Long (1995, p. 57). This process has been called "Creating Sanctuary in the Classroom" (Bloom, 1995a, 1997).

In this model, the classroom would become a sanctuary-type environment from elementary school through high school. With our present system this would be somewhat easier to accomplish in the elementary years since the children spend the entire year with the same group of students and teachers. An essential goal of the entire classroom group would be to create a "cooperative context" for learning in which students learn how to resolve conflicts constructively (Johnson and Johnson, 1995). This learning can proceed in parallel with more traditional educational goals as the social context itself becomes the medium within which the message of the educational discussion is actively learned. At any point in the school day a child or teacher could call a "council meeting" to immediately resolve interpersonal problems that are interfering with learning (Mercogliano, 1995). Such changes require "significant changes in the content and process of education . . . there's absolutely no choice but trying to create change on multiple levels" (O'Neil, 1995). This type of thinking requires change at the paradigmatic level, at the level of basic assumptions and structure and without such change, simple instrumental changes were useless.

One of the fundamental changes that needs to be made is an effort to understand and redirect disruptive and deviant behavior rather than condemning it or punishing it. We still have much to learn from our Native American neighbors. In the Seneca tradition, children are not punished for their wrongdoing because each offense contains a lesson to be learned (Mercogliano, 1995). But, if children are to learn from their mistakes rather than just repeating them, their social support system must have in place specific structures that are required for learning to take place and a philosophy that encourages and supports such learning. In a system that really works—a family, a hospital, a school, a prison—these structures are in place and people do learn. When learning does not occur and children continually make the same mistakes then we need to pay more attention to what is lacking in the structure of a learning organization than in what is lacking in the child.

In such a self-governing, conflict-resolution, cooperative system children can learn to resolve their own problems. They can think for themselves, cooperatively govern and problem solve without violence. In such a community atmosphere, children have the opportunity to develop attachments with many different people. If these attachments are promoted early enough in a child's life, much of the damage that occurs in their family of origin can be undone or at least mitigated. Even problem children can learn to modulate their emotional experiences, can learn to accept the soothing of others and learn to self-soothe. In such a system, children can have experiences with authority figures that are not abusive and in doing so, they can learn the real practice of basic democracy. As a result, they learn how to protect themselves more effectively from abusive authority. If reading, writing, arithmetic, literature, science, and history are learned in parallel with the skills that go into developing emotional intelligence, then all learning and awareness is enhanced.

Children who have other people to turn to who can help them manage overwhelming feelings, are far less likely to turn to addictive substances or other self-destructive behaviors that serve as inadequate substitutes for loving human relationships. In a community setting where open and honest communication is valued, children can see the consequences of each other's behavior and can insist that each other assume responsibility for those behaviors. Children are capable of establishing equitable systems of justice and restitution that teach them important and far-reaching life skills.

In referring to school reform, Seymour Sarason has summed up his evaluation of efforts to change the school system:

> Schools have been intractable to change and the attainment of goals set by reformers. A major failure has been the inability of reformers to confront this intractability. As a result, each new wave of reform learns nothing from earlier efforts and comes up with recommendations that have failed in the past. What is called reform is based on an acceptance of the system as it has been and is. Change will not occur unless there is an alteration of power relationships among those in the system and within the classroom. Altering these power relationships is necessary, but it is not a sufficient condition for obtaining desired changes. This is especially true for proposals that seek to give a greater role in decision making to teachers. There are two basic issues. The first is the assumption that schools exist primarily for the growth and development of children. That assumption is invalid because teachers cannot create and sustain the conditions for the productive development of children if those conditions do not exist for teachers. The second issue is that there is now an almost unbridgeable gulf that students perceive between the world of the school and the world outside of it. Schools are uninteresting places in which the interests and questions of children have no relevance to what they are required to learn in the classroom. Teachers continue to teach subject matter, not children. Any reform effort that does not confront these two issues and the changes they suggest is doomed. (Sarason, 1990, p. xiv)

MAKING THE WORKPLACE SAFE

According to a survey in 1993, only 28 percent of companies in the United States have a formal plan for preventing violence and only 22 percent had plans to introduce a strategy (Anfuso, 1994). In 1994, the American Management Association found that slightly less than half of private-sector companies surveyed provided counseling to victimized employees. Only 35 percent had policies and procedures that instructed workers on how to deal with a violent threat or incident (Yarborough, 1994).

The initial corporate response is usually to improve basic safety, just as creating physical safety is the first vital mission in any attempt to "create sanctuary." Hiring guards, installing security cameras, adding locks, installing bullet-proof glass are all measures that may be recommended. Prescreening to keep potentially violent people out of the workplace is another common intervention, but fraught with difficulties because of the impossibility of predicting behavior far into the future as well as the possibility of getting inaccurate information. It is possible to hire companies to do full background checks and this may be helpful. One useful technique is to use "behavior-based" interviewing in which the interviewer actually asks the job candidate how he or she would respond in certain provocative or challenging situations (Anfuso, 1994).

On the job, managers should be trained in how to recognize and manage violent behaviors, and action plans need to be developed that include processes for reporting threats. Many companies are providing managers' workshops designed to help managers understand how to support workers who have been involved in a crime (Anfuso, 1994). Some companies are using hotlines as the answer to threat reporting. Hardee's has a twenty-four-hour crisis-reporting center run by the loss prevention staff. The U.S. Postal Service has two toll-free numbers for help. Threats are taken very seriously and are promptly investigated by Postal Service crisis intervention teams, a response to the deaths of thirty-six postal workers since 1986. (Anfuso, 1994). The results for the Postal Service have been impressive. In 1993, investigators devoted more than 100,000 hours to investigating incidents and threats, along with many other changes in management and training. Reported assaults at post office facilities began to drop steadily; in 1990, 424 were reported and in 1993, 214 (Toufexis, 1994).

The necessity for crisis management teams who could defuse crises as they began to develop, and to manage them should they escalate, has been a strategy utilized in many emergency settings. Similar recommendations have been made for the business community. Says Michael R. Losey, president and CEO of the Society for Human Resource Management, "An established crisis management team, which has been trained to anticipate the needs of a workforce after a crisis, gives employees a sense of stability and security" *(USA Today,* 1995a). Dupont created a Corporate Threat Management team to develop an action plan for handling threats, harassment, and physical attacks that included representatives from security, external affairs, human resources, and company's, Employee Assistance Program (EAP) (Anfuso, 1994). According to Charles Labig, a management consultant, every company should have a violence response team in place. This team's mandate is to gather facts about a potentially violent situation, decide if the company should intervene, and, if so, identify the most appropriate method of doing so. The team develops a course of action to resolve any threat of violence, while protecting potential victims. (Labig, 1995, p. 15)*

Changing the Culture

But physical and behavioral safety measures, along with trying to keep violent people out of the workplace, are not enough. More important is creating a "violence-free company culture" (Barrier, 1995a). There are many different aspects to the creation of such a culture, some of which involve setting much clearer limits and firmer expectations, and others of which place a strong emphasis on education, personal communication, openness, democratic and consensus decision making, and freedom of expression.

Joseph Kinney, of the National Safe Workplace Institute observes that "The boundaries of allowable behavior have changed. We've allowed people to get away with too much. Companies need to go back and redefine those boundaries. If somebody's abusive toward somebody else, they need to be disciplined" (Anfuso, 1994). This means setting a "zero tolerance" for violence whether it is physical, verbal, or nonverbal (Barrier, 1995b). The cultural norm must be established that violence is to be taken extremely seriously—any threat of violence whether it is subtle or direct. Such incidents must be documented and investigated. Actions must be reported to the authorities and prosecuted to the fullest extent (Duncan, 1995; Barrier 1995b). Procedures must be put in place to guide employees in various potentially dangerous situations (Duncan, 1995). It is important to emphasize that a threat of violence is an act of violence. Garry G. Mathiason, a lawyer and specialist in workplace violence points out that "a threat can do independent damage and have tremendous psychological consequences . . . it is in fact, the growth of threatening words and behavior that has turned workplace violence into a major national phenomenon" (Barrier, 1995b, p. 19).

Many businesses are using the new concern about violence as a way of defining cultural values within the company. Liz Claiborne, Inc., and

---

Polaroid Corporation are providing programs about domestic violence. Liz Claiborne offers an EAP and family stress seminars, and a national outreach campaign about domestic abuse. Polaroid offers its employees flextime, short-term paid leave, and extended leave without pay to seek protection and legal recourse against domestic violence, as well as providing EAP services (McMurry, 1995). These companies are taking a strong position and in doing so are establishing a different social norm and set of expectations in relation to violence, at work and at home.

Wainwright Industries in St. Peters, Missouri, and Arlington, Texas, has made even more progress and as a result, violence at their two plants is virtually nonexistent. Wainwright is a family-owned business that manufactures stamped and machined products. The corporate policy from the top down is one of open communications in problem solving. They provide all employees with basic skills training in interpersonal relationships with an established norm in how to "treat people with the kind of respect and dignity you would expect to be treated with. It's pretty much Golden Rule training," says vice president David Robbins. The company relies on a suggestion system that last year yielded fifty-four implemented recommendations per employee. The managers are committed to responding to suggestions within twenty-four hours and to developing a plan for implementation of accepted suggestions within seventy-two hours. All their employees are salaried so they are paid whether they come to work or not, but consistently since 1984, they have had a 99 percent attendance. Everybody—from the president on down—wears the same uniform. Wainwright is a team-oriented company and the pressure to perform up to standard comes from peers and teammates, not from bosses. In 1994, Wainwright won the Malcolm Baldridge National Quality Award, established by Congress in 1987 (Barrier, 1995a).

HEALTH CARE RE-REFORM
AND THE COST OF VIOLENCE

If what we presently call health care is reformed, then we need to re-reform it as soon as possible. Health care has been almost totally taken over by moneyed interests and the quality of care is desperately jeopardized. It is simply absurd that a country of our size and wealth cannot provide high quality health care to all its citizens. The present situation, which is driven almost solely by market forces, must be stopped. Large proportions of the health care provider network have already been thoughtlessly deconstructed and it will take time for recovery, but it must be done. As always, mental health services have suffered the hardest, despite the fact that the economic losses that follow in the wake of mental illness are enormous and, to a large extent, preventable. Probably, the most important change that has occurred to the health care system is the radical departure from the traditional physician/patient relationship, wherein the physician is regarded as an advocate for the patient, to a new paradigm in which the patient is viewed as an individual to be manipulated to increase the profit of the third party/stockholder/physician (Warner, 1996).

The provision of good, thorough, and responsible health care for everyone is essential for primary, secondary, and tertiary prevention. But under the current system, none of the three levels of care can be guaranteed. The "invasion by commercialism of an arena formerly governed by professionalism poses severe hazards to the care of the sick and the welfare of communities: the health of the public and the public health" (McArthur and Moore, 1997). There are inherent ethical disruptions and corruption in a system in which incentives to underutilize services, delays in care, postponement of consultation or hospitalization, gatekeeping, a lack of concern for patient satisfaction, a lack of concern for physician satisfaction, and a seal on information disclosure about these practices are a part of expected practice (Rosner, 1997). Clinicians are calling for a medical ethic that is centered on the patient's "damaged humanity," rather the commercial needs of investor-owned, for-profit managed care companies (Churchill, 1997), a system of care that is based on social justice (Webb, 1996).

> Health care itself is more than a commodity, it is a personal healing activity carried out through institutions that embody values such as respect for persons, the value of human life, and duties to care for individuals who suffer. These issues fall under major overarching concerns on the macro level. Reform, however, often functions as a euphemism for changing the health care system to provide greater profitability, and for controlling costs. Admittedly, such changes can be disguised under reforming the health care system, and indeed, some of them are capable of enhancing and simultaneously making more efficient, our care for one another when sick. Most changes, nonetheless, are clearly driven from less noble ideals. Every schema for providing care also embodies values since these schemas presuppose various competing notions of justice and equity. Further, they may endanger long-held values of health care providers in meeting the needs of patients. (Thomasma, 1996, p. 233)

All of this is set within a larger social context of a need for escalating services to victims of violence. Since the arguments in favor of this kind of reform have been wholly based on economics and an insistence on cost savings, then perhaps it would be wise to review the economic costs of violence to the society and weigh treating violence against not treating it.

The Cost of Violence

It is the contention of these authors and many others that a significant proportion of mental illness and substance abuse is directly and indirectly related to exposure to violence. The burden of mental illness and substance abuse on American society has been known for some time, although indirect costs are always difficult to measure. It is estimated that in 1985, the total economic costs of mental illness were $103.7 billion and direct treatment and support accounted for $42.5 billion or 11.5 percent of the total personal health care spending for all illnesses (Rice, Kelman, and Miller, 1992). Adding alcohol and drug abuse to mental illness for estimate of total losses to the economy, the 1988 estimate was $273.3 billion, including $85.8 billion for alcohol abuse and $58.3 billion for drug abuse. This figure included $47.5 billion in other related costs, including the costs of crime, motor vehicle crashes, fire destruction, and the value of productivity losses for victims of crime, incarceration, crime careers, and caregiver services. The cost of acquired immunodeficiency syndrome associated with drug abuse was estimated at $1 billion, and the cost of fetal alcohol syndrome was estimated at $1.6 billion (Rice, Kelman, and Miller, 1991).

Approaching the problem from a slightly different point of view we can look at some specific costs of violence. For instance, one researcher in the ophthalmology department of an inner-city hospital on the East Coast, determined the number of ocular injuries secondary to trauma and then calculated that just for the 48 percent of patients who had to be hospitalized, the direct costs for hospitalization were $975,089 (Hemady, 1994). Another group looked at how much it cost to provide acute care for violence-related injuries in one hospital for a year—they estimated $8 million, and 80 percent of that was paid for with public funds (Sumner, Mintz, and Brown, 1987). Another group looked at the financial impact of intentional violence on a community hospital and calculated that in a four-year period there were 108 firearm injuries and 103 injuries related to cutting or piercing incidents, with hospital charges of over $2 million. The hospital was only reimbursed for 30 percent of these charges (Clancy et al., 1994). Reviewing the use of hospital resources by children admitted for intentionally inflicted injuries, investigators noted that these children use more hospital resources and consequently incur higher hospital charges than those with unintentional injuries. (Wright and Litaker, 1996). Another group examined gunshot wounds to children in an urban pediatric hospital from 1986-1992 and calculated that there were 4,587 admissions costing an estimated $1.63 million to the hospital since so many of the patients had public or no insurance. (Nance, Templeton, O'Neill, 1994). Domestic violence already costs companies nationwide $3 to $5 billion annually in absenteeism, reduced productivity, and increased health care costs (Anfuso, 1994). Irazuta and colleagues found that the child abuse cases at a pediatric intensive care unit had the highest severity of illness, the highest hospital charges, and the highest mortality rates. The medical bills for the acute care of the child abuse patient averaged $35,641 per case and even with these expenditures, 70 percent died and 60 percent of the survivors had severe residual morbidity (1997).

Available data shows that in 1992, gunshots killed 37,776 Americans; cut/stab wounds killed 4,095. Another 134,000 gunshot survivors and 3,100,000 cut/stab wound survivors received medical treatment. Annually, gunshot wounds cost an estimated U.S. $126 billion. Cut/stab wounds cost another U.S. $51 billion. The gunshot and cut/stab totals include U.S. $40 billion and U.S. $13 billion respectively in medical, public services, and work-loss costs. For medically treated cases, costs average U.S. $154,000 per gunshot survivor and U.S. $12,000 per cut/stab survivor. Gunshot wounds are more than three times as common in the U.S. than in Canada, which has strict handgun control. With the same quality of life loss per victim, gunshot costs per capita are an estimated U.S. $495 in the United States versus U.S. $180 in Canada (Miller and Cohen, 1997).

In 1993, Miller, Cohen, and Rossman calculated the victims' costs of violent crime for the United States using figures from 1987 and dollars valued at 1989 prices. According to their findings, in 1987 physical injury to people age twelve and older as a result of rape, robbery, assault, murder, and arson caused about $10 billion in potential health-related costs, including some unmet mental health care needs. This led to $23 billion in lost productivity and almost $145 billion in reduced quality of life. If associated deaths and cases resulting in psychological injury only are included, costs average $47,000 for rape, $19,000 for robbery, $15,000 for assault, and $25,000 for arson. Considering only survivors with physical injury, rape cost $60,000, robberies $25,000, assaults $22,000, and arson $50,000. Costs are almost $2.4 million per murder. Lifetime costs for all intentional injuries totaled $178 billion during 1987 to 1990 (Miller, Cohen, and Rossman, 1993). When the cost of pain, suffering, and the reduced quality of life is taken into consideration, the cost of crime to victims is an estimated $450 billion a year (Miller, Cohen, and Weirsema, 1996).

After examining these figures, one is forced to asked why we would destroy the best health care system the world has ever known—flawed as it may have been—rather than systematically addressing the causes of violence. Banning handguns, banning corporal punishment, providing adequate social services, mental health, and substance abuse treatment to families could go along way to reducing our health care bill and improving individual and social health. Does it make sense instead, to sacrifice the health care system, ultimately driving costs even higher? Pay now or pay later are the only two options.

Physicians' Call to Action

Physicians in Pennsylvania have organized to form the Pennsylvania Committee to Defend Health Care and their "Call to Action" was published in the *Journal of the American Medical Association* in December, 1997. The organization is sponsored by Philadelphia Physicians for Social Responsibility and the Ad Hoc Committee to Defend Health Care, led by Bernard Lown, MD, the 1985 Nobel Peace Prize recipient. Among any group of physicians there will be areas of disagreement, but this group has defined some clear areas of common ground:

1. Medicine and nursing must not be diverted from their primary tasks: the relief of suffering, the prevention and treatment of illness, and the promotion of health. The efficient deployment of resources is critical, but must not detract from these goals.
2. Pursuit of corporate profit and personal fortune have no place in caregiving.
3. Potent financial incentives that reward overcare or undercare weaken doctor-patient and nurse-patient bonds, and should be prohibited. Similarly, business arrangements that allow corporations and employers to control the care of patients should be proscribed.
4. A patient's right to a physician of choice must not be curtailed.
5. Access to health care must be the right of all.

This group is hoping to help mobilize a national effort to health care out of the hands of profiteers and put it back where it belongs—between patients and their health care providers.

We believe a colleague from Mount Sinai in New York, sums up the situation most accurately and that these sentiments apply to all health care providers, whether they are physicians or not: "Medicine is, at its center, a moral enterprise grounded in a covenant of trust. Only by caring and advocating for the patient can the integrity of our profession be affirmed" (Cassel, 1996, p. 291).

PRISONS AND THE CRIMINAL JUSTICE SYSTEM

We are the most violent society in the western world and have a greater percentage of citizens in jail than any other western country.

Norman Q. Brill, MD
Professor Emeritus, UCLA School of Medicine

Looking at the Problem

Building more prisons, and incarcerating more people, without doing anything about the nature of prison environments is just plain stupid. Prisons are hotbeds of trauma, both because they are filled with people who are already traumatized and violent and because they are traumatogenic environments in which brutality is the expected norm (Gilligan, 1996, Wachtler, 1997). It is clear that if we are to establish safety for all of us, then we need to get the most dangerous offenders off the street and away from us. But, when they get to prison we cannot pretend that punishing them is going to do anything except make them even less socially responsible. These people need treatment—for drugs, for the effects of violence, for the special issues surrounding perpetrations against others. Some of them will show no benefit from treatment whatsoever, presumably because the damage done to them in childhood has been so extensive and pervasive that it has irreparably damaged basic biological systems that are involved in social bonding, the formation of conscience and values, and the control of impulses. These unfortunates will need to stay locked away from everyone else forever, or until some time when we know how to help them. The rest deserve help, regardless of what they have done, to the extent that we know, or can learn, how to help them in ways that produce definite results—a decrease in criminal behavior.

Criminal behavior needs to be understood as "social pathology" not simply "bad" behavior. These people do not *really* make choices—they are so programmed to behave in asocial or antisocial ways that there is no viable choice, no real free will. This does *not* mean that they are not accountable for their behavior. They must be held accountable if we are to maintain safety. But let's not pretend that they have the same options in their lives as someone who is loved, well-treated, and provided with opportunities for normal development. Why are we wasting time, money, and human lives focused on "punishing" offenders when what we should be worried about is protecting society from people who cannot control their destructive impulses and preventing the development of criminal behavior? Why are we placing men who are already badly socialized into environments that are more barbaric and unrelenting then the environments they came from? What are the results? Does it work?

For antisocial adults, their social group has already proven to be an abysmal failure, for all kinds of very complicated reasons. They are part of the whole and we cannot scapegoat them and pretend we have solved the problem of criminal behavior. If we want fewer criminals than we must stop abusing children. If we want the criminals we have made to straighten out, then we must stop abusing them as well. As alluded to earlier, victims of trauma who are also perpetrators are among the most difficult to treat. The shame, guilt, and fear of punishment is so great that it interferes with the capacity to be honest with themselves and with those who try to help, and makes them feel even less deserving of help from others. There appears to be a downward spiral of degradation that begins at the moment when the victim "decides" to become a perpetrator. Every act of perpetration drags the person further down this slippery slope. The earlier the perpetration began, the more difficult it is to pull oneself up again. Our prisons are overfilled with people who have suffered severe abuse and deprivation as children. Our inclination to punish those who break social norms is, at least in part, out of our need for revenge. And those who have grown up in situations in which adults routinely broke the social norms about how to treat children, also are motivated to seek revenge. Their revenge, however, is usually directed at the society, not their families.

It would be difficult to create environments more brutalizing than many of our present prisons. Although we are frightened about crime, with good reason, some of our present approaches to the problem are nonsensical. Unless we are planning to execute everyone who is convicted of a crime, then we need to be prepared for the fact that these men and women are going to be back out on the streets, sooner or later. Since that is the case, it seems that it would be in our best interest—forget what is humane—to see that they come out of prison at least in no worse shape then when they went in. Even more sane would be a fervent effort to help them become better socialized and able to live constructive lives (Elikann, 1996; Gilligan, 1996).

Keeping the system the way it is makes no sense at all if we really want to stop the violence. Judge Dennis Challeen of Wisconsin has pointed out some of the absurdities of our present system as he describes what our goals are for offenders and what we actually get as a result of our punitive methods (Challeen, 1986; Zehr, 1994a, p. 8):

- We want them to have self-worth . . . so we destroy their self-worth.
- We want them to be responsible . . . so we take away all responsibilities.
- We want them to be part of our community . . . so we isolate them from our community.
- We want them to be positive and constructive . . . so we degrade them and make them useless.
- We want them to be nonviolent . . . so we put them where there is violence all around them.
- We want them to be kind and loving people . . . so we subject them to hatred and cruelty.
- We want them to quit being the tough guy . . . so we put them where the tough guy is respected.
- We want them to quit hanging around losers . . . so we put all the losers in the state under one roof.
- We want them to quit exploiting us . . . so we put them where they exploit each other.
- We want them to take control of their own lives, own their own problems, and quit being a parasite . . . so we make them totally dependent on us.

We have set about creating environments that are as traumatogenic as possible, short of reinstituting the use of torture devices and the methods of the Inquisition. Given all we now know about the long-term effects of violence, we can say with certainty that being raped, beaten, terrorized, threatened, humiliated, and made to feel constantly helpless are not good for anyone's physical or mental health. There are people in prison who must never be let out. We have, as yet, no sure-fire way to prevent violence once it has come to dominate a person's existence. We do not yet know how much physiology, brain injury, and genetics may play a role in the etiology of violence. But we do know that violence is a fairly good predictor of more violence. It makes absolutely no sense to put violent and nonviolent prisoners together. It is well-established that prisons are extreme "macho" environments, in which dominance and masculinity are fully equated and only the strongest survive (Rideau and Wikberg, 1994; Toch, 1992). We have to ask whether it even makes sense to put nonviolent people in prison at all; what can we possibly hope to gain? Does prison do anything that will help prevent them from committing crime again? Is prison a deterrent? There is an abundance of evidence that it is not. Let's look at some facts.

Do Prisons Work?

Aggressive, antisocial children tend to become delinquent adolescents and violent adults (Dishion, French, and Patterson, 1994). This is not theoretical information. This has been so firmly established, in so many studies, that the only bizarre thing about it is that the studies have had so little impact on social policy! Some people would like to bury their heads in the sand and say it is all genetic and all we can do is cage them. But, there are virtually no inherited behavior characteristics that do not depend on environment to materialize into actual behavior (Dishion, French, and Patterson, 1994). We do know that maltreated children have an elevated risk for psychopathology and in particular for antisocial behavior and chemical dependency. "A criminal is a misraised, mistrained person, unsuccessfully socialized" (Friedman, 1993).

When these children grow up and keep doing the same things that they have always been doing, they now have bodies and brains large enough to do some real damage. If they have not found a way to be violent in socially acceptable ways, they turn to domestic violence and street crime. When they are caught, we send them to prison. Historically, prisons originated as an attempt to do away with brutal and inhuman punishment. They had four major functions: deterrence, incapacitation, rehabilitation, and punishment. Have prisons accomplished any of these functions? Lois Forer was a trial court judge for many years in Philadelphia until she left the bench protesting a decision she was being forced to make because of mandatory sentencing. She believes an abundance of evidence supports that imprisonment has not deterred crime; the more prisons we build, the more crime there is and the crime rapidly outstrips prison capacity. It has not deterred or incapacitated criminals—they often continue to commit some crimes while in prison and certainly do commit crimes again when they leave. It has not rehabilitated them, since 80.3 percent of male state prisoners and 67.8 percent of female prisoners are recidivists. Whether or not they have been sufficiently punished depends on one's views of what punishment is supposed to do in a civilized society. How does one decide what punishment a person "deserves"?

Prison conditions were horrendous in this country until lawyers involved in civil rights law, such as the National Prison Project, organized for reforms. By the end of the 1970s, prisons had improved throughout the country under the pressure of law. But as the war on drugs has doubled the prison population since 1980, severe crowding has ensued. The present mood of the country appears set on eliminating or severely curbing most of the hard-earned reforms that were instituted throughout these years. Although, our prisons are still better than those of Eastern Europe and the third world, they compare very unfavorably with the more enlightened penal institutions of Europe (Cass, 1995).

Despite an increasingly punitive attitude toward crime, the U.S. rates of robbery, murder, and rape have tripled since 1960 (Brill, 1993). More people are behind bars in America than in any other country in the world (Forer, 1994). The U.S. homicide rate is four to seventy times that of other countries. For every homicide there are 100 assaults reported to emergency rooms. This behavior does not start in adulthood but in children: ten- to seventeen-year-olds are responsible for more than one-half of serious crime the in United States (Brill, 1993). In fact, as has been shown, antisocial and aggressive behavior is one of the most stable of the behavioral characteristics. Nonetheless, we keep building more prisons and spending more of our wealth in doing so. The majority of those in prison are young, and most were convicted of nonviolent property crimes and drug offenses (Forer, 1994).

After people are released from prison, their lives are all but ruined. Many parents have not seen their children for years. Social networks have been destroyed. Often prisoners are forgotten and find it very hard to reestablish family and friendship ties. They have usually been brutalized, often repeatedly raped, and sometimes even enslaved by other inmates. Rape is epidemic in prisons as a show of dominance, an assertion of masculinity, and for sexual pleasure (Gilligan, 1996; Wachtler, 1997). Weaker inmates can find safety only by becoming the "whore" of a stronger inmate to protect them. Sexual assault by one man beats repeated gang rape, endless beatings, or death (Rideau and Wikberg, 1992). For years, inmates are exposed to the enforced helplessness and powerlessness that is prison life. Crowding, ceaseless noise, lack of privacy, constant fear of violence, and enforced passivity are all conditions known to seriously stress even the most stable human being. Release from prison is no guarantee that anything will get better. Even if the prisoners serve their time and "go straight," the stigma of being ex-cons travels with them. Prisons are classified as "total institutions" (Goffman, 1961, p. 5) and the effects of such institutionalization are known to be frequently damaging to healthy subsequent functioning. In addition, our society provides few pathways for the fallen to redeem themselves.

We have no idea yet about the long-term posttraumatic impact of such environments. But, anything that was normal about them before they were imprisoned has been permanently altered. Jobs are extremely hard to obtain for an ex-con, and so is any kind of normal relationship. Before recent "reforms," prisoners may have at least learned how to read in prison, or achieved some higher educational status. But, as James Gilligan, former Director of Mental Health for the Massachusetts prison systems has pointed out, "We know that the single most effective factor which reduces the rate of recidivism in the prison population is education, and yet education in the prisons is the first item to be cut when an administration 'gets tough on crime'" (Gilligan, 1996, p. 188). We do know something about the long-term effects of institutionalization and its impact on a person's indentity. Prison society has its own structure, mores, and status (Wilmer, 1964). Any prisoner who survives has learned the rules of that society and it is extremely difficult to return to "normal" society once he or she has spent years being indoctrinated into another world. Goffman and others wrote prolifically in the 1950s and 1960s about the destructive impact of institutionalization. These critiques in part led to the closure of state institutions for the mentally ill (Goffman, 1961). As a result of the aftereffects of the Vietnam War, we know something about how difficult it is for a man who has been a killer—even a socially sanctioned killer—to return to the rules and mores of normal society. Our prisons are laboratories for the systematic desocialization of people who are already seriously damaged.

What Is to Be Done?

As has been said many times, the behavior of many of the people who end up in prison resembles that of a young child rather than a grown adult.

> It is relatively easy to condone the behavior of a child of two because no ordinary person doubts that the child is not responsible for most of its actions. It tends to take (and eat) what attracts its attention, knock down and wound its rival sibling, play with fire, expose its genitals, and so on. (Jones, 1968, p. 121)

This is not to say that we should condone criminal behavior, but it does give us something to think about regarding our current treatment of criminals. If these are people who are, in fact, developmentally arrested, is such a developmental arrest permanent? Are there interventions that might be more effective than punishment? After all, the "rage to punish" as Judge Forer calls our preoccupation with punishing criminals, can be seen as the childish equivalent response to the criminal's behavior. Punishment may help the punisher feel better, but it does not do much good for the person who is punished. "Making criminals pay" for their crimes is supposed to reinforce and support the social order, but it is us who are paying—with enormous amounts of wealth, with whatever guilt we may feel at the treatment these people receive, and with an escalating level of crime. Is this the behavior of sensible adults?

More important than asking 'How do we punish?" is to ask ourselves: What kind of behavior on our part stands the best chance of bringing about a better outcome on the part of the criminal? We want him (her) to make some sort of restitution for the crime that has been committed, but just as important we want him (her) not to break the law again when he or she is released. We want him (her) to be better socialized and able to live peacefully with other people. If change on the part of the criminal is simply not possible—and many of them will probably never change—then we want them to be in a facility that is safe and that encourages, instead of discourages, whatever socially acceptable skills and abilities the inmates can develop. They may be socially disabled and never able to live outside prison walls again, but as citizens, we do not want to participate in committing unethical or, under other circumstances, criminal, acts toward them. And we certainly want such an environment to be safe enough so that those who refuse or are unable to change cannot do further damage to victimize others.

Workers in the therapeutic community field have recognized the possibility of developing prisons as therapeutic milieus. Maxwell Jones, one of the founders of the therapeutic community model, was the first to write an entire chapter devoted to therapeutic communities in prison in *Social Psychiatry in Practice* (1968). In fact, the mission of his original unit at Belmont Hospital in Great Britain in the late 1940s was to try and do something to rehabilitate the chronically, "hard core" unemployed and certainly included people who now could easily end up in the prison system: "inadequate and aggressive psychopaths, schizoid personalities, early schizophrenia, various drug addictions, sexual perversions" (Jones et al., 1953). His results with long-term treatment in such a program were gratifying. The average length of stay was two to four months, with some staying up to a year. On follow-up six months after discharge, of eighty-two patients, 44 percent had made a satisfactory and 22 percent a fair adjustment as measured by level of symptoms, employment history, wages, social adjustment, environmental conditions, and absenteeism from work. In another study in which he participated, this time in a U.S. Navy facility designated for offenders, a highly positive response occurred when the inmates were designated by levels of maturity, while the same environment was detrimental for inmates demonstrating a low maturity level (Jones, 1968).

Harry Wilmer, as consultant to the Department of Corrections, State of California, wrote a description of a therapeutic community started in 1961 in

San Quentin. He said of these men, "They are dependent and prisonized. They wish not so much to be rehabilitated as to be deinstitutionalized. It is a complex task to help the prisoners free themselves from the dependent gratification of prison and crime, and renounce the rewards and types of satisfaction inherent in the criminal life" (Wilmer, 1964, p. 10). In another study, Turner describes a therapeutic community prison program for adult felons who were considered favorable for selection if they were under twenty-five years of age, had at some time had a close relationship with some adult, had some ability to relate to peers, and rated at the higher levels of a maturity scale. Their median period of treatment was eight months. Between 74 percent and 84 percent of the men showed a favorable outcome after one year (Turner, 1972).

The widest applicability of therapeutic community concepts to prisons was derived from the development of therapeutic communities in the drug treatment, self-help sphere within the general community. These programs tended to be more authoritarian and more highly structured than therapeutic communities within mental hospitals. The treatment results in these programs in the community were gratifying (Barr, 1986). One twelve-year follow-up study of heroin addicts showed that only 23 percent of the original population were using opiates daily. Forty-six percent had no daily use and no major criminal involvement over the years (Simpson, 1986).

Wexler founded a therapeutic community program for incarcerated drug abusers in 1977 in the New York prison system, called "Stay 'N' Out." Of the inmates studied in 1979, the parole revocation rate for the male part of the program was 6 percent, while the control group was 19 percent, and for the female 0 percent compared to 6 percent. He noted five important conditions for successful rehabilitation in the prisons: an isolated treatment unit, motivated participants, a committed and competent staff, adequate treatment duration, and continuity of care that extends into the community (Wexler, 1986). More recently, Wexler published a review article (1995) in which he demonstrates that therapeutic community treatment for incarcerated substance abusers is the treatment of choice; should be widely expanded; and should be increased in effectiveness by providing treatment for comorbid conditions.

At a therapeutic community program in the Delaware correctional system, inmates had to qualify for admission to the substance abuse program and had to strictly follow the rules in order to stay. Violence was not permitted, nor drug use. Supervised by staff, the inmates ran their own community. The men were required to behave appropriately with their fellow community members and with staff, and to the extent that they could not, they were expected to learn. Confrontation of deviant behavior was a generally accepted standard. A firm twelve-step program provided much of the structure for the unit. Men joined the community eighteen months before their discharge from the prison and then were sent to a transitional therapeutic community when they left. Assessment thus far indicates that men who joined the transitional therapeutic community or who were a part of the therapeutic community in the prison and outside had significantly lower rates of drug relapse and criminal recidivism after release. Men who only attended the prison therapeutic community did better than their untreated peers but not as well as those who attended both (Martin, Butzin, and Inciardi, 1995).

Another example of a more humane, enlightened penal institution is McKean, the federal correctional institution in Bradford, Pennsylvania, subject of an article in *Atlantic Monthly* (Worth, 1995). It was considered the most successful medium-security prison in the country. It was badly overcrowded but cost only $15,370 per year for each inmate, compared to the national average of $21,350. It cost about two-thirds of what many state prisons cost, and when it opened in 1989 until 1995, it had an amazing record: no escapes, no homicides, no sexual assaults, no suicides. In six years there were only three serious assaults on staff and six recorded assaults on inmates. This record was achieved under the leadership of Dennis Luther, who managed the prison in a manner similar to a therapeutic community. The root of his approach was unconditional respect for the inmates. His "Beliefs about the Treatment of Inmates" were recorded on plaques throughout the prison and included the beliefs that inmates had been sent to prison *as* punishment not *for* punishment, that correctional workers have a responsibility to send the inmates out to the community better off then they were, that inmates are entitled to a safe and humane environment, that people can change, and that the environment should be as normal as possible given the constraints of order and security.

Therapeutic communities are difficult to maintain, but therapeutic communities are even more difficult in a setting such as a prison because of the inherent contradictions in the philosophical underpinnings of the two systems. The fate of the therapeutic community is often determined by the general social climate and the last few decades have seen great changes in that social climate. We have witnessed a change from the late 1960s era of liberalism to one of authority and control, and now one of overt repression and punitiveness (Hinshelwood and Manning, 1979). As Clark pointed out in 1975:

> Most of these experiments, however, have remained on the fringe of the penal system, and the main reason for this seems to be the basic contract which the prisons have with the larger society that pays for

their upkeep. This contract demands secure custody quite openly, and contains a scarcely concealed wish for punishment. . . . this process actively contributes to the production of recidivists, men who return to jail again and again. (Clark, 1975, p. 99)

These difficulties are compounded by the inevitability of traumatic reenactment. A community setting of people who have acted out violently will need to have very strict, often authoritarian positions and behaviors in order to curb the repetition of violent acting out. The reactions to the reenactment can easily undermine the tenets of the therapeutic community.

The other significant problem that has not been adequately addressed in the prison system is, of course, the issue of trauma. As in the mental health system, workers in the prison system have lacked a cohesive theoretical way of understanding what has happened to the people they must treat. Although we know a great deal now about victimization, we are only beginning to develop a knowledge base about perpetration. What unique aspects of personality functioning are affected by inflicting harm on others as a repetition of what you have experienced yourself? Unless we can develop more programs in prison systems using a trauma-based approach, we cannot answer the question.

The bottom line is that the system is not working—not if we want to have less dangerous people roaming the streets. In the past decade state and federal prison expenses have risen from approximately $12 billion to $24.6 billion with no end in sight (Worth, 1995). In 1986, only 34.3 percent of all male state prison inmates were convicted of violent crimes (Forer, 1994). As has been demonstrated in the mental health system, if we are to be maximally successful in helping people lead more socially acceptable lives, we need at least a multitiered system of evaluation, treatment, and maintenance. Where people are in the system does not have to be based on some complicated psychological system but on their performance.

People who turn to crime are the most alienated members of our society. They have never learned, or have rejected, the basic rules of social functioning. Instead they have developed an alternative meaning system that gives structure and direction to their existence, but which makes it impossible for them to live by society's rules. Their early learning experiences have usually occurred in an abusive or neglectful context and they presumably suffer from many of the same symptoms that other victims of childhood abuse experience (Gilligan, 1996; Lewis, 1998). Their defenses against these symptoms, however, often lead them to risk taking, compulsive violence, substance abuse, sadism, and the like—behaviors that begin in childhood. This early trauma is then compounded by the exposure to death, violence, witnessing violence, and the terror that surrounds their lifestyle.

They need experiences with healthier, more reliable, and more consistent attachments; an opportunity to experience and work through their denied and suppressed emotions; a different kind of experience with authority that is strong but not abusive; experience and training in resolving problems through conflict resolution rather than through wielding weapons; and attention to their problems of awareness. The rate of dissociation among the criminal population has yet to be measured. As we have seen, addiction is an enormous problem both in and out of prison and we can reliably predict that without treating the addiction, relapse will occur. We must remain aware of the reality, however, that repetition is an essential part of human existence and is compounded by the force of traumatic reenactment. A strong propensity for criminals to reenact their behavior continues in the same way we all reenact behavior that we have learned as normal. This reenactment will continue to be a problem and will therefore require a sophisticated set of supports after discharge from the prison to help keep the ex-inmate on the right path. In focusing on crime and punishment, we support and encourage the criminals' avoidance of confronting their own pain—of what has been done to them and what they have done to others and themselves. They want to be labeled bad; that gives their lives a precise definition and meaning without the burden of dealing with more mature and complex developmental tasks—such as wrestling with remorse, restitution, forgiveness, responsibility, guilt, culpability, accountability.

The only resolution for alienation is social acceptance. They cannot do it alone. People who have taken a criminal life course need to be convinced that their social group can and wishes to accept them back and yet will not encourage, tolerate, or support continued antisocial behavior. They need to see that there is some consistency instead of abject hypocrisy in the society from which they have become so estranged. There will be many people who simply cannot come back, who are so lost in their own personal hell, that they cannot be reached and will defeat all efforts to do so. That is the price we pay for what we do to our children. These have to be set aside from those who are willing to change in order to preserve safety and order for the social group. It is probably this last necessity that of changing the attitudes of the social group, that is the most difficult challenge. We need criminals to be criminals. They are playing a social role that we cannot presently do without (Elikann, 1996). They are acting out our submerged conflicts and if we dare to decide that they do still belong to the human race, we are in danger of having to deal with our conflicts ourselves. But if we hope to stop the cycles of violence, we must at least stop the wheel from turning as rapidly as it does today.

SPIRITUAL SUPPORT FOR NONVIOLENCE

What role does religion and spiritual belief have to play in containing the spread of violence? Churches around the country have actively initiated all kinds of antiviolence programs and seminars. Churches are the primary location of twelve-step meetings for all different kinds of addictions in many communities. Religious organizations have been holding trainings in family violence, sexual abuse, and community violence. They have provided day care centers for the young, after-school programs for older children, and elder care for the seniors. These are all activities that help contain the spread of violence by providing support within the community for activities that reduce violence.

As a major social institution, what role can the church play in helping a society to heal? We believe that all religious organizations have a grand opportunity to play a vital and constructive role in stopping the violence so endemic to our culture. But this can only come about by actively preaching nonviolence from the pulpits and by initiating communitywide programs that provide nonviolent solutions to complex problems.

The Religious Roots of Nonviolence

The thinking on nonviolence spans thousands of years and many different cultures. Christianity was understood by the earlier followers of Jesus as a definitively nonviolent practice. In three brief centuries, by its witness of love and sacrifice, Christianity grew from a tiny Jewish sect to become a religion professed by the majority in the most populous areas of mankind. In the words of K. S. Latourette, a leading historian of the period,

> Never in so short a time has any other religious faith or, for that matter, any other set of ideas, religious, political or economic, without the aid of physical force or of social or cultural prestige, achieved so commanding a position in such an important culture. (Apsey, 1990, p. 27)

In the United States, the nonviolence preached by Jesus has been most consistently displayed by groups such as the Amish, the Mennonites, and the Quakers.

Nonviolence has roots in Judaism as well, going back at least to Palestinian Talmudic sources of the middle third century (Kimelman, 1990). Truth, justice, and peace are the three tools, according to Jewish thought, for the preservation of the world.

> While Judaism does not appear to require a commitment to nonviolence in order to fulfill its precepts, it so sharply curtails the use of violence that nonviolence becomes more often than not the only meaningful way to fulfill a life dedicated to truth, justice and peace. (Solomonow, 1990, pp. 153-154)

Buddhism is fundamentally nonviolent. According to Buddhism, for a man to be perfect there are two qualities that he should develop equally: compassion and wisdom. Right Action aims at promoting moral, honorable and peaceful conduct, admonishing us to abstain from destroying life, stealing, dealing dishonestly with each other, engaging in illegitimate intercourse, and encouraging us to lead a peaceful life in every way (Rahula, 1959).

The Bhagavad-Gita had a major influence on Thoreau and through him, Tolstoy, and King. It also was the single most influential work in forming Gandhi's thought (Holmes, 1990). Gandhi said, "I object to violence, because, when it appears to do good, the good is only temporary; the evil it does is permanent" (Wallis, 1994, p. 190). In his letter from the Birmingham jail, Martin Luther King Jr. wrote,

> I have earnestly opposed violent tension, but there is a type of tension which is necessary for growth. Just as Socrates felt that it was necessary to create a tension in the mind so that individuals could rise from the bondage of myths and half-truths to the unfettered realm of creative analysis and objective appraisal, so must we see the need for nonviolent gadflies to create the kind of tension in society that will help men rise from the dark depths of prejudice and racism to the majestic heights of understanding and brotherhood. (King, 1990, p. 69)

The National Conference of Christians and Jews (Community and Justice)

One national organization that has been addressing bigotry and racism since 1927 is the National Conference of Christians and Jews, recently renamed the National Conference for Community and Justice. This is a nonsectarian civic organization established to promote religious, racial, and ethnic inclusiveness in American society. The National Conference promotes understanding and respect among all races, religions, and cultures through advocacy, conflict resolution, and education. Originally organized as a response to hate campaigns following World War I, particularly against Catholics, the National Conference has developed and adapted its activities within an ever shifting American scene. Today there are over sixty offices nationwide whose programs share three common objectives: (1) to nurture individual self-worth, (2) to encourage the acceptance and appreciation of persons different from one's self, and (3) to discover ways in which all persons can cooperate in the enjoyment and sustenance of a democratic society.

Chapter 9

Primary Prevention: Ending the Cycles of Violence

As with tertiary and secondary prevention efforts, we already know what needs to be done. Let's look first at family violence.

PREVENTING FAMILY VIOLENCE

We Do Know What to Do

The American Psychological Association in their report *Violence and the Family* (1996), made a number of recommendations aimed at primary prevention which are entirely consistent with all that we have discussed in this manual. Their recommendations for universal interventions include:

- Media efforts that educate about the connection between gender role expectations and family violence.
- Programs that reduce unemployment and poverty, which are strongly associated with increased rates of family violence.
- Enforcement of existing handgun laws; creation of handgun laws where none exist.
- Change laws to criminalize family violence.
- Advocate for community agency support.
- Change the physical structure of schools to reduce opportunities for expression of highly aggressive behavior.
- Media efforts to deglamorize violence and more accurately portray its consequences.
- School-based programs to teach conflict, problem solving, and anger-management skills to all children.
- School programs to counter traditional gender role stereotypes and expectations.

- Alcohol and drug abuse prevention programs.
- Parenting education programs.
- Documentaries about family violence shown on network television.
- Sex abuse prevention programs such as "good touch, bad touch" for young children.
- Training legal, medical, and mental health professionals to better understand the dynamics of family violence.
- Sermons delivered by religious leaders declaring family violence immoral.
- Community-based activities, such as clean-up and beautification projects or midnight basketball, that bring people—particularly adolescents or young adult men—together in productive activities.

The National Conference on Family Violence: Health and Justice, whose recommendations we reviewed earlier, also made extensive recommendations for the prevention of family violence.

Prevention

Prevention of family violence should be viewed in terms of social justice and affirmation of basic human rights, rather than retributive criminal justice. We support the shift of social, economic, and political resources toward strengthening communities and families in their many forms. This means ensuring equitable access to employment, education, housing, and health care.

Strategies

- Collaboration among health, criminal justice, and the private sector to regulate products that increase the potential for family violence or magnify its consequences (i.e., alcohol and other drugs and firearms).
- Ratification and implementation by the United States of the United Nations Convention on the Rights of the Child and other human rights conventions.
- Inclusion of representatives of groups with the highest rate of victimization at every level of decision making concerning issues of family violence.
- Development and employment of alternatives to violence and aggression as a means to resolve conflict at all levels of society.

Effective primary prevention programs must be implemented through the sustained allocation of human and financial resources at the federal, state, and local levels. Primary prevention must encompass the cooperation, integration, and sharing of information by the health, justice, social service and education systems, both public and private, in allocating funding and resources in culturally responsive, community-empowered efforts. Programs of proven effectiveness should be funded by reallocating existing funding and allocating new resources.

- Instead of building more prisons, use the money to fund community-based, community-controlled systematically evaluated prevention programs that build on strengths. Develop, systematically evaluate, and disseminate new, effective primary prevention programs.
- Primary prevention should be sustained over the long term as a core public health function by generating new revenue (e.g., surcharge on marriage licenses, taxes on alcohol, ammunition).

Because violent behaviors are learned within the context of family, community, and society, the unlearning of these behaviors and the substitution of more appropriate behaviors must take place within the context of the family, community, and society. Therefore, we recommend the establishment of community-based, community-controlled prevention systems that would include:

- A vehicle to foster communication and coordination among public and private entities.
- Violence prevention community educational efforts, with a focus on early interventions that are comprehensive and multidisciplinary.
- Home visitation programs of proven effectiveness to reduce violence to children and elders and to improve maternal health.
- Life skills education, including conflict resolution, goal setting, caregiving, etc.
- Parenting and caregiving education and support.
- Programs that focus on perpetrators as well as victims.
- Comprehensive public school violence-prevention education, beginning in preschool years and available to all families, which includes training in stress management, conflict resolution, parenting and caregiver skills, substance abuse, and gender relationships.

Individuals in high-risk situations such as job loss, divorce, child custody, HIV, elder care situations, and adolescent transition stages should be included. Services for family violence prevention must be made available to all persons in need of services without regard to race, ethnicity, gender, sexual orientation, or ability to pay.

- Comprehensive public school violence-prevention education, beginning in preschool years and available to all families, which includes training in stress management, conflict resolution, parenting and caregiver skills, substance abuse, and gender relationships.

Recognizing that all human beings are valuable, we must design and implement a national public awareness and educational campaign to convince the American people that family abuse, neglect, and exploitation are not okay. Strategies include:

- Promote the formation of broad-based community boards representing public and private systems to further a national agenda aimed at preventing family violence through education, promotion of legislation, identification of service gaps, and development of resources.

Professional Education

Family violence is a public health crisis in the United States. We are speaking on behalf of those whose lives have been affected by violence and whose voices are too often unheard.

- Mandatory comprehensive education about family violence throughout the life span must become a standard component in undergraduate, graduate, and continuing education curricula in all health, justice, and other helping professions.
- As a central component, professional education must include the perspectives and participation of survivors and/or advocates in its development and delivery. Education should utilize appropriate interactive and experiential models and should be integrated throughout the professional curriculum.
- Education of family violence for health, justice, and social service professionals must be fully valued. Those who provide such instruction should be given professional recognition and support. Professional education activities, including resource and faculty development, implementation and evaluation, must be adequately funded.
- Professional education requires an interdisciplinary approach; didactic and practical/clinical educational programs should include approaches to facilitate interdisciplinary contact and collaboration
- The educators must reflect the diversity of our society.
- Family violence content must be a component of the licensure and certification for all health and justice professions.
- The AMA working with other organizations, should quickly develop and widely disseminate a "Patient to Plaintiff" video/instructional

guide that incorporates the response of various disciplines to all forms of family violence.
- The U.S. Department of Health and Human Services and Department of Justice should fund the development and dissemination of publications on model professional educational programs as well as directories of all educational programs on family violence.
- The federal government, professional associations, private foundations, and educational institutions should foster the development and continuation of high-quality research on family violence.
- Federal incentives should be provided for expansion of family violence professional education.

Professional associations should join with accrediting bodies for educational institutions, postgraduate programs, and continuing education courses to develop and support core family violence curricula that incorporate the following educational principles. Each professional organization will establish a time frame, with specific measurable goals, for instituting these reforms. Professional schools and associations should examine, modify, and develop curricula, as appropriate, to include these principles.

All family violence professional education from the undergraduate level through continuing education programs should:

- Foster awareness and sensitivity to cultural diversity.
- Formally address interrelationships among (and the uniqueness of) each form of family violence.
- Explore how power and control affect relationships (i.e., victim-victimizer, professional-professional, and professional-victim/victimizer).
- Develop awareness and understanding of the language, culture, responsibilities, and needs of the other disciplines.
- Teach that violence as a primary means of resolving conflict is not acceptable.
- Incorporate and value skill development.
- Teach how to establish, maintain, and value the relationship with one's community and its resources.
- Encourage continuous evaluation and improvement of the system's effectiveness.
- Be provided in an empathic and caring environment.
- Acknowledge that professional groups will include survivors and/or perpetrators of family violence at various stages of awareness, defenses, and healing; be prepared to provide link to appropriate services for these individuals.

Breaking the Cycle of Family Violence—Peaceful Posse

> *Posse:* Any body of men who have authority to aide in maintaining
> the peace

> Who is about Peace? We are about Peace
> Walk away from violence and say yes to Peace

> > Boys of Peaceful Posse:
> > Sean, Juan, David, Cyrus, Kenneth,
> > Mike, John, Matt, Darnell

> I can't do nothing by myself. It's *we* that gotta do something. That's
> what the Peaceful Posse means to me.

> > Tyrone, age 14

The Peaceful Posse, a violence prevention program of Philadelphia
Physicians for Social Responsibility, offers boys new relationships, mentoring, and an opportunity to share and heal in a safe space. The eight- to
fourteen-year-old boys meet weekly in after-school groups led by a mature
male, who models nonviolent solutions to life's problems for them. In every
group meeting, boys are listened to as they describe situations in which
violence occurred. They learn to express their feelings about this violence and
validate each other in a context that promotes mutual healing and support.

> After watching the film on domestic violence, Louis talked for the
> first time about hating his father for beating up his mother. His
> mother, he said, hated the word "sorry" because his father said it all
> the time. Tyrone also talked about his father beating up their mother.
> Cleo talked about how violent a man his father is. Cleo says his
> father was abusive to everyone. (Progress notes, May 6, 1996)

The thirty boys who make up the Peaceful Posse live in two Philadelphia public housing communities. Every day they are faced with pressures
to conform to a hyperviolent image of masculinity:

> Brother Rob [the leader of Peaceful Posse] was late for our in-ser-
> vice training. He was obviously upset, so at the break I asked him
> what was wrong. He told me that on the way to the meeting, he had
> been stopped by one of his boys from the Peaceful Posse. This child
> had just been held up at gunpoint—for the third time in a year—for a

thin gold chain he wore around his neck, a single memento from his usually absent father. Brother Rob was proud of the boy, because this time, he didn't fight back, thereby possibly saving his life.

This vignette describes everyday life for many boys growing up amid the viciousness of today's city neighborhoods, and for the adults trying to save them. Since violence, not harmony, is normal for these kids, the skills of nonviolent engagement need to be taught. According to a preliminary appraisal of Peaceful Posse conducted by an evaluator from the City University of New York, "The majority of the boys believe that hitting, screaming, being mean, getting into a fight or otherwise being physical, is typically wrong behavior." The evaluator also found the boys to be receptive to a goal of gender justice, building on the close relationships the boys typically have with their mothers to enable the boys to develop empathy for women. Pending adequate funding, future plans for expanding this two-year program include training new adult leaders, creating more Peaceful Posse groups, creating Senior Posses to provide ongoing support for graduates of Peaceful Posse, and creating Parent Posses in order to foster the development of parent peer support.

PROMOTING RESILIENCY

Earlier we defined resiliency and began to develop some ideas about how to encourage its development. Promoting resilience is a vital aspect of primary prevention. Violent and traumatic events threaten the ability of human communities to foster health and resilience, as do such ecological "pollutants" as racism, sexism, and poverty (Harvey, 1996). Garbarino and colleagues have discussed the human ecological threat posed by high-risk communities as conferring "social toxicity" on the residents of those communities (1997). Nonetheless, we need to be reminded that although the failure rate is higher, most children who grow up in toxic family environments and communities still succeed in spite of their surroundings. For children in violent neighborhoods to grow up into healthy and competent adults, three factors appear to be critical: (1) a warm and affectionate relationship with an adult who cares for and supports the child; (2) an environment that includes high expectations for the child and faith in the child's ability; and (3) opportunities for the child to participate in the life and work going on around him or her (Benard, 1991). Promoting resiliency is something everyone can do, in every interaction with another human being.

How Families Can Promote Resilience

Families can promote resilience in some clearly defined ways. In the studies undertaken by Virginia Demos, the families who showed high resilience shared certain characteristics:

- They maximized opportunities of the shared experience of good feelings by doing things that made each other feel good as frequently as possible.
- They were quick to reestablish good feelings after a break occurred, such as an angry scolding or an experience of bad feelings on the part of the child.
- They found ways to help their children when they were over-whelmed by bad feelings such as distress, anger, fear, or shame by acknowledging the negative feeling and helping the child reestablish a positive feeling. (Demos, 1989)

The management of positive and negative emotional states is extremely important and can be learned by anyone, thus increasing the number of options we have in dealing with other people and increasing the chances for resilient types of responses to stress. Perhaps the most overlooked parental failure is the tendency of parents to focus on behavior and completely overlook the sequence of feelings that the child experiences and as a consequence, the most powerful tool in shaping behavior is lost.

Rutter (1990) has explored the very important concept of "turning points," the particular experiences in a child's life that can change the developmental trajectory from that point on. He focuses on the kinds of protective processes that can be put into place to reduce the risk of damage and increase the likelihood of resiliency. The first necessary step in supporting protective processes is to reduce the risk impact. The first and most logical way of accomplishing this task is to alter the child's exposure to, or intimate involvement with, the risk situation. But when this is not possible, then sometimes it *is* possible to alter the meaning or riskiness of the risk variable for that child. This introduces the concept of *stress inoculation*— controlled exposure to stress in circumstances in which successful coping or adaptation can take place. Thus children who are exposed to normal experiences of separation, e.g., baby-sitters, in situations that are not overwhelming, begin to develop coping skills that serve them when they are exposed to a higher degree of separation stress. Stress inoculation involves the promotion of coping with the hazards when the exposure is of a type and degree that is manageable in the context of the child's capacities and social situation.

A second vital protective process is the reduction of negative chain reactions. Negative chain reactions occur, for instance when the child is traumatized in some way, say sexually abused, and then further traumatized when the caregivers deny the abuse or blame the child. Often the chain reaction response does more long-term harm then the trauma itself. Here the protective function does not simply reside within the individual, but within the interaction between the individual and other people's reactions.

A third protective process resides in the establishment and maintenance of self-esteem and self-efficacy. Two types of experiences are most influential: the establishment of secure and harmonious love relationships and success in accomplishing tasks that are identified by individuals as central to their interests. Various kinds of research studies including short-term prospective studies, retrospective recall of adults, and intergenerational studies of high-risk populations all show that early childhood attachments provide a degree of protection against later risk environments. It is important to remember however, that self-concepts continue to be modified according to the nature of life experiences encountered so that positive interpersonal experiences in adulthood can also be transformative.

The fourth protective process includes anything that opens up opportunities for children to find other alternative sources of empathic experiences with others, other coping strategies, and other ways of getting their needs met (Rutter, 1990).

Recommendations from Resilient Adults

Resilient adults have made some constructive recommendations for anyone hoping to enhance resiliency in others. They recommend a focus on strengths, on how persons survived as well as they have, rather than a focus on weakness, vulnerability, or pathology. Helpers need to ask, "What were the coping skills that were effective, even if in a limited way"? It is important to help the person look for the beacons of hope that have sustained them—in themselves and in others. These beacons often come in the form of surrogates who become symbols of opportunity, of possibility—a teacher, a therapist, a family friend, a distant relative. It is vital never to underestimate the importance of simple kindness in the lives of those who are downtrodden and betrayed. Even small doses of kindness can last a lifetime in memory. Likewise it is important to openly admire the successes of each person—their capacity to learn and love which overcomes their history of abuse (Higgins, 1994).

Another interesting recommendation made by resilient survivors relates to the qualities inherent in the helper, in the person—therapist, physician, teacher, or friend—who hopes to be of help to others:

> Clinicians and educators need to have both technical knowledge and ability; but in addition, I feel it's absolutely essential for the person to be highly developed as a human being: capable of caring for others, capable of loving others, . . . a realized person. You cannot get good work done by defective individuals who just have the right credentials. . . . The people who helped me the most helped me partially because of who they *were*, modeling for me how to be as a human being. (Higgins, 1994, p. 327)

As Higgins points out, it is important that anyone hoping to help encourage resilience in others recognize that these individuals have grown up with models of exploitation, cruelty, and boundary violation. They lack a positive role model of human interaction and often do not recognize how bizarre their childhood treatment has been. This is an essential role of other people—to communicate positive regard, to provide an alternative to abusive relationships, to validate their perceptions of the destructive nature of their experiences.

SHARING THE WEALTH

Business as Perpetrator of Violence

The present level of economic inequality, both nationally and internationally, cannot hold. Without changes in our system of distributing wealth we are destined to become our worst nightmare. These are George Kennan's prophetic and disturbing words from 1948 when he was head of the state department's policy planning staff:

> We have about 50 percent of the world's wealth, but only 6.3 percent of its population. In this situation, we cannot fail to be the object of envy and resentment. Our real task in the coming period is to devise a pattern of relationships which will permit us to maintain this position of disparity without positive detriment to our national security. To do so we will have to dispense with all sentimentality and daydreaming; and our attention will have to be concentrated everywhere on our immediate national objectives. We need not

deceive ourselves that we can afford today the luxury of altruism and world-benefaction. . . . We should cease to talk about vague and . . . unreal objectives such as human rights, the raising of the living standards, and democratization. The day is not far off when we are going to have to deal in straight power concepts. The less we are then hampered by idealistic slogans, the better. (Kovel, 1994, p. 58)

The time is coming, and coming rapidly, when we are either going to have to move away from what Ralph Nader has termed "malignant capitalism," or we are going to have to give up any pretense of upholding the basic tenets that are the bedrock of the American identity—democracy, freedom, tolerance, fair play, compassion, and human rights—both abroad *and* at home. A system based on taking from the poor to give to the rich cannot maintain its stability without increasing oppression and the invocation of authoritarian rule. Depriving whole populations of the poor with the means to feed their children, while at the same time arming them with lethal weapons, forces an insurrection bound to deprive us all of our basic civil rights in the name of increased security. Changing government policy now could prevent disaster in the near future.

On January 17, 1961, Dwight Eisenhower, President of the United States, stood to give his Farewell Address to the nation. The Cold War was waging and America was prospering, so his warning, somewhat surprising since he was a firmly entrenched military man, elicits surprise even thirty-seven years later.

Until the latest of our world conflicts, the United States had no armaments industry. American makers of plowshares could, with time and as required, make swords as well. But we can no longer risk emergency improvisation of national defense. We have been compelled to create a permanent armaments industry of vast proportions. Added to this, three and a half million men and women are directly engaged in the defense establishment. We annually spend on military security alone more than the net income of all United States corporations.

Now this conjunction of an immense military establishment and a large arms industry is new in the American experience. The total influence—economic, political, even spiritual—is felt in every city, every state house, every office of the Federal Government. We recognize the imperative need for this development. Yet we must not fail to comprehend its grave implications. Our toil, resources and livelihood are all involved; so is the very structure of our society. In the councils of Government, we must guard against the acquisition of unwarranted influence, whether sought or unsought, by the military-industrial complex. The potential for the disastrous rise of misplaced power exists and will persist.

We must never let the weight of this combination endanger our liberties or democratic processes. We should take nothing for granted. Only an alert and knowledgeable citizenry can compel the proper meshing of the huge industrial and military machinery of defense with our peaceful methods and goals, so that security and liberty may prosper together. Akin to, and largely responsible for the sweeping changes in our industrial-military posture has been the technological revolution during recent decades.

. . . It is the task of statesmanship to mold, to balance, and to integrate these and other forces, new and old, within the principles of our democratic system—ever aiming toward the supreme goals of our free society. . . . As we peer into society's future, we—you and I, and our Government—must avoid the impulse to live only for today, plundering, for our own ease and convenience, the precious resources of tomorrow. We cannot mortgage the material assets of our grandchildren without risking the loss also of their political and spiritual heritage. We want democracy to survive for all generations to come, not to become the insolvent phantom of tomorrow.

During the long lane of the history yet to be written, America knows that this world of ours, ever growing smaller, must avoid becoming a community of dreadful fear and hate, and be, instead, a proud confederation of mutual trust and respect. Such a confederation must be one of equals. The weakest must come to the conference table with the same confidence as do we, protected as we are by our moral, economic and military strength. That table, though scarred by many past frustrations, cannot be abandoned for the certain agony of the battlefield.

Disarmament, with mutual honor and confidence, is a continuing imperative. Together we must learn how to compose differences—not with arms, but with intellect and decent purpose. Because this need is so sharp and apparent, I confess that I lay down my official responsibilities in this field with a definite sense of disappointment. As one who has witnessed the horror and the lingering sadness of war, as one who knows that another war could utterly destroy this civilization which has been so slowly and painfully built over thousands of years, I wish I could say tonight that a lasting peace is in sight.

As it turns out, Eisenhower's warning that "In the councils of Government, we must guard against the acquisition of unwarranted influence, whether sought or unsought, by the military-industrial complex" has not been well heeded. Thanks to the military-industrial complex the most important sector in international trade is not oil, cars, or planes—it is armaments. Arms sales are incredibly large—at least $900 billion annually. Some experts place the real figures for arms sales at two, three, even four times higher (Saul, 1992). Even though the Cold War supposedly ended the U.S. defense budget continues to escalate; in 1995 the House approved funding that the Pentagon had not even requested (Dellums, 1995). We will spend $2.5 trillion from 1995 to 2005 under Clinton's deficit reduction proposal for the military (Hartung, 1995). What does it say about us as a society, when in 1997, only $10 million was earmarked exclusively for child abuse research by the National Institute of Health, but we can spend $2.5 trillion for guns?

We cannot have strict gun control laws here because it is just too big a business. Too much of our economy—33 percent of the federal budget alone (Saul, 1992)—now depends on armaments, while total expenditure for education, social services, and highway construction only amounts to 15 percent (Saul, 1992). Forty percent of all U.S. scientists are employed on defense-related projects. Because our economy—and increasingly the economies of other countries—are so interconnected, everyone is affected by weapons sales. As a civilized country we cannot really decide that this is insane because this business is an essential part of our economy. Our behavior is similar to that of traumatized patients. They eventually come to base their existence on strange, destructive behavior that originates with some response to perpetration against them, and then defend that behavior with every conceivable rationalization and fight strongly against any attempt to get them to give it up. As Americans, we have decided that safety = gun ownership and many of us are now prepared to die for this belief. If we are afraid to really look at the roots of the problem—as troubled patients are afraid to look at the reality of the homes they grew up in—then we will lie to ourselves and lie to everyone else to protect our cherished belief systems.

But it is not only armaments that drive our present economic system. It is also competition and the eternal search for the best bottom line, the most profitable outcome for the shareholders and the executives. "Competition to make the largest possible profit exceeds every other motive for economic expansion. In no other civilization has this drive for money become such a central power as it has in ours" (Bahro, 1994, p. 99). Earl Shorris (1994) has called America a "nation of salesmen" *"homo vendens,"* operating on the principle that all value is exchange value, set by the market and no one else. The market determines the value of everything and nothing, neither the utility of the thing nor its intrinsic qualities (durability, beauty, happiness, economy, healthfulness) have any role to play in the judgment of the market. Nothing has value in and of itself. It is this paradigm that allows us to base an economy on weapons, to spoil the environment, to sell dangerous substances, to deny medical and social services, and it cannot easily be changed without catastrophic upheaval.

As Jim Garbarino has noted,

> It has become a tenet of our society that "The business of America is business," and the world has listened. We've heard it over and over: What's the bottom line? Discussions of the sustainable society seem to run aground on the shoals of profitability. Will this measure pay off? Will it maintain or increase dividends? Will such a program meet the payroll? No analysis of the sustainable society can proceed without accounting for the role of corporate economic enterprise— the private "for-profit" sector. (Garbarino, 1992, pp. 193-194)

Socially Responsible Business

As early as the 1920s there was at least one person in business who, with uncanny prescience, wrote about changes that were necessary for business to prosper. Her name was Mary Parker Follett. The prevailing management theory in her day was similar to what persists in many corporate settings—a fondness for command-style, hierarchical organizations inspired by the military model. Follett advocated an entirely different approach characterized by flatter hierarchies, teamwork and participative management, leadership based on ability, cooperative conflict resolution, and a shared corporate vision. Says London School of Economics Chairman, Sir Peter Parker, "People often puzzle about who is the father of management. I don't know who the father was, but I have no doubt about who was the mother" (Linden 1995, p. 77).

Today, many companies are struggling with the issues Mary Parker Follett described. There is an increasing focus on corporate social responsibility, and a new paradigm does appear to be struggling to be born. Under various titles such as the "learning organization," "workplace community," the "Third Way," the "humane corporation," and the "living organization," many businesspeople appear to be arriving at conclusions similar to medical and mental health workers, some criminal justice thinkers, and many educators (Nirenberg, 1993; Senge, 1990). We stand on the brink of enormous opportunity; our actions will determine whether the world as we know it descends into destructive chaos or emerges as a new liberating order.

Business for Social Responsibility (BSR) is a nonprofit organization that provides access to successful corporate strategies and practices through member education and information programs and materials. BSR focuses not just on the well-being of the bottom line but also on practices that ensure the well-being of the workforce, the environment, and the surrounding communities.

Influenced by the work of modern physicists, biologists, and ecologists, some business organizations are beginning to view themselves as living systems and are finding that paying attention to all the aspects of the system pays off in dividends, both financial and psychological. In such organizations, workers are treated as whole human beings with families and extended networks, rather than as cogs in some huge industrial machine. Peter Senge, one of the gurus of this movement and author of the *The Fifth Discipline,* warns companies that survival depends on the ability to think systematically, seeing patterns, interrelationships, and interdependencies rather than chains of cause and effect. He calls the type of organization he describes a "learning organization" and says that, "The organizations that will truly excel in the future will be the organizations that discover how to tap people's commitment and capacity to learn at *all* levels in an organization" (Senge 1990, p. 4). The concept of fifth discipline derives from the five disciplines Senge believes are essential ingredients for a learning organization: systems thinking, personal mastery (learning to be open with others), mental models (putting aside old ways of thinking), shared vision (forming a plan that everyone can agree on), and team learning (working together to achieve the plan) (Dumain, 1994). Such companies as Federal Express, GS Technologies, and Ford have been using the concepts of Senge and his colleagues with positive results to change the way they do business (Dumain, 1994).

Shaffer and Anundsen (1993) have highlighted eight qualities of the workplace community that seem consistent across the literature: alignment of values between all members of the workplace, an employee-based structure, teamwork, open communication, mutual support, respect for individuality, permeable boundaries, and opportunities for group renewal. These qualities of the workplace community bear a strong likeness to those of the therapeutic community and the therapeutic school. Management consultant Walter Bennis suggests a complete overhaul of our present way of doing business, from the top down. He comments on the repetition compulsion: "A lot of companies still don't understand. . . . Einstein's definition of insanity is when you continue to repeat over and over the same practice, hoping to get different results" (Bennis, 1993, p. 30).

But, to accomplish the creation of a "workplace community" we must address our idolization of competition, one of the great American myths. As Alfie Kohn (1986) points out, we are under the illusion that even minimal profitability and productivity, to say nothing of excellence, is entirely dependent on competing with each other and that competition brings out the best in us. The real situation is quite different. Johnson and Johnson surveyed 122 studies from 1924 to 1980, including every North American study on the subject of competition and performance. The evidence was clear and overwhelmingly consistent—competition almost never improves performance, in fact, superior performance seems to require the absence of competition. Competition sometimes produces better results only if the task is simple, such as rote decoding, and not interdependent at all. Cooperation within and between groups is the real motivator for performance (Kohn, 1986).

John Paluszek, President of Ketchum Public Affairs and winner of the 1994 Gold Anvil Award given by the Public Relation's Society of America, says that there will be an "integrated standard" of success for companies in the future. The new age company will be judged not just on bottom-line profits but also on its "corporate citizenship," that corporations will adopt social responsibility as a part of their own enlightened self-interest. "Post-modern society requires that many voices need to be heard in solutions to society's common problems. As we've progressed, consensus, messy as it may be, is more important that it has ever been in order to avoid conflict" (Bovet, 1994, p. 32).

Apparently, the idea of "corporate social responsibility" dates back to at least the mid-1920s when business executives were beginning to speak of the need for corporate directors to act as trustees for the interests, not just of stockholders, but other social claimants as well. These ideas were accompanied by a growing belief that business and society were linked by what we now call interconnectedness or interdependency. Some writers of the day began to advocate that businesses had an obligation to provide "service" beyond profits, yet without denying profits (Frederick, 1994 [1978]).

Experts who have studied the rise of ethics as a central corporate responsibility trace concerns surfaced during the Watergate scandal of the early 1970s, when some companies were convicted of setting up illegal political slush funds. Later came the disclosure of bribe payments by U.S. firms to obtain foreign military sales, followed by defense-procurement scandals and more recently by insider-trading revelations as well as the savings and loans debacle (Miller, 1995). The fundamental idea embedded in "corporate social responsibility" is that business corporations have an obligation to work for social betterment. Recently, Hyman and Blum (1995) have described "just" companies. "A just company is a morally driven organization, the long-term economic success of which demands that it serve most participants well . . . Harm done by one party to another always affects both parties" (p. 48).

Harry Van Buren (1995), in writing about business ethics for the next millennium writes of five basic principles, all of which are good for business in the long run. He defines a just society as one that does not tolerate employment discrimination because employees deserve a living wage and safe working conditions. He promotes the idea that corporate responsibility requires the business community to regard the environment as a resource to be protected for future generations. Included in this sense of responsibility are corporate decisions not to create products that kill or maim. For him, a healthy business ethic also decries the government repression of democracy, unions, and free speech as creating environments that are inappropriate for business.

Interestingly and encouragingly, the public appears to agree. According to the results of a 1993 study on "cause-related marketing" (CRM) consumers believe business has a responsibility to help improve social ills. Seventy-one percent say they think CRM is a good way to help solve social problems, while 64 percent of consumers believe that CRM should be a standard part of a company's activities. A whopping 84 percent say they have a more positive image of a company it if is doing something to make the world a better place (Caudron, 1994).

And, there are companies who are listening. New England Electric System ranks first of all electric utilities because of its environmentally sound energy conservation programs. Colgate is collaborating with the New York City School District to rebuild schools and develop "theme" schools. The Timberland Company has invested millions in the development of urban "peace corps" through City Year. Their mission statement makes a social commitment directly by stating "Each individual can and must, make a difference in the way we experience life on this planet." Additionally, the company's Standards for Social Responsibility creates international guidelines for choosing business partners including those who offer medical and insurance benefits, pay the at least the minimum wage, compensate for overtime, do not employ children under age fourteen, and provide a safe workplace—and inspections confirm compliance. The Coca-Cola Company has made a significant contribution to supporting women and minority-owned businesses, supports minority youth through internships, encourages all employees to volunteer in the community in various programs, and has been sited as one of the best places to work for minorities. Polaroid has instituted one of the most comprehensive AIDS education and prevention plans in the country and has strongly supported women and minorities. Merck and Company has formed a partnership with a Costa Rican institution that supplies Merck with plant and insect samples that ensures the Costa Rican company will benefit from any developments of pharmaceuticals that arise from their efforts. Merck is also helping to fund conservation efforts to preserve the rainforests (Will, 1995). All of these companies realize that good citizenship is also good business. The behavior and value system of those at the top is directly conveyed throughout the entire company and with consistency, can change the entire corporate climate.

At present, we are in a situation that is extremely destructive and dangerous for any democracy—an increasing economic inequity. The trend over the last century had been in the direction of a more equitable distribution of wealth until the 1980s. During the 1980s the real income of most American families has stagnated or fallen while that of the top percent increased by 115 percent. During the 1980s the number of individuals in poverty rose from 23 million to 35 million while the number of millionaires increased from 642 in 1975 to 60,667 in 1991. Managerial salaries average 100 times the average pay of employees, ten times greater than the ratio in other advanced capitalist countries (Heilbroner, 1995).

As we mentioned in Part I, the rich have gotten richer while the poor—most often women and children—have gotten poorer. Between 1947 and the mid-seventies the ratio of the income of the top 5 percent of families to the lower 20 percent dropped from a ratio of 14 to 1 to 11 to 1. Since then the ratio has risen to 19-1. Newly released census data also show that incomes fell on average for the bottom 60 percent of households over the past seven years. Not only have real wages continued to decline but the share of workers covered by health insurance and pension plans has also declined. In addition there has been a steady increase in the share of workers forced to work under part-time and other nonstandard work arrangements, making Manpower, a temporary employment agency, the largest private employer in the United States. In 1974, the average CEO of a major company was paid thirty-four times the earnings of the average worker. Today he is making about 180 times the worker's pay. Poverty rates in the United States, despite economic expansion, are two to three times those of Western Europe. The poverty rate for children under six in France is 6 percent (Faux, 1997). According to the National Center for Children in Poverty, 24 percent of all American children under the age of 6 are poor (Herbert, 1995).

We desperately need a strong dose of universal corporate social responsibility and it is going to require overturning some strongly held shibboleths about the importance of competition, obedience to the bottom line, and the sanctity of money. As Michael Linton warns,

> It all comes down to money in the end. The problems of the world come from our actions, and our actions, both as a society and as individuals, are largely determined by the way money works. Many trivial and even damaging things are happening—simply because some people have the money and the will to do them. In contrast, other things of real value, many essential to the survival of the planet, are not happening—simply because those who have the will, have not the money. People are working in ways detrimental to their personal health, to that of the environment, both locally and globally, and to the well-being of their community because they need the money. (Linton, 1993, p. 65)

PRIMARY PREVENTION AND THE MEDIA

Violence in America, including increased portrayals of violence in the media against children, adults, and the elderly, has reached such epidemic proportions that media consumers, providers, and professionals must take action to reverse this trend. As television becomes more sophisticated and interactive, the commercial media has an extraordinary opportunity to change the present direction of the public will and experience. At present, much criticism is justifiably aimed at the media moguls for their extraordinary influence in maintaining standards of violence, cruelty, sadism, and meanness that are unprecedented. But it does not have to stay this way. Media giants have families too and are a fundamental and important part of this massive web we call American society. As such, they have a vital role to play in generating a much greater sense of social responsibility. The educational possibilities of the media are endless. If they chose to do so, television producers and moviemakers could as deliberately provide models for peace, nonviolent conflict resolution, and compassion as they do models of violence. Different choices are there to be made but it is unlikely to happen until concerned citizens organize in great enough numbers to exert sufficient pressure to bring about changes.

Television could also help change the national climate by generating more thoughtful, in-depth analyses of issues that serve to show the public how truly complex and interconnected problems are instead of attempting to dazzle the public with sensationalistic, unbalanced presentations of issues through soundbites. Both television and radio could do an extraordinary service to the public in modeling how to think about, discuss, and problem solve very complicated, multidimensional issues, rather than presenting oversimplified and unbalanced presentations of ideas, social movements, and events. News programs could show some good news *as* news instead of concentrating solely on one disaster after another. In actual fact, extraordinarily positive things are happening every day and yet if they get any play at all, they come at the end of the regular news reports as the final laugh of the evening. Good, but not good enough.

The Media Can Promote Safety, Not Violence

In their recommendations, the National Conference on Family Violence addressed the issue of the relationship between the media and other social institutions. They noted that in the past, consumers and media providers have endured an adversarial relationship and urged that future efforts to address the problem should be inclusive and collaborative in nature. In service of this, they urged consumers, providers, and professionals to participate in creating a new climate of socially responsible perspective on violence. They hoped that the American Medical Association and the American Bar Association would provide the leadership necessary to promote such an initiative (Witwer and Crawford, 1995). Here are the media recommendations that were made by the work groups:

> Establish a national coalition of professional organizations (including health, justice, education, and child advocacy groups) to promote safe, nonviolent families and society. This group will work in partnership with the media, to examine violence in the media, and to promote socially responsible approaches.

Strategies

- Create a national resource center.
- Collect sources of data.
- Identify experts.
- Encourage continued research.
- Educate the media and the public.
- Provide media with resources, media kits, etc.
- Develop forums for sharing information and strategic planning.
- Encourage development of media education efforts to help prevent violence.

- Outreach with state and local violence prevention efforts.
- Acknowledge excellence.
- Establish multidisciplinary criteria for media excellence in violence prevention.
- Encourage media organizations to give awards for promotion of nonviolence.
- Include award recipients on national advisory board.
- Market nonviolence.
- Create public service announcements to raise awareness.
- Encourage health and justice professionals to form liaisons with local media.
- Produce programs in partnership with media to promote alternatives to violence.

AMA Guidelines on Media Violence

But in the meantime, what can each of us do to prevent media violence from having such an impact on our children and families? The American Medical Association has publicized the potential adverse health and social consequences from excess media activity (1996). These include: increased violent behavior, obesity, decreased physical activity and fitness, increased cholesterol levels, excess sodium intake, repetitive strain injury (video and computer games), insomnia, photic seizures in vulnerable individuals, impaired school performance, increased use of tobacco and alcohol, increased sexual activity, decreased attention span, decreased family communication, excess consumer focus (resulting in envy, entitlement, etc.). The list of national organizations concluding that violent entertainment causes violent behavior is by now extensive and includes: American Academy of Child and Adolescent Psychiatry, American Academy of Pediatricians, American Medical Association, American Psychiatric Association, American Psychological Association, Centers for Disease Control and Prevention, National Institute of Mental Health and the Surgeon General's Office. How much more convincing do we need?

The AMA has produced a *Physician's Guide to Media Violence* (1996) and in that document, they provide a list of suggestions for parents about media use:

- *Be alert to the shows your children see.* These suggestions are important for all children, and most important for young children: the younger the child, the more impressionable he or she is.
- *Avoid using television, videos, or video games as a baby-sitter.* It might be convenient for busy parents, but it can begin a pattern of

always turning to media for entertainment or diversion. Simply turning the sets off is not nearly as effective as planning some other fun activity with the family.

- *Limit the use of media.* Television use must be limited to no more than one or two quality hours per day. Set situation limits, too—no television or video games before school, during daytime hours, during meals, or before homework is done.

- *Keep television and video player machines out of your children's bedrooms.* Putting them there encourages more viewing and diminishes your ability to monitor their use.

- *Turn the television off during mealtimes.* Use this time to catch up and connect with one another.

- *Turn television on only when there is something specific you have decided is worth watching.* Don't turn the TV on "to see if there's something on." Decide in advance if a program is worth viewing. Identify high-quality programs, using evaluations of programs in your selection process.

- *Don't make the TV the focal point of the house.* Avoid placing the television in the most prominent location in your home. Families watch less television or play fewer videos if the sets are not literally at the center of their lives.

- *Watch what your children are watching.* This will allow you to know what they're viewing and will give you an opportunity to discuss it with them. Be active: talk and make connections with your children while the program is on.

- *Be especially careful of viewing just before bedtime.* Emotion-invoking images may linger and intrude into sleep.

- *Learn about movies that are playing and the videos available for rental or purchase.* Be explicit with children about your guidelines for appropriate movie viewing and review proposed movie choices in advance.

- *Become "media literate."* This means learning how to evaluate media offerings critically. First learn yourself and then teach your children. Learn about advertising and teach your children about its influences on the media they use.

- *Limit your own television viewing.* Set a good example by your moderation and discrimination in viewing. Be careful when children are around and may observe material from "your" program.

- *Let your voice be heard.* We all need to raise our voices so that they are heard by program decision makers and sponsors. We need to insist on better programming for our children. (*Physician's Guide to Media Violence,* American Medical Association, copyright © 1996)

RESTITUTION NOT RETRIBUTION: REWORKING THE JUSTICE SYSTEM

Justice and Religion

Ask many people today what should be done with a murderer and they will quickly answer "fry 'em." Retribution is the byword of the day, punishment the apparent solution to our epidemic of crime. The justification that is repeatedly used for this attitude is biblical, an "eye for an eye." But few of those calling loudly for this principle appear to be aware of how biblically misguided they are. According to Howard Zehr, Professor of Sociology and Restorative Justice at Eastern Mennonite University's Conflict Transformation Program, an "eye for an eye," a phrase that only appears three times in the Bible, is not at all what it seems. The Bible opens in Genesis with a recognition of the human tendency to take unlimited revenge, called the "Law of Lamech"; it is described as seventy times seven, a number representing infinity. The "eye for an eye" idea was meant to set a limit on this unrestricted desire for revenge by establishing a law of proportion that laid the basis for restitution—not that you were to take an eye for an eye, but that you were not allowed to take *more than* an eye for an eye. These same voices, who call so loudly for retribution are often Christians, who perhaps forget that the New Testament message of Jesus was that we love not just our own kind but our enemies as well— until seventy times seven, an unlimited number of times. In putting it this way, Jesus was apparently intending to set the law of retaliation on its head (Zehr, 1994a).

In the past, there have been other systems of achieving justice that were not based solely on retribution and revenge. As documented by Herman Bianchi, retired Dean of the Law School of the Free University of Amsterdam, there was a role for penance for a crime, for making restitution, for restoring wholeness to a damaged relationship or community (Bianchi, 1995). Before modern times, crime was a violation of people and of community and such wrongs created obligations. Justice called for situations to be made right. The options of vengeance or courts existed, but were largely backups used when negotiation and restitution did not work. Crime was not a monopoly of the state; even when victims and offenders resorted to courts, they retained power to settle when they wished (Zehr,

1994a). "It is beyond doubt that the ancient legal systems that preceded our modern Western system—Hebrew, Greek, Roman, and Teutonic—did not favor punitive crime control as we have it today" (Bianchi, 1995, p. 15).

Zehr has compared biblical justice with contemporary justice and has found some dramatic differences (1990, p. 151):

Contemporary Justice

    1. Justice divided into areas, each with different rules
    2. Administration of justice as an inquiry into guilt
    3. Justice tested by rules, procedures
    4. Focus on infliction of pain
    5. Punishment as an end
    6. Rewards based on just deserts, "deserved"
    7. Justice opposed to mercy
    8. Justice neutral, claiming to treat all equally
    9. Justice as maintenance of the status quo
   10. Focus on guilt and abstract principles

Biblical Justice

    1. Justice seen as integrated whole
    2. Administration of justice as a search for solutions
    3. Justice defined by outcome, substance
    4. Focus on making right
    5. Punishment in context of redemption
    6. Justice based on need, undeserved
    7. Justice based on mercy and love
    8. Justice both fair and partial
    9. Justice as active, progressive, seeking to transform status quo
   10. Focus on harm done

The origin of modern punitive law dates from thirteenth-century European culture and reached its full organization in late eighteenth century. According to Bianchi, between 1200 and 1750, it gradually developed from a civil system of repair and compensation into the system of painful public repression we know today. The first crime in this modern sense was not murder—it was heresy against the Church, followed by witchcraft. The punitive system we know today has its roots in the Roman Catholic Inquisition and was rapidly adopted by secular authorities to increase their own power and control over the people. Gradually, crime was no longer seen as a conflict between citizens but as a conflict between the state and the accused, just as religious beliefs were no longer between God and man but between church/state and man (Bianchi, 1995). At this point God was interpreted as an increasingly punitive and legalistic judge resulting in a Western obsession with the retributive theme in the Bible that so affects our social milieu today. We must not forget that this attitude served the needs of those in power, and served powerful political strivings then, just as it does today.

In the process of this shift, the voices of the victims have been lost and thus an opportunity to heal the victims, the offenders, and the shattered community is lost as well.

> Healing requires opportunities for meaning and empowerment but the criminal justice response usually ignores victims, often not even informing them of events. It steals their experience and denies them meaning. Moreover it reinterprets the whole experience in foreign, legal terms. So victims feel fundamentally disrespected not only by the offenders but then by justice. (Zehr, 1994a, p. 7)

Restorative Justice

The alternative to the present system of retributive justice is restorative justice. In a restorative system of justice, the fundamental concerns are entirely different and focus on the restoration of relationship as well as individual and social healing. The first question is "Who has been hurt?" Once established, the next consideration is "What are the needs of victims, offenders, and communities?" The last consideration is "What are the obligations and whose are they?" Under such guidelines the aim of justice is to meet needs and promote healing of (a) victims, (b) the community, (c) offenders, and (d) of relationships between them. In a restorative system of justice, there is a recognition that violations create obligations and these obligations are bilateral—the offender must acknowledge and take responsibility for the harm done to victims and communities, and society acknowledges a responsibility to both victims and offenders.

We are really describing two very different paradigms for a criminal justice system. In a system of retributive justice, crime violates the state and its laws, justice focuses on establishing guilt so that does of pain can be measured out, justice is sought through a conflict between adversaries in which the offender is pitted against the state, and rules and intentions outweigh outcomes. One side wins and the other loses. In a system of restorative justice, crime violates people and relationships, justice aims to identify needs and obligations so that things can be made right. Justice encourages dialogue and mutual agreement, gives victims and offenders central roles, and is judged by the extent to which responsibilities are assumed, needs are met, and healing of individuals and relationships is encouraged (Zehr, 1994a).

Attempts to implement this philosophy have been in effect since the 1970s. Called Victim-Offender Reconciliation Programs (VORP), the current focus is usually on property crimes and acts of vandalism, although some programs are beginning to deal with more serious offenses as well. In these programs, offenders must deal directly with those they have harmed and are helped to understand the "three dimensions of harm" involved in their offenses—harm to victims, to the community, and to themselves. They are encouraged to develop and carry out their own sentence proposals. Reoffense rates tend to be remarkably low, at least at the Juvenile Reparations Program in Elkhart, Indiana—home of the original United States VORP. Programs that involve juveniles have been studied more than those with adults but so far the results are encouraging. Eighty-nine percent of VORP restitution agreements are fulfilled as opposed to 50 to 60 percent for restitution ordered by the court. In one study, 79 percent of victims and 85 percent of offenders said they were satisfied and in an earlier study 97 percent of victims said they would go through the process again if necessary. Victim fear was reduced, stereotypes were changed, offenders see these programs as a "tough response," and recidivism is reduced. Both the victims and the offenders have a true experience with justice. In one study of burglary victims, those who had gone through the VORP were twice as likely to say they had experienced justice as those who only went through the normal criminal justice process (Zehr, 1994b).

DEALING WITH BULLIES: REFUSING TO BE A VICTIM OR A BYSTANDER

Bullies come in all shapes and sizes—but originally they come in the form of very little boys and girls. Grown-up bullies have learned that the skills of intimidation, threat, and manipulation learned as children continue to get results as adults. The screaming boss, the batterer, the abusive radio talk show host, the leaders of gun organizations, and even the guy that pulls a gun can only be taken seriously because they have the power to enforce their threats—in terms of emotional development, they are still badly behaved children.

Richard Hazler (1996) has written a long overdue book about bullying. He defines bullying as

> repeatedly harming others. This can be done by physical attack or by hurting other's feelings through words, actions, or social exclusion. Bullying may be done by one person or by a group. It is an unfair match since the bully is either physically, verbally, and/or socially stronger than the victims. (p. 6)

In reviewing the literature, he notes that bullies apparently share a number of characteristics:

- They must demonstrate power or be seen as failures. The need for power and control is a compensation for underlying fears of inadequacy.
- They see no alternatives other than aggression to preserve dignity and self-image.
- They have difficulty in reaching out to others for help.
- They generally feel unloved, unimportant, and inferior—feelings they then project upon their victims.
- The bullying behavior is learned. Bullies are often victimized at home; their families have three times more problems; they have few good role models for constructive conflict resolution; the discipline they receive is harsh and inconsistent; there is little empathy expressed in their families; and the aggressive patterns of behavior are transmitted from generation to generation.
- Bullying by girls typically takes the form of verbal and social attacks. Bullies are more likely to demonstrate paranoid types of thinking and thus are likely to see hostile intent in the actions of potential victims.
- Bullies are less likely than others to recognize prosocial responses to threatening situations.
- They are quicker to anger and to use force.
- Typically, they have greater than average strength, are more energetic, are generally older than their victims, and place a great deal of importance on physical image.
- They are less positive about schoolwork and are more likely to have a variety of violence and crime-related problems as adults.

The book suggests interventions for victims and bystanders to manage bullies. These suggestions can be used toward preventing cycles of violence from starting in the family, at work, on the streets, and within communities. Here are some of the suggestions:

Ideas for Victims

- *Avoid giving the bully an emotional payoff.* Victims who can find ways to rob the bully's emotional payoff will take the pleasure out of the bully's behaviors and decrease the likelihood that these behaviors will continue over time.
- *Be physically and verbally assertive (not aggressive).* Bullies do not want to be challenged; they are only interested in easy targets. Choose assertive words and behaviors that convey confident messages without demeaning the other person. Take an assertive and direct physical stance. Avoid being aggressive or making threatening gestures.
- *Do something unexpected.* Bullies want victims who are predictable.
- *Practice necessary behaviors.* Don't just ruminate after the fact, but plan ahead for different responses that may work, but practice where it is safe and with someone who is safe to be with.
- *Strengthen continuing friendships and make new ones.* Bullying requires that victims be isolated in some way. Reversing isolation is a good way of decreasing the possibility of victimization.
- *Seek support when necessary.* Victims need to know that they are not alone.

Ideas for Bystanders

- *Recognize and give permission to act on your feelings and discomfort.* Bystanders are frequently embarrassed, feel inadequate, and are afraid when confronted by the acts of a bully. Find other people who feel similarly and start sharing feelings together.
- *Decide on specific actions to take.* To overcome inadequacy bystanders have to act. Thinking about specific actions and doing something is better than doing nothing at all. Not all interventions work, but we can learn from the ones that do not.
- *Provide immediate and/or follow-up support for victims.* Bystanders can become involved by helping victims either through direct intervention or personal support. The larger the number of bystanders available and the more united their approach, the greater will be the possibility of success.
- *Spend time with victims.*
- *Get physically and personally closer to victims rather than keeping your distance.*
  - Talk with victims about casual things.
  - Invite victims to be involved in a variety of group activities.
  - Be encouraging of victims efforts and accomplishments.

- Talk about serious things and problems when the victims want to do so.
- Express your desire to find additional ways to help.
- Give support regularly.
- *Help bullies change in ways that are positive for themselves and others.* Condemn the behavior, not the person.
- *Seek help in appropriate ways and situations.*

If we all took these recommendations seriously, in every social setting, most victimization would stop before it even started. We all have known people who fit this description. We probably still do. Bullies are not only hoodlums on the streets. They also run corporations, sit in houses of Congress, and dominate our airwaves. The problem is that bullying works. Bullies gain power, prestige, and wealth. But as many observers have pointed out, they only get away with it because of the power of the bystander effect. When groups of people join together to say no to bullies, the bullies are forced to back down. We all must stop being bystanders and instead, become witnesses.

A COMMUNITY RESPONSE TO VIOLENCE

Bucks County, Pennsylvania, is one of the wealthiest counties in the United States. North of Philadelphia, it is the site of the original home of William Penn and contains the exact point where Washington crossed the Delaware. For our purposes, Bucks County is interesting because of its demographics. Large for a northeastern region, it encompasses wealthy suburbs, rural farmlands, old small towns, trailer parks, and suburban ghettos. Every major ethnic group and every religion is represented. A stronghold of Republican voters, it has a county government that has historically tended toward conservatism. But faced with rising crime in the streets, in the schools, and at work, the movers and shakers of the county decided to take action and in May 1995, presented an antiviolence plan which they have been busily putting into place ever since.

William Eastburn is a prominent local attorney who survived a shot to the heart by an assailant. He joined forces with Judge Kenneth Biehn, President Judge of the Bucks County Court of Common Pleas and husband of the Education Director of the local Network of Victims Assistance. Together and with the support of three County Commissioners, Charles Martin, Michael Fitzpatrick, and Sandra Miller, they spearheaded the development of a countywide Task Force on Violence. The task force participants rapidly swelled to over 300 individuals representing more than 150 organizations in the county.

Among those included were grassroots community groups, civic associations, schools, police departments, churches and synagogues, hospitals and health agencies, cultural organizations, criminal justice agencies, corporations, small businesses, and the media. These active volunteers gave freely of their time and talents, willingly traveling to attend meetings, often early in the morning and in the evening hours, and spending many hours in between meetings organizing, preparing reports, making calls, writing up minutes, recruiting more people, and doing what it takes to get a massive effort off the ground. The United Way of Bucks County provided some one-year support to get the effort under way and this was supplemented by a planning grant from the Pennsylvania Commission on Crime and Delinquency through its "Communities That Care" program.

The charge of the task force was this:

> To reduce violence in Bucks County's homes, schools, and communities by identifying model public and private prevention efforts and by developing a countywide action plan to design and implement the most effective programs.

In the executive summary, the task force outlined six major strategies with implementation plans for each strategy.

Strategy 1

Build strong violence prevention relationships among community members, schools, social agencies, governmental agencies, religious institutions, law enforcement agencies, and mass media.

- Create an ongoing working group of diverse community members and professionals to establish priorities and to evaluate progress in all areas of the plan.
- Establish a council of social service agencies and community organizations that includes a business and industry link to promote continued resource sharing and collaboration.
- Promote media involvement by assisting in communication between media and community resources, promoting public discussion on violence prevention and related issues, and encouraging media sensitivity in handling stories involving violence.

Strategy 2

Prevent violence by acknowledging existing positive efforts and by identifying and implementing additional prevention and intervention programs for our families, our schools, and communities.

- Promote culturally sensitive parenting programs for physical, psychological, and social safety in families.
- Encourage increased use of Student Assistance Programs and Instructional Support Teams in the schools to help children at risk.
- Establish a domestic violence treatment network for abusive partners.
- Promote increased awareness and use of prevention and intervention services by older adults and people with disabilities.
- Integrate alcohol and drug prevention programs with violence prevention programs.

Strategy 3

Strive to build community programs that provide social, economic, and recreational opportunities with special focus on youth.

- Present models to motivate adults to take positive roles in the development of youth and to provide youth with more opportunities for leadership and cultural awareness.
- Promote the growth of a variety of mentoring programs.
- Present a model to increase recreational alternatives through community partnerships.
- Gather and disseminate job and volunteer opportunities for youth; encourage the development of increased opportunities.
- Encourage employers and employees to get involved with youth through community service activities such as adopt-a-school programs.

Strategy 4

Promote the implementation of violence prevention education.

- Establish a central data bank through the Bucks County Free Library for violence prevention resources and information and explore ways to keep citizens abreast of state-of-the-art prevention information.
- Link trainers and mentors with organizations and neighborhood groups to assist them in implementing violence prevention programs.
- Encourage every public and private school to designate a violence prevention facilitator.
- Provide community education and professional training in sexual and domestic violence prevention and treatment in understanding the management and supervision of sex offenders in the community.

- Provide community education and professional training about the mental health system and methods of crisis intervention.

Strategy 5

Improve the Justice System in Bucks County to provide a system of response to diminish incidences of violence.

- Create a Violence Against Women coordinating team to develop a unified systems response to domestic and sexual violence.
- Investigate the establishment of a Family Resource Center for supervised visitations, information, and referral.
- Promote ways to increase communication between the justice system and the drug and alcohol systems.
- Encourage and assist self-identified communities in stopping the cyclical patterns of drug abuse and violence.
- Coordinate justice agencies with treatment providers to help in the supervision, management, and treatment of sex offenders in the community.

Strategy 6

Create a sense of community and foster leadership development in all our neighborhoods.

- Encourage individual communities to build neighborhood identity through more opportunities for resident contact and communication.
- Provide leadership skills training for volunteers who seek to improve their communities.
- Develop opportunities for interaction and communication among municipalities and communities.
- Establish a countywide council dedicated to ending discrimination based on age, race, color, gender, religion, creed, culture, socioeconomic status, sexual orientation, ancestry, handicap, or disability.
- Recognize and promote neighborhood models of successful, nonviolent approaches to problem solving.

Two years into the development of the plan, the task force has formed an implementation committee of about eleven members representing the president judge, the head of the largest charitable organization in the county, the publisher of the local newspaper, representatives of: district justices, juvenile justice, children and youth, schools, clergy, hospitals, law enforcement, human health services, and the county commissioners. Significant progress has already been made in covering many areas of the action plan. Violence in the workplace has been strongly addressed with positive results through seminars, meetings, and agency involvement. With the cooperation of law enforcement and several public agencies, the schools have received increased funding for antidrug and antiviolence programs. A Human Relations Council has formed and has been involved in the investigation of several violent situations involving problems in several different communities. Because of the unity of the council, it was able to respond quickly and forcefully to a recent incidence of violence involving area students. The media has been integrally involved in all of the antiviolence efforts and have made commitments to do more extensive stories that present the stories of the victims and the follow-up to violence, rather than just sensationalizing the acts of perpetration. Parenting centers have been established in three different communities. Every school has appointed an antiviolence coordinator who integrates services with the drug and alcohol agencies and law enforcement. Mentoring programs have dramatically increased and local industries and chambers of commerce have become involved in adopting schools. This example of one community action plan was designed to bring about long-term change over the next decade, but already the residents of this county are able to see positive change as a result of local empowerment.

BEARING WITNESS AND HUMAN LIBERATION

As physicians and health care providers, we are convinced that the kinds of major interventions and changes that we have described in this book are necessary. Our work with individual patients has shown us why this is so. It is not possible to curb an epidemic as long as the disease carriers are allowed free access to other vulnerable people. It is not possible to correct potentially fatal physiological problems on a battlefield. The first step in any situation in which there is the potential for a high casualty rate is triage, to sort out the most life-threatening cases from others. The next step is to establish some kind of order, to restore even a minimal element of safety to the situation. Our debates over gun control, media violence, corporal punishment, domestic violence, prison, affirmative action, child abuse, health care, and welfare reform make about as much sense as two surgeons in a MASH tent arguing about which kind of suture material to use while the patient is bleeding to death.

We do not need any more studies to prove that there is a correlation between guns and gunshot wounds, between violence on TV and violence in vulnerable children, between corporal punishment and the perpetuation of violence, between domestic violence and many forms of psychological and social problems, between prison environments and the learning of violence, between discrimination and identity problems, between child abuse and adult psychiatric and social problems, between poor health care and poor health, between poverty and environments that promote trauma. We do, however, need more research to help us understand what the most effective strategies are to deal with these very complex problems. Because of the complicated and often provocative nature of the problems, perhaps it is only natural that we would want to avoid wrestling with these issues. Or that we would keep trying to label the problems as being less complex and interconnected than they are. After all, committing ourselves to reversing the structural violence that comprises much of the normal behavior in our society will take enormous effort, time, and money. The changes that are required necessitate a total mobilization of social resources, the kind of activation that we usually only see in response to a declared war. Turn on the news or read a newspaper and one could begin to believe that perhaps we are in a war, but this war is much more difficult to fight—this is a war against ourselves.

We have titled this book *Bearing Witness* because we wanted to convey the vital importance of the need for all those who are presently silent to speak up and bear witness to what they have seen. This is a particularly urgent call to health care workers and other service providers who spend a lifetime in the "trenches," attempting to fix what is already broken, while trying to prevent more damage from occurring. The idea of bearing witness derives from the concept of testimony that came out of Chile in the 1970s, when psychologists, priests, nuns, and other caregivers put their own lives on the line by collecting testimonies from former political prisoners who had been tortured (Agger and Jensen, 1990). This process of listening to, recording, and transmitting the details of pain and moral outrage has also been a process that Holocaust survivors such as Victor Frankl, Bruno Bettelheim, Primo Levi, and Elie Wiesel have used for themselves and to help others.

Ignacio Martin-Baró was a El Salvadoran Jesuit priest, theologian, and psychologist who was assassinated by the U.S.-trained government soldiers in November 1989 because of his alignment with the Salvadoran people in their collective resistance to oppression and their struggle for peace and justice. In a manuscript he finished just before his murder, he wrote about a "liberation psychology," a sister discipline to the "liberation theology" that grew out of war-torn Latin America. He noted that psychology—and by extension all caregiving professions—have served directly and indirectly to strengthen oppressive political structures that exist by drawing attention away from themselves and toward individual and subjective factors. He called for a new psychology that would engage initially in three major tasks. The first task is the recovery of historical memory,

> to discover through collective memory, those elements of the past which have proved useful in the defense of the interests of exploited classes and which may be applied to the present struggles. . . . Thus, the recovery of a historical memory supposes the reconstruction of models of identification that, instead of chaining and caging the people, open up the horizon for them, toward their liberation and fulfillment. (Martin-Baró, 1994, p. 30)

The second task is to de-ideologize everyday experience, since

> we know that knowledge is a social construction. Our countries live burdened by the lie of a prevailing discourse that denies, ignores, or disguises essential aspects of reality . . . this process of de-ideologizing common sense must be realized as much as possible through critical participation in the life of the poorer people. (Ibid., p. 31)

The third task is to utilize the people's virtues because

> current history confirms, day by day, their uncompromising solidarity with the suffering, their ability to deliver and to sacrifice for the collective good, their tremendous faith in the human capacity to change the world, their hope for a tomorrow that keeps being violently denied to them. (Ibid., p. 31)

For healing to occur, victims of violence need to "speak out to power," whether that power is invested in their parents, their spouse, their teacher, their boyfriend, their employer, their neighbor, their clergyman, or their government. In an interconnected, interdependent world there simply is no room for violence.

In his essay on postmodernism and the prospects for a new world order, philosopher and legal scholar Richard Falk (1992) reminds us that

> The human species has a special coevolutionary capacity and responsibility. Unlike other species we are aware of our roles in the world and

bear the burdens of awareness of having disrupted the ecological order to such a dangerous and unnecessary degree. As humans, we can respond to the pain of the world by devoting our energies to various kinds of restorative action, building institutional forms and popular support for such a dramatic reorientation of behavior. This "conversion" from secularism is under way but to an uneven degree, and virtually not at all in relations to the powerfully entrenched governmental and market structures associated with modernist enterprise. . . . We remain at a stage of postmodern consciousness in which our discernment of negations has formed a consensus but our imaginative attempts at alternatives remain at the experimental stage, hence fraught with controversy and disillusion. (p. 36)

There is no logical reason why our world cannot become a place of peace, tolerance, compassion, and care if we have sufficient dedication, imagination, and perseverance to overcome time-honored obstacles. But it will not happen without the active participation of those who are presently still silent, fearful of their own voice and the bullies that surround us. It is our hope that this book has offered those silent ones a different way of thinking about, understanding, and integrating much of what we already know at a deeper, soul level about what needs to change and that this knowledge will help us all find courage for the struggle that lies ahead. We must commit ourselves to some higher vision, some greater spiritual, moral, or religious reality that allows us at least a momentary glimpse of wholeness, health, and integrity. Once we have experienced wholeness, we will never want to be fragmented again.

Human rights are universal and indivisible. Human freedom is not separate from these: if it's denied to anyone anywhere, it is therefore denied, indirectly, to all. This is why we can't remain silent in the countenance of evil or violence; silence merely encourages evil and violence. . . . Respect for the universality of human and civil rights, their inalienability and indivisibility, is perforce possible only when it's understood—at least in the philosophical or existential sense— that one is "responsible for the whole world" and that one must behave in the manner in which all ought to behave, even if not all do.

Vaclav Havel
"True Democracy Demands Moral Conviction"
1993, p. 607

Bibliography

AAUW. (1992). *How Schools Shortchange Girls*. The AAUW Educational Foundation.

AAUW. (1993). *Hostile Hallways*. The AAUW Educational Foundation.

Agger, I., and Jenson, S. B. (1990, January). Testimony as ritual and evidence in psychotherapys for political refugees. *Journal of Traumatic Stress, 3* (1), 115-130.

Aho, J. (1994). *This thing of darkness: A sociology of the enemy.* Seattle: University of Washington Press.

Alexander, B. H., Franklin, G. M., and Wolf, M. E. (1994). The sexual assault of women at work in Washington State, 1980 to 1989. *The American Journal of Public Health, 84* (4), 640-643.

Alexander, P .C. (1992). Application of attachment theory to the study of sexual abuse. *Journal of Consulting and Clinical Psychology, 60* (2), 185-195.

Alford, J. D., Mahone, C., and Fielstein, E. M. (1988). Cognitive and behavioral sequelae of combat: Conceptualization and implications for treatment. *Journal of Traumatic Stress, 1* (4), 489-501.

American Academy of Pediatrics (AAP), Committee on Communication. (1990). Children, adolescents, and television. *Pediatrics, 85,* 1119-1120.

American Medical Association. (1996). Family Violence Report Card. On AMA Web site, http://www.ama-assn.org/ad-com/releases/1996/fvcard.htm.

American Medical Association. (1996). *Physician's guide to media violence.* Chicago, IL: American Medical Association.

American Psychiatric Association. (1952). *Diagnostic and Statistical Manual of Mental Disorders.* Washington, DC: American Psychiatric Press.

American Psychiatric Association. (1968). *Diagnostic and Statistical Manual of Mental Disorders* (Second Edition). Washington, DC: American Psychiatric Press.

American Psychiatric Association. (1980). *Diagnostic and Statistical Manual of Mental Disorders* (Third Edition). Washington, DC: American Psychiatric Press.

American Psychiatric Association. (1987). *Diagnostic and Statistical Manual of Mental Disorders* (Third Revised Edition). Washington, DC: American Psychiatric Press.

American Psychiatric Association. (1994). *Diagnostic and Statistical Manual of Mental Disorders* (Fourth Edition). Washington, DC: American Psychiatric Press.

American Psychological Association. (1996). *Violence and the Family: Report of the American Psychological Association Presidential Task Force on Violence and the Family.* Washington, DC: American Psychological Association. Copyright © 1996 by the American Psychological Association. Reprinted with permission.

Amir, M., Kaplan Z., Neumann, L., Sharabani, R., Shani, N., and Buskila, D. (1997). Post-traumatic stress disorder, tenderness, and fibromyalgia. *Journal of Psychosomatic Research, 42* (6), 607-613.

Anderson, E. (1990). *Streetwise Chicago.* Chicago: University of Chicago Press.

Anderson, E. (1994, May 15). Living hard by the code of the streets. *Philadelphia Inquirer,* p. C7.

Anfuso, D. (1994). Deflecting workplace violence. *Personnel Journal, 73* (10), 66-78.

Apsey, L. S. (1990). How transforming power has been used in the past by early Christians. In Holmes, R. L. (Ed.), *Nonviolence in theory and practice* (pp. 27-28). Belmont, CA: Wadsworth Publishing.

Arbetter, S. (1995). Violence: A growing threat. *Current Health, 21* (6), 6-13.

Arbuckle, J., Olson, L., Howard, M., Brillman, J., Anctil, C., and Sklar, D. (1996). Safe at home? Domestic violence and other homicides among women in New Mexico. *Annals of Emergency Medicine, 27* (2), 210-215.

Attala, J.M. (1996). Detecting abuse against women in the home. *Home Care Provider, 1* (1), 12-18.

Baars, B. J., and McGovern, K. (1995). Steps toward healing: False memories and traumagenic amnesia may coexist in vulnerable populations. *Consciousness and Cognition, 4* (1), 68-74.

Bach, M., and Bach, D. (1995). Predictive value of alexithymia: A prospective study in somatizing patients. *Psychotherapy and Psychosomatics, 64* (1), 43-48.

Badura, A. S., Reiter, R. C., Altmaier, E. M., Rhomberg, A., and Elas, D. (1997). Dissociation, somatization, substance abuse, and coping in women with chronic pelvic pain. *Obstetrics and Gynecology, 90* (3), 405-410.

Bahro, R. (1994). *Avoiding social and ecological disaster: The politics of world transformation.* Bath, England: Gateway Books.

Baker, S. P. (1985). Without guns, do people kill people? *American Journal of Public Health 75,* 587.

Barash, D. P. (1994). *Beloved enemies: Our need for opponents.* Amherst, NY: Prometheus Books.

Baron, S. A. (1993). *Violence in the workplace: A prevention and management guide for businesses.* Ventura, CA: Pathfinder Publishing of California.

Barr, H. (1986). Outcome of drug abuse treatment in two modalities. In G. DeLeon and J. T. Ziegenfuss (Eds.), *Therapeutic communities for addictions* (pp. 97-108). Springfield, IL: Charles C Thomas.

Barrier, M. (1995a). Creating a violence-free company culture. *Nation's Business, 83* (2), 22-23.

Barrier, M. (1995b). The enemy within. *Nation's Business, 83* (2), 18-24.

Bartlett, D. L., and Steele, J. B. (1992). *America: What went wrong?* Kansas City: Andrews and McMeel.

Baum, A. (1991). *Toxins, technology, and natural disasters.* In G. R. Varden Bos and B. K. Bryant (Eds.), *Cataclysms, crises, and catastrophes: Psychology in action* (pp. 176-197). Washington, DC: American Psychological Association.

Beck, J. (1972). Meditation I, 1963. New York City—Dreams of a free society. *The life of the theatre.* San Francisco: City Lights Books.

Becker, C. (1994). Introduction: Presenting the problem. In C. Becker (Ed.), *The subversive imagination: Artistis, society, and social responsibility.* New York: Routledge.

Benard, B. (1991). *Fostering resiliency in kids: Protective factors in the family, school, and community.* Portland, OR: Northwest Regional Educational Laboratory.

Benedek, E. P. (1989). Baseball, apple pie, and violence: Is it American? In L. J. Dickstein, and C. C. Nadelson (Eds.), *Family violence: Emerging Issues of a national crisis* (pp. 1-13). Washington, DC: American Psychiatric Press.

Benedikt, R. A., and Kolb, L. C. (1986). Preliminary findings on chronic pain and post-traumatic stress disorder. *American Journal of Psychiatry, 143* (7), 908-910.

Bennis, W. (1993). A talk with Warren Bennis. *Psychology Today, 26* (6), 30-32.

Bentovim, A. (1992). *Trauma organized systems.* London: Karnac Books.

Berenbaum, H. (1996). Childhood abuse, alexithymia, and personality disorder. *Journal of Psychosomatic Research, 41* (6), 585-595.

Bergmann, M. S. (1992). *In the shadow of Moloch: The sacrifice of children and its impact on Western religions.* New York: Colombia University Press.

Berkowitz, L. (1986). Situational influences on reactions to observed violence. *Journal of Social Issues, 42* (3), 93-106.

Berman, L. H. (1992). The effects of living with violence. *Journal of the American Academy of Psychoanalysis, 20* (4), 671-675.

Berry, J. (1992). *Lead us not into temptation: Catholic priests and the sexual abuse of children.* New York: Doubleday.

Besson, A., Privat, A. M., Eschalier, A., and Fialip, J. (1996). Effects of morphine, naloxone, and their interaction in the learned-helplessness paradigm in rats. *Psychopharmacology (Berlin), 123* (1), 71-78.

Betson, D. M., and Michael, R. T. (1997). Why so many children are poor. *Future Child, 7* (2), 25-39.

Bianchi, H. (1995). *Justice as sanctuary: Toward a new system of crime control.* Bloomington, IN: Indiana University Press.

Bills, L. J. (1997). Personal communication.

Bills, L. J., and Kreisler, K. (1993). Treatment of flashbacks with naltrexone. *American Journal of Psychiatry, 150* (9), 1430.

Biondi, M., and Zannino, L. G. (1997). Psychological stress, neuroimmunomodulation, and susceptibility to infectious diseases in animals and man: A review. *Psychotherapy and Psychosomatics, 66* (1), 3-26.

Bleich, A., Dolev, A., Koslowski, M., Vozner, Y., and Lerer, B. (1994). Psychiatric morbidity following psychic trauma of combat origin. *Harefuah, 126* (9), 493-496.

Bloom, M. (1996). *Primary prevention practices.* Thousand Oaks: Sage.

Bloom, S. L. (1994). The sanctuary model: Developing generic inpatient programs for the treatment of psychological trauma. In M. B. Williams and J. F. Sommer (Eds.), *Handbook of post-traumatic therapy: A practical guide to intervention, treatment, and research,* (pp. 474-491). New York: Greenwood Publishing.

Bloom, S. L. (1995a). Creating sanctuary in the classroom. *Journal for a Just and Caring Education, 1* (4), 403-433.

Bloom, S. L. (1995b). When good people do bad things: Meditations on the "backlash." *Journal of Psychohistory, 22* (3), 273-304.

Bloom, S. L. (1996). Trauma and the nature of evil. *Trauma and Controversy,* Twelfth Annual Meeting, International Society for Traumatic Stress Studies. Sheraton Palace Hotel, San Francisco, CA, November 9-13, 1996.

Bloom, S. L. (1997). *Creating sanctuary: Towards the evolution of sane communities.* New York: Routledge.

Boccia, M. L., Scanlan, J. M., Laudenslager, M. L., Berger, C. L., Hijazi, A. S., and Reite, M. L. (1997). Juvenile friends, behavior, and immune responses to separation in bonnet macaque infants. *Physiological Behavior, 61* (2), 191-198.

Bollerud, K. (1990). A model for the treatment of trauma-related syndromes among chemically dependent inpatient women. *Journal of Substance Abuse Treatment, 7* (2), 83-87.

Boraine, A. (1996). Alternatives and adjuncts to criminal prosecutions. Speech presented at "Justice in Cataclysm: Criminal Tribunals in the wake of mass violence," Brussels, Belgium, July 20-21, 1996.

Bovet, S. F. (1994). Make companies more socially responsible. *Public Relations Journal, 50* (8), 30-33.

Bowlby, J. (1982). *Attachment.* New York: Basic Books.

Bowlby, J. (1984). Violence in the family as a disorder of the attachment and caregiving systems. *American Journal of Psychoanalysis, 44* (9), 9-27.

Bowlby, J. (1988). *A secure base: Parent-child attachment and healthy human development.* New York: Basic Books.

Braudel, F. (1994). *A history of civilizations.* New York: Allen Lane.

Breakey, G., and Pratt, B. (1991). Healthy growth for Hawaii's "Healthy Start": Toward a systematic statewide approach to the prevention of child abuse and neglect. *Bulletin of National Center for Clinical Infant Programs, 11* (4), 16-22.

Bremner, J. D., Davis, M., Southwick, S. M., Krystal, J. H., and Charney, D. S. (1993). Neurobiology of post-traumatic stress disorder. In J. M. Oldham, M. B. Riba, and A. Tasman (Eds.), *Review of Psychiatry, 12,* (pp. 183-204). Washington, DC: American Psychiatric Press.

Bremner, J. D., Krystal, J. H., Southwick, S. M., and Charney, D. S. (1995). Functional neuroanatomical correlates of the effects of stress on memory. *Journal of Traumatic Stress, 8* (4), 527-553.

Bremner, J. D., Krystal, J. H., and Charney, D. S., and Southwick, S. M. (1996). Neural mechanisms in dissociative amnesia for childhood abuse: Relevance to the current controversy surrounding the "false memory syndrome." *American Journal of Psychiatry, 153* (7), 71-82.

Brende, J. O. (1993). A 12-step recovery program for victims of traumatic events. In J. P. Wilson and B. Raphael (Eds.), *International handbook of traumatic stress syndromes*. New York: Plenum Press.

Brendtro, L., and Long, N. (1995). Breaking the cycle of conflict. *Educational Leadership, 52* (5), 52-57.

Brent, D. A., Perper, J. A., Allman, C. J., Moritz, G. M., Wartella, M. E., and Zelenak, J. P. (1991). The presence and accessibility of firearms in the homes of adolescent suicides: A case control study. *Journal of the American Medical Association, 266* (21), 2989.

Breslau, N., Davis, G. C., Andreski, P., and Peterson, E. (1991). Traumatic events and post-traumatic stress disorder in an urban population of young adults. *Archives of General Psychiatry, 48* (3), 216-222.

Brill, N. Q. (1993). *America's psychic malignancy*. Springfield, IL: Charles C Thomas.

Brinkerhoff, M. B., Grandin, E., and Lupri, E. (1992). Religious involvement and spousal violence. The Canadian case. *Journal for the Scientific Study of Religion 31* (1), 15-31.

Brooks-Gunn, J., and Duncan, G. J. (1997). The effects of poverty on children. *Future Child, 7* (2), 55-71.

Brown, D., Scheflin, A. W., and Hammond, D. C. (1998). *Memory, trauma treatment, and the law*. New York: W. W. Norton.

Brown, L. M., and Gilligan, C. (1992). *Meeting at the crossroads: Women's psychology and girls' development*. New York: Ballantine Books.

Browne, A. (1993). Violence against women by male partners. *American Psychologist, 48* (10), 1077-1097.

Burgess, A.W., Hartman, C. R., and Clements, P. T. (1995). Biology of memory and childhood trauma. *Journal of Psychosocial Nursing and Mental Health Services, 33* (3), 16-26.

Burgess, A. W., Hazelwood, R. R., Rokous, F. E., Hartman, C. R., and Burgess, A. G. (1988). Serial rapists and their victims: Reenactment and repetition. In R. A. Prentky and V. L. Quinsey (Eds.), *Human sexual aggression: Current perspectives* (pp. 277-295). New York: New York Academy of Sciences.

Burgess, A. W., and Holmstrom, L. L. (1974). Rape trauma syndrome. *American Journal of Psychiatry, 131* (9), 981-986.

Calabrese, R. L. (1986, April/May). Teaching as a dehumanizing experience. *The High School Journal, 69* (4), 255-259.

Caldwell, M. F. (1992, August). Incidence of PTSD among staff victims of patient violence. *Hospital and Community Psychiatry, 43* (8), 838-839.

Callahan, C. M. and Rivara, F. P. (1992). Urban high school youths and handguns, A school-based survey. *Journal of the American Medical Association, 267* (22), 3038-3048.

Canada, G. (1995). *Fist, stick, knife, gun*. Boston: Beacon Press.

Capra, F. (1982). *The turning point: Science, society, and the rising culture*. New York: Simon and Schuster.

Card, K. K. (1974). Lethality of suicide methods and suicide risks: Two distinct concepts. *Omega, 5*, 37.

Carrey, N. J., Butter, H. J., Persinger, M. A., and Bialik, R. J. (1995). Physiological and cognitive correlates of child abuse. *Journal of the American Academy of Child and Adolescent Psychiatry, 34* (8), 1067-1075.

Carton, P. (1991). Mass media and young people. *Nieman Reports, 45* (4), 24-30.

Cass, J. (1995, March 2). Hard time. *Philadelphia Inquirer*, p. G-01.

Cassel, C. K. (1996). The patient-physician covenant: An affirmation of Asclepios. *Connecticut Medicine, 60* (5), 291-293.

Caudron, S. (1994). Fight crime, sell products: Socially responsible companies that join the fight against crime may find new consumers in the process. *Industry Week, 243* (20), 49-52.

Cavendish, R. 1980. *Mythology: An illustrated encyclopedia.* New York: Rizzoli International Publications.

Centerwall, B. S. (1992). Television and violence. The scale of the problem and where to go from here. *Journal of the American Medical Association, 267* (22), 3059-3063.

Challeen, D. A. (1986). *Making it right: A common sense approach to criminal justice.* Aberdeen, SD: Melius and Peterson Publishing.

Chemtob, C. M., Roitblat, H. L., Hamada, R. S., Carlson, J. G., and Twentyman, C. T. (1988). A cognitive action theory of post-traumatic stress disorder. *Journal of Anxiety Disorders, 2*, 253-275.

Chira, S. (1994, July 10). Worry and distrust of adults beset teen-agers, poll says. *The New York Times*, Section I, page 1, col. 3.

Chodorow, N. (1978). *The reproduction of mothering.* Berkeley: University of California Press.

Christian, C. W., Scribano, P., Seidl, T., and Pinto-Martin, J. A. (1997). Pediatric injury resulting from family violence. *Pediatrics, 99* (2), E8.

Churchill, L. R. (1997). "Damaged humanity": The call for a patient-centered medical ethic in the managed care era. *Theoretical Medicine, 18* (1-2), 113-126.

Clancy, T. V., Misick, L.N., Covington, D., Churchill, M. P., and Maxwell, J. G. (1994). The financial impact of intentional violence on community hospitals. *Journal of Trauma, 37* (1), 1-4.

Clark, D. (1975). *Social therapy in psychiatry.* New York: Jason Aronson.

Clinton, H. R. (1996). *It takes a village: And other lessons children teach us.* New York: Simon and Schuster.

Coates, D., Wortman, C. B., and Abben, A. (1979). Reactions to victims. In I. H. Friez, D. Bar-Tal, and J. S. Carroll (Eds.), *New approaches to social problems.* San Francisco: Jossey-Bass.

Cobb, W. H., and Grier, P. M. (1968). *Black rage.* New York: Basic Books.

Cochrane, C. E., Brewerton, T. D., Wilson, D. B., and Hodges, E. L. (1993). Alexithymia in the eating disorders. *International Journal of Eating Disorders, 14* (2), 219-222.

Cole, P. M., and Putnam, F. W. (1992). Effect of incest on self and social functioning: A developmental psychopathology perspective. *Journal of Consulting and Clinical Psychology, 60,* (2), 174-184.

Cole, S. L. 1985. *The absent one: Mourning ritual, tragedy, and the performance of ambivalence.* University Park, PA: Pennsylvania State University Press.

Connell, R. W. (1995). *Masculinities.* Berkeley: University of California Press.

Corcoran, M. E. and Chaudry, A. (1997). The dynamics of childhood poverty. *Future Child, 7* (2), 40-54.

Costela, C., Tejedor-Real, P., Mico, J. A., Gibert-Rahola, J. (1995). Effect of neonatal handling on learned helplessness model of depression. *Physiology and Behavior, 57* (2), 407-410.

Courtois, C. (1988). *Healing the incest wound: Adult survivors in therapy.* New York: W. W. Norton and Co.

Cramer, E., and McFarlane, J. (1994, August 11). Pornography and abuse of women. *Public Health Nursing, 11* (4), 268-272.

Craven, D. (1997). *Sex differences in violent victimization, 1994.* Washington, DC: U.S. Department of Justice, Bureau of Justice Statistics.

Crewdson, J. (1988). *By silence betrayed: Sexual abuse of children in America.* Boston: Little, Brown and Co.

Crews, W. D. Jr., Bonaventura, S., Rowe, F. B., and Bonsie, D. (1993). Cessation of long-term naltrexone therapy and self-injury: A case study. *Research in Developmental Disabilities, 14* (4), 331-340.

Crouch, E., and Williams, D. (1995). What cities are doing to protect kids. *Educational Leadership, 52* (5), 60-63.

Danielli, Y. (1985). The treatment and prevention of long-term effects and intergenerational transmission of victimization: A lesson from Holocaust survivors and their children. In C. R. Figley (Ed.), *Trauma and its wake: The study and treatment of post-traumatic stress disorder.* New York: Brunner/Mazel.

Danielli, Y. (1997). International handbook of multigenerational legacies of trauma. *PTSD Research Quarterly, 8* (1), 1-6.

D'Aquili, E. G., Laughlin, C. D. Jr., and McManus, J. (Eds.). (1979). *The spectrum of ritual: A biogenetic structural analysis.* New York: Columbia University Press.

Davidson, J. R., Hughes, D., Blazer, D. G., and George, L. K. (1991). Post-traumatic stress disorder in the community: An epidemiological study. *Psychological Medicine, 21* (3), 713-721.

Davies, D. (1991). Intervention with male toddlers who have witnessed parental violence. *Families in Society, 72* (9), 515-524.

Davies, P. 1983. *God and the new physics.* New York: A Touchstone Book.

Davis, J. W., Kaups, K. L., and Rhames, M. P. III. (1997). More guns and younger assailants: A combined police and trauma center study. *Archives of Surgery, 132* (10), 1067-1070.

De Becker, G. (1997). *The gift of fear.* Boston: Little Brown.

De Bellis, M. D., Burke, L., Trickett, P. K., and Putnam, F. W. (1996). Antinuclear antibodies and thyroid function in sexually abused girls. *Journal of Traumatic Stress, 9* (2), 369-378.

Dean, E. T. (1997). *Shook over hell: Post-traumatic stress, Vietnam, and the Civil War.* Cambridge, MA: Harvard University Press.

DeGroot, J. M., Rodin, G., and Olmsted, M. P. (1995). Alexithymia, depression, and treatment outcome in bulimia nervosa. *Comprehensive Psychiatry, 36* (1), 53-60.

Dellums, R. V. (1995). Stealth bombing America's future. *The Nation, 261* (10), 350-353.

DeMause, L. (1982). The evolution of childhood. In DeMause, L. (Ed.), *Foundations of psychohistory* (pp. 1-83). New York: Creative Roots.

DeMause, L. (1990). The history of child assault. *The Journal of Psychohistory, 18* (1), 1-24.

DeMause, L. (1991). The Gulf War as mental disorder. *The Journal of Psychohistory, 19* (1), 1-22.

Demos, E. V. (1989). Resiliency in infancy. In T. F. Dugan and R. Coles (Eds.), *The child in our times: Studies in the development of resiliency.* New York: Brunner/Mazel.

Dillon, S. (1993, November 24). Board reports played down school crime, Cortines says. *The New York Times,* B1, 2.

Dillon, S. (1994, July 7). Report finds more violence in the schools. *The New York Times,* B1, 5.

Dilworth, D. D. (1994). 1 million victimized at work annually. *Trial, 30* (10), 109-111.

Dishion, T. J., French, D. C., and Patterson, G. P. (1994). The development and ecology of antisocial behavior. In D. Cicchetti and D. J. Cohen (Eds.), *Developmental psychopathology, Volume 2: Risk, disorder, and adaptation.* New York: John Wiley and Sons.

Dissanayake, E. (1992). *Homoaestheticus: Where art comes from and why.* New York: The Free Press.

Dodge, K. A., Bates, J. E., and Pettit, G. S. (1990). Mechanisms in the cycle of violence. *Science, 250* (4988), 1678-1683.

Donald, M. (1991). *Origins of the modern mind: Three stages in the evolution of culture and cognition.* Cambridge, MA: Harvard University Press.

Dossey, L. 1993. *Healing words: The power of prayer and the practice of medicine.* San Francisco: HarperSanFrancisco.

Driver, T. F. (1991). *The magic of ritual: Our need for liberating rites that transform our lives and our communities.* San Francisco: HarperSan Francisco.

Drossman, D. A. (1995). Sexual and physical abuse and gastrointestinal illness. *Scandinavian Journal of Gastroenterology Supplment, 208,* 90-96.

Drummond, P. D., and Hewson-Bower, B. (1997). Increased psychosocial stress and decreased mucosal immunity in children with recurrent upper respiratory tract infections. *Journal of Psychosomatic Research, 43* (3), 271-278.

Dumain, Brian. (1994). Mr. Learning organization. *Fortune, 130* (8), 147-154.

Duncan, G. J., Brooks-Gunn, J., and Klebanov, P. K. (1994). Economic deprivation and early childhood development. *Child Development, 65* (2Spec No), 296-318.

Duncan, R. D., Saunders, B. E., Kilpatrick, D. G., Hanson, R. F., and Resnick, H. S. (1996). Childhood physical assault as a risk factor for PTSD, depression, and substance abuse: Findings from a national survey. *American Journal of Orthopsychiatry, 66* (3), 437-448.

Duncan, T. S. (1995). Death in the office: Workplace homicides. *FBI Law Enforcement Bulletin, 64* (4), 20-26.

Dunn, G. E., Paolo, A. M., Ryan, J. J, and Fleet, J. V. (1993, July 7). Dissociative symptoms in a substance abuse population. *American Journal of Psychiatry, 150* (7), 1043.

Durant, R. H., Getts, A. G., Cadenhead, C., and Woods, E. R. (1995, December 17). The association between weapon carrying and the use of violence among adolescents living in and around public housing. *Journal of Adolescent Health, 17* (6), 376-380.

Duster, T. 1971. Conditions for guilt-free massacre. In N. Sanford and C. Comstock (Eds.), *Sanctions for evil: Sources of social destructiveness* (pp. 25-36). San Francisco: Jossey-Bass, Inc.

Dworkin, A. (1979) *Pornography: Men possessing women.* New York: Penguin Books.

Dworkin, A. (1992). Against the male flood: Censorship, pornography, and equality. In C. Itzen (Ed.), *Pornography: Women, violence and civil liberties* (pp. 515-535). New York: Oxford University Press, Inc.

Dyson, F. (1992). *From Eros to Gaia.* New York: Pantheon.

Earle, R. B. (1995). *Helping to prevent child abuse—and future criminal consequences: Hawaii Healthy Start.* Washington, DC: U.S. Department of Justice, National Institute of Justice.

Eby, K. K., Campbell, J. C., Sullivan, C. M., and Davidson, W. S. Jr. (1995). Health effects of experiences of sexual violence for women with abusive partners. *Health Care Women International, 16* (6), 563-576.

Edelman, S. E. (1978, July). Managing the violent patient in a community mental health center. *Hospital and Community Psychiatry, 29* (7), 460-462.

Egeland, B., and Susman-Stillman, A. (1996). Dissociation as a mediator of child abuse across generations. *Child Abuse and Neglect, 20* (11), 1123-1132.

Ehrenreich, B. (1997). *Blood rites: Origins and history of the passions of war.* New York: Metropolitan Books.

Eisenman, R. (1993). Characteristics of adolescent felons in prison treatment programs. *Adolescence, 28* (111), 695-699.

Eitinger, L. (1961). Pathology of the concentration camp syndrome: A.M.A. *Archives of General Psychiatry, 9* (5), 79-87.

Ekman, P., Levenson, R. W., and Friesen, W. V. (1983). Autonomic nervous system activity distinguishes among emotions. *Science, 221* (4616), 1208-1210.

Elikann, P. T. (1996). *The tough-in-crime myth: Real solutions to cut crime.* New York: Insight Books.

Elium, D., and Elium, J. (1992). *Raising a son.* Hillsboro, OR: Beyond Words Publishing, Inc.

Ellason, J. W., Ross, C. A., Sainton, K., and Mayran, L. W. (1996). Axis I and II comorbidity and childhood trauma history in chemical dependency. *Bulletin of the Menninger Clinic, 60* (1), 39-51.

Ellison, C. G., and Bartkowski, J. P. (1997). Religion and the legitimation of violence. In J. Turpin and L. R. Kurtz (Eds.), *The web of violence: From interpersonal to global* (pp. 46-67). Urbana, IL: University of Illinois Press.

Else, L., Wonderlich, S. A., Beatty, W. W., Christie, D. W., and Staton, R. D. (1993). Personality characteristics of men who physically abuse women. *Hospital and Community Psychiatry, 44* (1), 54-58.

Emergency Nurses Association (1995). Fact Sheet on 1994 Emergency Nurses Association survey on prevalence of violence in U. S. emergency departments. Unpublished.

Eron, L. D., Gentry, J. H., and Schlegel, P. (1994). *Reason to hope. A psychosocial perspective on violence and youth.* Washington, DC: American Psychological Association.

Eslin, M. 1976. *The anatomy of drama.* New York: Hill and Wang.

Evans, D. L., Leserman, J., Pedersen, C. A., Golden, R. N., Lewis, M. H., Folds, J. A., and Ozer, H. (1989). Immune correlates of stress and depression. *Psychopharmacology Bulletin, 25* (3), 319-324.

Everly, G. S. (1989). Stress-related disease: A review. In G. S. Everly (Ed.), *A clinical guide to the treatment of the human stress response* (pp. 61-77). New York: Plenum Press.

Falk, R. (1992). *Explorations at the end of time: The prospects for world order.* Philadelphia: Temple University Press.

Faludi, S. (1991). *Backlash.* New York: Doubleday.

Family Violence Prevention Fund (1993). *Men beating women: Ending domestic violence, a qualitative and quantitative study of public attitudes on violence against women.* New York: EDK Associates.

Farrell, W. (1993). *The myth of male power.* New York: Simon and Schuster.

Faux, J. (1997, October 27). The "American Model" exposed. *The Nation,* pp. 18-22.

Federal Bureau of Investigation. (1996). *Crime in the United States, 1995.* Washington, DC: United States Government Printing Office.

Fergusson, D. M., and Lynskey, M. T. (1997). Physical punishment/maltreatment during childhood and adjustment in young adulthood. *Child Abuse and Neglect, 21* (7), 617-630.

Fialkov, M. J. (1992). Children of chemically dependent parents: Multiperspectives from the cutting edge. *American Journal of Addictions, 1* (2).

Fierman, E. J., Hunt, M. F., Pratt, L. A., Warshaw, M. G., Yonkers, K. A., Peterson, L. G., Epstein-Kaye, T. M., and Norton, H. S. (1993). Trauma and post-traumatic stress disorder in subjects with anxiety disorders. *American Journal of Psychiatry, 150* (12), 1872-1874.

Figley, C. R. (1995). *Compassion fatigue: Coping with secondary traumatic stress disorder in those who treat the traumatized.* New York: Brunner/Mazel.

Fingerhut, L.A. and Kleinman, J. C. (1990). International and interstate comparisons of homicide among young males. *Journal of the American Medical Association, 263* (24), 3292.

Finkel, K. (1994). Philadelphia in the 1820s: A new civic consciousness. In Johnston, N. (Ed.), *Eastern State Penitentiary: Crucible of good intentions* (pp. 9-20). Philadelphia: University of Pennsylvania Press.

Finkelhor, D., and Dziuba-Leatherman, J. (1994). Victimization of children. *American Psychologist, 49* (3), 173-183.

Fischer, K. W., and Ayoub, C. (1994). Affective splitting and dissociation in normal and maltreated children. In D. Cichetti and S. Toth (Eds.), *Disorders and dysfunctions of the self: Rochester symposium on developmental psychopathology (Vol. 5)* (pp. 149-222). Rochester: Rochester University Press.

Fish-Murray, C. C., Koby, E. V., and Van der Kolk, B. A. (1987). Evolving ideas: The effect of abuse on children's thought. In B. A. Van der Kolk, (Ed.). *Psychological trauma* (pp. 89-110). Washington, DC: American Psychiatric Press.

Fogelman, E. (1994). *Conscience and courage: Rescuers of Jews during the Holocaust.* New York: Anchor Books.

Forer, L. (1994). *The rage to punish.* New York: W. W. Norton and Company.

Forrest, D. (1996). Torture through the ages. In Forrest, D. (Ed.) for Amnesty International. *A glimpse of hell: Reports on torture worldwide.* New York: New York University Press.

Forsyth, D. R. 1990. *Group dynamics,* Second Edition. Pacific Grove: CA: Brooks/Cole.

Foucault, M. (1973). *Madness and civilization.* New York: Vintage Press.

Frank, R. H., and Cook, P. J. (1995). *The winner-take-all society.* New York: Martin Kessler Books.

Frankl, V. E. (1959). *Man's search for meaning.* Boston: Beacon Press.

Frederick, C. J. (1991). Psychic trauma in victims of crime and terrorism. In *Cataclysms, crises, and catastrophes.* Washington, DC: American Psychological Association.

Frederick, W. C. (1994). (Reprint of classic paper from 1978). From CSR1 to CSR2: The maturing of business-and-society thought. *Business and Society, 33* (2), 150-67.

Freedman, J. (1993). *From cradle to grave: The human face of poverty in America.* New York: Atheneum.

Friedlander, B. Z. (1993). Community violence, children's development, and mass media: In pursuit of new insights new goals, and new strategies. *Psychiatry, 56* (1), 66-81.

Friedlander, L., Lumley, M. A., Farchione, T., and Doyal, G. (1997). Testing the alexithymia hypothesis: Physiological and subjective responses during relaxation and stress. *Journal of Nervous and Mental Disease, 185* (4), 233-239.

Friedman, L. M. (1993). *Crime and punishment in American history.* New York: BasicBooks.

Friedman, L., and Cooper, S. (1987). *The cost of domestic violence.* New York: Victims Services Research Department.

Friedman, M. J. (1990). Interrelationships between biological mechanisms and pharmacotherapy of post-traumatic stress disorder. In M. E. Wolf and A. D. Mosnaim (Eds.), *Post-traumatic stress disorder: Etiology, phenomenology, and treatment* (pp. 204-205). Washington, DC: American Psychiatric Press.

Fuchs, E. (1987). *Plays of the Holocaust: An international anthology.* New York: Theatre Communications Group.

Fukudo, S., Nomura, T., Muranaka, M., and Taguchi, F. (1993). Brain-gut response to stress and cholinergic stimulation in irritable bowel syndrome. A preliminary study. *Journal of Clinical Gastroenterology, 17* (2), 133-141.

Fukunishi, I., Kaji, N., Hosaka, T., Berger, D., and Rahe, R. H. (1997). Relationship of alexithymia and poor social support to ulcerative changes on gastrofiberscopy. *Psychosomatics, 38* (1), 20-26.

Fulghum, R. (1989). *All I really need to know I learned in kindergarten.* New York: Villard Books.

Gabbard, G. O. (1989). *Sexual exploitation in professional relationships* (pp. 177-192). Washington, DC: American Psychiatric Press.

Galin, D. (1974). Implications for psychiatry of left and right cerebral specialization. *Archives of General Psychiatry, 31* (4), 572-583.

Gallo, S. (1997, August). Book cites poverty as top kid's problem. *The Medical Herald,* p. S-16.

Gallup Organization, Inc. (1995, December). *Disciplining children in America: A Gallup Poll report.* Princeton, NJ: Gallup Poll News Service.

Gallup Organization, Inc, as reported in K. Maguire and A. L. Pastore, (Eds.). (1996). *Sourcebook of criminal justice statistics 1995.* Washington, DC: U. S. Department of Justice, Bureau of Justice Statistics.

Gallup Organization, Inc. (1997, March). *Americans' relationship with their children.* Princeton, NJ: Gallup Poll News Service.

Galvin, M. R., Stilwell, B. M., Shekhar, A., Kopta, S. M., and Goldfarb, S. M. (1997). Maltreatment, conscience functioning, and dopamine beta hydroxylase in emotionally disturbed boys. *Child Abuse and Neglect, 21* (1), 83-92.

Garbarino, J. (1992). *Towards a sustainable society: An economic, social, and environmental agenda for our children's future.* Chicago: The Noble Press.

Garbarino, J., Dubrow, N., Kostelny, K., and Pardo, C. (1992). *Children in danger: Coping with the consequences of community violence.* San Francisco: Jossey-Bass.

Garbarino, J., Kostelny, K., and Barry, F. (1997). Value transmission in an ecological context: The high-risk neighborhood. In J. E. Grusec and L. Kuczynski (Eds.), *Parenting and children's internalization of values* (pp. 307-332). New York: Wiley.

Garland, D. (1990). *Punishment and modern society.* Chicago: University of Chicago Press.

Garrett, P., Ng'andu, N., and Ferron, J. (1994). Poverty experiences of young children and the quality of their home. *Child Development, 65* (2 Spec No), 331-345.

Geisser, M.E., Roth, R. S., Bachman, J. E., and Eckert, T. A. (1996). The relationship between symptoms of post-traumatic stress disorder and pain, affective disturbance and disability among patients with accident and non-accident related pain. *Pain, 66* (2-3), 207-214.

Gelles, R. J., and Straus, M. A. (1988). *Intimate violence.* New York: A Touchstone Book.

Gerbner, G. (1993). Violence on television. *Challenging media images of women, 5* (2), 1, 4, 8.

Gerbner, G. (1994, July). Television violence. The art of asking the wrong question. *The World and I,* 385-392.

Gerbner, G. (1996). TV violence and what to do about it. *Nieman Reports,* L (3), 10-12.

Gersons, B. (1989, July). Patterns of PTSD among police officers following shooting incidents: A two-dimensional model and treatment implications. *Journal of Traumatic Stress, 2* (3), 247-257.

Gilligan, C. (1982). *In a different voice.* Cambridge, MA.: Harvard University Press.

Gilligan, J. (1996). *Violence: Our deadly epidemic and its causes.* New York: G. P. Putnam's Sons.

Gilmore, M. (1991). Family album. *Granta, 37,* 11-52.

Girard, R. (1972). *Violence and the sacred.* Baltimore: Johns Hopkins.

Glover, H. (1992). Emotional numbing: A possible endorphin-mediated phenomenon associated with post-traumatic stress disorders and other allied psychopathologic states. *Journal of Traumatic Stress, 5* (4), 643-675.

Glover, H. (1993). A preliminary trial of nalmefene for the treatment of emotional numbing in combat veterans with post-traumatic stress disorder. *Israel Journal of Psychiatry and Related Sciences, 30* (4), 255-263.

Goffman, E. (1961). *Asylums.* New York: Doubleday.

Goldberg, C. 1996. *Speaking with the devil: Dialogue with evil.* New York: Viking.

Goldstein, A. P., Harootunian, B., and Conoley, J. C. (1994). *Student aggression: Prevention, management, and replacement training.* New York: Guilford.

Goldstein, M. Z. (1989). Elder neglect, abuse, and exploitation. In L. J. Dickstein and C. C. Nadelson (Eds.), *Family violence: Emerging issues of a national crisis.* Washington, DC: American Psychiatric Press.

Grace, M. C., Green, B. L., Lindy, J. D., and Leonard, A. C. (1993). The Buffalo Creek disaster: A 14-year follow-up. In J. P. Wilson and B. Raphael (Eds.), *International handbook of traumatic stress syndromes.* New York: Plenum Press.

Grasmick, H. G., Bursik, R. J. Jr., and Kimpel, M. (1991). Protestant fundamentalism and attitudes toward corporal punishment of children. *Violence and Victims, 6* (4), 283-298.

Green, A. (1993). Childhood sexual and physical abuse. In J. P. Wilson and B. Raphael (Eds.), *International handbook of traumatic stress syndromes.* New York: Plenum Press.

Green, B. L. (1982). Assessing levels of psychological impairment following disaster. *Journal of Nervous and Mental Disease, 170* (9), 544-552.

Green, B. L. (1994). Psychosocial research in traumatic stress: An update. *Journal of Traumatic Stress Studies, 7* (3), 341-362.

Green, B. L., Lindy, J. D., Grace, M. C., Gleser, G. C., Leonard, A. C., Korol, M., and Winget, C. (1990). Buffalo Creek survivors in the second decade: Stability of stress symptoms. *American Journal of Orthopsychiatry, 60* (1), 43-54.

Green, M. B. (1993). Chronic exposure to violence and poverty: Interventions that work for youth. *Crime and Delinquency, 39* (1), 106-124.

Green, R. G., and Thomas, S. L. (1986). The immediate effects of media violence on behavior. *Journal of Social Issues, 42* (3), 7-27.

Grevin, P. (1990). *Spare the child: The religious roots of punishment and the psychological impact of physical abuse.* New York: Vintage.

Grisso, J .A., Wishner, A. R., Schwartz, D. F., Weene, B. A., Holmes, J. H., and Sutton, R. L. (1991). A population-based study of injuries in inner-city women. *American Journal of Epidemiology, 134* (1), 59-68.

Gurian, M. (1996). *The wonder of boys.* New York: Putnam Books.

Guyer, B., Lescohier, I., Gallagher, S., Hausman, A., and Azzara, C. V. (1989). Intentional injuries among children and adolescents in Massachusetts. *The New England Journal of Medicine, 321* (23), 1584-1589.

Haan, N. (1989). Coping with moral conflict as resiliency. In T. F. Dugan and R. Coles (Eds.), *The child in our times: Studies in the development of resiliency* (pp. 23-42). New York: Brunner/Mazel.

Hanh, T. N. (1987). *Being peace.* Berkeley, CA; Parallax Press.

Harber, K. D., and Pennebaker, J. W. (1992). Overcoming traumatic memories. In S. A. Christianson (Ed.), *The handbook of emotion and memory: Research and theory* (pp. 359-387). Hillsdale, NJ: Lawrence Erlbaum Associates.

Harrison, P. A., Fulkerson, J. A., and Beebe, T. J. (1997). Multiple substance use among adolescent physical and sexual abuse victims. *Child Abuse and Neglect, 21* (6), 529-539.

Hartung, W. D. (1995). Notes from the underground: An outsider's guide to the defense budget debate. *World Policy Journal, 12* (3), 15-19.

Harvey, M. R. (1996). An ecological view of psychological trauma and trauma recovery. *Journal of Traumatic Stress, 9* (1), 3-23.

Hatfield, E., Cacioppo, J. T., and Rapson, R. L. (1994). *Emotional contagion.* Paris: Cambridge University Press.

Havel, V. (1990). *Disturbing the peace: Conversations with Karel Hvizdala.* New York: Alfred A. Knopf.

Havel, V. (1993). True democracy demands moral conviction. In D. Gioseffi (Ed.), *On prejudice: A global perspective.* New York: Anchor Books.

Hazler, R. J. (1996). *Breaking the cycle of violence: Interventions for bullying and victimization.* Bristol, PA: Accelerated Development.

Hearst, P. *Every secret thing.* New York: Doubleday.

Heath, L., Bresolin, L. B., and Rinaldi, R. C. (1989). Effects of media violence on children. *Archives of General Psychiatry, 46* (4), 376-379.

Hedeboe, J., Charles, A. V., Nielsen, J., Grymerf, F., Moller, B. N., Moller-Madson, B., and Jensen, S. E. (1985). Interpersonal violence: Patterns in a Danish community. *American Journal of Public Health, 75* (6), 651.

Heilbroner, R. (1995). *Visions of the future: The distant past, yesterday, today, and tomorrow.* New York: Oxford University Press.

Hellwege, J. (1995). Claims for domestic violence in the workplace may be on the rise. *Trial, 31* (5), 94-96.

Hemady, R. K. (1994). Ocular injuries from violence treated at an inner-city hospital. *Journal of Trauma, 37* (1), 5-8.

Heninger, G. R. (1995). Neuroimmunology of stress. In M. J. Friedman, D. S. Charney, and A. Y. Deutch (Eds.), *Neurobiological and clinical consequences of stress: From normal adaptation to post-traumatic stress disorder* (pp. 381-401). Philadelphia: Lippincott-Raven.

Herbert, B. (1994, May 15). Call to arms. *The New York Times*, p. A18.

Herbert, B. (1995, March 22). What special interest? *The New York Times*, p. A19.

Herman, B. H., Hammock, M. K., Egan, J., Arthur-Smith, A., Chatoor, I., and Werner, A. (1989). Role for opioid peptides in self-injurious behavior: Dissociation from autonomic nervous system functioning. *Developmental Pharmacology and Therapeutics, 12* (2), 81-89.

Herman, J. L. (1992). *Trauma and recovery.* New York: Basic Books.

Herman, J. L., Perry, J. C., and Van der Kolk, B. A. (1989). Childhood trauma in borderline personality disorder. *American Journal of Psychiatry, 146* (4), 490-495.

Herzog, J. (1982). World beyond metaphor: Thoughts on the transmission of trauma. In M. S. Bergmann and M. E. Jucovy (Eds.), *Generations of the Holocaust* (pp. 103-119). New York: Basic Books.

Hewitt, J. B., and Levin, P. F. (1997). Violence in the workplace. *Annual Review of Nursing Research, 15,* 81-99.

Higgins, G. O. (1994). *Resilient adults: Overcoming a cruel past.* San Francisco: Jossey-Bass.

Hinshelwood, R. D., and Manning, N. (1979). *Therapeutic communities: Reflections and progress.* London: Routledge and Kegan Paul.

Hoffman, L. P., Watson, D., Wilson, G., and Mongomery, J. (1989). Low plasma beta-endorphin in post-traumatic stress disorder. *Australia and New Zealand Journal of Psychiatry 23* (2), 269-273.

Holmes, R. L. (1990). Three modern philosophers of nonviolence: Tolstoy, Gandhi, and King. In R. L. Holmes, *Nonviolence in theory and practice.* (pp. 41-44). Belmont, CA: Wadsworth Publishing.

Holton, J. K. (1995). Witnessing violence: Making the invisible visible. *Journal of Health Care for the Poor and Underserved, 6* (2), 152-159.

Hood, R. W., Spilka, B., Hunsberger, B. and Gorsuch, R. (1996). *The psychology of religion: An empirical approach.* New York: Guilford.

Horowitz, M. J. (1986). *Stress response syndromes.* Northvale, NJ: Jason Aronson.

Horowitz, M. J. (1992). Stress-response syndromes: A review of posttraumatic stress and adjustment disorders. In J. P. Wilson and B. Raphael (Eds.), *The international handbook of traumatic stress syndromes* (pp. 49-60). New York: Plenum.

Huesmann, L. R. (1986). Psychological processes promoting the relationship between exposure to media violence and aggressive behavior by the viewer. *Journal of Social Issues, 42* (3), 125-139.

Huesmann, L. R., Eron, L. D., Lefkowitz, M. M., and Walder, L. O. (1984). The stability of aggression over time and generations. *Developmental Psychology, 20* (6), 1120-1134.

Hunter, M. (1990). *Abused boys.* New York: Fawcett Columbine.

Hutson, H. R., Anglin, D., Stratton, G., and Moore, J. (1997, June 19). Hate crime violence and its emergency department management. *Annals of Emergency Medicine, 29* (6), 786-791.

Hyman, M. R., and Blum, A. A. (1995). "Just" companies don't fail: The making of the ethical corporation. *Business and Society Review, 93,* 48-50.

Igartua, J., and Paez, D. (1997). Art and remembering traumatic collective events: The case of the Spanish Civil War. In J. W. Pennebaker, D. Paez, and B. Rimé, (Eds.), *Collective memory of political events* (pp. 79-102). Mahwah, NJ: Lawrence Erlbaum.

Irazuzta, J. E., McJunkin, J. E., Danadian, K., Arnold, F., Zhang, J. (1997). Outcome and cost of child abuse. *Child Abuse and Neglect, 21* (8), 751-757.

Ironson, G., Wynings, C., Schneiderman, N., Baum, A., Rodriguez, M., Greenwood, D., Benight, C. C., Antoni, M. H., LaPerriere, A. Huang, H., Klimas, N., and Fletcher, M. A. (1997). Post-traumatic stress symptoms, intrusive thoughts, loss, and immune function after Hurricane Andrew. *Psychosomatic Medicine, 59* (2), 128-141.

Irwin, C., Falsetti, S. A., Lydiard, R. B., Ballenger, J. C., Brock, C. D., and Brener, W. (1996). Comorbidity of post-traumatic stress disorder and irritable bowel syndrome. *Journal of Clinical Psychiatry, 57* (12), 576-578.

Irwin, J., and Austin, J. (1994). *It's about time.* New York: Wadsworth Publishing.

ISTSS, International Society for Traumatic Stress Studies (1998). Childhood remembered: A report on the current scientific knowledge base and its applications. Northbrook, IL: International Society for Traumatic Stress Studies.

Itzen, C., (Ed.) (1992). *Pornography: Women, violence, and civil liberties.* New York: Oxford University Press, Inc.

James, B. (1989). *Treating traumatized children: New insights and creative interventions.* New York: Lexington Books.

James, B. (1994). *Handbook for treatment of attachment-trauma problems in children.* New York: Lexington Books.

James, W. (1902). *The varieties of religious experience.* New York: Modern Library.

Janis, I. L. 1972. *Victims of groupthink.* Boston: Houghton Mifflin.

Janis, I. L. (1982). Decision making under stress. In L. Goldberger and S. Breznitz (Eds.), *Handbook of stress: Theoretical and clinical aspects* (pp. 69-87). New York: Free Press.

Janoff-Bulman, R. (1992). *Shattered assumptions: Towards a new psychology of trauma.* New York: Free Press.

Jenkins, E. L. (1996a). Violence against women in the workplace. *Journal of the American Medical Women's Association, 51* (3), 118-119.

Jenkins, E. L. (1996b). Workplace homicide: Industries and occupations at high risk. *Occupational Medicine, 11* (2), 219-225.

Jenkins, E. L., Layne, L. A., and Kisner, S. M. (1992, May). Homicide in the workplace: The U. S. experience, 1980-1988. *AAOHN Journal, 40* (5), 215-218.

Jenkinson, W. R. (1993). Attacks on postmen in Northern Ireland. What features of the attack are associated with prolonged absence from work? *Occupational Medicine, 43* (1), 39-42.

Jimerson, D. C., Wolfe, B. E., Franko, D. L., Covino, N. A., and Sifneos, P. E. (1994). Alexithymia ratings in bulimia nervosa: Clinical correlates. *Psychosomatic Medicine, 56* (2), 90-93.

Johansen, B. E. (1982). *Forgotten founders: How the American Indian helped shape democracy.* Boston: The Harvard Common Press.

Johnson, D. W., and Johnson, R. T. (1995). Why violence prevention programs don't work and what does. *Educational Leadership, 52* (5), 63-69.

Johnston, N. (1994). Reforming criminals. In N. Johnston (Ed.), *Eastern State Penitentiary: Crucible of good intentions* (pp. 21-30). Philadelphia: University of Pennsylvania Press.

Jones, M. (1968). *Social psychiatry in practice.* Middlesex, England: Penguin Books.

Jones, M., Baker, A., Freeman, T., Merry, J., Pomryn, B. A., Sandler, J., and Tuxford, J. (1953). *The therapeutic community: A new treatment method in psychiatry.* New York: Basic Books.

Joukamaa, M., Karlsson, H., Sholman, B., and Lehtinen, V. (1996). Alexithymia and psychological distress among frequent attendance patients in health care. *Psychotherapy and Psychosomatics, 65* (4), 199-202.

Kars, H., Broekema, W., Glaudemans-van, Gelderen I., Verhoeven, W. M., and van Ree, J. M. (1990). Naltrexone attenuates self-injurious behavior in mentally retarded subjects. *Biological Psychiatry, 27* (7), 741-746.

Katz, M. (1989). *The undeserving poor: From the war on poverty to the war on welfare.* New York: Pantheon.

Kaufman, M. (1993). *Cracking the armour: Power, pain, and the lives of men.* Toronto, Canada: Viking.

Kauhanen, J., Kaplan, G. A., Cohen, R. D., Julkunen, J., and Salonen, J. T. (1996). Alexithymia and risk of death in middle-aged men. *Journal of Psychosomatic Research, 41* (6), 541-549.

Kawachi, I., and Kennedy, B. P. (1997, April 5). Health and social cohesion: Why care about income inequality? *British Medical Journal, 314* (7086), 1037-1040.

Keep, N., and Gilbert, P. (1992). California Emergency Nurses Association informal survey of violence in California emergency departments. *Journal of Emergency Nursing, 18* (5), 433-439.

Kellerman, A. L. (1986). Protection or peril? An analysis of firearm-related
deaths in the home. *New England Journal of Medicine, 314,* 1557.

Kellerman, A. L. (1991). Suicide in the home in relation to gun ownership. *New
England Journal of Medicine, 327,* 467.

Kellerman, A. L. (1993). Gun ownership as a risk factor for homicide in the home.
New England Journal of Medicine, 329, 1084.

Kellerman, A. L., Rivaro, F. P., Lee, R. K., Banton, J. G., Cummings, P., Hack-
man, B. B., and Somes, G. (1996). Injuries due to firearms in three cities. *New
England Journal of Medicine, 335* (19), 1438-1444.

Kempe, R., and Kempe, C. H. (1978). *Child abuse.* Cambridge: Harvard University Press.

Kilborn, P. T. (1995, March 17). Women and Minorities Still Face "Glass Ceiling," *The New York Times,* p. A22.

King, M. L. Jr. (1990). Letter from the Birmingham Jail. In Holmes, R. L. *Nonviolence in theory and practice* (pp. 68-77). Belmont, CA: Wadsworth Publishing.

Kilpatrick, D. G., Edmunds, C. N., and Seymour, A. K. (1992). *Rape in America:
A report to the nation.* Arlington, VA: National Victim Center.

Kilpatrick, D. G., and Resnick, H. S. (1993). PTSD associated with exposure to
criminal victimization in clinical and community populations. In J. R. T. Davidson
and E. B. Foa (Eds.), *Post-traumatic stress disorder: DSM IV and beyond*
(pp. 113-143). Washington, DC: American Psychiatric Press.

Kilpatrick, D., and Saunders, B. (1997). *The prevalence and consequences of
child victimization: Summary of a research study.* Washington, DC: U.S.
Department of Justice, National Institute of Justice.

Kimelman, R. (1990). Nonviolence in the Talmud. In Holmes, R. L. *Nonviolence
in theory and practice,* (pp. 20-26). Belmont, CA: Wadsworth Publishing.

Kimmel, M. S. (Ed.). (1990). *Men confront pornography.* New York: Crown
Publishers, Inc.

Kimmel, M. (1996). *Manhood in America.* New York: The Free Press.

Kirkhorn, M. J. (1996). Violent crime. *Nieman Reports, L* (3), 4-9.

Kivel, P. (1992). *Men's work: How to stop the violence that tears our lives apart.*
New York: Ballantine Books.

Kluft, R. P. (1996). Dissociative identity disorder. In L. K. Michelson and W. J.
Ray (Eds.), *Handbook of dissociation: Theoretical, empirical, and clinical
perspectives* (pp. 337-366). New York: Plenum Press.

Kochanska, G. (1997). Mutually responsive orientation between mothers and
their young children: Implications for early socialization. *Child Development,
68* (1), 94-112.

Kohn, A. (1986). *No contest: The case against competition.* Boston: Houghton
Mifflin Company.

Kokopeli, B., and Lakey, G. (1990). More power than we want. In F. Abbott (Ed.),
Men and intimacy. Freedom, CA: The Crossing Press.

Koss, M. P., Goodman, L. A., Browne, A., Fitzgerald, L. F., Keita, G. P., and Russo, N. F. (1994). *No safe haven: Male violence against women at home, at work, and in the community.* Washington, DC: American Psychological Association Press.

Koss, M. P., Koss, P. G., and Woodruff, W. J. (1991). Deleterious effects of criminal victimization on women's health and medical utilization. *Archives of Internal Medicine, 151* (2), 342-347.

Koss, M. P., Woodruff, W. J., and Koss, P. G. (1990). Relation of criminal victimization to health perceptions among women medical patients. *Journal of Consulting and Clinical Psychology, 58* (2), 147-152.

Kosten, T. R., and Krystal, J. (1988). Biological mechanisms in post-traumatic stress disorder: Relevance for substance abuse. *Recent Advances in Alcoholism, 6,* 49-68.

Kovel, J. (1994). *Red hunting in the promised land: Anticommunism and the making of America.* New York: Basic Books.

Krevans, J., and Gibbs, J. C. (1996). Parents' use of inductive discipline: Relations to children's empathy and prosocial behavior. *Child Development, 67* (6), 3263-3277.

Kristiansen, C. M., Felton, K. A., and Hovdestad, W. E. (1996). Recovered memories of child abuse: Fact, fantasy or fancy? *Women and Therapy, 19* (1), 47-59.

Krystal, H. (1988). *Integration and self-healing: Affect, trauma, alexithymia.* Hillsdale, NJ: Analytic Press.

Krystal, H. (1992). Beyond the DSM-III-R: Therapeutic considerations in post-traumatic stress disorder. In J. P. Wilson and B. Raphael (Eds.). *The international handbook of traumatic stress syndromes* (pp. 841-854). New York: Plenum.

Kubany, E. S., McKenzie, W. F., Owens, J. A., Leisen, M. B., Kaplan, A. S., and Pavich, E. (1996, September). PTSD among women survivors of domestic violence in Hawaii. *Hawaii Medical Journal, 55* (9), 164-165.

Kuhn, T. S. (1970). *The structure of scientific revolutions.* Chicago: University of Chicago Press.

Kurz, D. (1996). Separation, divorce, and woman abuse. *Violence against women, 2* (1), 63-81.

Kutchinsky, B. (1991). Pornography and rape: Theory and practice? *International Journal of Law and Psychiatry, 14* (1-2), 47-64.

Labig, C. E. (1995). Forming a violence response team. *HR Focus, 72* (8), 15-17.

Lande, R. G. (1993, April). The video violence debate. *Hospital and Community Psychiatry, 44* (4), 347-351.

Lansky, M. R., and Bley, C. R. (1995). *Posttraumatic nightmares: Psychodynamic explorations.* Hillsdale, NJ: The Analytic Press.

Lantieri, L. (1995). Waging peace in our schools: Beginning with the children. *Phi Delta Kappan, 76* (5), 386-389.

Larson, E. (1993, January). The story of a gun. *Atlantic Monthly,* 48-78.

Latane, B., and Darley, J. M. (1970). *The unresponsive bystander: Why doesn't he help?* New York: Appleton-Century-Crofts.

Laub, D., and Auerhahn, N. (1984). Reverberations of genocide: Its expression in the conscious and unconscious of post-Holocaust generations. In S. Luel and P. Marcus (Eds.), *Psychoanalytic reflections on the Holocaust: Selected essays* (pp. 150-167). Denver: Holocaust Awareness Institute, Center for Judaic Studies, University of Denver.

Laub, J. H., and Lauritsen, J. L. (1995). Violent criminal behavior over the life course: A review of the longitudinal and comparative research. In R. B. Ruback and N. A. Weiner (Eds.), *Interpersonal violent behaviors: Social and cultural aspects.* (pp. 43-62). New York: Springer Publishing.

LeDoux, J. E. (1992). Emotion as memory: Anatomical systems underlying indelible neural trances. In S. A. Christianson (Ed.), *The handbook of emotion and memory: Research and theory.* (pp. 269-288). Hillsdale, NJ: Lawrence Erlbaum Associates.

LeDoux, J. E. (1994). Emotion, memory, and the brain. *Scientific American, 270* (6), 50-57.

Lefkowitz, B. (1997). *Our guys.* Berkeley: University of California Press.

Lerner, M. 1996. *The politics of meaning: Restoring hope and possibility in an age of cynicism.* Reading, MA: Addison-Wesley.

Leserman, J., Drossman, D. A., Li, Z., Toomey, T. C., Nachman, G., and Glogau, L. (1996). Sexual and physical abuse history in gastroenterology practice: How types of abuse impact health status. *Psychosomatic Medicine, 58* (1), 4-15.

Levin, P. F., Hewitt, J. B., and Misner, S. T. (1996). Workplace violence: Female occuaptional homicides in metropolitan Chicago. *AAOHN Journal, 44* (7), 326-331.

Lew, M. (1988). *Victims no longer.* New York: Harper Collins.

Lewis, D. O. (1998). *Guilty by reason of insanity: A psychiatrist explores the minds of killers.* New York: Fawcett Columbine.

Lex, B. (1979). The neurobiology of ritual traunce. In E. G. D'Aquili, C. D. Laughlin Jr., and J. McManus (Eds.), *The spectrum of ritual: A biogenetic structural analysis* (pp. 117-151). New York: Columbia University Press.

Lieberman, T. (1998). Hunger in America, *The Nation,* March 30, pp. 11-16.

Lifton, R. J. (1993). From Hiroshima to the Nazi doctors. In J. P. Wilson and B. Raphael (Eds.), *The international handbook of traumatic stress syndromes* (pp. 11-23). New York: Plenum.

Linden, D. W. (1995). The mother of them all: Early business management theorist Mary Parker Follett. *Forbes, 155* (2), 75-77.

Lindquist, B., and Molnar, A. (1995). Children learn what they live. *Educational Leadership, 52* (5), 50-52.

Lindy, J. D., and Titchener, J. L. (1983) "Acts of God and man": Long-term character change in survivors of disasters and the law. *Behavioral Sciences and the Law, 1* (3), 85-96.

Linton, M. (1993). Money and community economics. In C. Whitmyer, (Ed.), *In the company of others: Making community in the modern world* (pp. 65-70). New York: Jeremy Tarcher.

Lira, E. (1997). Remembering: Passing back through the heart. In J. W. Pennebaker, D. Paez, and B. Rimé (Eds.), *Collective memory of political events* (pp. 223-235). Mahwah, NJ: Lawrence Erlbaum.

Loas, G., Fremaux, D., Otmani, O., Lecercle, C., and Delahousse, J. (1997). Is alexithymia a negative factor for maintaining abstinence? A follow-up study. *Comprehensive Psychiatry, 38* (5), 296-299.

Lumley, M. A., and Norman, S. (1996). Alexithymia and health care utilization. *Psychosomatic Medicine, 58* (3), 197-202.

Lumley, M. A., and Roby, K. J. (1995). Alexithymia and pathological gambling. *Psychotherapy and Psychosomatics, 63* (3-4), 201-206.

Lumley, M. A., Mader, C., Gramzow, J., and Papineau, K. (1996). Family factors related to alexithymia characteristics. *Psychosomatic Medicine, 58* (3), 211-216.

Lystad, M. (Ed.). (1986). *Violence in the home: Interdisciplinary perspectives.* New York: Brunner/Mazel.

Macfarlane, A. 1985. The root of all evil. In D. Parkin (Ed.). *The anthropology of evil* (pp. 57-76). New York: Basil Blackwell.

MacKinnon, C. A. (1992). Pornography, civil rights, and speech. In Itzen, C., (Ed.), *Pornography: Women, violence, and civil liberties* (pp. 456-512). New York: Oxford University Press, Inc.

Main, M., and Hess, E. (1990). Parents' unresolved traumatic experiences are related to infant disorganized attachment status: Is frightened and/or frightening parental behavior the linking mechanism? In M. T. Greenberg, D. Cicchetti, and E. M. Cummings (Eds.), *Attachment in the preschool years: Theory, research, and intervention* (pp. 161-182). Chicago: University of Chicago Press.

Mainellis, K. A. (1996). How bad is violence in hospitals? *Safety and Health, 153* (1), 50-55.

Makower, J. (1994). *Beyond the bottom line: Putting social responsibility to work for your business and the world.* New York: Simon and Schuster.

March, J. S. (1993). What constitutes a stressor? The "Criterion A" Issue. In J. R. T. Davidson and E. B. Foa (Eds.), *Post-traumatic stress disorder: DSM-IV and beyond* (pp. 37-54). Washington, DC: American Psychiatric Press.

Margalit, A. (1996). *The decent society.* Cambridge, MA: Harvard University Press.

Margenau, H., and Varhese, R. A. (1992). *Cosmos, bios, theos: Scientists reflect on science, God, and the origins of the universe, life, and homo sapiens.* LaSalle, IL: Open Court.

Marshall, J. Jr. (1996). *Street soldier.* New York: Delacorte Press.

Martin, S. S., Butzin, C. A., and Inciardi, J. A. (1995). Assessment of a multistage therapeutic community for drug-involved offenders. *Journal of Psychoactive Drugs, 27* (1), 109-116.

Martin-Baró, I. (1994). *Writings for a liberation psychology.* Cambridge: Harvard University Press.

Matsakis, A. (1994). *Post-traumatic stress disorder: A complete treatment guide.* Oakland, CA: New Harbinger Publications.

Maxfield, M. G., and Widom, C. S. (1996). The cycle of violence. Revisited 6 years later. *Archives of Pediatric and Adolescent Medicine, 150* (4), 390-395.

Mayer, J. D., and Salovey, P. (1997). What is emotional intelligence? In P. Salovey and D. J. Sluyter (Eds.), *Emotional development and emotional intelligence: Educational implications.* New York: Basic Books.

McArthur J. H., and Moore F. D. (1997). The two cultures and the health care revolution. Commerce and professionalism in medical care. *JAMA, 277* (12), 985-989

McCall, N. (1994). *Makes me wanna holler.* New York: Random House.

McCann, I. L., and Pearlman, L. A. (1990). Vicarious traumatization: A framework for understanding the psychological effects of working with victims. *Journal of Traumatic Stress, 3* (3), 131-147.

McCauley, J., Kern, D. F., Kolodner, K., Dill, L., Schroeder, A. F., DeChant, H. K., Ryden, J., Bass, E. B., and Derogatis, L. R. (1995). The "battering syndrome": Prevalence, and clinical characteristics of domestic violence in primary care internal medicine practices. *Annals of Internal Medicine, 123* (10), 737-746.

McFarlane, A. C., and Van der Kolk, B. A. (1996). Trauma and its challenge to society. In B. A. Van der Kolk, A. C. McFarlane, L. Weisaeth (Eds.), *Traumatic stress: The effects of overwhelming experience on mind, body, and society* (pp. 24-46). New York: Guilford Press.

McLaughlin, C., and G. Davidson. 1994. *Spiritual politics: Changing the world from the inside out.* New York: Ballantine Books.

McLean, C. (1996). The politics of men's pain. In C. McLean, M. Carey, and C. White, (Eds.), *Men's ways of being.* Boulder, CO: Westview Press.

McMurry, K. (1995). Workplace violence: Can it be prevented? *Trial, 31* (12), 10-13.

Meier, C. A. (1989). *Healing dream and ritual.* Switzerland: Daimon Verlag.

Mercogliano, C. (1995). Making it up as we go along: The story of the (Albany) Free School. Unpublished manuscript.

Mercy, J. A., and Houk, V. N. (1986). Firearm injuries: A call for science. *New England Journal of Medicine, 319* (19), 1283.

Messadié, G. 1996. *A history of the devil.* New York: Kodansha America, Inc.

Miedzian, M. (1991). *Boys will be boys.* New York: Doubleday.

Milgram, S. (1974). *Obedience to authority.* New York: Harper Colophon.

Miller, A. (1983). *For your own good: Hidden cruelty in child-rearing and the roots of violence.* New York: Farrar, Straus, and Giroux.

Miller, T. R., and M. A. Cohen. (1997). Costs of gunshot and cut/stab wounds in the United States, with some Canadian comparisons. *Accident Analysis and Prevention, 29* (3), 329-341.

Miller, T. R., Cohen, M. A., and Rossman, S. B. (1993). Victim costs of violent crime and resulting injuries. *Health Affairs (Millwood), 12* (4), 186-197.

Miller, T., Cohen, M., and Weirsema, B. (1996). *Victim costs and consequences: A new look.* Washington, DC: U. S. Department of Justice, National Institute of Justice.

Miller, W. H. (1995). More than just making money: The last 25 years have seen industry assume a new mission—social responsibility. *Industry Week, 244* (15), 91-96.

Milner, J. S., Halsey, L. B., and Fultz, J. (1995). Empathic responsiveness and affective reactivity to infant stimuli in high- and low-risk for physical child abuse mothers. *Child Abuse and Neglect, 19* (6), 767-780.

Mirsky, A. F. (1995). Perils and pitfalls on the path to normal potential: The role of impaired attention. *Journal of Clinical and Experimental Neuropsychology, 17* (4), 481-498.

Mitchell, J. T., and Dyregrov, A. (1993). Traumatic stress in disaster workers and emergency personnel: Prevention and intervention. In J. P. Wilson and B. Raphael (Eds.), *International handbook of traumatic stress syndromes* (pp. 905-914). New York: Plenum Press.

Moeran, B. (1985). Confucian confusion: The good, the bad and the noodle western. In D. Parkin (Ed.) *The anthropology of evil* (pp. 92-109). New York: Basil Blackwell.

Mullen, P. E., Martin, J. L., Anderson, J. C., Romans, S. E., and Herbison, G. P. (1996). The long-term impact of the physical, emotional, and sexual abuse of children: A community study. *Child Abuse and Neglect, 20* (1), 7-21.

Nadel, L. (1995). The psychobiology of trauma and memory. Symposium presented at Fourth European Conference on Traumatic Stress, Paris, France. May 7-11.

Nance, M. L., Stafford, P. W., and Schwab, C. W. (1997). Firearm injury among urban youth during the last decade: An escalation in violence. *Journal of Pediatric Surgery, 32* (7), 949-952.

Nance, M. L., Templeton, J. M. Jr., and O'Neill, J. A. Jr. (1994). Socioeconomic impact of gunshot wounds in an urban pediatric population. *Journal of Pediatric Surgery, 29* (1), 39-43.

Nathanson, D. L. (1992). *Shame and pride: Affect, sex, and the birth of the self.* New York: W. W. Norton and Company.

National Institute of Justice. (1996). *Victim costs and consequences: A new look.* (NIJ Research Report, National Institute of Justice, U. S. Department of Justice). Washington, DC: U. S. Government Printing Office.

National Victim Center. (1993). *Crime and victimization in America: Statistical overview.* Arlington, VA: National Victim Center.

Nelson, N. A., and Kaufman, J. D. (1996). Fatal and nonfatal injuries related to violence in Washington workplaces, 1992. *Amercian Journal of Industrial Medicine, 30* (4), 438-446.

Nichols, W. D. (1995). Violence on campus: The intruded sanctuary. *The FBI Law Enforcement Bulletin, 64* (6), 1-6.

Nightingale, C. H. (1993). *On the edge.* New York: Basic Books.

Nirenberg, J. (1993). The Living Organization: Transforming teams into workplace communities. *The Futurist, 27* (6), 39-40.

Noddings, N. 1989. *Women and evil.* Berkeley: University of California Press.

Nordheimer, J. (1971). From Dakto to Detroi: Death of a troubled hero. *The New York Times, 12* (41), 325, May 26.

Norris, F. H. (1992). Epidemiology of trauma: Frequency and impact of different potentially traumatic events on different demographic groups. *Journal of Consulting and Clinical Psychology, 60* (3), 409-418.

Ochberg, F. (1996). A primer on covering victims. *The Neiman Report L* (3), 21-26.

Oliner, S. P., and Oliner, P. M. (1988). *The altruistic personality.* New York: Free Press.

Oliver, J. E. (1993). Intergenerational transmission of child abuse: Rates, research, and clinical implications. *American Journal of Psychiatry, 150* (9), 1315-1324.

Olson, L. M., Christoffel, K. K., and. O'Connor, K. G. (1997). Pediatrician's experience with attitudes towards firearms: Results of a national survey. *Archives of Pediatric and Adolescent Medicine, 151* (4), 352-359.

Omar, D. (1996). *Introduction by the Minister of Justice, Mr. Dullah Omar* [On line]. Available: Truth Commission Web Site. www.truth.org.za.

O'Neil, J. (1995). On schools as learning organizations: A conversation with Peter Senge. *Educational Leadership, 52* (7), 20-24.

Orenstein, P. (1994). *School girls.* New York: Doubleday.

Orsillo, S. M., Weathers, F. W., Litz, B. T., Steinberg, H. R., Huska, J. A., and Keane T. M. (1996). Current and lifetime psychiatric disorders among veterans with war zone-related post-traumatic stress disorder. *Journal of Nervous and Mental Disease, 184* (5), 307-313.

Orwell, G. (1981). *1984.* New York: Penguin Books.

Osherson, S. (1986). *Finding our fathers.* New York: Fawcett Columbine.

Osofsky, J. (1995). The effects of exposure to violence on young children. *American Psychologist, 50* (9), 782-788.

Paez, D., Basabe, N., and Gonzalez, J. L. (1997). Social processes and collective memory: A cross-cultural approach to remembering political events. In J. W. Pennebaker, D. Paez, and B. Rimé (Eds.), *Collective memory of political events* (pp. 147-174). Mahwah, NJ: Lawrence Erlbaum.

Pagnozzi, A. (1994, May). Killer girls. *Elle,* 122-123.

Pargament, K. I. (1997). *The psychology of religion and coping: Theory, research, practice.* New York: Guilford Press.

Parker, J. D., Taylor, G. J., Bagby, R. M., and Acklin, M. W. (1993). Alexithymia in panic disorder and simple phobia: A comparative study. *American Journal of Psychiatry, 150* (7), 1105-1107.

Parkin, D. (1985). Introduction. In D. Parkin (Ed.), *The anthropology of evil* (pp. 1-25). New York: Basil Blackwell.

Patterson, J., and Kim, P. (1991). *The day America told the truth.* New York: Prentice Hall.

Pecukonis, E. V. (1996). Childhood sex abuse in women with chronic intractable back pain. *Social Work in Health Care, 23* (3), 1-16.

Peipher, M. (1994). *Reviving Ophelia.* New York: Ballantine.

Pennebaker J. W. (1989). Confession, inhibition, and disease. *Advances in Experimental Social Psychology, 22,* 211-244.

Pennebaker, J. W. (1990). *Opening up: The healing power of confiding in others.* New York: Morrow.

Pennebaker, J. W. (Ed.). (1995). *Emotion, disclosure, and health.* Washington, DC: American Psychological Association.

Pennebaker, J. W. (1997a). On the creation and maintenance of collective memories: History as social psychology. In J. W. Pennebaker, D. Paez, and B. Rimé (Eds.), *Collective memory of political events* (pp. 3-19). Mahwah, NJ: Lawrence Erlbaum.

Pennebaker, J. W. (1997b). *Opening up: The healing power of expressing emotions.* New York: Guilford Press.

Pennebaker, J. W., Paez, D. and Rimé, B. (Eds.). (1997). *Collective memory of political events* (pp. 1, 14-18). Mahwah, NJ: Lawrence Erlbaum.

Pennebaker, J. W., and Susman, J. R. (1988). Disclosure of traumas and psychosomatic processes. *Social Science and Medicine, 26* (3), 327-332.

Perry, B. D. (1993). Neurodevelopment and the neurophysiology of trauma I: Conceptual considerations for clinical work with maltreated children. *The Advisor: American Professional Society on the Abuse of Children, 6* (1), 14-18.

Perry, J. C., Herman, J. L., Van der Kolk, B. A., and Hoke, L. A. (1990). Psychotherapy and psychological trauma in borderline personality disorder. *Psychiatric Annals, 20* (1), 33-43.

Petty, F., Chae, Y., Kramer, G., Jordan, S., and Wilson, L. (1994a). Learned helplessness sensitizes hippocampal norepinephrine to mild restress. *Biological Psychiatry, 35* (12), 903-908.

Petty, F., Kramer, G., Wilson, L., and Jordan, S. (1994b). In vivo serotonin release and learned helplessness. *Psychiatry Research, 52* (3), 285-293.

Pike, J. L., Smith, T. L., Hauger, R. L., Nicassio, P. M., Patterson, T. L., McClintick, J., Costlow, C., and Irwin, M. R. (1997). Chronic life stress alters sympathetic, neuroendocrine, and immune responsivity to an acute psychological stressor in humans. *Psychosomatic Medicine, 59* (4), 447-457.

Pitman, R. K. (1993). Posttraumatic obsessive-compulsive disorder: A case study. *Comprehensive Psychiatry, 34* (2), 102-107.

Pitman, R. K., and Orr, S. (1990). The black hole of trauma. *Biological Psychiatry, 27* (5), 469-471.

Pitman, R. K., Van der Kolk, B. A., Orr, S. P., and Greenberg, M. S. (1990). Naloxone-reversible analgesic response to combat-related stimuli in post-traumatic stress disorder. *Archives of General Psychiatry, 47* (6), 541-544.

Plichta, S. B., and Abraham, C. (1996). Violence and gynecologic health in women <50 years old. *American Journal of Obstetrics and Gynecology, 174* (3), 903-907.

Pocock, D. (1985). Unruly evil. In D. Parkin (Ed.), *The anthropology of evil* (pp. 42-56). New York: Basil Blackwell.

Pollack, W. S. (1995). No man is an island: Toward a new psychoanalytic psychology of men. In R. F. Levant and W. S. Pollack (Eds.), *A new psychology of men* (pp. 2-31). New York: Basic Books.

Porcelli, P., Leoci, C., Guerra, V., Taylor, G. J., and Bagby, R. M. (1996). A longitudinal study of alexithymia and psychological distress in inflammatory bowel disease. *Journal of Psychosomatic Research, 41* (6), 569-573.

Porcelli, P., Zaka, S., Leoci, C., Centonze, S., and Taylor, G. J. (1995). Alexithymia in inflammatory bowel disease. A case-control study. *Psychotherapy and Psychosomatics, 64* (1), 49-53.

Powell, E. C., Sheehan, K. M., and Christoffel, K. K. (1996). Firearm violence among youth: Public health strategies for prevention. *Annals of Emergency Medicine, 28* (2), 204-212.

Prothrow-Stith, D. (1992). Can physicians help curb adolescent violence? *Hospital Practice, 27* (6), 193-196.

Putnam, F. W. (1990). Disturbances of "self" in victims of childhood sexual abuse. In R. P. Kluft (Ed.), *Incest-related syndromes of adult psychopathology.* (pp. 113-132). Washington, DC: American Psychiatric Press.

Putnam, F. W. (1991). Dissociative phenomena. In A. Tasman and S. M. Goldfinger (Eds.), *Review of psychiatry: Vol. 10* (pp. 145-160). Washington, DC: American Psychiatric Press.

Putnam, F. W. (1996). Developmental pathways in sexually abused girls: Psychological and biological data from the longitudinal study. Presented at Psychological Trauma: Maturational Processes and Therapeutic Intervention, March 29-30, 1996. Swissotel, Boston, Harvard Medical School, Department of Continuing Education.

Rahula, W. (1959). *What the Buddha taught.* New York: Grove Press.

Raphael, B. (1986). *When disaster strikes.* New York: Basic Books.

Rauch, S. L., Van der Kolk, B. A., Fisler, R. E., Alpert, N. M., Orr, S. P., Savage, C. R., Fischman, A. J., Jenike, M. A., and Pitman, R. K. (1996). A symptom provocation study of post-traumatic stress disorder using positron emission tomography and script-drive imagery. *Archives of General Psychiatry, 53* (5), 380-387.

Ray, M., and Rinzler, A. (1993). *The new paradigm in business: Emerging strategies for leadership and organizational change.* New York: G.P. Putnam's Sons.

Reite, M., and Boccia, M. L. (1994). Physiological aspects of adult attachment. In M. B. Sperling and W. H. Berman (Eds.), *Attachment in adults: Clinical and developmental perspectives* (pp. 98-127). New York: Guilford Press.

Resnick, H. S., Kilpatrick, D. G., Dansky, B. S., Saunders, B. E., and Best, C. L. (1993). Prevalence of civilian trauma and post-traumatic stress disorder in a representative national sample of women. *Journal of Consulting and Clinical Psychology, 6* (6), 984-991.

Rhea, M. H., Chafey, K. H., Dohner, V. A., and Terragno, R. (1996). The silent victims of domestic violence. *Journal of Child and Adolescent Psychiatric Nursing, 9* (3), 7-15.

Rice, D. P., Kelman, S., and Miller, L. S. (1991). Estimates of economic costs of alcohol and drug abuse and mental illness, 1985 and 1988. *Public Health Report, 106* (3), 280-292.

Rice, D. P., Kelman, S., and Miller, L. S. (1992). The economic burden of mental illness. *Hospital and Community Psychiatry, 43* (12), 1227-1232.

Richards, A., and Handy, K. (1995). Vietnam veterans and family decision making. In D. K. Rhoades, M. R. Leaveck, and J. C. Hudson (Eds.), *The legacy of Vietnam veterans and their families: Survivors of war: Catalysts for change* (pp. 410-419). Washington, DC: Agent Orange Class Assistance Program.

Rideau, W., and Wikberg, R. (1992). *Life sentences: Rage and survival behind bars.* New York: Times Books.

Rogers, M. P., Weinshenker, N. J., Warshaw, M. G., Goisman, R. M., Rodriguez-Villa, F. J., Fierman, E. J., and Keller, M. B. (1996). Prevalence of somatoform disorders in a large sample of patients with anxiety disorders. *Psychosomatics, 37* (1), 17-22.

Rosenbaum, R. (1995, May 1). Explaining Hitler. *The New Yorker,* 50-70.

Rosenberg, T. (1995). *The haunted land.* New York: Vintage Press.

Rosenheck, R. A. (1986). Impact of post-traumatic stress disorder of World War II on the next generation. *Journal of Nervous and Mental Disease, 174* (6), 319-327.

Rosner, F. (1997). The ethics of managed care. *Mt. Sinai Journal of Medicine, 64* (1), 8-19.

Ross, C. A., Kronson, J., Koensgen, S., Barkman, K., Clark, P., and Rockman, G. (1992, August). Dissociative comorbidity in 100 chemically dependent patients. *Hospital and Community Psychiatry, 43* (8), 840-842.

Roszak, T., Gomes, M. E. and Kanner, A. D. (1995). *Ecopsychology: Restoring the earth, healing the mind.* San Francisco: Sierra Club Books;

Roth, A. S., Ostroff, R. B., and Hoffman, R. E. (1996). Naltrexone as a treatment for repetitive self-injurious behaviour: An open-label trial. *Journal of Clinical Psychiatry, 57* (6), 233-237.

Russell, D. (1993). *Philadelphia Daily News,* 3.

Russell, D. E. H. (1993) *Against pornography.* Berkeley, CA: Russell Publications.

Russell, J. B. (1988a). *The prince of darkness: Radical evil and the power of good in history.* Ithaca: Cornell University Press.

Russell, J. B. (1988b). The evil one. In P. Woodruff and H. A. Wilmer (Eds.), *Facing evil: Light at the core of darkness* (pp. 47-61). LaSalle, IL: Open Court.

Rutter, M. (1990). Psychosocial resilience and protective mechanisms. In J. Rolf, A. S. Masten, D. Cicchetti, K. Neuchterlein, and S. Weintraub (Eds.), *Risk and protective factors in the development of psychopathology* (pp. 181-214) New York: Cambridge University Press.

Saarijarvi, S., Salminen, J. K., Tamminen, T., and Aarela, E. (1993). Alexithymia in psychiatric consultation-liaison patients. *General Hospital Psychiatry, 15* (5), 330-333.

Sadker, M., and Sadker, D. (1994). *Failing at fairness.* New York: Charles Scribner's Sons.

Salasin, S. E., and Rich, R. F. (1993). Mental health policy for victims of violence: The case against women. In J. P. Wilson and B. Raphael (Eds.), *International handbook of traumatic stress syndromes* (pp. 947-956). New York: Plenum Press.

Salminen, J. K., Saarijarvi, S., Aairela, E., and Tamminen, T. (1994). Alexithymia—state or trait? One-year follow-up study of general hospital psychiatric consultation out-patients. *Journal of Psychosomatic Research, 38* (7), 681-685.

Salmon, P., and Calderbank, S. (1996, March). The relationship of childhood physical and sexual abuse to adult illness behavior. *Journal of Psychosomatic Research, 40* (3), 329-336.

Saltzman, L. E. (1992). Weapon involvement and injury outcome in family and intimate assaults. *Journal of the American Medical Association, 267* (22), 3043.

Sampson, R. J., and Laub, J. H. (1994). Urban poverty and the family context of delinquency: A new look at structure and process in a classic study. *Child Development, 65* (2 Spec No), 523-540.

Sanford, N. 1971. Authoritarianism and social destructiveness. In N. Sanford and C. Comstock. *Sanctions for evil: Sources of social destructiveness.* San Francisco: Jossey-Bass, Inc.

Saporta, J., and Van der Kolk, B. A. (1992). Psychobiological consequences of severe trauma. In Basoglu, M. (Ed.), *Torture and its consequences: Current treatment approaches* (pp. 151-181). New York: Cambridge University Press.

Sarason, S. (1990). *The predictable failure of educational reform: Can we change course before it's too late?* San Francisco: Jossey-Bass.

Saul, J. R. (1992). *Voltaire's bastard.* New York: Vintage Books.

Saxe, G. N., Chinman, G., Berkowitz, R., Hall, K., Lieberg, G., Schwartz, J., and Van der Kolk, B. A. (1994). Somatization in patients with dissociative disorders. *American Journal of Psychiatry, 151* (9), 1329-1334.

Scarry, E. (1985) *The body in pain.* New York: Oxford University Press.

Schetky, D. H. (1990). A review of the literature on the long-term effects of childhood sexual abuse. In R. P. Kluft (Ed.), *Incest-related syndromes of adult psychopathology* (pp. 35-54). Washington, DC: American Psychiatric Press.

Schmidt, U., Jiwany, A., and Treasure, J. (1993). A controlled study of alexithymia in eating disorders. *Comprehensive Psychiatry, 34* (1), 54-58.

Schooler, C., and Flora, J. A. (1996). Pervasive media violence. *Annual Review of Public Health, 17,* 275-298.

Schor, J. B. (1992). *The overworked American.* New York: Basic Books.

Schwab, C. W. (1993). Presidential address, Sixth Scientific Assembly of the Eastern Association for the Surgery of Trauma, January 14.

Schwartz, J. (1992). *The creative moment: How science made itself alien to modern culture.* London: Jonathan Cape.

Schwarz, D. F., Grisso, J. A., Miles, C. G., Holmes, J. H., Wishner, A. R., and Sutton, R. L. (1994). A longitudinal study of injury morbidity in an African-American population. *Journal of the American Medical Association, 271* (10), 755.

Schwarz, E. D., and Perry, B. D. (1994). The post-traumatic response in children and adolescents. In D. A. Tomb (Ed.), *Psychiatric clinics of North America, Vol. 17, No. 2, Post-traumatic stress disorder* (pp. 311-326). Philadelphia: W. B. Saunders.

Scott, K. (1993). *The autobiography of an L. A. gang member.* New York: Penguin Books.

Scott, W. J. (1993). *The politics of readjustment: Vietnam veterans since the war.* New York: Aldin De Gruyter.

Sears, R. R., MacCoby, E. E., and Levin, L. (1957). *Patterns of child rearing.* Evanston, IL: Row, Peterson.

Segal, L. (1990). *Slow motion.* New Brunswick, NJ: Rutgers University Press.

Seligman, M. E. P. (1992). *Helplessness: On development, depression, and death.* New York: W. H. Freeman.

Sells, C. W., and Blum, R. W. (1996, April). Morbidity and mortality among U.S. adolescents: An overview of data and trends. *American Journal of Public Health. 86* (4), 513-519.

Senge, P. (1990). *The fifth discipline: The art and practice of the learning organization.* New York: Doubleday.

Sewell, J. D. (1993, January). Traumatic stress of multiple murder investigations. *Journal of Traumatic Stress, 6* (1), 103-118.

Shaffer, C. R., and Anundsen, K. (1993). *Creating community anywhere: Finding support and connection in a fragmented world.* Los Angeles: Jeremy P. Tarcher.

Shanahan, M. G. (1995). Solving campus-community problems. *The FBI Law Enforcement Bulletin, 64* (2), 1-6.

Shatan, C. (1972). Post-Vietnam syndrome. *The New York Times,* p. 35, May 6.

Shatan, C. F. (1985). Johnny, we don't want to know you: From DEROS and death camps to the diagnostic battlefield. Unpublished paper presented at the Founding Meeting of the Society for Traumatic Stress Studies, September 23, 1985, Atlanta, Georgia.

Shengold, L. (1989). *Soul murder: The effects of childhood abuse and deprivation.* New Haven: Yale University Press.

Sheridan, M. J. (1995). A proposed intergenerational model of substance abuse, family functioning, and abuse/neglect. *Child Abuse and Neglect, 19* (5), 519-530.

Shorris, E. (1994). *A nation of salesman: The tyranny of the market and the subversion of culture.* New York: W. W. Norton and Company.

Silove, D. (1996). Torture and refugee trauma: Implications of nosology and treatment of post-traumatic syndromes. In F. L. Mak and C. C. Nadelson (Eds.), *International review of psychiatry: Vol. 2* (pp. 211-232). Washington, DC: American Psychiatric Press.

Silverstein, O., and Rashbaum, B. (1994). *The courage to raise good men.* New York: Viking.

Simpson, D. D. (1986). 12-Year follow-up: Outcomes of opioid addicts treated in therapeutic communities. In G. DeLeon and J. T. Ziegenfuss (Eds.), *Therapeutic communities for addictions* (pp. 109-120). Springfield, IL: Charles C Thomas.

Singer, M. I., Anglin, T. M., Song, L. Y., and Lunghofer, L. (1995). Adolescents' exposure to violence and associated symptoms of psychological trauma. *JAMA, 273* (6), 477-482.

Sloan, J. H., Kellerman, A. L., Reay, D. T., Ferris, J. A., Koepsell, T., Rivara, F. P., Rice, C., Gray, L., and LoGerfo, J. (1988). Handgun regulations, crime, assaults, and homicide: A tale of two cities. *New England Journal of Medicine, 319*, 1256.

Smelser, N. J. 1971. Some determinants of destructive behavior. In N. Sanford and C. Comstock (Eds.). *Sanctions for evil: Sources of social destructiveness* (pp. 15-24). San Francisco: Jossey-Bass, Inc.

Smith, B. (1994). Cease fire! Preventing workplace violence. *HR Focus 71* (2), 1-4.

Smith, J. R., and Brooks-Gunn, J. (1997). Correlates and consequences of harsh discipline for young children. *Archives of Pediatric and Adolescent Medicine, 151* (8), 777-786.

Solomonow, A. (1990). Living truth: A Jewish perspective. In Holmes, R. L. *Nonviolence in theory and practice* (pp. 153-154). Belmont, CA: Wadsworth Publishing.

Sommerville, C. J. (1982). *The rise and fall of childhood.* New York: Vintage Books.

Southwick, S. M., Bremner, D., Krystal, J. H., and Charney, D. S. (1994). Psychobiologic research in post-traumatic stress disorder. In D. A. Tomb (Ed.), *Psychiatric clinics of North America, Vol. 17, No. 2, Post-traumatic stress disorder* (pp. 251-264). Philadelphia: W. B. Saunders.

Southwick, S. M., Yehuda, R., and Giller, E. L. (1993). Personality disorders in treatment-seeking combat veterans with post-traumatic stress disorder. *American Journal of Psychiatry, 150* (7), 1020-1023.

Southwick, S. M., Yehuda, R., and Morgan, C. A. (1995). Clinical studies of neurotransmitter alterations in post-traumatic stress disorder. In M. J. Friedman, D. S. Charney, and A. Y. Deutch (Eds.), *Neurobiological and clinical consequences of stress: From normal adaptation to post-traumatic stress disorder* (pp. 335-349). Philadelphia: Lippincott-Raven.

Spaccarelli, S., Coatsworth, J. D., and Bowden, B. S. (1995). Exposure to serious family violence among incarcerated boys: Its association with violent offending and potential medicating variables. *Violence and Victims, 10* (3), 163-182.

Spitz, R. A. (1945). Hospitalism: An inquiry into the genesis of psychiatric conditions of early childhood. *Psychoanalytic Study of the Child, 1*, 53-74.

Squire, L. (1987). *Memory and brain.* New York: Oxford University Press.

Stamm, B. H. (Ed.). (1995). *Secondary traumatic stress: Self-care issues for clinicians, researchers, and educators.* Lutherville, MD: Sidran Press.

Starer, D. (1995). *Hot topics.* New York: A Touchstone Book.

Staub, E. (1989). *The roots of evil: The origins of genocide and other group violence.* New York: Cambridge University Press.

Staub, E. (1992). Transforming the bystanders: Altruism, caring, and social responsibility. In H. Fein (Ed.), *Genocide watch.* New Haven: Yale University Press.

Staub, E. (1996). Cutural-societal roots of violence: The examples of genocidal violence and of contemporary youth violence in the United States. *American Psychologist, 51* (2), 117-132.

Steiner, G. (1961). *The death of tragedy.* London: Faber and Faber.

Steinmetz, S. K., and Straus, M.A. (1973). The family as a cradle of violence. *Society, 10* (6), 50-56.

Stevenson, H. C. Jr. (1997). "Missed, dissed and pissed": Making meaning of neighborhood risk, fear, and anger management in urban black youth. *Cultural Diversity and Mental Health, 3* (1), 37-52.

Stillion, J. M. (1995). Premature death among males. In D. Sabo and D. F. Gordon, (Eds.), *Men's health and illness* (pp. 160-183). Thousand Oaks, CA: Sage Publications.

Stilwell, B. M., Galvin, M., Kopta, S. M., Padgett, R. J., and Holt, J. W. (1997). Moralization of attachment: A fourth domain of conscience functioning. *Journal of American Academy of Child and Adolescent Psychiatry, 36* (8), 1140-1147.

Stine, S. M., and Kosten, T. R. (1995). Complications of chemical abuse and dependency. In M. J. Friedman, D. S. Charney, and A. Y. Deutch (Eds.), *Neurobiological and clinical consequences of stress: From normal adaptation to post-traumatic stress disorder* (pp. 447-464). Philadelphia: Lippincott-Raven.

Straus, M. A. (1994). *Beating the devil out of them: Corporal punishment in American families.* New York: Lexington Books.

Straus, M. A., Sugarman, D. B., and Giles-Sims, J. (1997). Spanking by parents and subsequent antisocial behavior of children. *Archives of Pediatric and Adolescent Medicine, 151* (8), 761-767.

Strenz, T. (1982). The Stockholm Syndrome. In F. Ochberg and D. Soskis (Eds.), *The victims of terrorism* (pp. 149-164). Boulder, CO: Westview.

Sugarmann, J. (1994, March 10). Ceasefire. *Rolling Stone.*

Sumner, B. B., Mintz, E. R., and Brown, P. L. (1987). Injuries caused by personal violence. *Injury, 18* (4), 258-260.

Sutherland, S. M., and Davidson, J. R. T. (1994, June). Pharmacotherapy for post-traumatic stress disorder. In D. A. Tomb (Ed.), *Post-Traumatic Stress Disorder, The Psychiatric Clinics of America, 17* (2), 409-423.

Sutker, P. B., Allain, A. N. Jr., and Winstead, D. K. (1993). Psychopathology and psychiatric diagnoses of World War II Pacific Theater prisoner of war survivors and combat veterans. *American Journal of Psychiatry, 150* (2), 240-245.

Taylor, D. 1985. Theological thoughts about evil. In D. Parkin (Ed.) *The anthropology of evil* (pp. 26-41). New York: Basil Blackwell.

Tejedor-Real, P., Mico, J. A., Maldonado, R., Roques, B. P., and Gibert-Rahola, J. (1995). Implication of endogenous opioid system in the learned helplessness model of depression. *Pharmacology, Biochemistry, and Behavior, 52* (1), 145-152.

Terr, L. (1990). *Too scared to cry: Psychic trauma in childhood.* New York: Harper and Row.

Terr, L. (1994). *Unchained memories: True stories of traumatic memories, lost and found.* New York: Basic Books.

Thomasma, D. C. (1996). The ethics of managed care: Challenges to the principles of relationship-centered care. *Journal of Allied Health, 25* (3), 233-246.

Time Magazine, January 25, 1993, p. 23.

Toch, Hans. (1992). *Living in prison: The ecology of survival.* Washington, DC: The American Psychological Association.

Toch, T., and Silver, M. (1993). Violence in schools. *US News and World Report, 115* (18), 30-36.

Todarello, O., Casamassima, A., Daniele, S., Marinaccio, M., Fanciullo, F., Valentino, L., Tedesco, N., Wiesel, S., Simone, G., and Marinaccio, L. (1997). Alexithymia, immunity, and cervical intraepithelial neoplasia: Replication. *Psychotherapy and Psychosomatics, 66* (4), 208-213.

Todarello, O., Casamassima, A., Marinaccio, M., La Pesa, M. W., Caradonna, L. Valentino, L., and Marinaccio, L. (1994). Alexithymia, immunity, and cervical intraepithelial neoplasia: A pilot study. *Psychotherapy and Psychosomatics, 61* (3-4), 199-204.

Todarello, O., Taylor, G. J., Parker, J. D., and Fanelli, M. (1995). Alexithymia in essential hypertensive and psychiatric outpatients: A comparative study. *Journal Psychosomatic Research, 39* (8), 987-994.

Tolan, P. H., and Henry, D. (1996). Patterns of psychopathology among urban poor children: Comorbidity and aggression effects. *Journal of Consulting and Clinical Psychology, 64* (5), 1094-1099.

Toscano, G. (1996). Workplace violence: An analysis of bureau of labor statistics data. *Occupational Medicine, 11* (2), 227-235.

Toufexis, Anastasia. (1994). Workers who fight fire with fire. *Time, 143* (17), 34-38.

Tuakli-Williams, J., and Carrillo, J. (1995). The impact of psychosocial stressors on African-American and Latino preschoolers. *Journal of the National Medical Association, 87* (7), 473-478.

Turnbull, C. M. 1972. *The mountain people.* New York: Simon and Schuster.

Turner, C. W., Hess, B. W., and Peterson-Lewis, S. (1986). Naturalistic studies of the long-term effects of television violence. *Journal of Social Issues, 42* (3), 51-73.

Turner, M. (1972). Norman House. In S. Whiteley, D. Briggs, and M. Turner (Eds.), *Dealing with deviants* (pp. 175-224). London: The Hogarth Press.

United Nations (1996). Human Rights Fact Sheet No. 10 (Rev. 1) The Rights of the Child. New York: United Nations.

U.S. Advisory Board on Child Abuse and Neglect. (1991). *Creating caring communities: Blueprint for an effective federal policy on child abuse and neglect.* Washington, DC: U. S. Government Printing Office.

U.S. Advisory Board on Child Abuse and Neglect. (1992). *The continuing child protection emergency: A challenge to the nation.* Washington, DC: U.S. Government Printing Office.

U.S. Advisory Board on Child Abuse and Neglect. (1993). *Neighbors helping neighbors: A new national strategy for the protection of children.* Washington, DC: U. S. Government Printing Office.

U.S. Department of Health and Human Services. (1996). *The third national incidence study of child abuse and neglect.* Washington, DC: U. S. Government Printing Office.

U.S. Department of Health and Human Services. (1997). *Child maltreatment 1995: Reports from the states to the National Child Abuse and Neglect data system.* Washington, DC: U. S. Government Printing Office.

U.S. Department of Justice. (1995). *National Crime Victimization Survey.* Washington, DC: U. S. Government Printing Office.

Uddo, M., Vasterling, J. J., Brailey, K., and Sutker, P. B. (1993). Memory and attention in combat-related post-traumatic stress disorder (PTSD). *Journal of Psychopathology and Behavioral Assessment, 15* (1), 43-52.

United Nations. (1996). *The Rights of the Child. Human Rights Fact Sheet No. 10 (Rev. 1).* Geneva: United Nations.

Ursano, R. J. (1985). Vietnam-era prisoners of war: Studies of U.S. Air Force prisoners of war. In S. M. Sonnenberg, A. S. Blank, and J. A. Talbott (Eds.). *The trauma of war: Stress and recovery in Vietnam veterans* (pp. 339-357). Washington: American Psychiatric Press.

USA Today. (1995a). Advance planning for workplace violence. *USA Today, 124* (2603), 3-4.

USA Today. (1995b). Company programs can prevent violence. *USA Today, 124* (2607), 6-8.

Van Buren, H. J. III. (1995). Business ethics for the new millenium. *Business and Society Review 93*, 51-55.

Van der Hart, O. 1983. *Rituals in psychotherapy: Transition and continuity.* New York: Irvington Publishers.

Van der Kolk, B. A. (1987a). *Psychological trauma.* Washington, DC: American Psychiatric Press.

Van der Kolk, B. A. (1987b). The separation cry and the trauma response: Developmental issues in the psychobiology of attachment and separation. In B. A. Van der Kolk (Ed.), *Psychological trauma* (pp. 31-62). Washington, DC: American Psychiatric Press.

Van der Kolk, B. A. (1988). The trauma spectrum: The interaction of biological and social events in the genesis of the trauma response. *Journal of Traumatic Stress, 1* (3), 273-290.

Van der Kolk, B. A. (1989). The compulsion to repeat the trauma: Reenactment, revictimization, and masochism. *Psychiatric clinics of North America, Vol. 12.*

Treatment of victims of sexual abuse, (pp. 389-411). Philadelphia: W. B. Saunders.

Van der Kolk, B. A. (1993). Biological considerations about emotions, trauma, memory, and the brain. In S. L. Ablon, D. Brown, E. J. Khantzian, and J. E. Mack (Eds.), *Human feelings: Explorations in affect development and meaning* (pp. 221-240). Hillsdale, NJ: The Analytic Press.

Van der Kolk, B. A. (1994). The body keeps the score: Memory and the evolving psychobiology of posttraumatic stress. *Harvard Review of Psychiatry, 1* (5), 253-265.

Van der Kolk, B. A. (1996a). The complexity of adaptation to trauma. In B. A. Van der Kolk, C. McFarlane, and L. Weisaeth (Eds.). *Traumatic stress: The effects of overwhelming experience on mind, body, and society.* New York: Guilford Press.

Van der Kolk, B. A. (1996b) Trauma and memory. In B. A. Van der Kolk, C. McFarlane, and L. Weisaeth (Eds.), *Traumatic stress: The effects of overwhelming experience on mind, body, and society* (pp. 279-302). New York: Guilford Press.

Van der Kolk, B. A., Brown, P., and Van der Hart, O. (1989). Pierre Janet on post-traumatic stress. *Journal of Traumatic Stress, 2* (3), 365-378.

Van der Kolk, B. A., Burbridge, J. A., and Suzuki, J. (1997). The psychobiology of traumatic memory: Clinical implications of neuroimaging studies. *Annals New York Academy of Sciences, 821,* 99-113.

Van der Kolk, B. A., and Ducey, C. P. (1989). The psychological processing of traumatic experience: Rorschach patterns in PTSD. *Journal of Traumatic Stress, 2* (2), 259-274.

Van der Kolk, B. A., and Fisler, R. (1995). Dissociation and the fragmentary nature of traumatic memories: Overview and exploratory study. *Journal of Traumatic Stress, 8* (4), 505-525.

Van der Kolk, B. A., and Greenberg, M. S. (1987). The psychobiology of the trauma response: Hyperarousal, constriction, and addiction to traumatic reexposure. In B. A. Van der Kolk (Ed.), *Psychological trauma.* (pp. 63-88). Washington, DC: American Psychiatric Press.

Van der Kolk, B. A., Greenberg, M., Boyd, H., and Krystal, J. (1985). Inescapable shock, neurotransmitters, and addiction to trauma: Toward a psychobiology of post-traumatic stress. *Biological Psychiatry, 20,* 314-325.

Van der Kolk, B. A., and Kadish, W. (1987). Amnesia, dissociation, and the return of the repressed. In B. A. Van der Kolk (Ed.). *Psychological trauma.* (pp. 173-190). Washington, DC: American Psychiatric Press.

Van der Kolk, B. A., and Saporta, J. (1993). Biological response to psychic trauma. In J. P. Wilson and B. Raphael (Eds.), *International handbook of traumatic stress syndromes* (pp. 25-33). New York: Plenum Press.

Van der Kolk, B. A., and Van der Hart, O. (1989). Pierre Janet and the breakdown of adaptation in psychological trauma. *American Journal of Psychiatry, 146* (12), 1530-1540.

Van der Kolk, B. A., and Van der Hart, O. (1991). The intrusive past: The flexibility of memory and the engraving of trauma. *American Imago, 48* (4), 425-454.

Vasile R. G., Goldenberg, I., Reich, J., Goisman, R. M., Lavori, P. W., and Keller, M. B. (1997). Panic disorder versus panic disorder with major depression; Defining and understanding differences in psychiatric morbidity. *Depression and Anxiety, 5* (1), 12-20.

Volavka, J. (1995). *Neurobiology of violence.* Washington, DC: American Psychiatric Press.

Volkan, V. D. (1988). *The need to have enemies and allies: From clinical practice to international relations.* Northvale, NJ: Jason Aronson Inc.

Wachtler, S. (1997). *After the madness: A judge's own prison memoir.* New York: Random House.

Waldron, I. (1995). Contributions of changing gender differences in behavior and social roles to changing gender differences in mortality. In D. Sabo and D. F. Gordon, (Eds.), *Men's health and illness* (pp. 25-34). Thousand Oaks, CA: Sage Publications.

Walker, E. A., Gelfand, A. N., Gelfand, M. D., Green, C., and Katon, W. J. (1996). Chronic pelvic pain and gynecological symptoms in women with irritable bowel syndrome. *Journal of Psychosomatic Obstetrics and Gynaecology, 17* (1), 39-46.

Walker, L. E. (1979). *The battered woman.* New York: Harper and Row.

Walling, M. K., O'Hara, M. W., Reiter, R. C., Milburn, A. K., Lilly, G., and Vincent, S. D. (1994). Abuse history and chronic pain in women: II. A multivariate analysis of abuse and psychological morbidity. *Obstetrics and Gynecology, 84* (2), 200-206.

Wallis, J. (1994). *The soul of politics.* New York: The New Press.

Wallis, S. (1995). Discipline and civility must be restored to America's public schools. *USA Today, 124* (2606), 32-35.

Warner, E. G. (1996). Ethics and morality vs. managed care. *Journal of the Oklahoma State Medical Association, 89* (8), 275-279.

Warshaw, L. J., and Messite, J. (1996). Workplace violence: Preventive and interventive strategies. *Journal of Occupational and Environmental Medicine, 38* (10), 993-1006.

Watson, R. (1995). A guide to violence prevention. *Educational Leadership, 52* (5), 57-60.

Webb, M. S. (1996). Medical ethics under managed care: How can the patient survive? *Annals of Plastic Surgery, 37* (3), 233-244.

Webster's Ninth New Collegiate Dictionary. (1996). Springfield, MA: Merriam-Webster.

Wexler, Harry K. (1986). Therapeutic communities within prisons. In G. DeLeon and J. T. Ziegenfuss (Eds.), *Therapeutic communities for addictions.* Springfield, IL: Charles C Thomas.

Wexler, Harry K. (1995). The success of therapeutic communities for substance abusers in American prisons. *Journal of Psychoactive Drugs, 27* (1), 57-66.

Wheeler, E. D., and Baron, S. A. (1994). *Violence in our schools, hospitals, and public places.* Ventura, CA: Pathfinder Publishing of California.

Widom, C. P., and Ames, M. A. (1994). Criminal consequences of childhood sexual victimization. *Child Abuse and Neglect, 18* (4), 303-318.

Widom, C. S., and Kuhns, J. B. (1996). Childhood victimization and subsequent risk for promiscuity, prostitution, and teenage pregnancy: A prospective study. *American Journal of Public Health, 86* (11), 1607-1612.

Will, R. (1995). Corporations with a conscience. *Business and Society Review, 93,* 17-20.

Wilmer, H. (1958). *Social psychiatry in action: A therapeutic community.* Springfield, IL: Charles C Thomas.

Wilmer, H. (1964). A living group experiment at San Quentin prison. *Corrective Psychiatry and Journal of Social Therapy, 10.*

Wilson, J. P. (1995). The historical evolution of PTSD diagnostic criteria: From Freud to DSM-IV. In. G. S. Everly Jr. and J. M. Lating (Eds.), *Psychotraumatology: Key papers and core concepts in post-traumatic stress* (pp. 9-26). New York: Plenum Press.

Wilt, S., and Olson, S. (1996, May). Prevalence of domestic violence in the United States. *Journal of the American Medical Women's Association, 51* (3), 77-82.

Windau, J., and Toscano, G. (1994). Murder, Inc.—Homicide in the American workplace. *Business and Society Review, 89,* 58-59.

Witwer, M. B., and Crawford, C. A. (1995). A coordinated approach to reducing family violence: Conference highlights. *National Institute of Justice Research Report, October, 1995.* Washington, DC: National Institute of Justice.

Wolfe, D. A., and Korsch, B. (1994). Witnessing domestic violence during childhood and adolescence: Implication for pediatric practice. *Pediatrics, 94* (4), 594-599.

Wolfgang, M. E. (1958). *Patterns in criminal homicide.* Philadelphia, PA: University of Pennsylvania Press.

Wolin, S. J., and Wolin, S. (1993). *The resilient self: How survivors of troubled families rise above adversity.* New York: Villard Books.

Wood, W., and Wong, F. Y. (1991). Effects of media violence on viewer's aggression in unconstrained social interaction. *Psychological Bulletin, 109* (3), 371-383.

Worth, R. (1995, November). A model prison. *Atlantic Monthly,* p. 38+.

Wright, M. S., and Litaker, D. (1996). Childhood victims of violence. Hospital utilization by children with intentional injuries. *Archives of Pediatric and Adolescent Medicine, 150* (4), 415-420.

Wright, R. (1994). *The moral animal: The new science of evolutionary psychology.* New York: Pantheon.

Yablonsky, L. (1972). *Robopaths: People as machines.* New York: Bobbs-Merrill.

Yablonsky, L. (1992). *Psychodrama: Resolving emotional problems through roleplaying.* New York: Brunner/Mazel.

Yarborough, M. H. (1994). Securing the American workplace. *HR Focus, 71* (9): 1-4.

Yehuda, R., Steiner, A., Kahana, B., Binder-Brynes, K., Southwick, S. M., Zemelman, S., and Giller, E. L. (1997). Alexithymia in Holocaust survivors with and without PTSD. *Journal of Traumatic Stress, 10* (1), 93-100.

Young, J. L., and Griffith, E. E. (1995). Regulating pastoral counseling practice: The problem of sexual misconduct. *Bulletin of the American Academy of Psychiatry and Law 23* (3), 421-432.

Zahn, T. P., Moraga, R., and Ray, W. J. (1996). Psychophysiological assessment of dissociative disorders. In L. K. Michelson and W. J. Ray (Eds.) *Handbook of dissociation: Theoretical, empirical, and clinical perspectives.* New York: Plenum.

Zavoski, R. W., Lapidus, G. D., Lerer, T. J., and Banco, L. I. (1995). A population-based study of firearm injury among children and youth. *Pediatrics, 96* (2 Pt 1), 278-282.

Zeanah, C. H., and Zeanah, P. D. (1989). Intergenerational transmission of maltreatment: Insights from attachment theory and research. *Psychiatry, 52* (2), 177-196.

Zehr, H. (1990). *Changing lenses: A new focus for crime and justice.* Scottsdale, PA: Herald Press.

Zehr, H. (1994a). Justice that heals: The vision. *Stimulus, 2* (3), 5-11.

Zehr, H. (1994b). Justice that heals: The practice. *Stimulus, 2* (3), 69-74.

Zeitlin, S. B., and McNally, R. J. (1993). Alexithymia and anxiety sensitivity in panic disorder and obsessive-compulsive disorder. *American Journal of Psychiatry, 150* (4), 658-660.

Zimring, F. E. (1991, November). Firearms, violence, and public policy. *Scientific American,* pp. 48-54.

Zimring, F. E., and Gordon, H. (1987). *The citizen's guide to gun control.* New York: Macmillan Publishing Company.

Ziolkowski, M., Gruss, T., and Rybakowski, J, K. (1995). Does alexithymia in male alcoholics constitute a negative factor for maintaining abstinence? *Psychotherapy and Psychosomatics, 63* (3-4), 169-173.

Index

Order Your Own Copy of
This Important Book for Your Personal Library!

BEARING WITNESS
Violence and Collective Responsibility

_____ in hardbound at $59.95 (ISBN: 0-7890-0477-1)

_____ in softbound at $29.95 (ISBN: 0-7890-0478-X)

COST OF BOOKS _____

OUTSIDE USA/CANADA/
MEXICO: ADD 20% _____

POSTAGE & HANDLING _____
(US: $3.00 for first book & $1.25
for each additional book)
Outside US: $4.75 for first book
& $1.75 for each additional book)

SUBTOTAL _____

IN CANADA: ADD 7% GST _____

STATE TAX _____
(NY, OH & MN residents, please
add appropriate local sales tax)

FINAL TOTAL _____
(If paying in Canadian funds,
convert using the current
exchange rate. UNESCO
coupons welcome.)

☐ **BILL ME LATER:** ($5 service charge will be added)
(Bill-me option is good on US/Canada/Mexico orders only;
not good to jobbers, wholesalers, or subscription agencies.)

☐ Check here if billing address is different from
shipping address and attach purchase order and
billing address information.

Signature _____

☐ **PAYMENT ENCLOSED: $** _____

☐ **PLEASE CHARGE TO MY CREDIT CARD.**

☐ Visa   ☐ MasterCard   ☐ AmEx   ☐ Discover
☐ Diners Club
Account # _____

Exp. Date _____

Signature _____

Prices in US dollars and subject to change without notice.

NAME _____

INSTITUTION _____

ADDRESS _____

CITY _____

STATE/ZIP _____

COUNTRY _____ COUNTY (NY residents only) _____

TEL _____ FAX _____

E-MAIL_____
May we use your e-mail address for confirmations and other types of information? ☐ Yes   ☐ No

Order From Your Local Bookstore or Directly From
The Haworth Press, Inc.
10 Alice Street, Binghamton, New York 13904-1580 • USA
TELEPHONE: 1-800-HAWORTH (1-800-429-6784) / Outside US/Canada: (607) 722-5857
FAX: 1-800-895-0582 / Outside US/Canada: (607) 772-6362
E-mail: getinfo@haworthpressinc.com
PLEASE PHOTOCOPY THIS FORM FOR YOUR PERSONAL USE.

BOF96